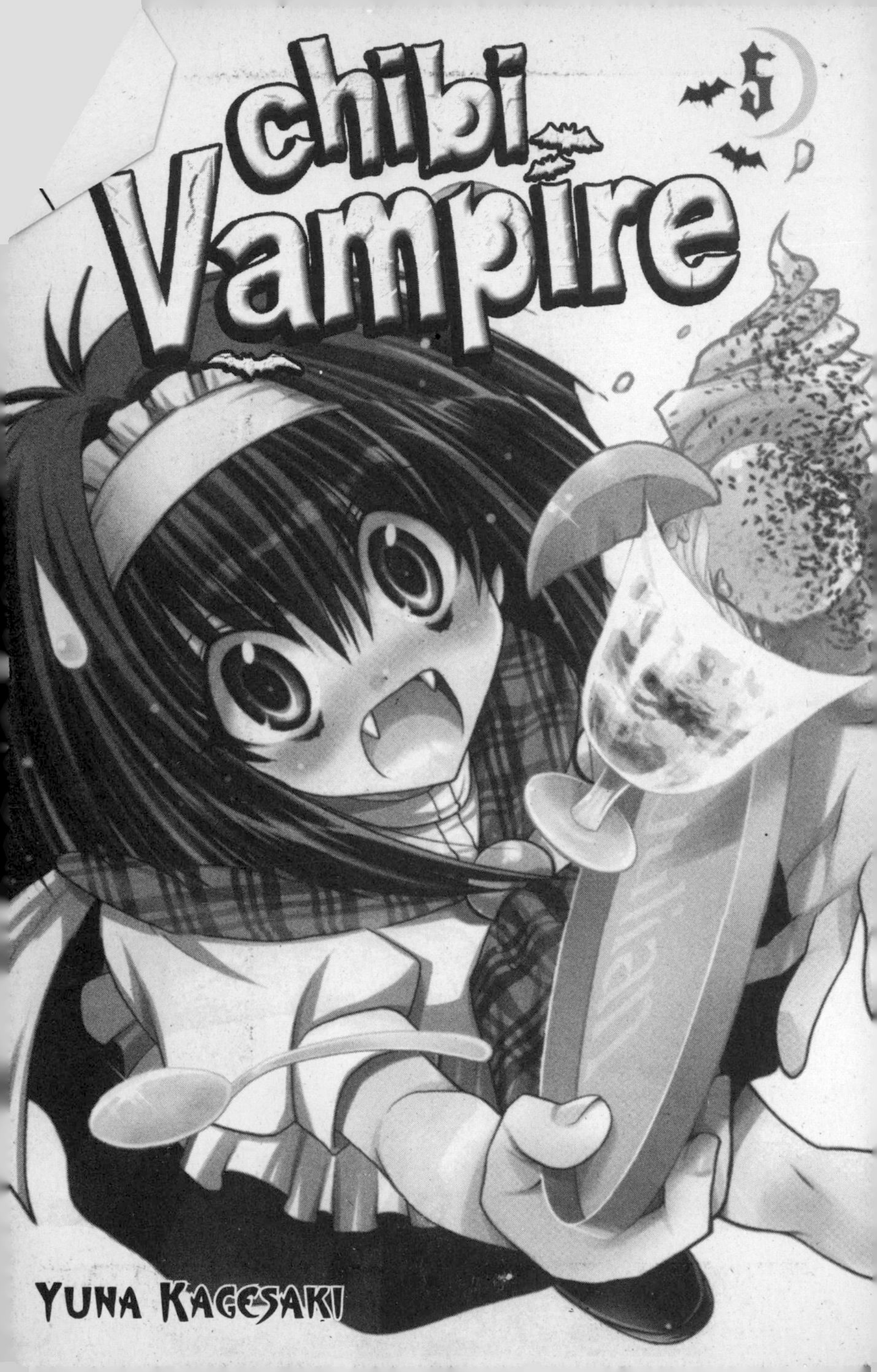
chibi
Vampire
5
YUNA KAGESAKI

Chibi Vampire Volume 5
Created by Yuna Kagesaki

Translation - Alexis Kirsch
Associate Editor - Christine Boylan
Retouch and Lettering - Star Print Brokers
Production Artist - Gavin Hignight
Graphic Designer - Jesselisa Moretti

Editor - Tim Beedle
Digital Imaging Manager - Chris Buford
Pre-Production Supervisor - Erika Terriquez
Art Director - Anne Marie Horne
Production Manager - Elisabeth Brizzi
Managing Editor - Vy Nguyen
VP of Production - Ron Klamert
Editor-in-Chief - Rob Tokar
Publisher - Mike Kiley
President and C.O.O. - John Parker
C.E.O. and Chief Creative Officer - Stuart Levy

A TOKYOPOP® Manga

TOKYOPOP Inc.
5900 Wilshire Blvd. Suite 2000
Los Angeles, CA 90036

E-mail: info@TOKYOPOP.com
Come visit us online at www.TOKYOPOP.com

KARIN Volume 5 © YUNA KAGESAKI 2005 First published in Japan in 2005 by FUJIMISHOBO CO., LTD., Tokyo.English translation rights arranged with KADOKAWA SHOTEN PUBLISHING CO., LTD., Tokyo through TUTTLE-MORI AGENCY, INC., Tokyo.
English text copyright © 2007 TOKYOPOP Inc.

ISBN: 978-1-59816-326-1
First TOKYOPOP printing: August 2007
10 9 8 7 6 5 4
Printed in the USA

Chibi Vampire

Volume 5

Created by

Yuna Kagesaki

TOKYOPOP®

HAMBURG // LONDON // LOS ANGELES // TOKYO

OUR STORY SO FAR...

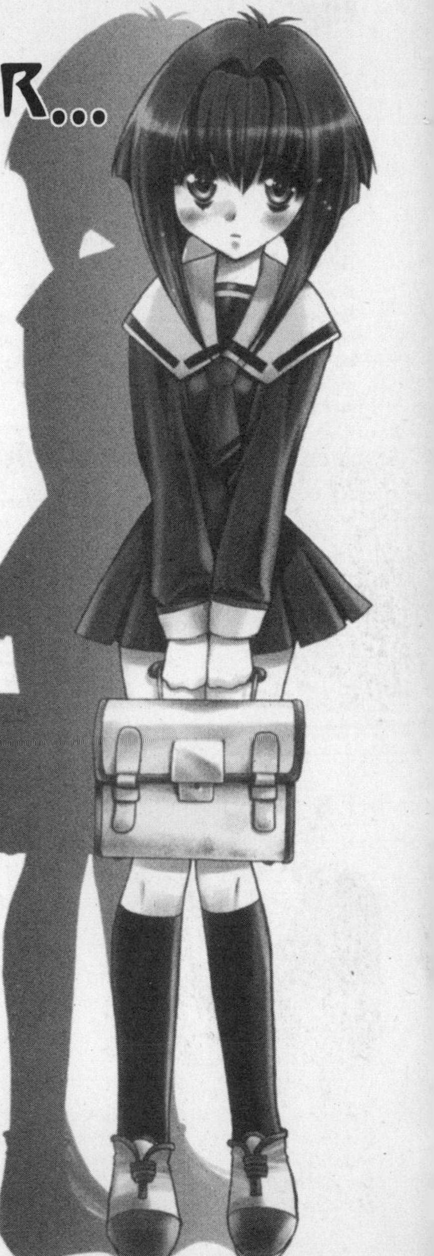

KARIN MAAKA ISN'T LIKE OTHER GIRLS. ONCE A MONTH, SHE EXPERIENCES PAIN, FATIGUE, HUNGER, IRRITABILITY–AND THEN SHE BLEEDS. FROM HER NOSE. KARIN IS A VAMPIRE, FROM A FAMILY OF VAMPIRES, BUT INSTEAD OF NEEDING TO DRINK BLOOD, SHE HAS AN EXCESS OF BLOOD THAT SHE MUST GIVE TO HER VICTIMS. IF DONE RIGHT, GIVING THIS BLOOD TO HER VICTIM CAN BE AN EXTREMELY POSITIVE THING. THE PROBLEM WITH THIS IS THAT KARIN NEVER SEEMS TO DO THINGS RIGHT...

KARIN IS HAVING A BIT OF BOY TROUBLE. KENTA USUI–THE HANDSOME NEW STUDENT AT HER SCHOOL AND WORK–IS A NICE ENOUGH GUY, BUT HE EXACERBATES KARIN'S PROBLEM. KARIN, YOU SEE, IS DRAWN TO PEOPLE WHO HAVE SUFFERED MISFORTUNE, AND KENTA HAS SUFFERED PLENTY OF IT. KARIN DISCOVERED THIS WHEN SHE BIT KENTA'S MOTHER, AN INCIDENT THAT WAS UNFORTUNATELY WITNESSED BY KENTA. NOW, KARIN'S CONVINCED THAT SHE CAN KEEP HER NOSEBLEEDS UNDER CONTROL AS LONG AS SHE KEEPS KENTA HAPPY, AND KENTA HAS PROMISED KARIN'S PARENTS THAT HE'D HELP HER OUT DURING THE DAYTIME. A SIMPLE ENOUGH PLAN, BUT IT'S ABOUT TO BECOME A LOT MORE COMPLICATED, AS IT'S BECOME CLEAR TO KARIN THAT HER FEELINGS FOR KENTA RUN MUCH DEEPER THAN SHE REALIZED. SHE'S IN LOVE WITH THE POOR CHAP.

THE MAAKA FAMILY

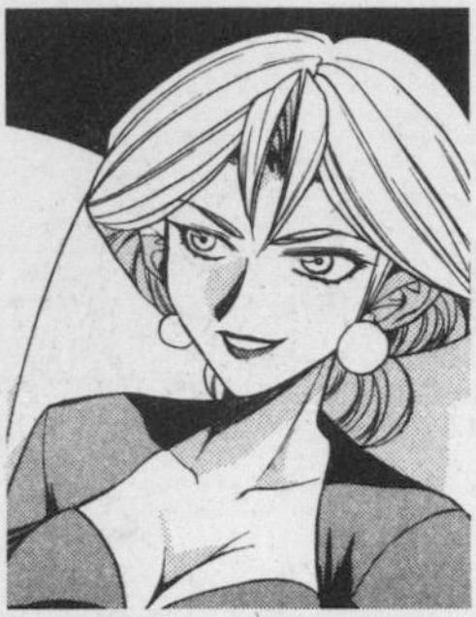

CALERA MARKER

Karin's overbearing mother. While Calera resents that Karin wasn't born a normal vampire, she does love her daughter in her own obnoxious way. Calera has chosen to keep her European last name.

HENRY MARKER

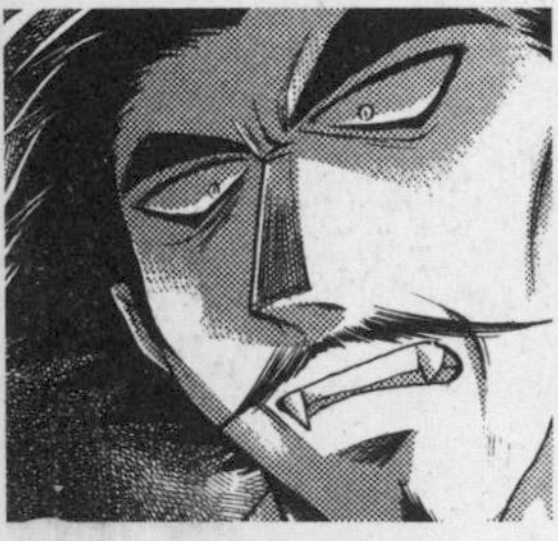

Karin's father. In general, Henry treats Karin a lot better than she's treated by her mother, but the pants in this particular family are worn by Calera. Henry has also chosen to keep his European last name.

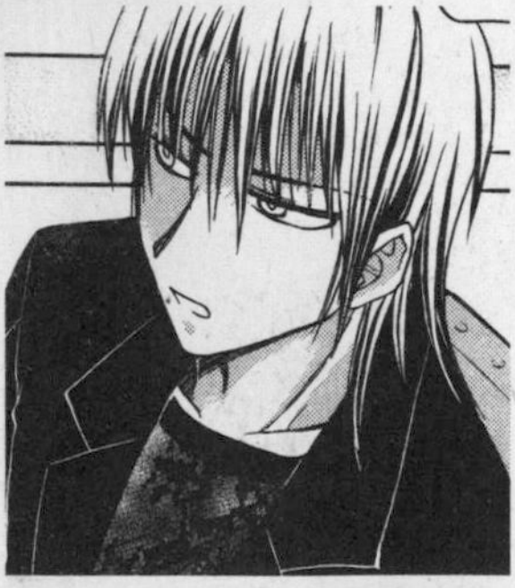

REN MAAKA

Karin's older brother. Ren milks the "sexy creature of the night" thing for all it's worth, and spends his nights in the arms (and beds) of attractive young women.

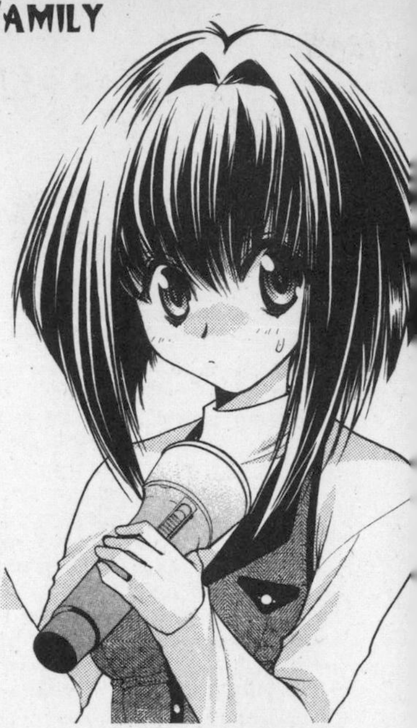

KARIN MAAKA

Our little heroine. Karin is a vampir living in Japan, but instead o sucking blood from her victims, sh actually GIVES them some of he blood. She's a vampire in revers

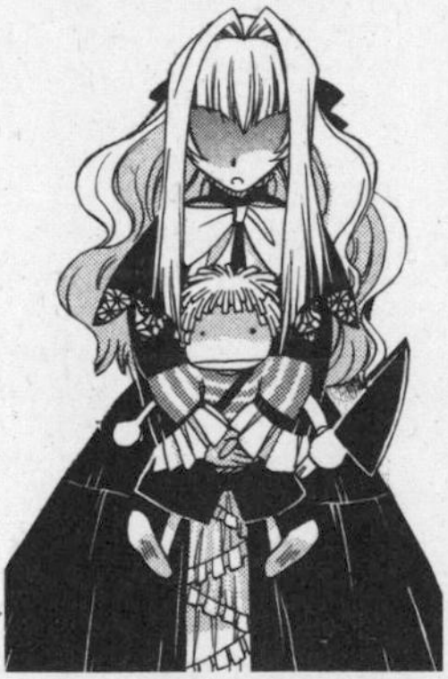

ANJU MAAKA

Karin's little sister. Anju has no yet awoken as a full vampire, bu she can control bats and is usually the one who cleans up after Karin's messes. Rarely seen without he "talking" doll, Boogie.

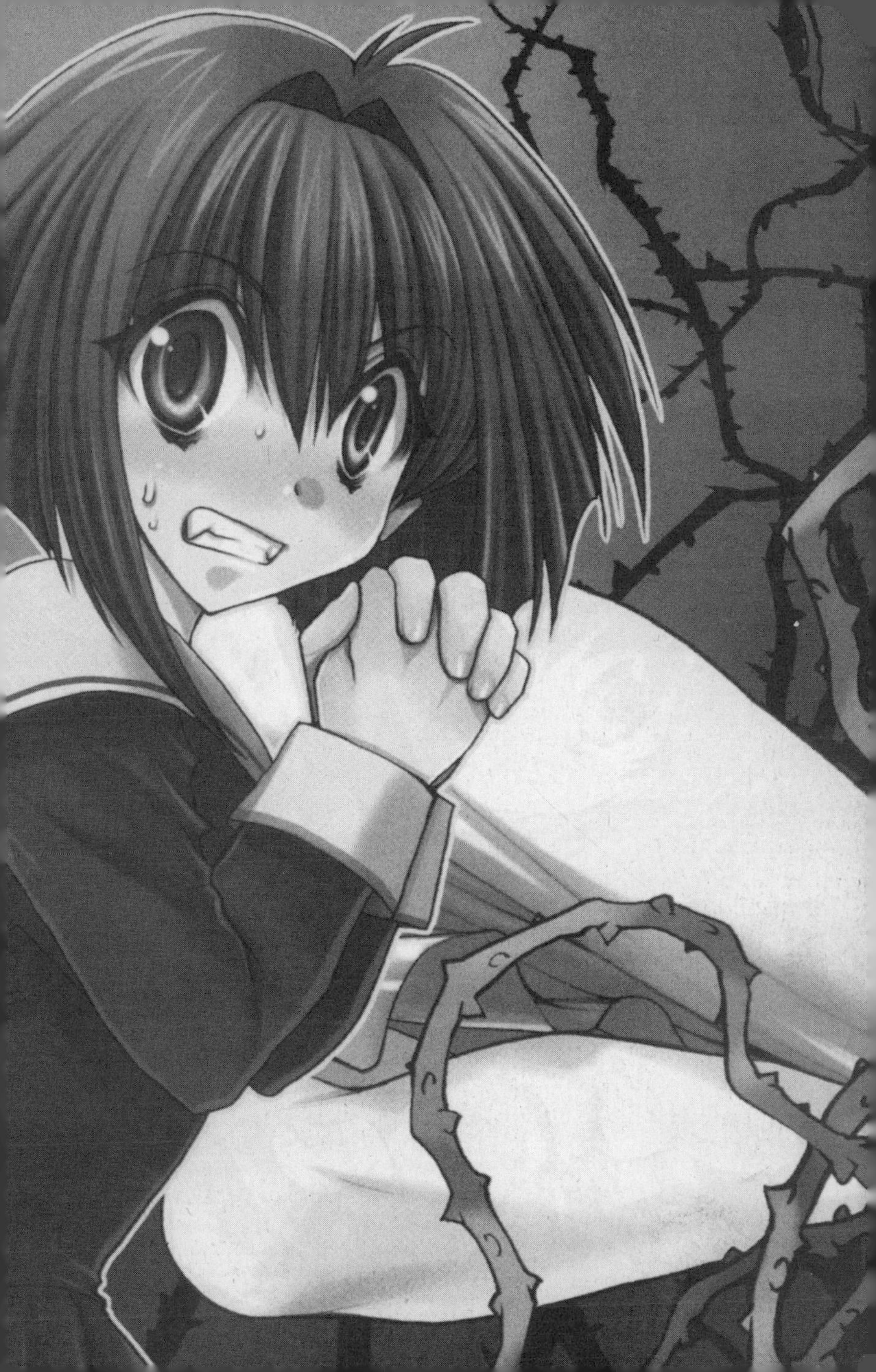

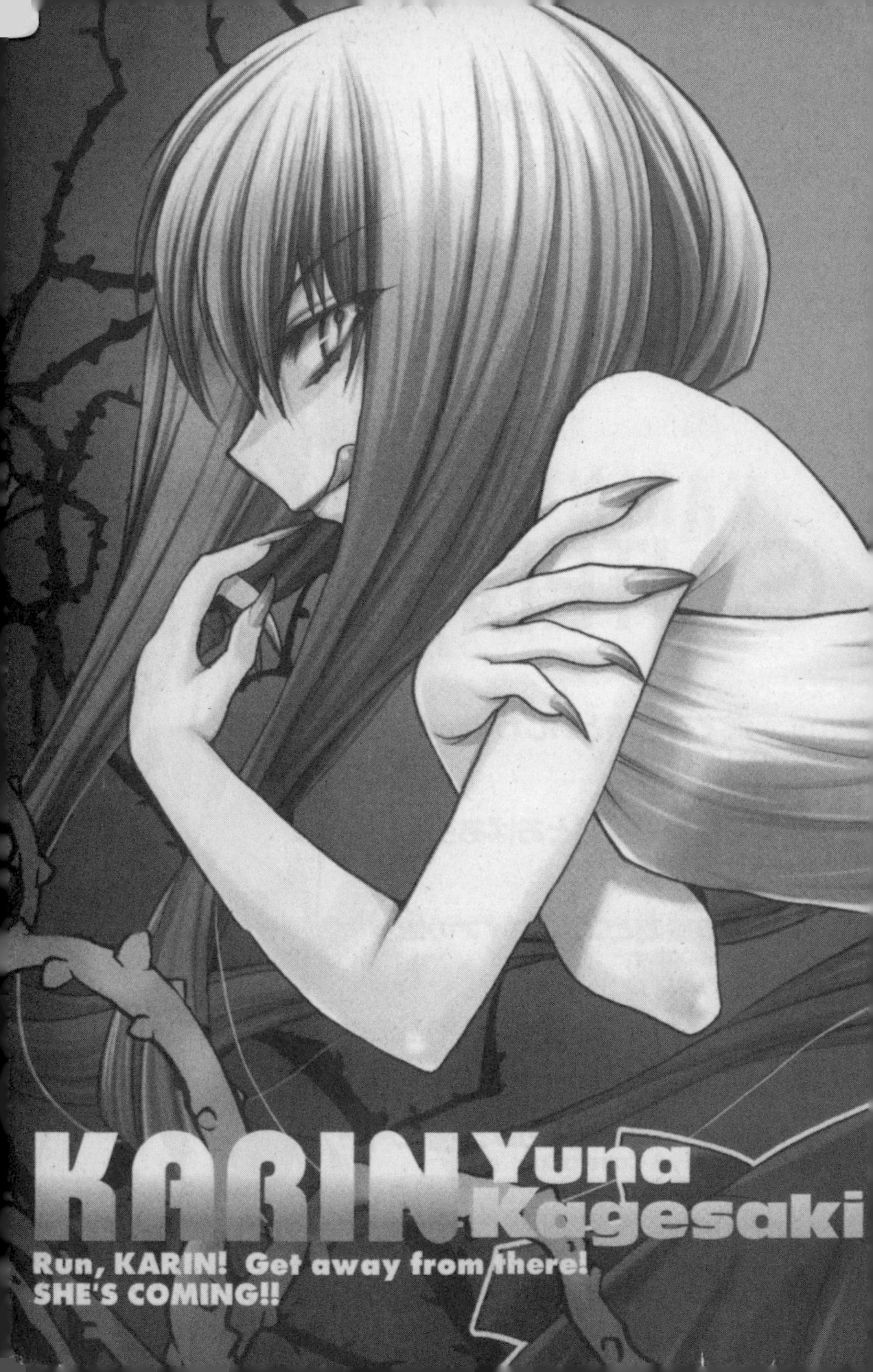
KARIN
Yuna Kagesaki
Run, KARIN! Get away from there!
SHE'S COMING!!

VOL.5

ONTENTS

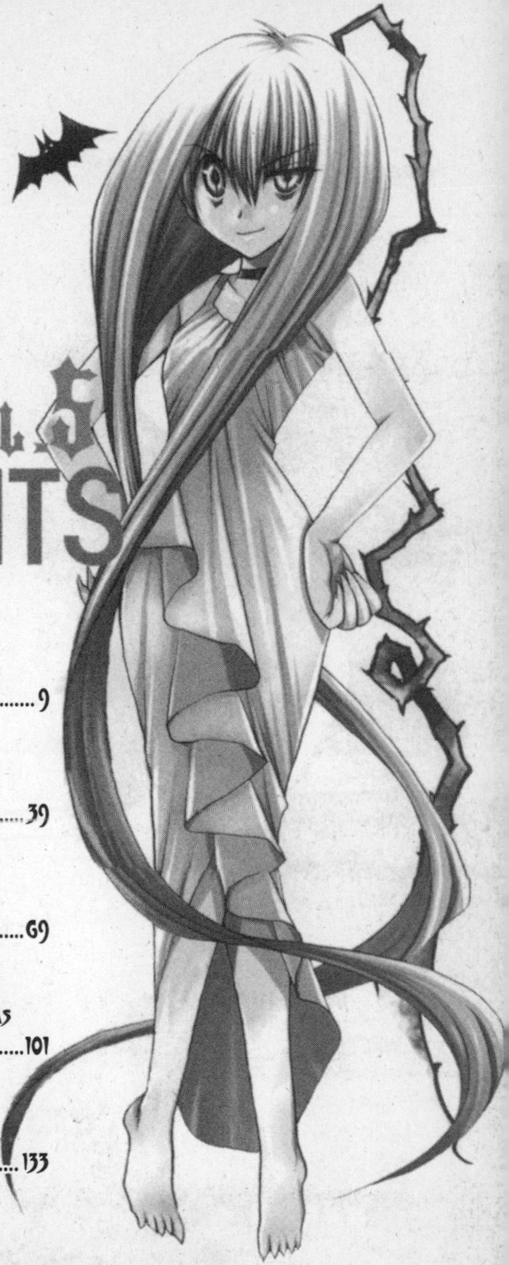

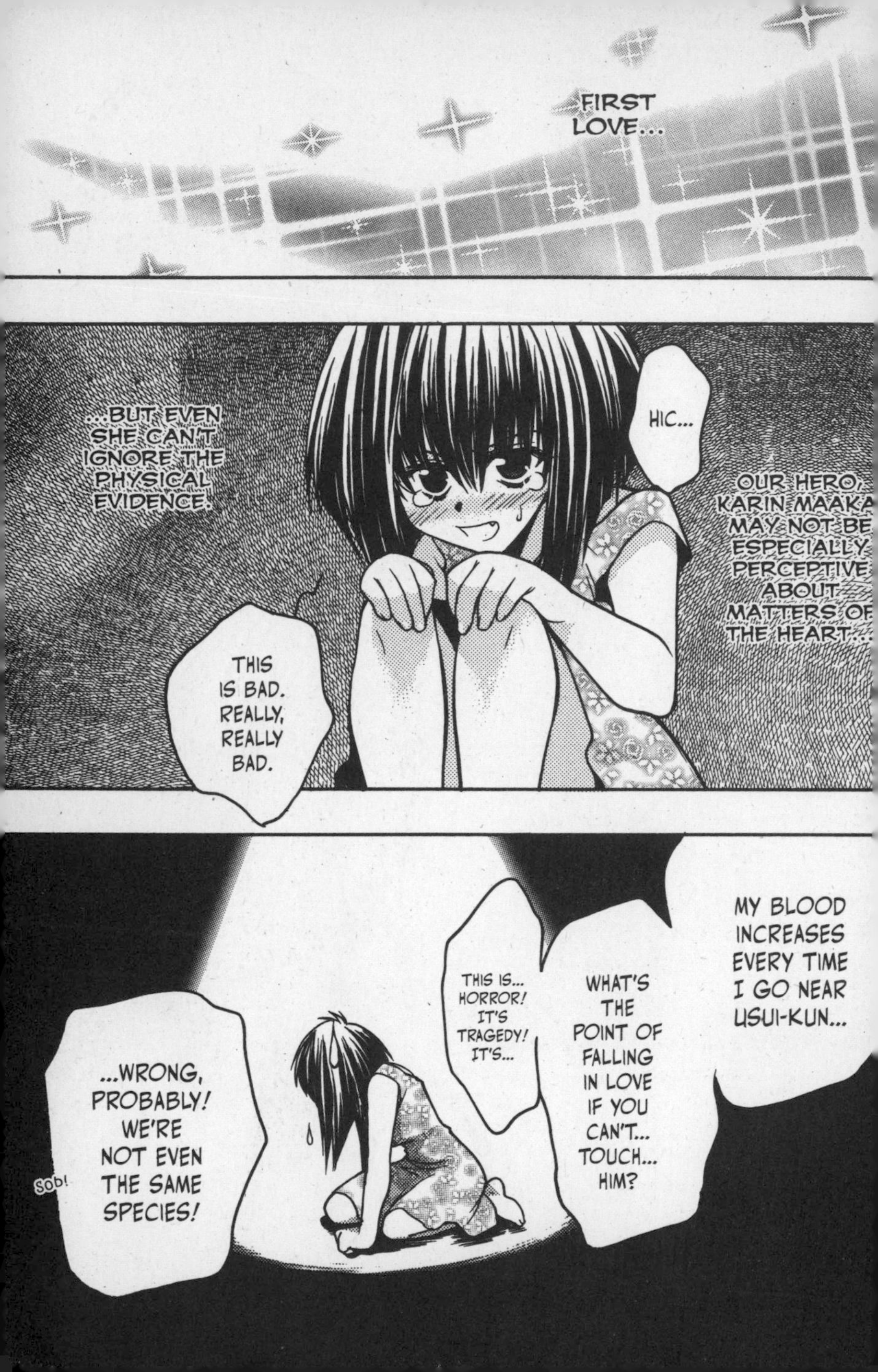
FIRST LOVE...
HIC...
OUR HERO, KARIN MAAKA, MAY NOT BE ESPECIALLY PERCEPTIVE ABOUT MATTERS OF THE HEART...
...BUT EVEN SHE CAN'T IGNORE THE PHYSICAL EVIDENCE.
THIS IS BAD. REALLY, REALLY BAD.
MY BLOOD INCREASES EVERY TIME I GO NEAR USUI-KUN...
WHAT'S THE POINT OF FALLING IN LOVE IF YOU CAN'T... TOUCH... HIM?
THIS IS... HORROR! IT'S TRAGEDY! IT'S...
...WRONG, PROBABLY! WE'RE NOT EVEN THE SAME SPECIES!
Sob!

TH EMBARRASSMENT) THE PANICKED FAMILY AND THE MEAN GRANDMA

~CONFUSION~

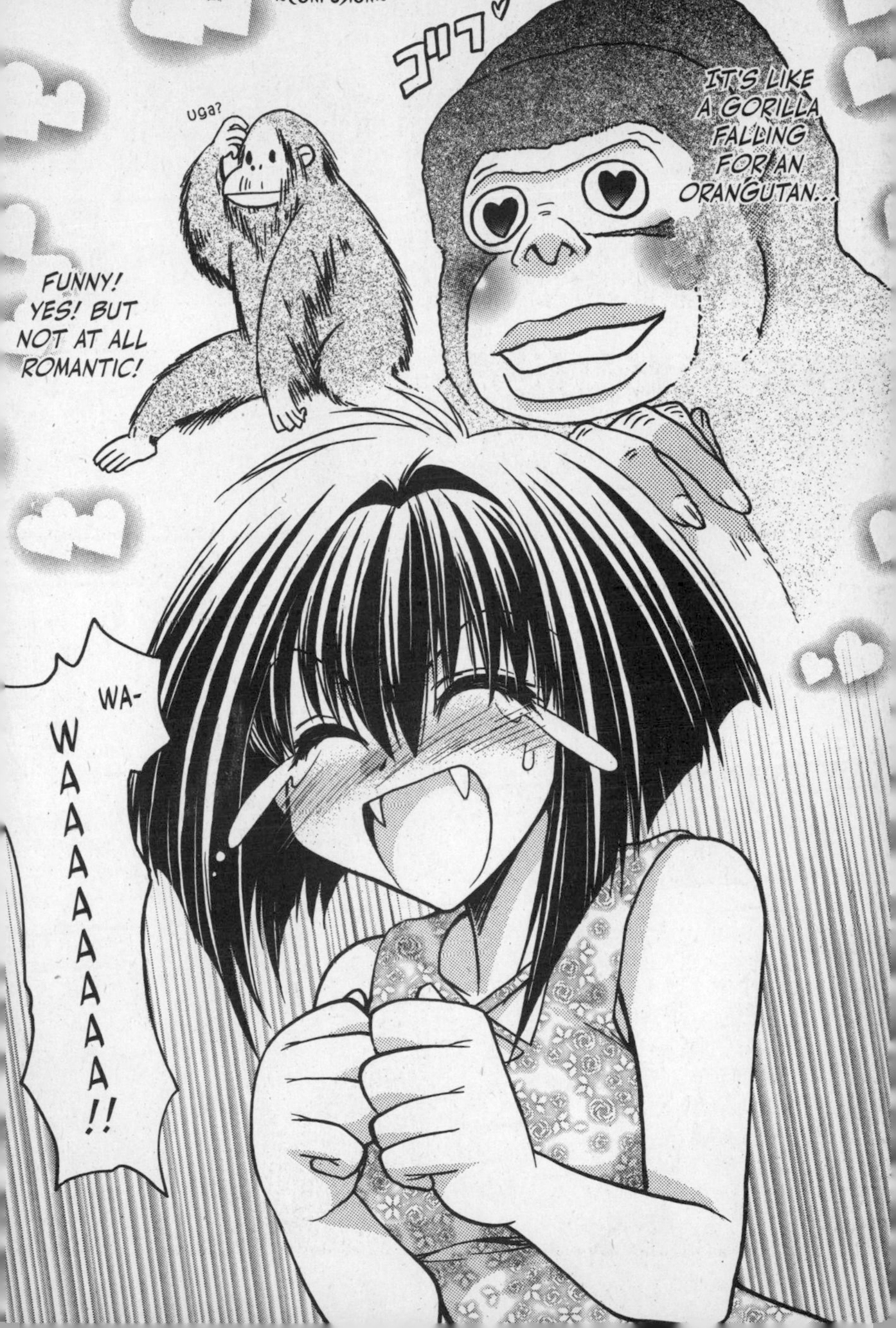
ゴリ♡
IT'S LIKE A GORILLA FALLING FOR AN ORANGUTAN...
Uga?
FUNNY! YES! BUT NOT AT ALL ROMANTIC!
WA-
WAAAAAAAAA!!

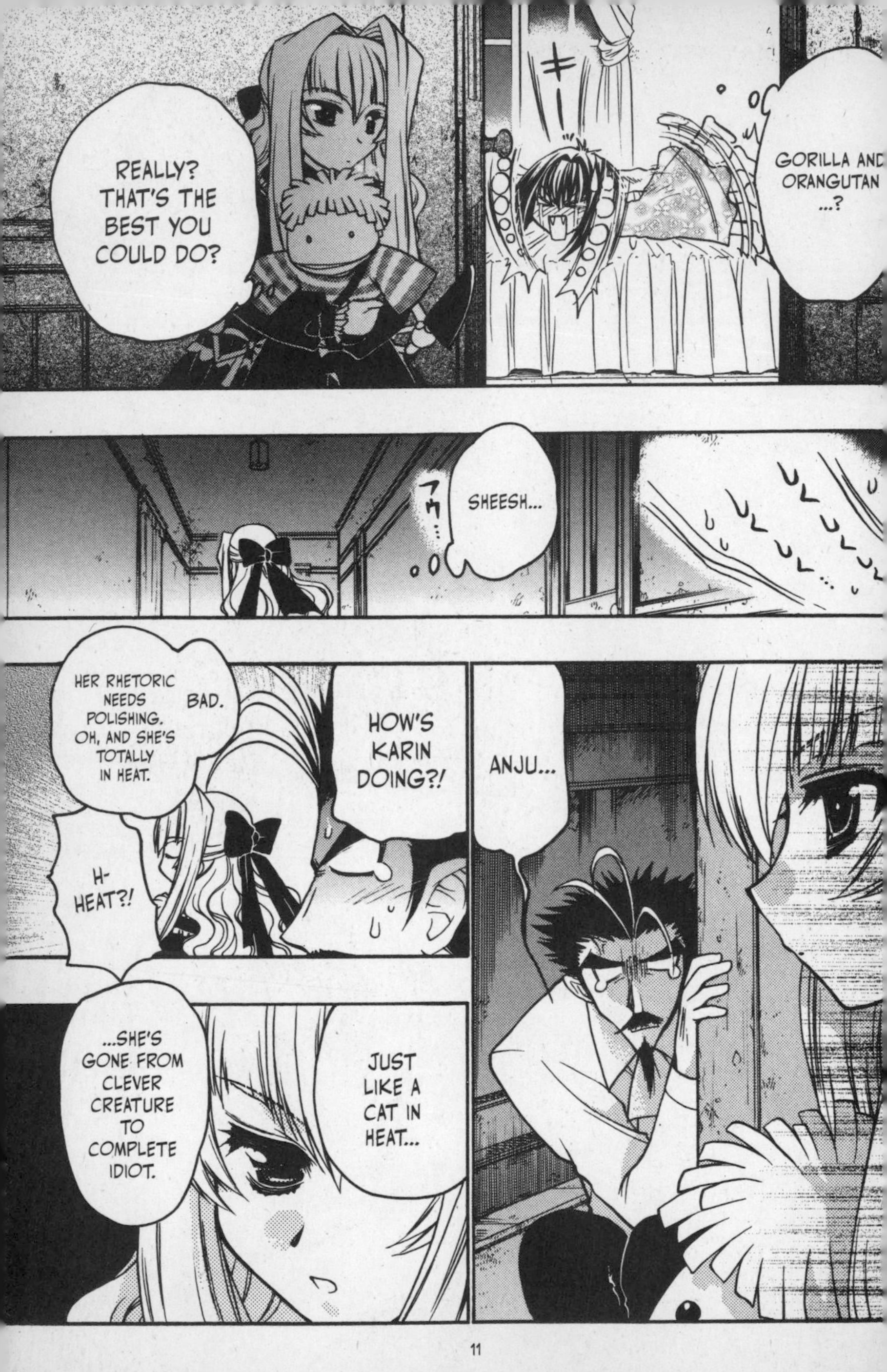
キー
GORILLA AND ORANGUTAN ...?
REALLY? THAT'S THE BEST YOU COULD DO?
UL UL UL UL UL...
SHEESH...
フゥ...
ANJU...
HOW'S KARIN DOING?!
BAD.
HER RHETORIC NEEDS POLISHING. OH, AND SHE'S TOTALLY IN HEAT.
H- HEAT?!
JUST LIKE A CAT IN HEAT...
...SHE'S GONE FROM CLEVER CREATURE TO COMPLETE IDIOT.

YOU DIDN'T HAVE TO BE SO... EXPLICIT!
......
T'S A HAME.
HE KNEW HER SECRET IDENTITY AND WAS WILLING TO KEEP IT A SECRET. HE WAS SOMEONE SHE COULD KEEP AROUND AND BITE WHENEVER SHE NEEDED TO.
THEN SHE FALLS FOR HIM AND CAN'T BRING HERSELF TO BITE HIM. IT'S SWEET, BUT IMPRACTICAL.
AND HE'S SOMEWHAT... IRREPLACE-ABLE.
THERE MUST BE A WAY TO FIX THIS.
AS ANJU PONDERED THE SITUATION...

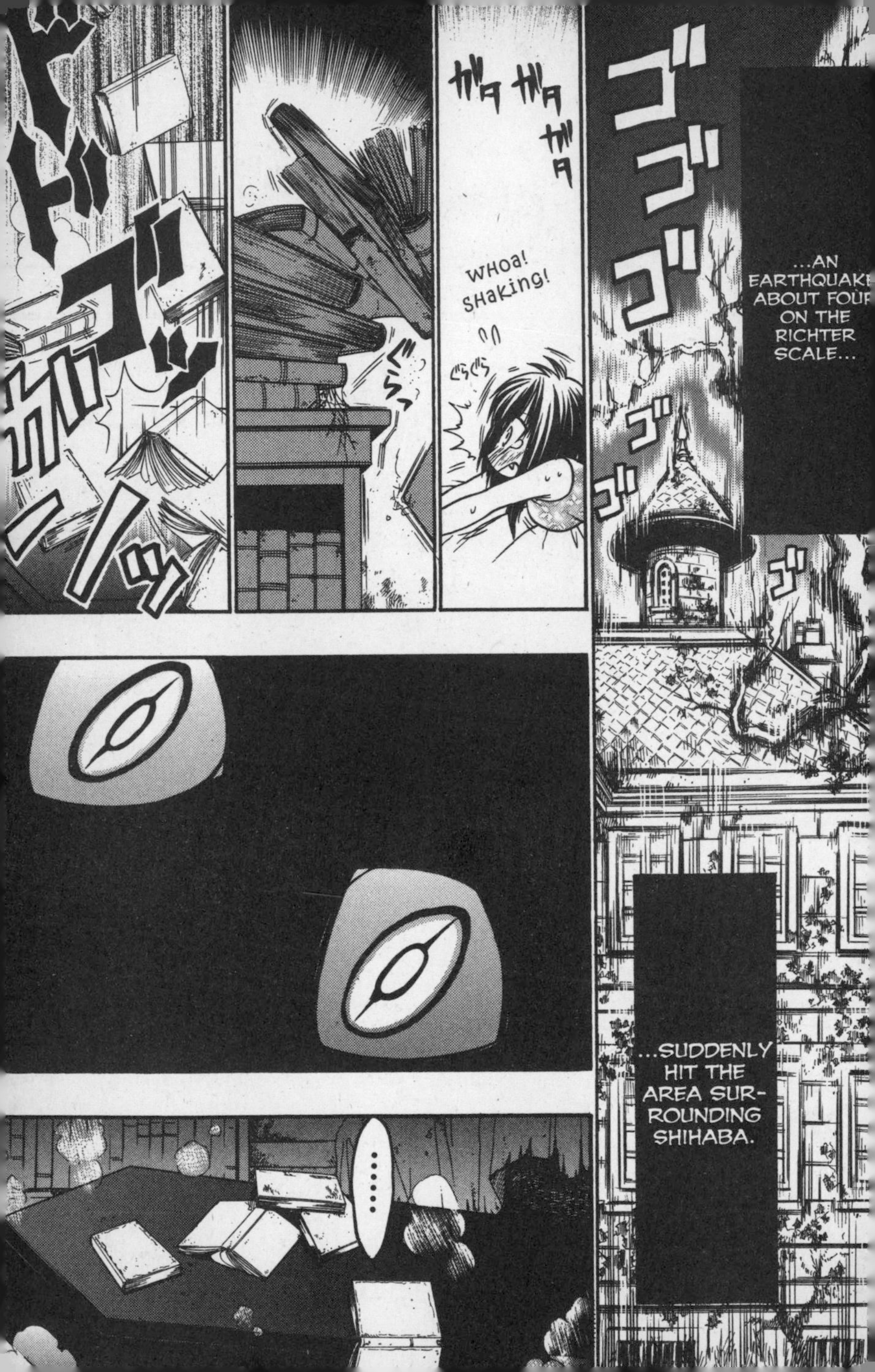

...AN EARTHQUAKE ABOUT FOUR ON THE RICHTER SCALE...
...SUDDENLY HIT THE AREA SUR-ROUNDING SHIHABA.
WHOa! SHAking!
......

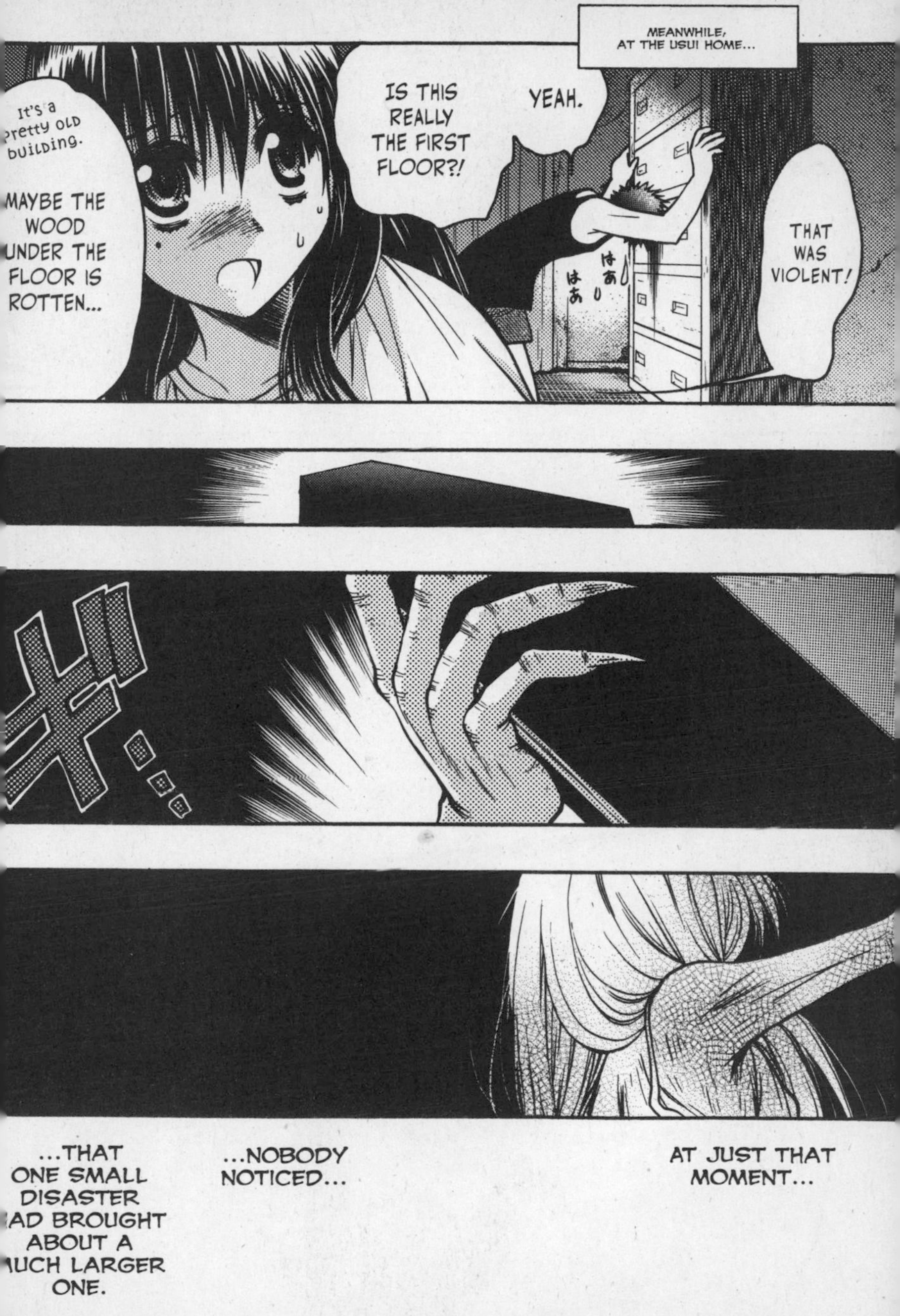
MEANWHILE, AT THE USUI HOME...
THAT WAS VIOLENT!
はあ はあ
YEAH.
IS THIS REALLY THE FIRST FLOOR?!
It's a pretty OLD building.
MAYBE THE WOOD UNDER THE FLOOR IS ROTTEN...
ギ...
AT JUST THAT MOMENT...
...NOBODY NOTICED...
...THAT ONE SMALL DISASTER AD BROUGHT ABOUT A UCH LARGER ONE.

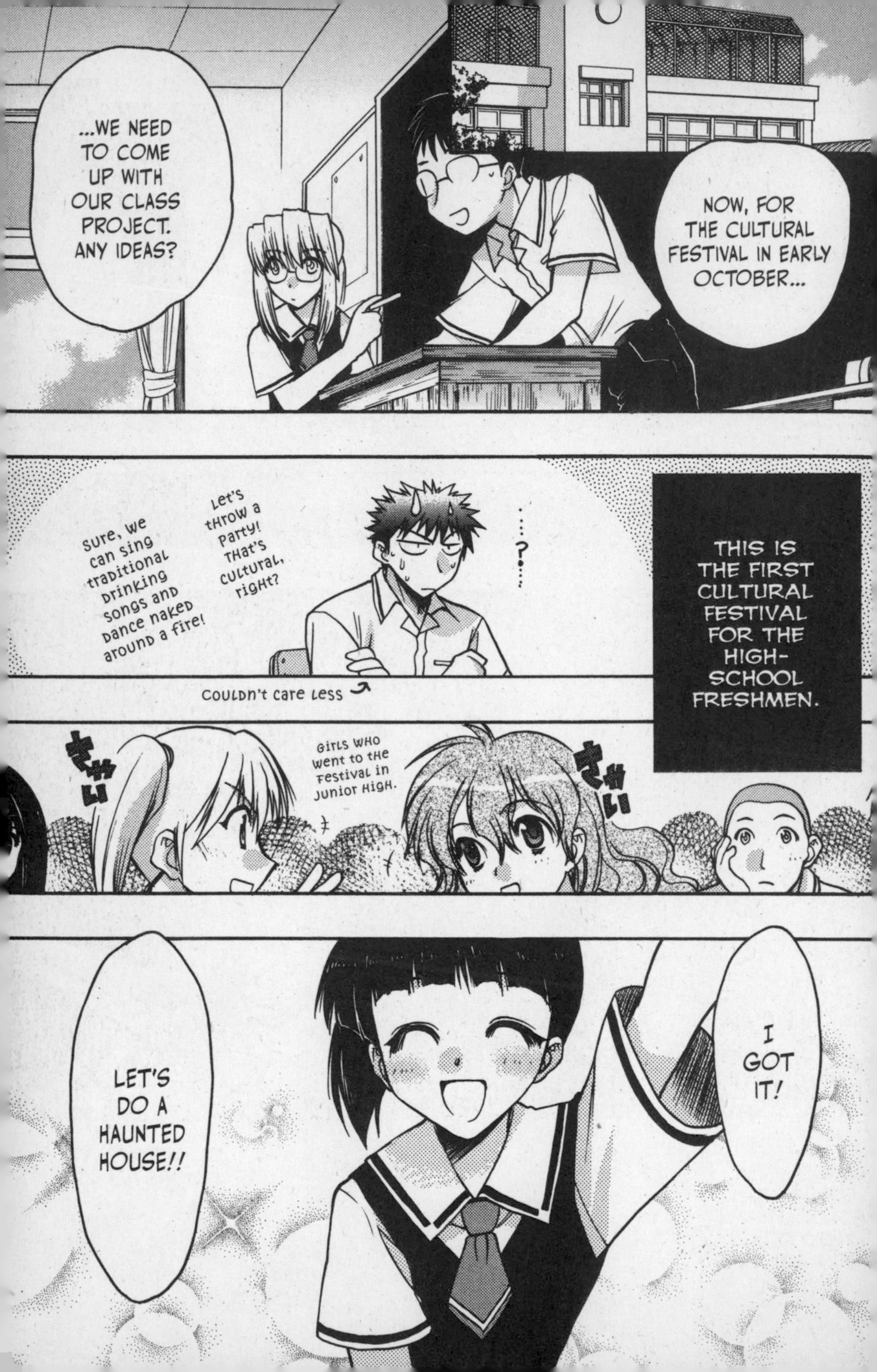
NOW, FOR THE CULTURAL FESTIVAL IN EARLY OCTOBER...
...WE NEED TO COME UP WITH OUR CLASS PROJECT. ANY IDEAS?
THIS IS THE FIRST CULTURAL FESTIVAL FOR THE HIGH-SCHOOL FRESHMEN.
...?...
Let's throw a party! That's cultural, right?
Sure, we can sing traditional drinking songs and dance naked around a fire!
Couldn't care less
きゃい
Girls who went to the festival in junior high.
きゃい
I GOT IT!
LET'S DO A HAUNTED HOUSE!!

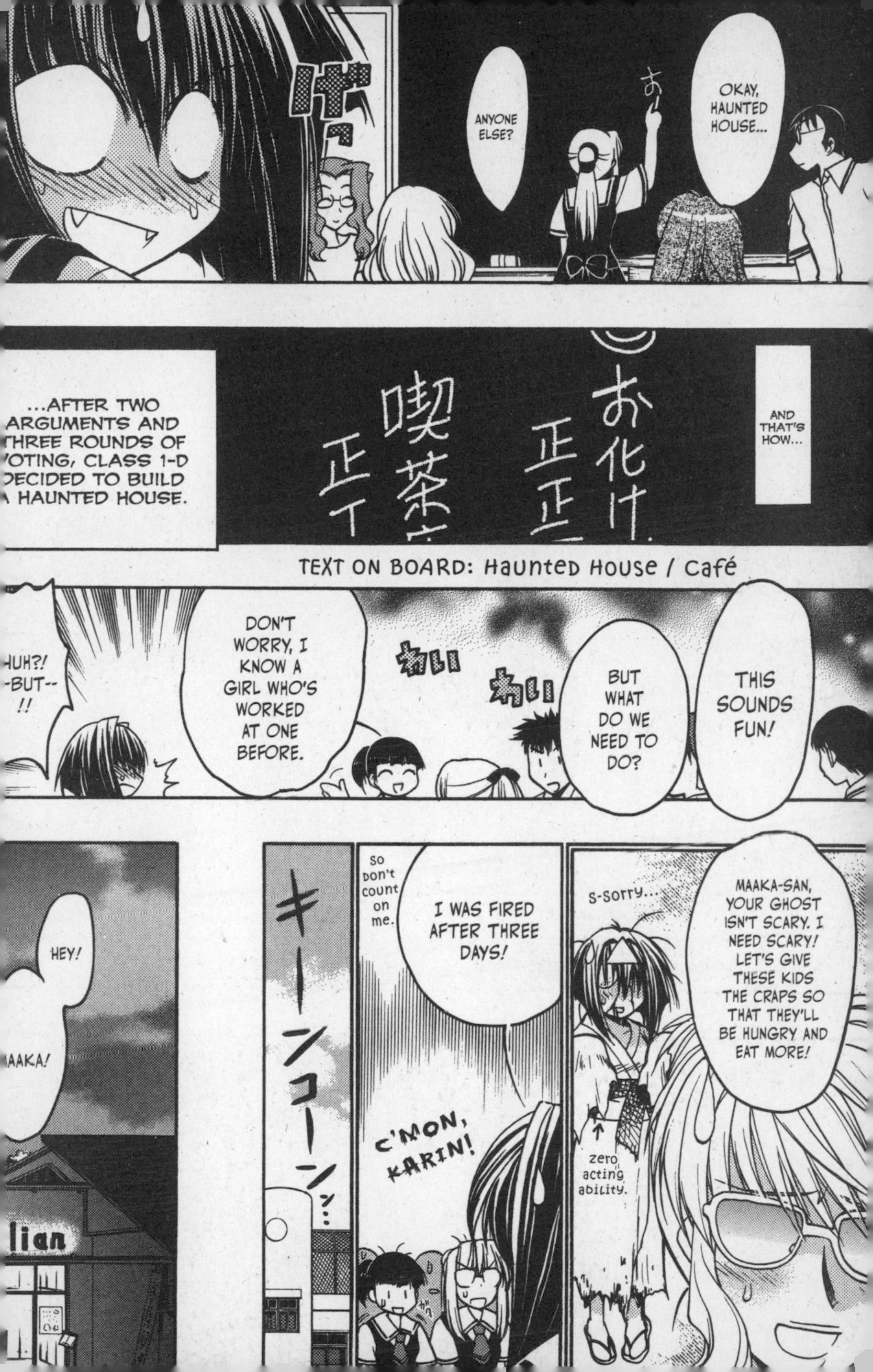
OKAY, HAUNTED HOUSE...
あ
ANYONE ELSE?
ゲッ
AND THAT'S HOW...
お化け 正正
喫茶 正T
...AFTER TWO ARGUMENTS AND THREE ROUNDS OF VOTING, CLASS 1-D DECIDED TO BUILD A HAUNTED HOUSE.
TEXT ON BOARD: Haunted House / Café
THIS SOUNDS FUN!
BUT WHAT DO WE NEED TO DO?
わい
わい
DON'T WORRY, I KNOW A GIRL WHO'S WORKED AT ONE BEFORE.
HUH?! --BUT-- !!
MAAKA-SAN, YOUR GHOST ISN'T SCARY. I NEED SCARY! LET'S GIVE THESE KIDS THE CRAPS SO THAT THEY'LL BE HUNGRY AND EAT MORE!
S-Sorry...
zero acting ability.
I WAS FIRED AFTER THREE DAYS!
So don't count on me.
キーンコーン...
C'MON, KARIN!
HEY!
AAKA!
lian

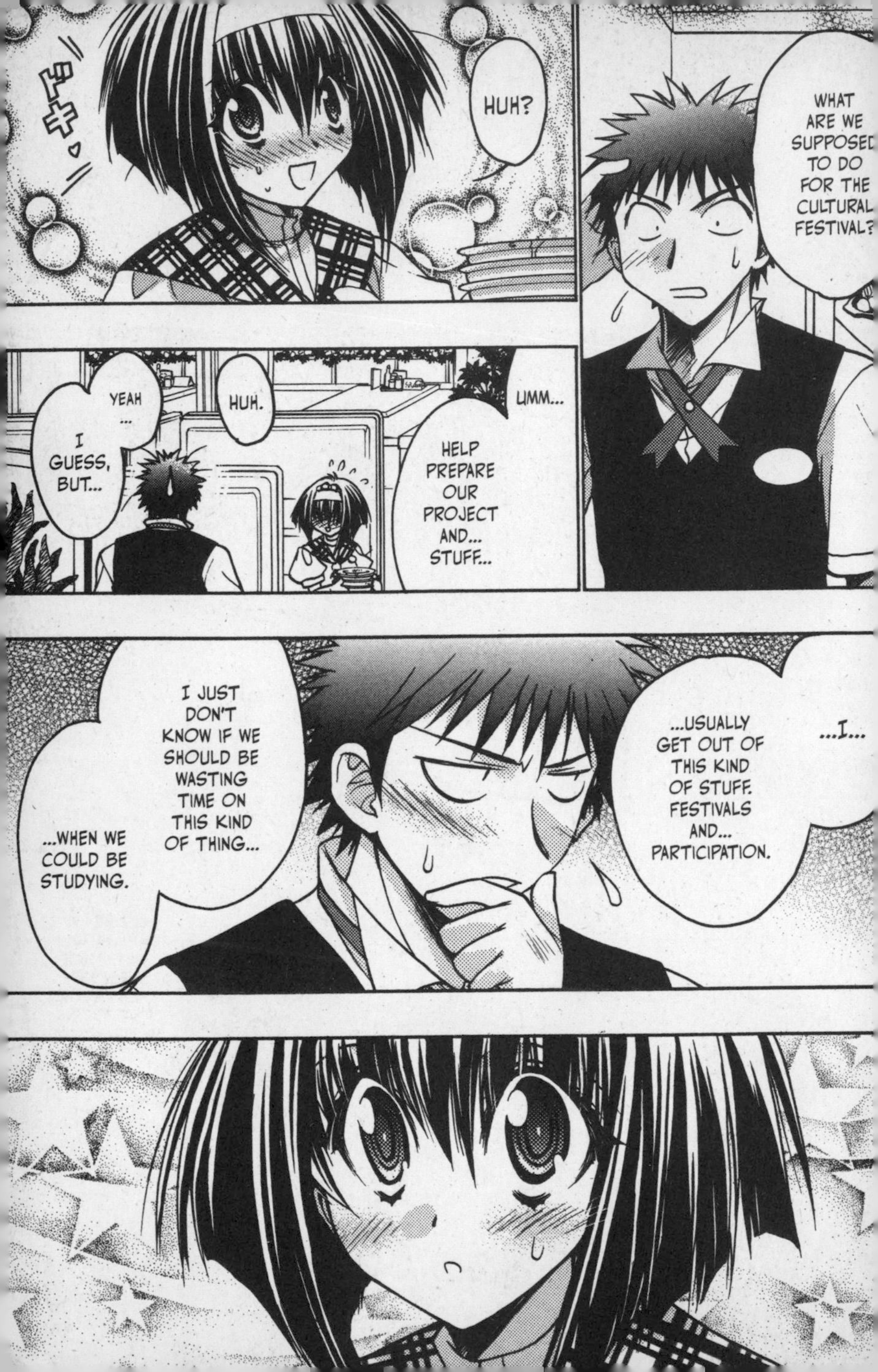
WHAT ARE WE SUPPOSED TO DO FOR THE CULTURAL FESTIVAL?
HUH?
ドキ
UMM...
HELP PREPARE OUR PROJECT AND... STUFF...
HUH.
YEAH... I GUESS, BUT...
...I...
...USUALLY GET OUT OF THIS KIND OF STUFF. FESTIVALS AND... PARTICIPATION.
I JUST DON'T KNOW IF WE SHOULD BE WASTING TIME ON THIS KIND OF THING...
...WHEN WE COULD BE STUDYING.

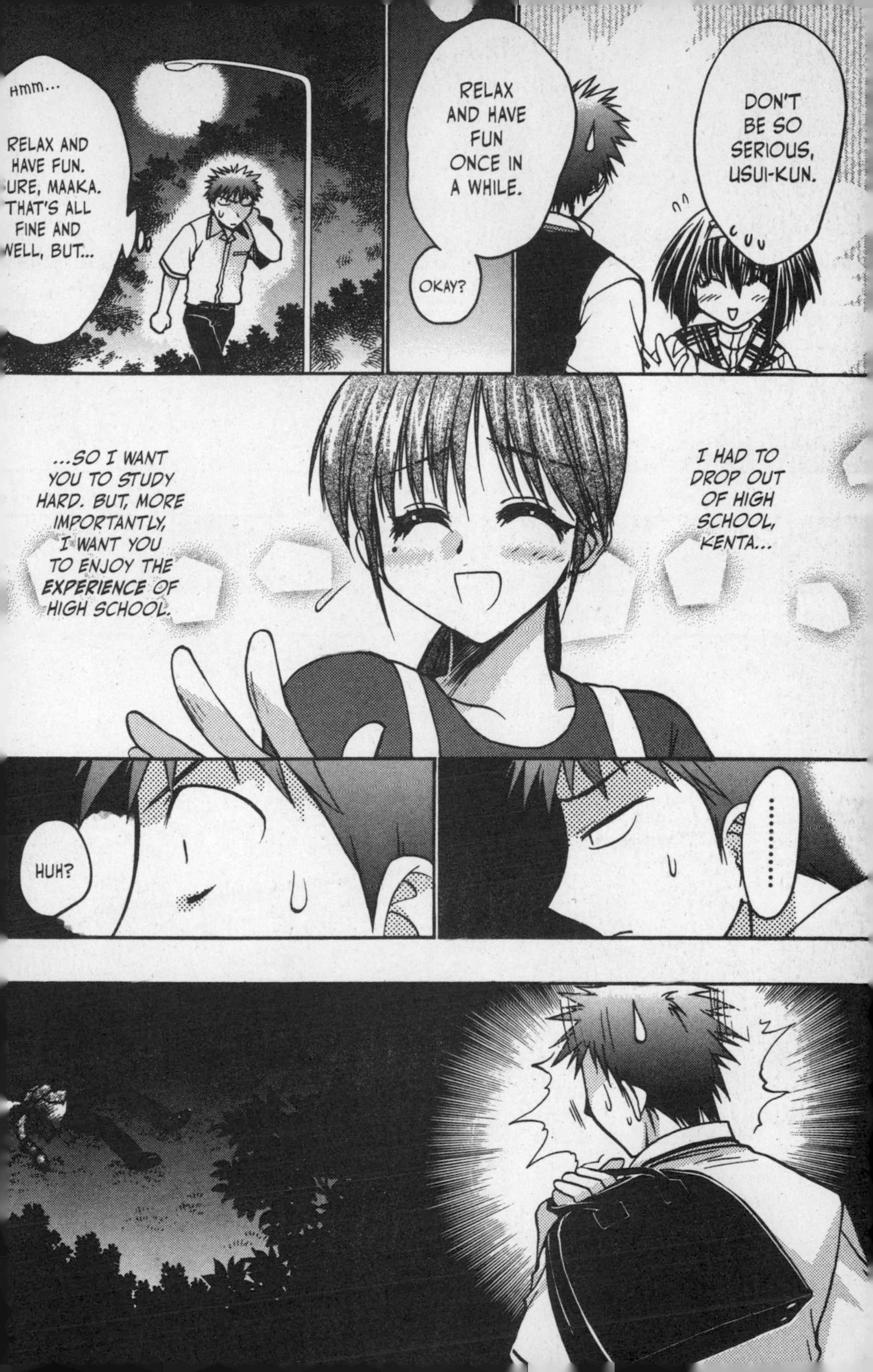
DON'T BE SO SERIOUS, USUI-KUN.
RELAX AND HAVE FUN ONCE IN A WHILE.
OKAY?
Hmm...
RELAX AND HAVE FUN. URE, MAAKA. THAT'S ALL FINE AND WELL, BUT...
I HAD TO DROP OUT OF HIGH SCHOOL, KENTA...
...SO I WANT YOU TO STUDY HARD. BUT, MORE IMPORTANTLY, I WANT YOU TO ENJOY THE **EXPERIENCE** OF HIGH SCHOOL.
....
HUH?

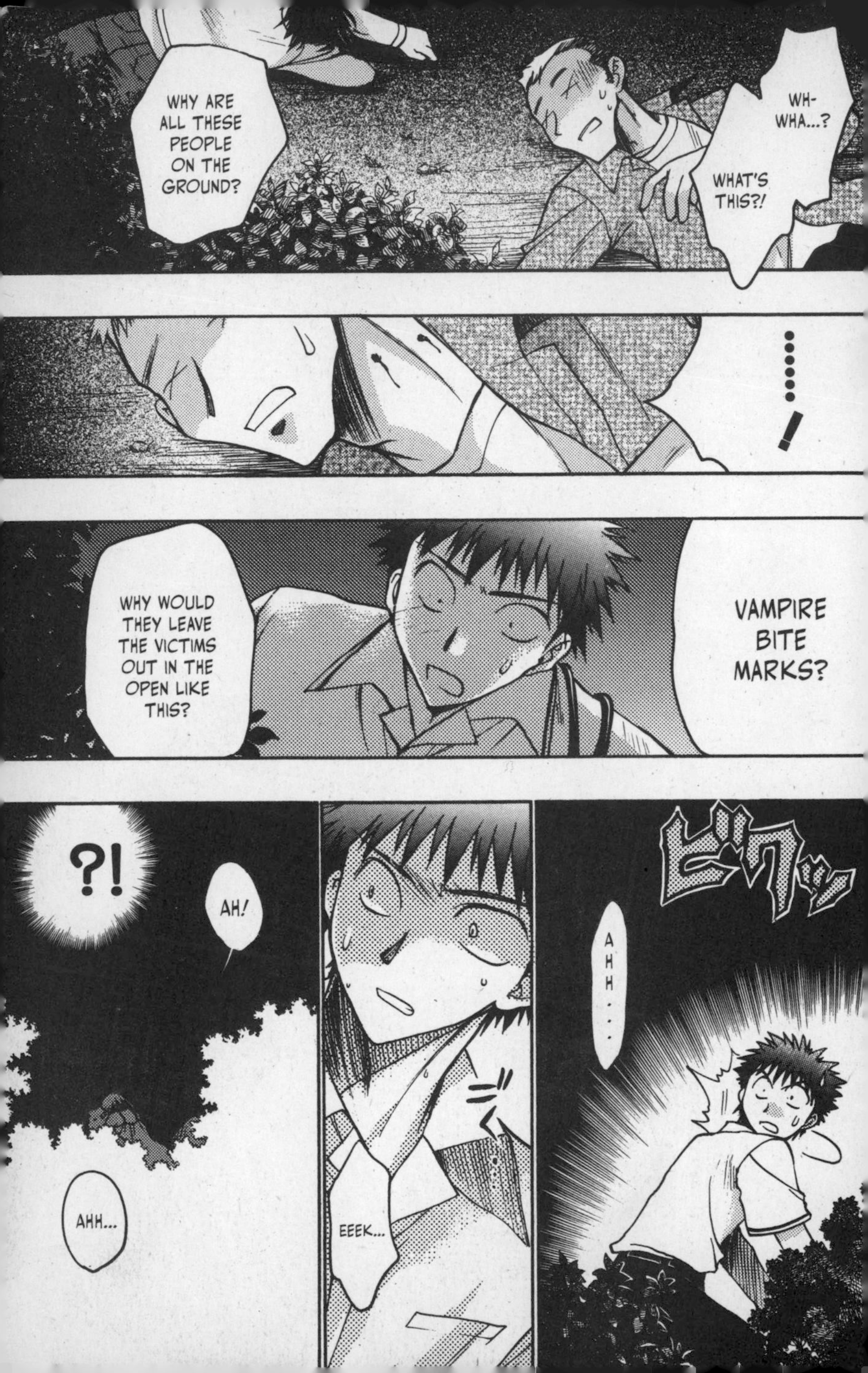
WH- WHA...?
WHAT'S THIS?!
WHY ARE ALL THESE PEOPLE ON THE GROUND?
......!
VAMPIRE BITE MARKS?
WHY WOULD THEY LEAVE THE VICTIMS OUT IN THE OPEN LIKE THIS?
ビクッ
AHH...
EEEK...
?!
AH!
AHH...

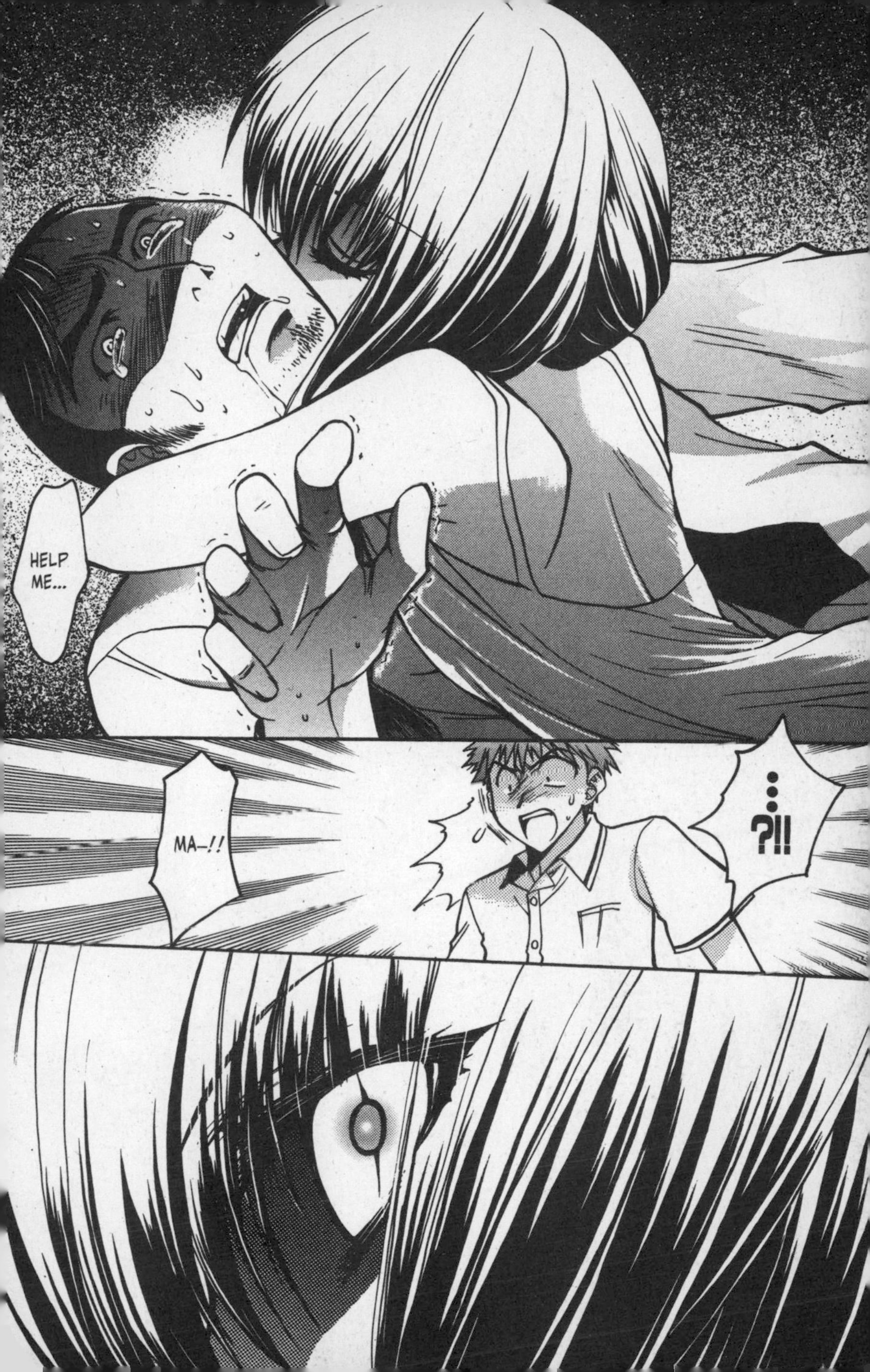
HELP ME...
...?!!
MA–!!

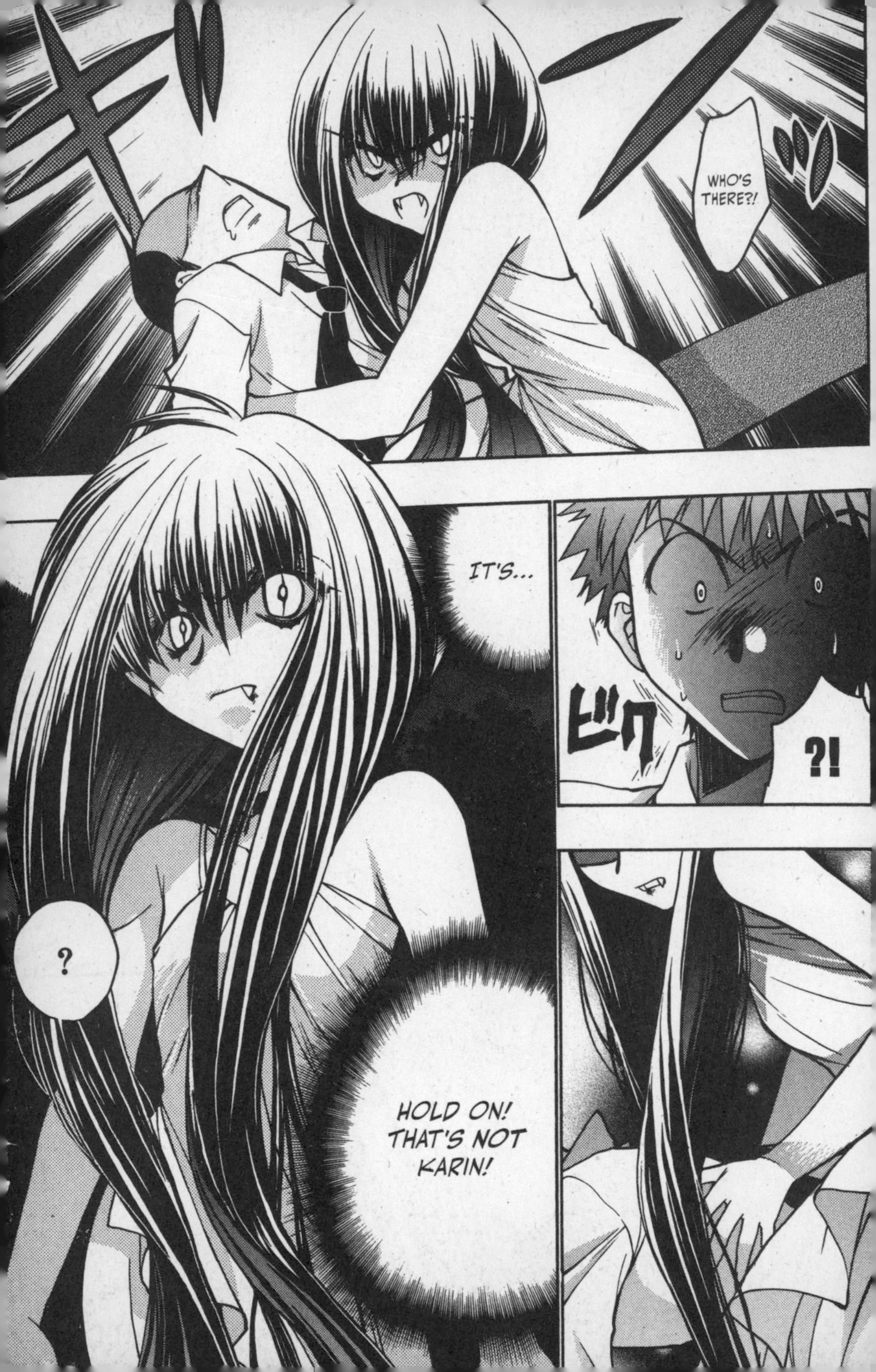
WHO'S THERE?!
ビク
?!
IT'S...
?
HOLD ON! THAT'S NOT KARIN!

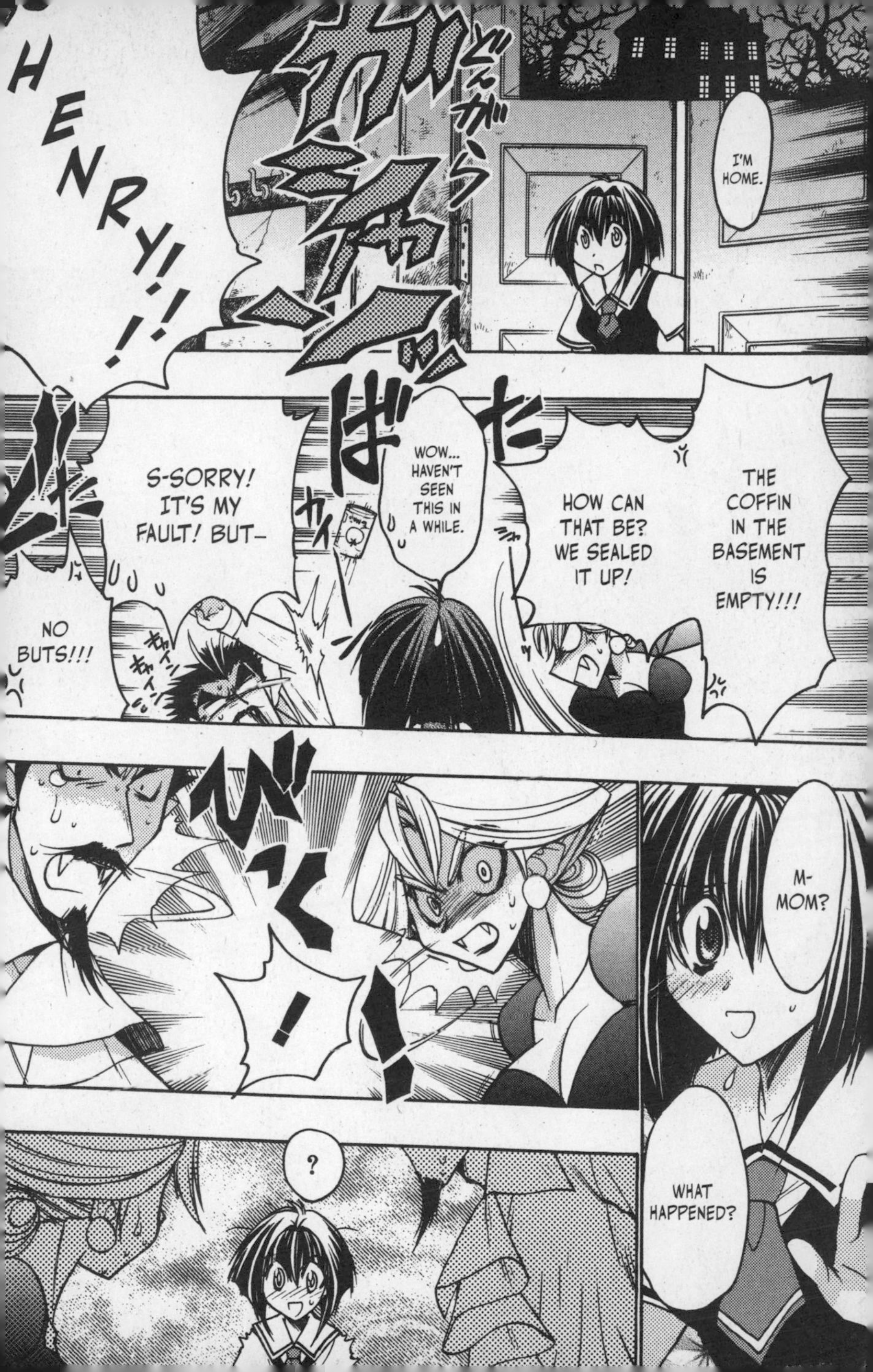
I'M HOME.
どんがら
HENRY!!!!
THE COFFIN IN THE BASEMENT IS EMPTY!!!
HOW CAN THAT BE? WE SEALED IT UP!
WOW... HAVEN'T SEEN THIS IN A WHILE.
S-SORRY! IT'S MY FAULT! BUT—
NO BUTS!!!
M-MOM?
!
WHAT HAPPENED?
?

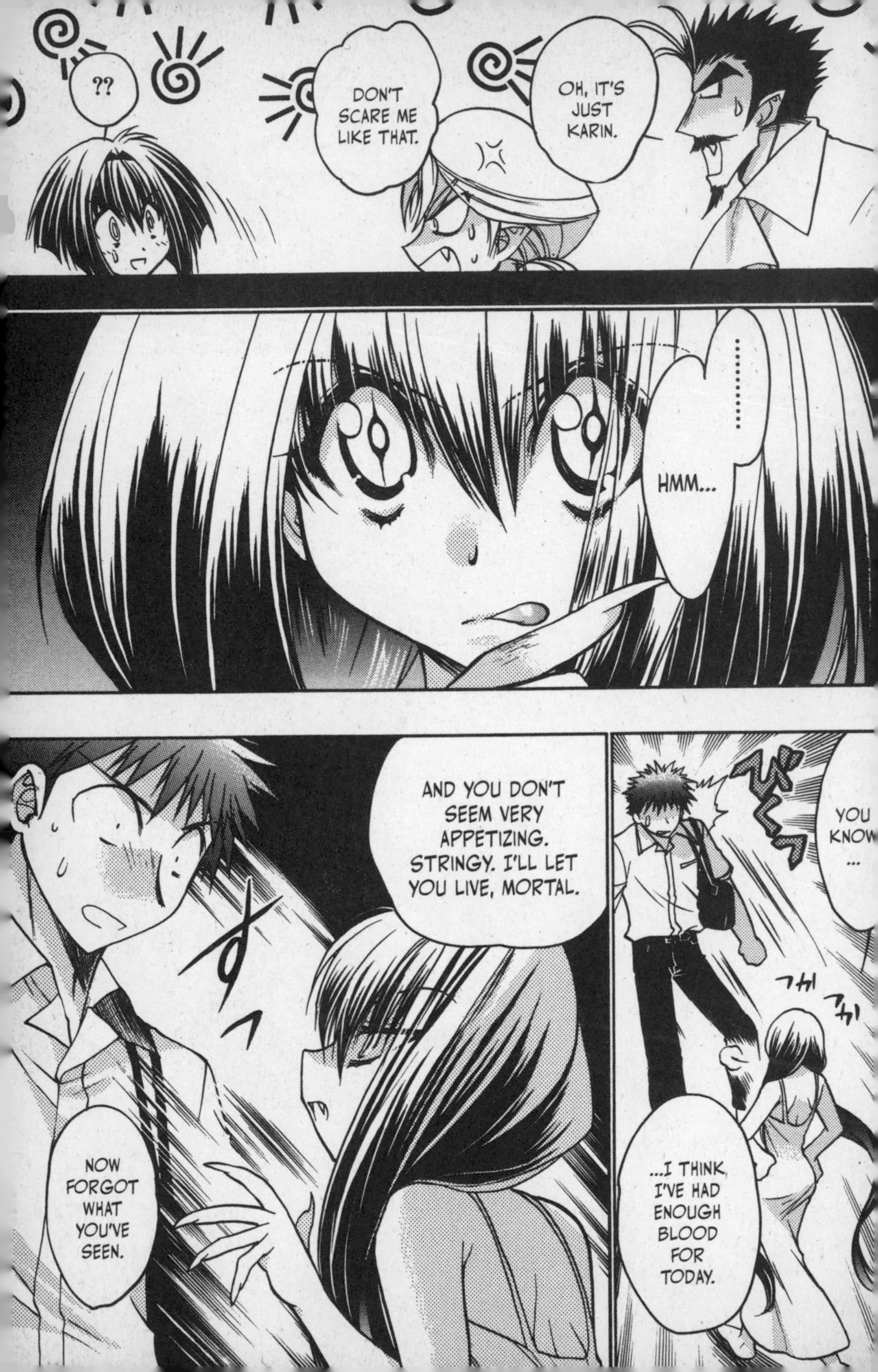
OH, IT'S JUST KARIN.
DON'T SCARE ME LIKE THAT.
??
......
HMM...
YOU KNOW ...
...I THINK, I'VE HAD ENOUGH BLOOD FOR TODAY.
AND YOU DON'T SEEM VERY APPETIZING. STRINGY. I'LL LET YOU LIVE, MORTAL.
NOW FORGOT WHAT YOU'VE SEEN.

OH...
ドサ!!
PHEW...
NOW, RETURN HOME...?
KNOWING THE FAMILY, THEY MAY HAVE ALREADY NOTICED.

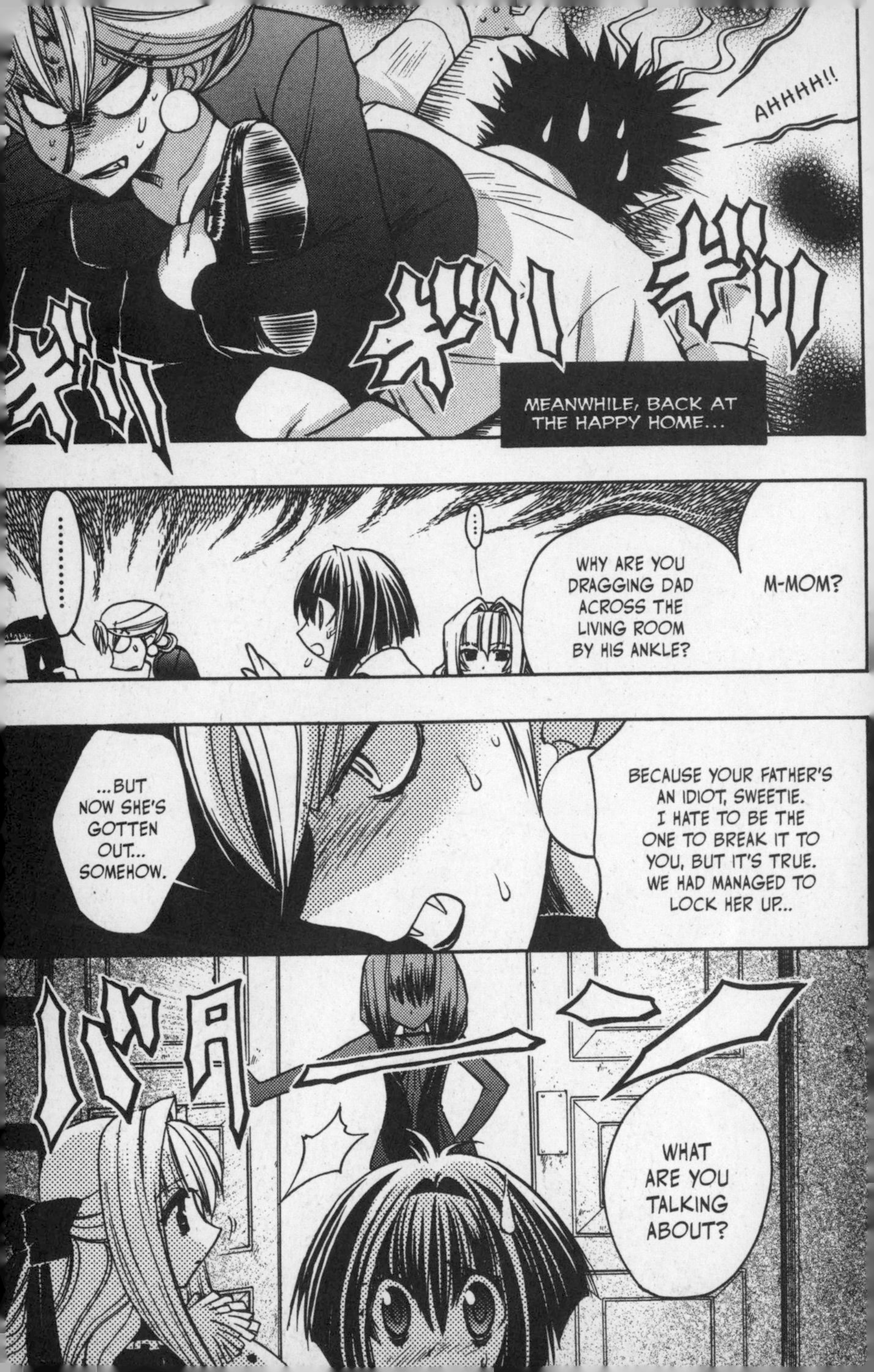
AHHHH!!
MEANWHILE, BACK AT THE HAPPY HOME...
M-MOM?
WHY ARE YOU DRAGGING DAD ACROSS THE LIVING ROOM BY HIS ANKLE?
...
......
BECAUSE YOUR FATHER'S AN IDIOT, SWEETIE. I HATE TO BE THE ONE TO BREAK IT TO YOU, BUT IT'S TRUE. WE HAD MANAGED TO LOCK HER UP...
...BUT NOW SHE'S GOTTEN OUT... SOMEHOW.
WHAT ARE YOU TALKING ABOUT?

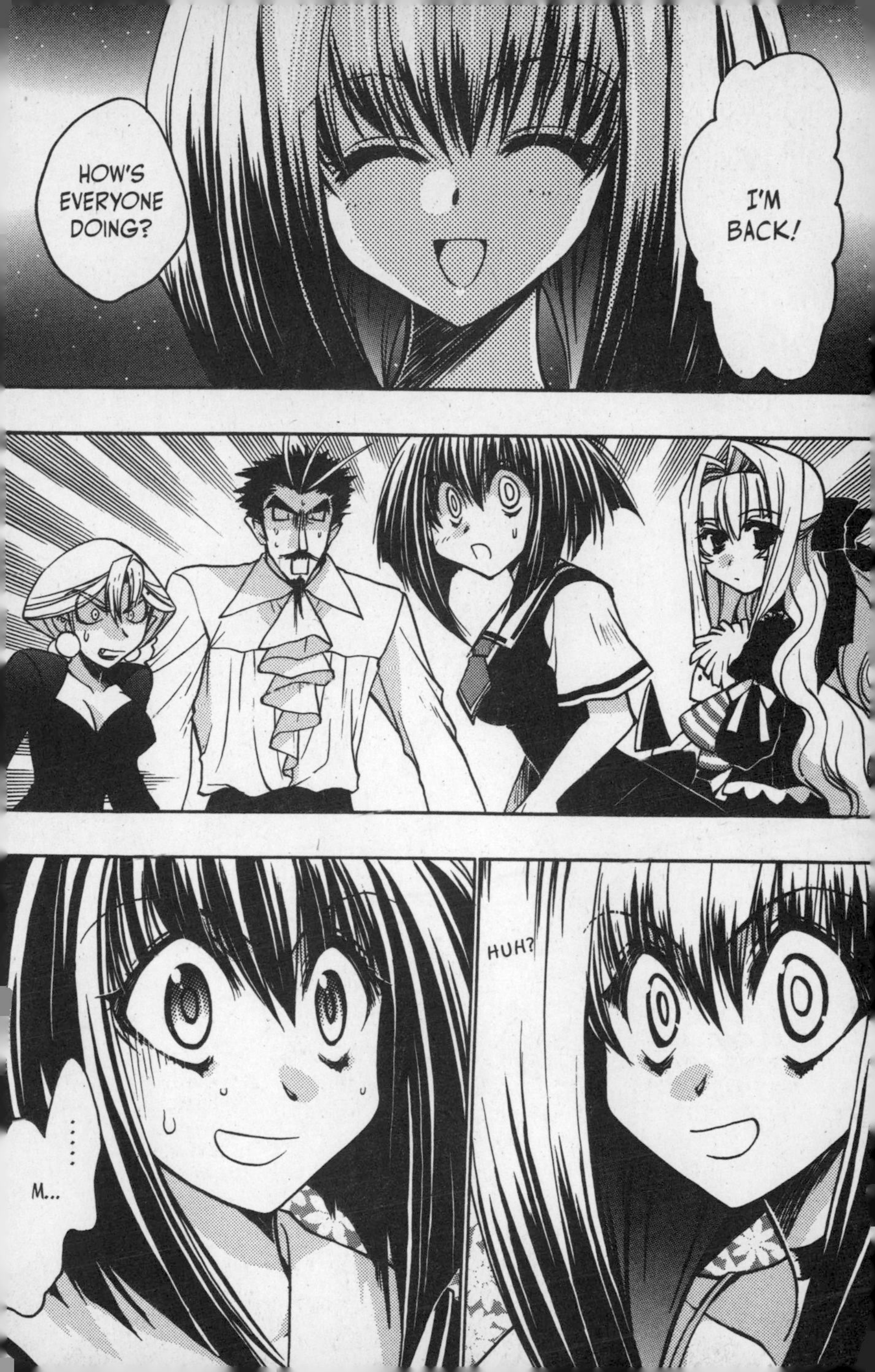
I'M BACK!
HOW'S EVERYONE DOING?
HUH?
......
M...

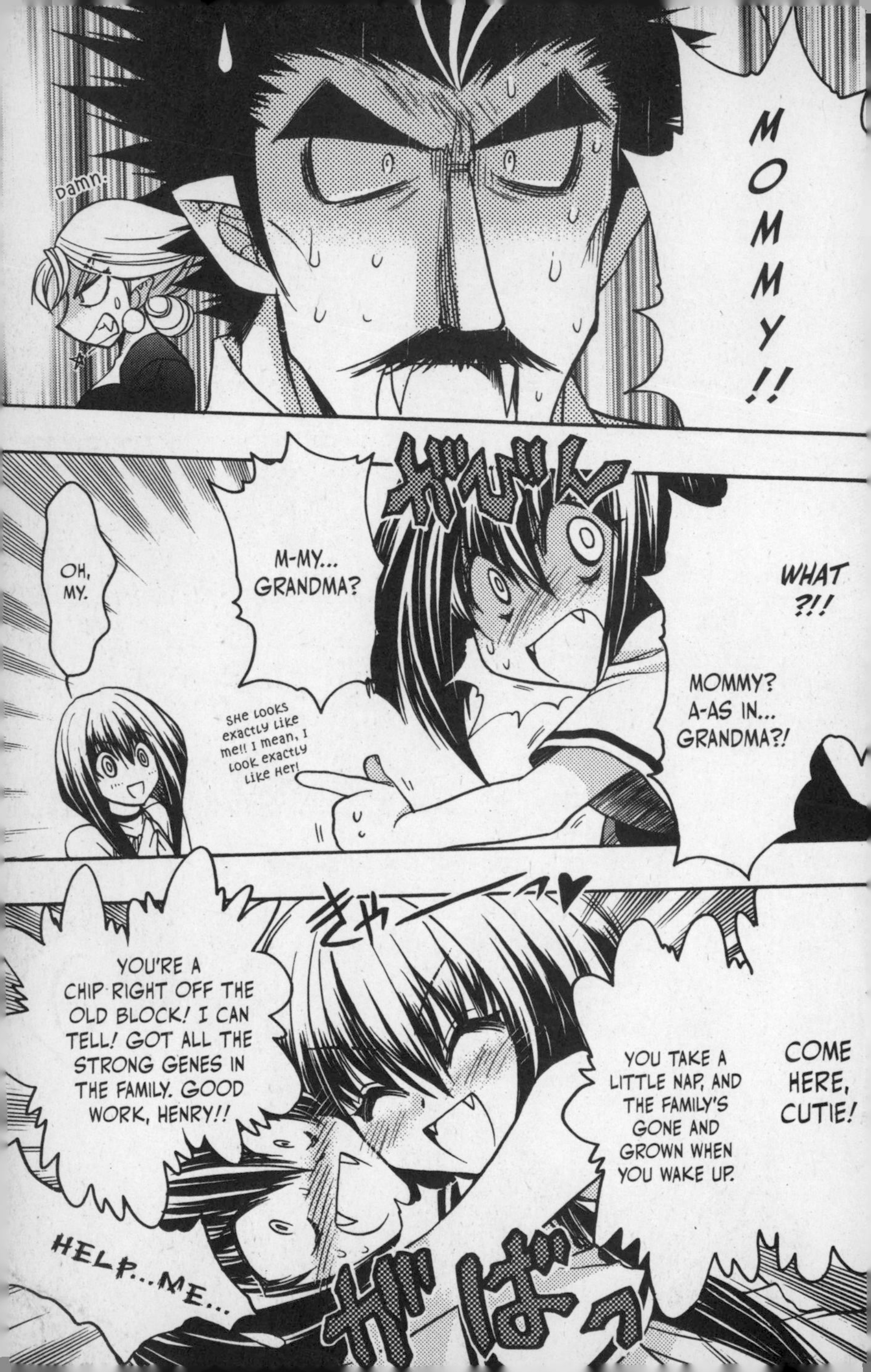
MOMMY!!
Damn.
WHAT?!!
MOMMY? A-AS IN... GRANDMA?!
M-MY... GRANDMA?
OH, MY.
She looks exactly like me!! I mean, I look exactly like her!
COME HERE, CUTIE!
YOU TAKE A LITTLE NAP, AND THE FAMILY'S GONE AND GROWN WHEN YOU WAKE UP.
きゃーーー♥
YOU'RE A CHIP RIGHT OFF THE OLD BLOCK! I CAN TELL! GOT ALL THE STRONG GENES IN THE FAMILY. GOOD WORK, HENRY!!
がばっ
HELP...ME...

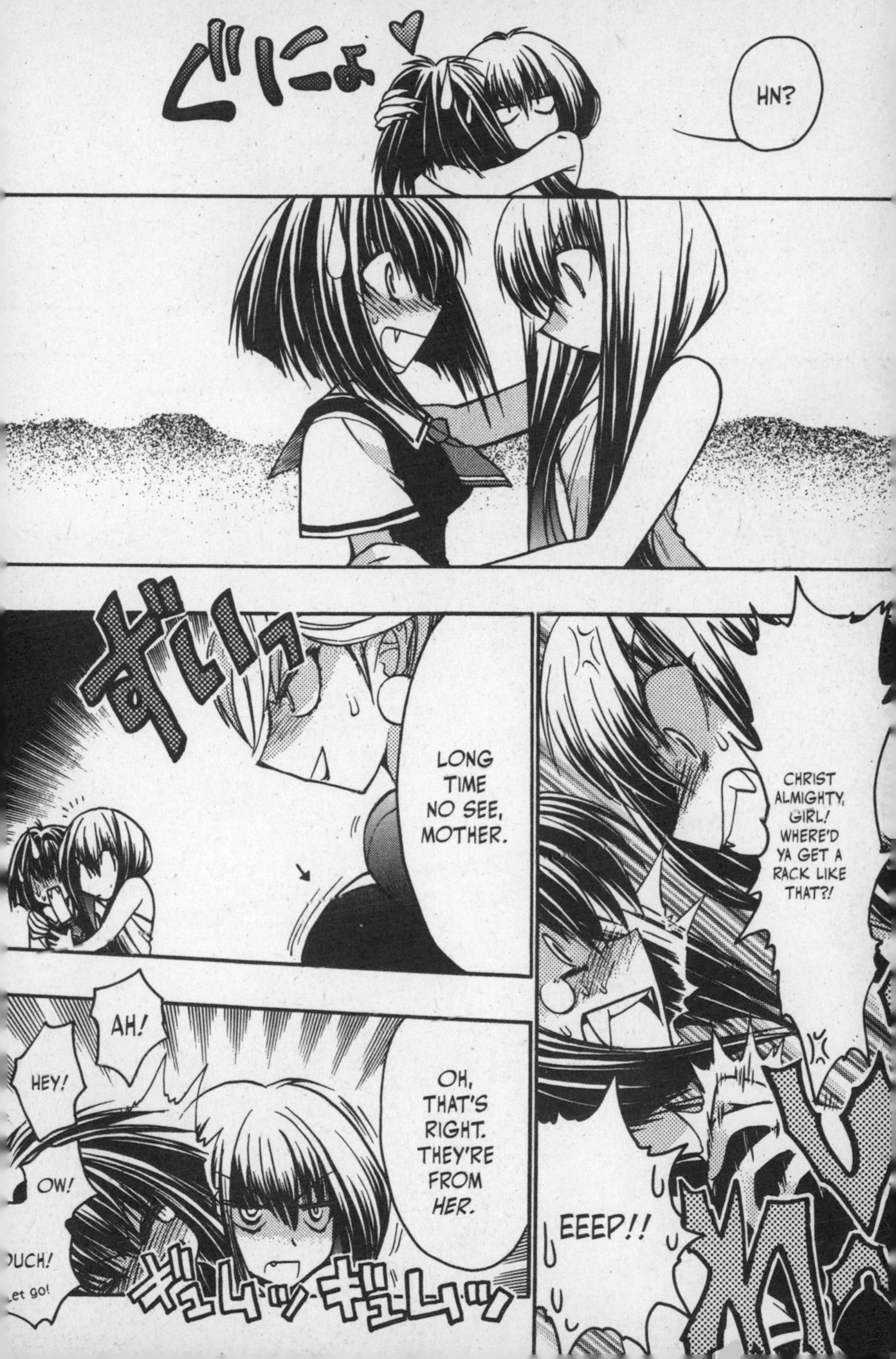
HN?
ぐにょ♥
CHRIST ALMIGHTY, GIRL! WHERE'D YA GET A RACK LIKE THAT?!
EEEP!!
ずいっ
LONG TIME NO SEE, MOTHER.
OH, THAT'S RIGHT. THEY'RE FROM HER.
AH!
HEY!
OW!
UCH!
et go!
ぎゅむっ ぎゅむっ

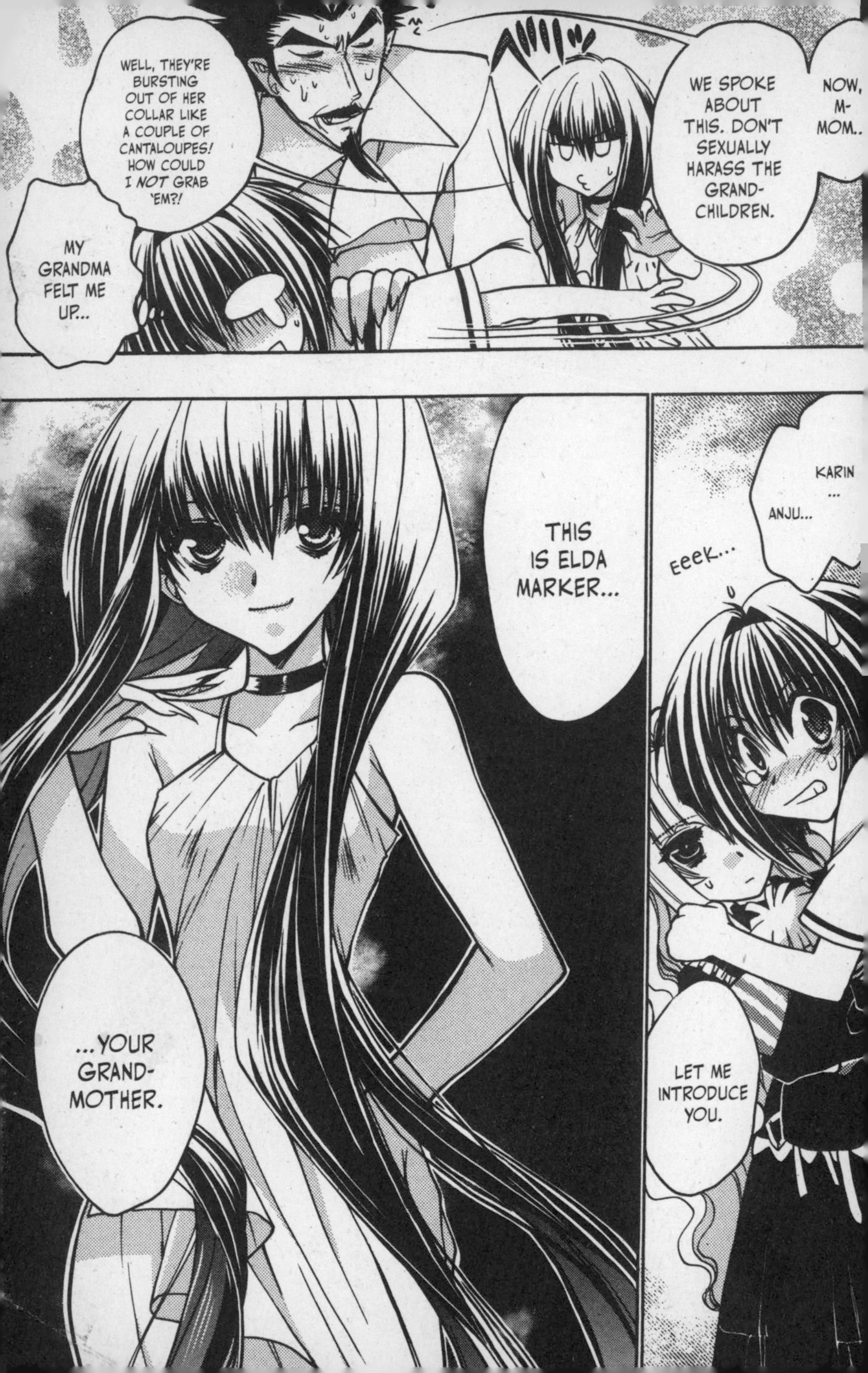
NOW, M-MOM..
WE SPOKE ABOUT THIS. DON'T SEXUALLY HARASS THE GRAND-CHILDREN.
WELL, THEY'RE BURSTING OUT OF HER COLLAR LIKE A COUPLE OF CANTALOUPES! HOW COULD I *NOT* GRAB 'EM?!
MY GRANDMA FELT ME UP...
KARIN...
ANJU...
Eeek...
LET ME INTRODUCE YOU.
THIS IS ELDA MARKER...
...YOUR GRAND-MOTHER.

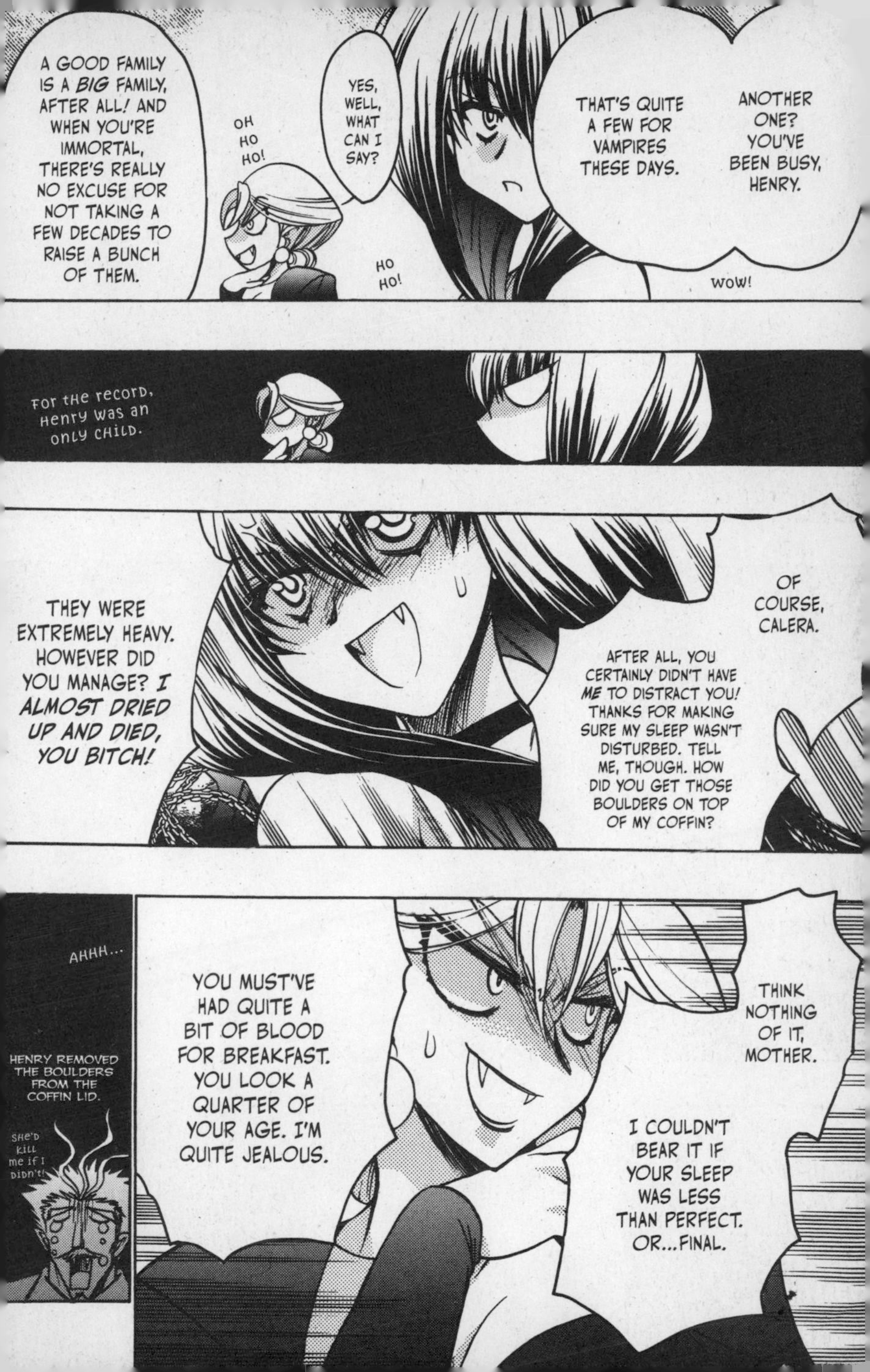

ANOTHER ONE? YOU'VE BEEN BUSY, HENRY.
THAT'S QUITE A FEW FOR VAMPIRES THESE DAYS.
WOW!
YES, WELL, WHAT CAN I SAY?
HO HO!
OH HO HO!
A GOOD FAMILY IS A *BIG* FAMILY, AFTER ALL! AND WHEN YOU'RE IMMORTAL, THERE'S REALLY NO EXCUSE FOR NOT TAKING A FEW DECADES TO RAISE A BUNCH OF THEM.
For the record, Henry was an only child.
OF COURSE, CALERA.
AFTER ALL, YOU CERTAINLY DIDN'T HAVE *ME* TO DISTRACT YOU! THANKS FOR MAKING SURE MY SLEEP WASN'T DISTURBED. TELL ME, THOUGH. HOW DID YOU GET THOSE BOULDERS ON TOP OF MY COFFIN?
THEY WERE EXTREMELY HEAVY. HOWEVER DID YOU MANAGE? ***I ALMOST DRIED UP AND DIED, YOU BITCH!***
THINK NOTHING OF IT, MOTHER.
I COULDN'T BEAR IT IF YOUR SLEEP WAS LESS THAN PERFECT. OR...FINAL.
YOU MUST'VE HAD QUITE A BIT OF BLOOD FOR BREAKFAST. YOU LOOK A QUARTER OF YOUR AGE. I'M QUITE JEALOUS.
AHHH...
HENRY REMOVED THE BOULDERS FROM THE COFFIN LID.
SHE'D KILL ME IF I DIDN'T!

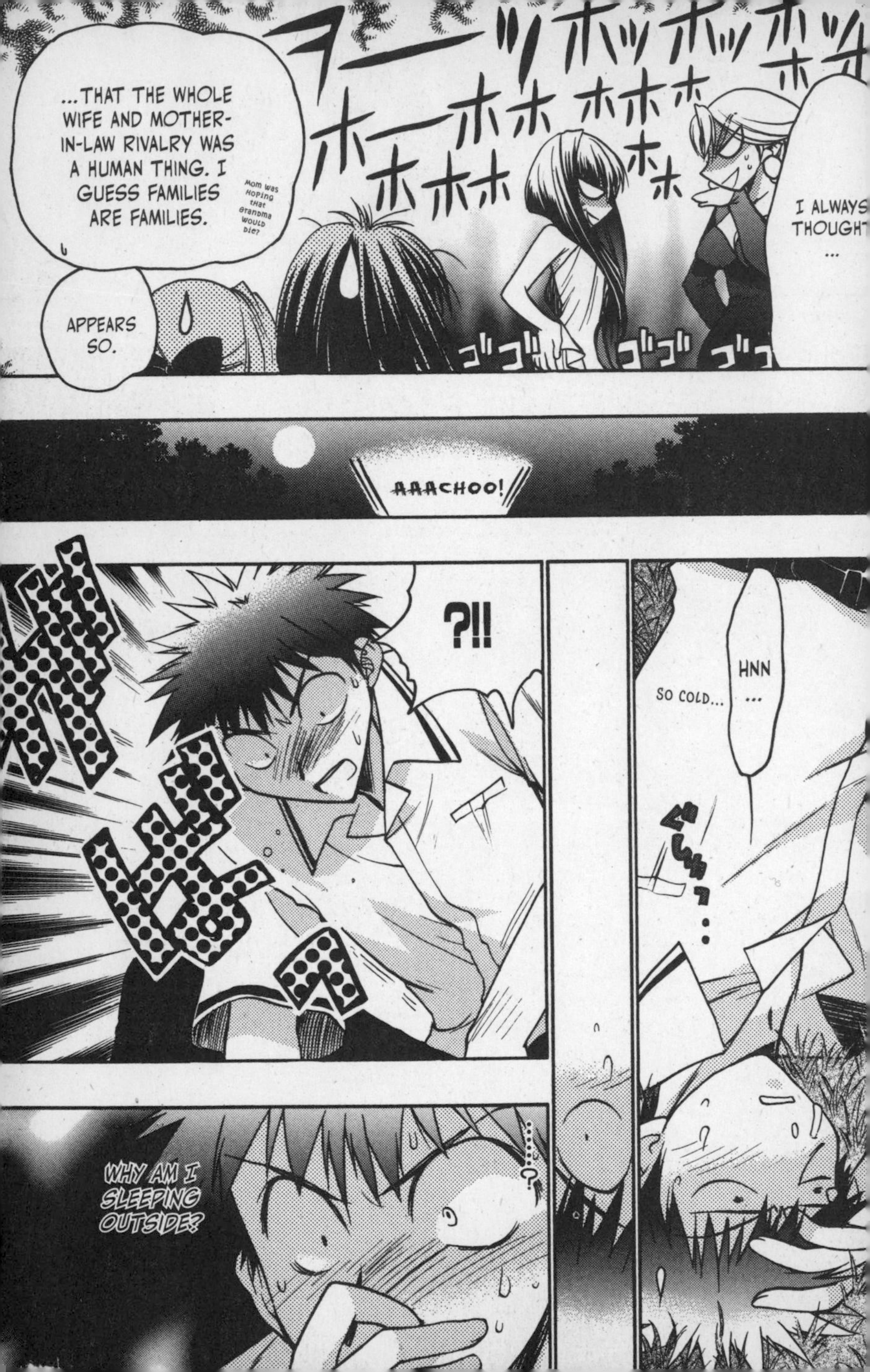
I ALWAYS THOUGHT ...
...THAT THE WHOLE WIFE AND MOTHER-IN-LAW RIVALRY WAS A HUMAN THING. I GUESS FAMILIES ARE FAMILIES.
Mom was hoping that grandma would die?
APPEARS SO.
AAACHOO!
HNN ...
SO COLD...
?!!
WHY AM I SLEEPING OUTSIDE?

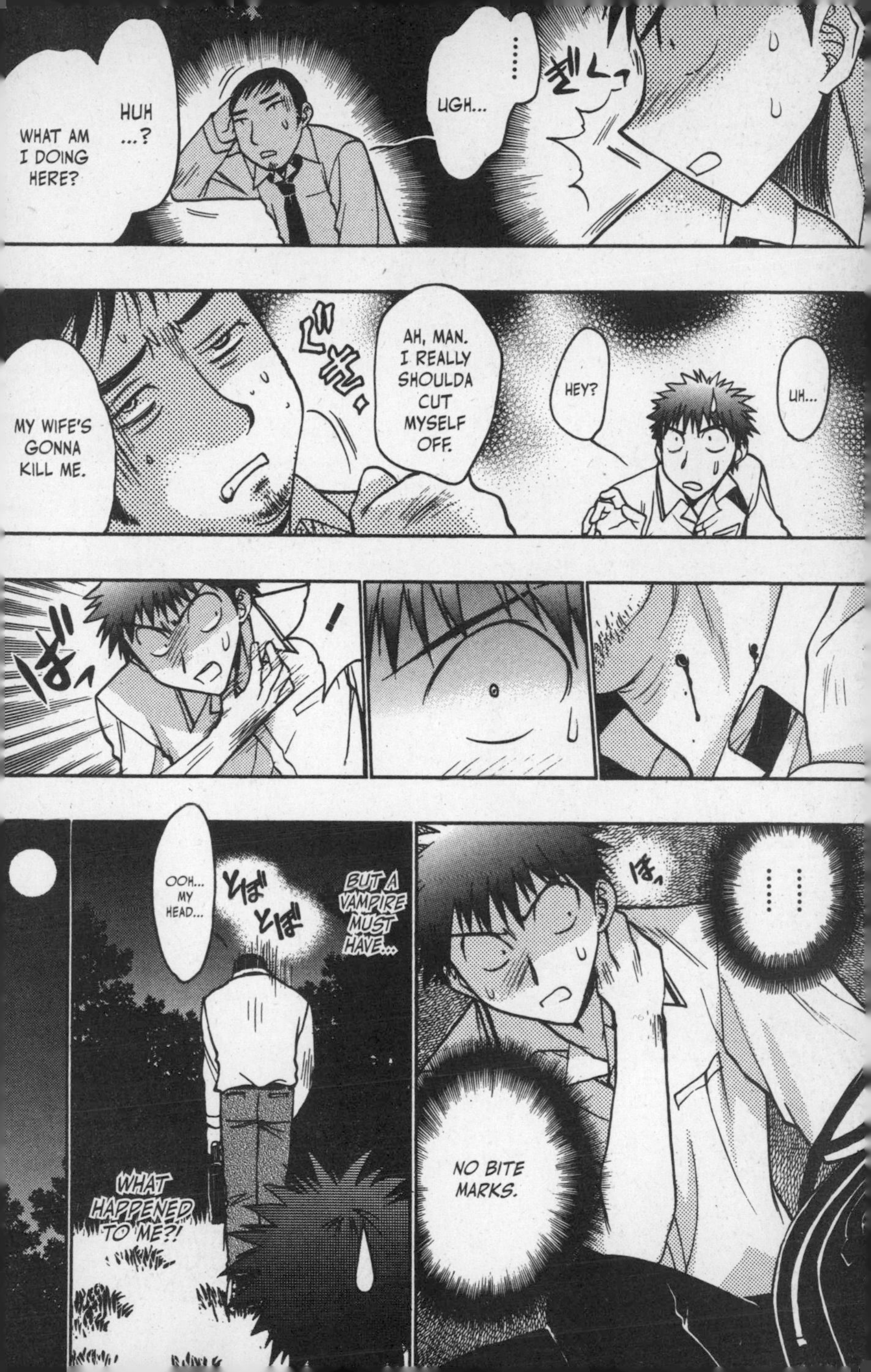
......
ぎくっ
UGH...
HUH ...?
WHAT AM I DOING HERE?
UH...
HEY?
AH, MAN. I REALLY SHOULDA CUT MYSELF OFF.
MY WIFE'S GONNA KILL ME.
!
ばっ
ほっ
......
NO BITE MARKS.
BUT A VAMPIRE MUST HAVE...
とぼ とぼ
OOH... MY HEAD...
WHAT HAPPENED TO ME?!

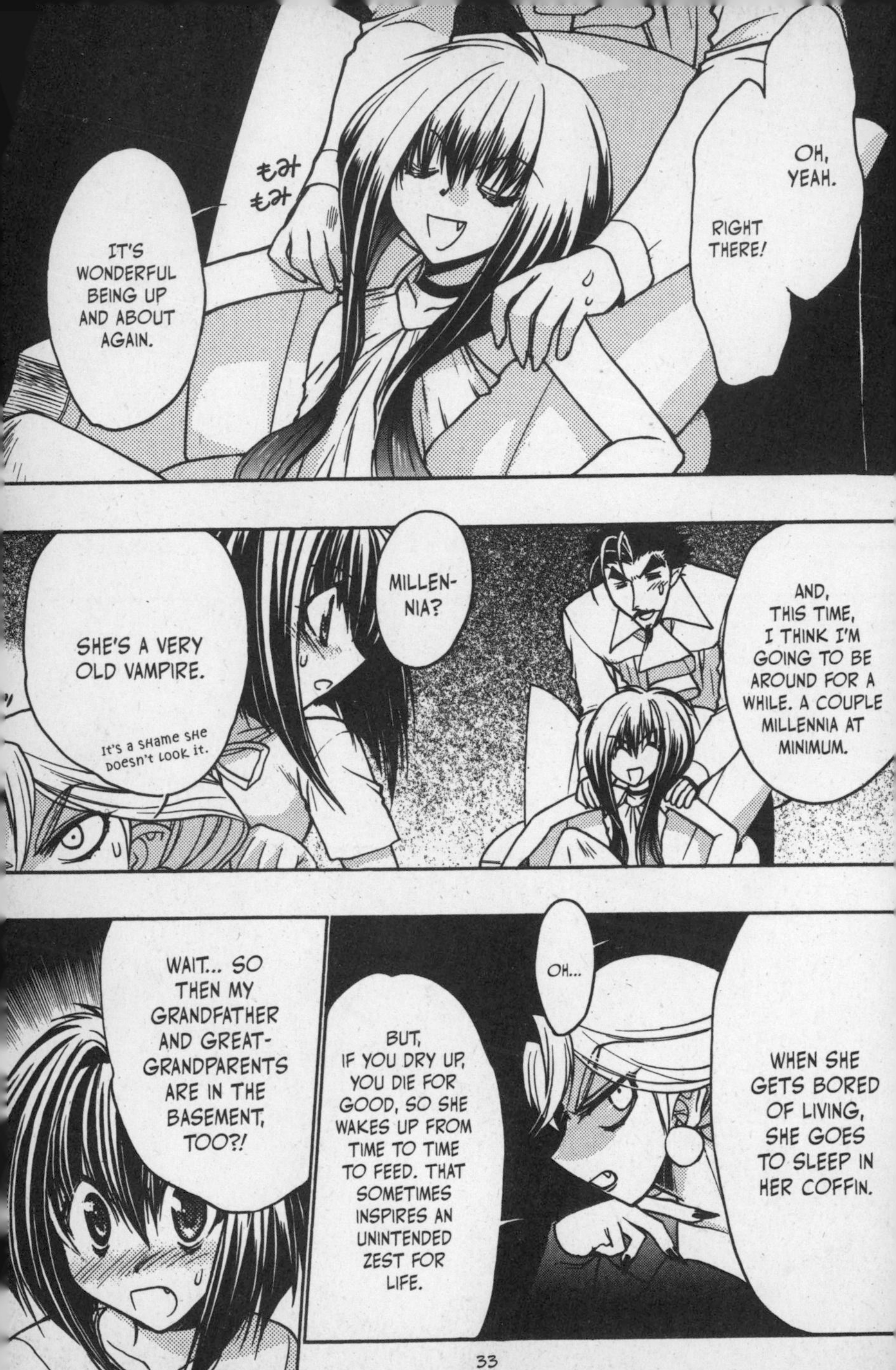
OH, YEAH.
RIGHT THERE!
もみ もみ
IT'S WONDERFUL BEING UP AND ABOUT AGAIN.
AND, THIS TIME, I THINK I'M GOING TO BE AROUND FOR A WHILE. A COUPLE MILLENNIA AT MINIMUM.
MILLEN-NIA?
SHE'S A VERY OLD VAMPIRE.
It's a shame she doesn't look it.
WHEN SHE GETS BORED OF LIVING, SHE GOES TO SLEEP IN HER COFFIN.
OH...
BUT, IF YOU DRY UP, YOU DIE FOR GOOD, SO SHE WAKES UP FROM TIME TO TIME TO FEED. THAT SOMETIMES INSPIRES AN UNINTENDED ZEST FOR LIFE.
WAIT... SO THEN MY GRANDFATHER AND GREAT-GRANDPARENTS ARE IN THE BASEMENT, TOO?!

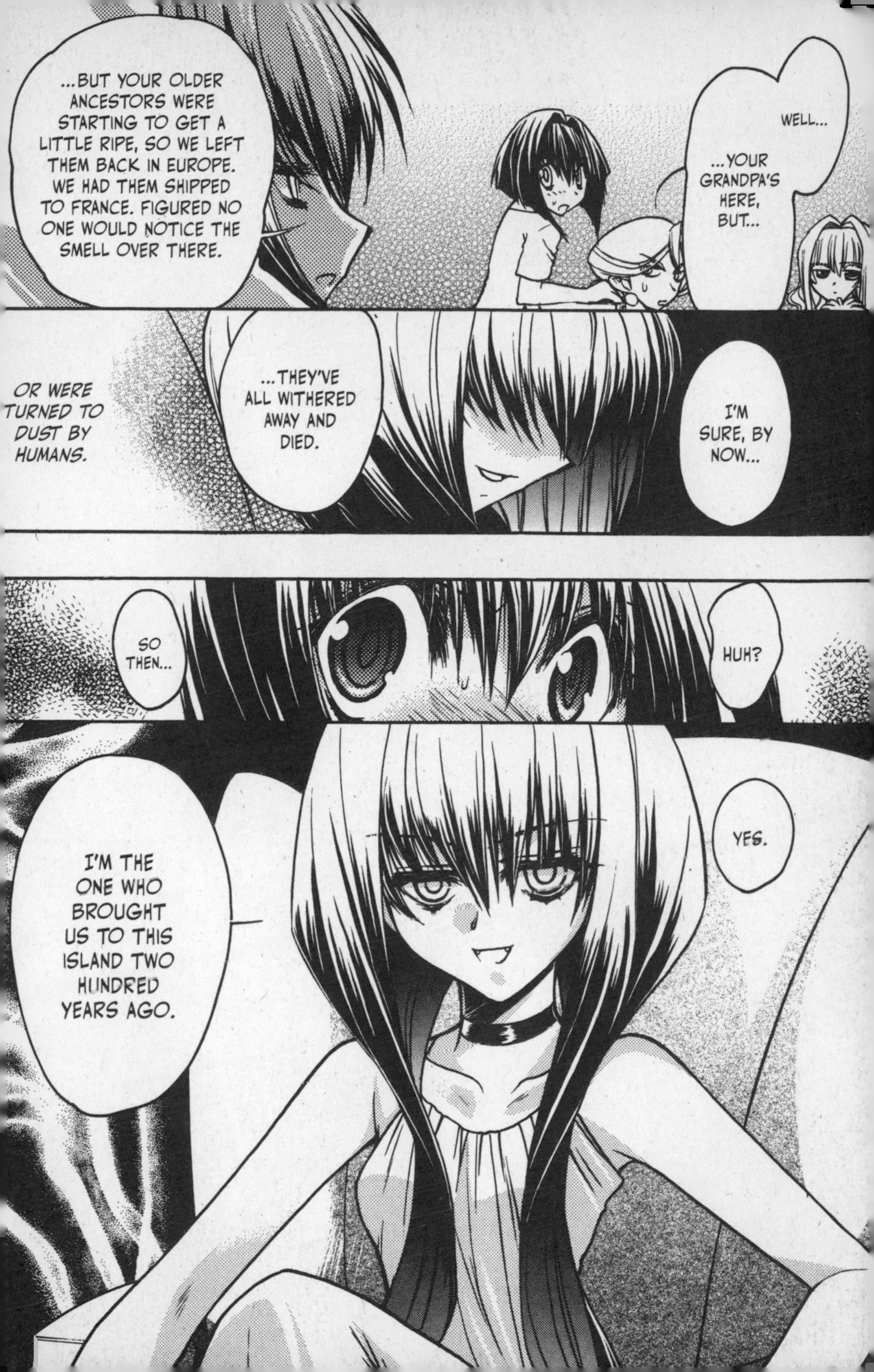
WELL...
...YOUR GRANDPA'S HERE, BUT...
...BUT YOUR OLDER ANCESTORS WERE STARTING TO GET A LITTLE RIPE, SO WE LEFT THEM BACK IN EUROPE. WE HAD THEM SHIPPED TO FRANCE. FIGURED NO ONE WOULD NOTICE THE SMELL OVER THERE.
I'M SURE, BY NOW...
...THEY'VE ALL WITHERED AWAY AND DIED.
OR WERE TURNED TO DUST BY HUMANS.
HUH?
SO THEN...
YES.
I'M THE ONE WHO BROUGHT US TO THIS ISLAND TWO HUNDRED YEARS AGO.

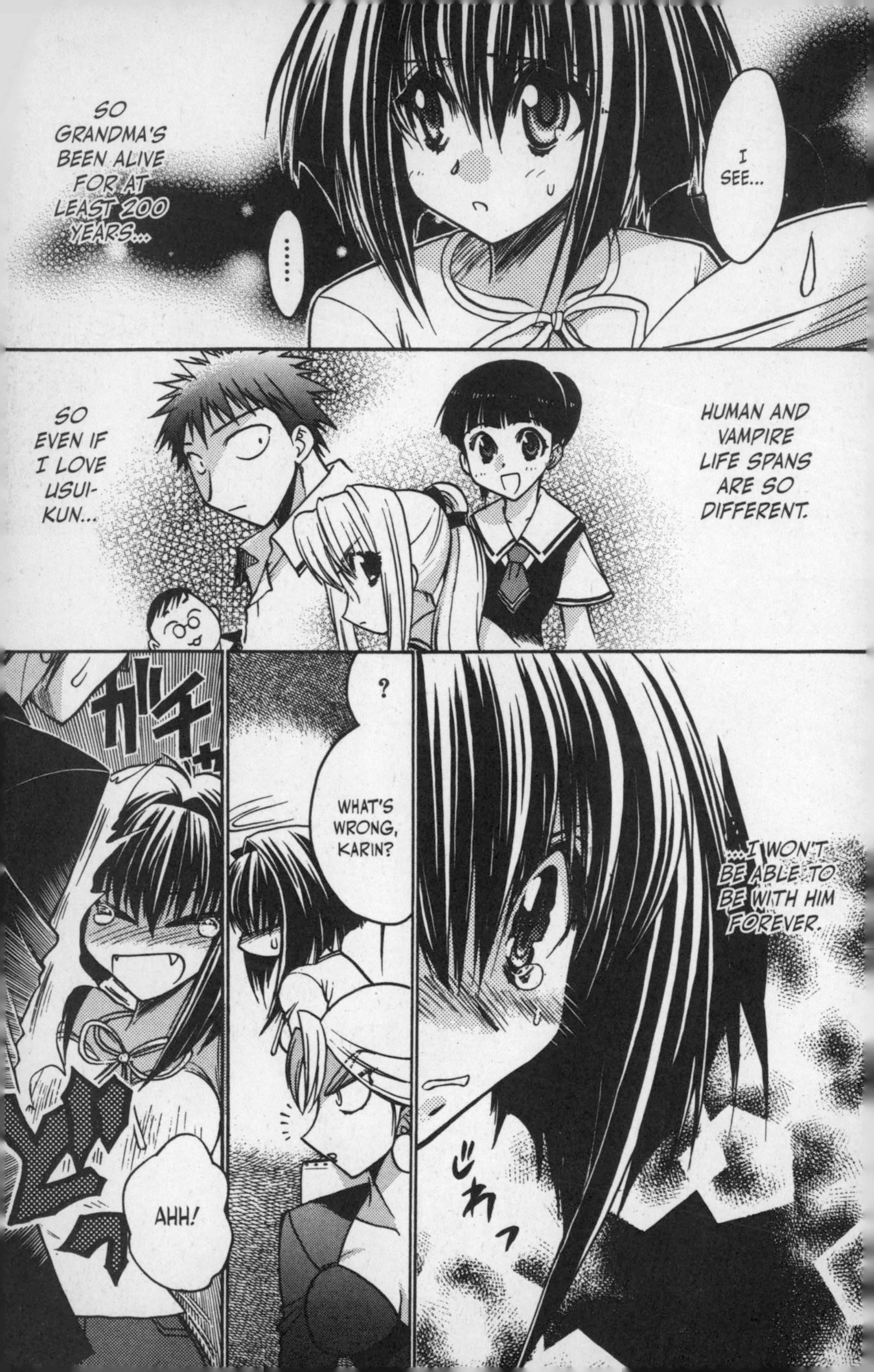
I SEE...
SO GRANDMA'S BEEN ALIVE FOR AT LEAST 200 YEARS...
......
HUMAN AND VAMPIRE LIFE SPANS ARE SO DIFFERENT.
SO EVEN IF I LOVE USUI-KUN...
...I WON'T BE ABLE TO BE WITH HIM FOREVER.
じわっ
?
WHAT'S WRONG, KARIN?
AHH!

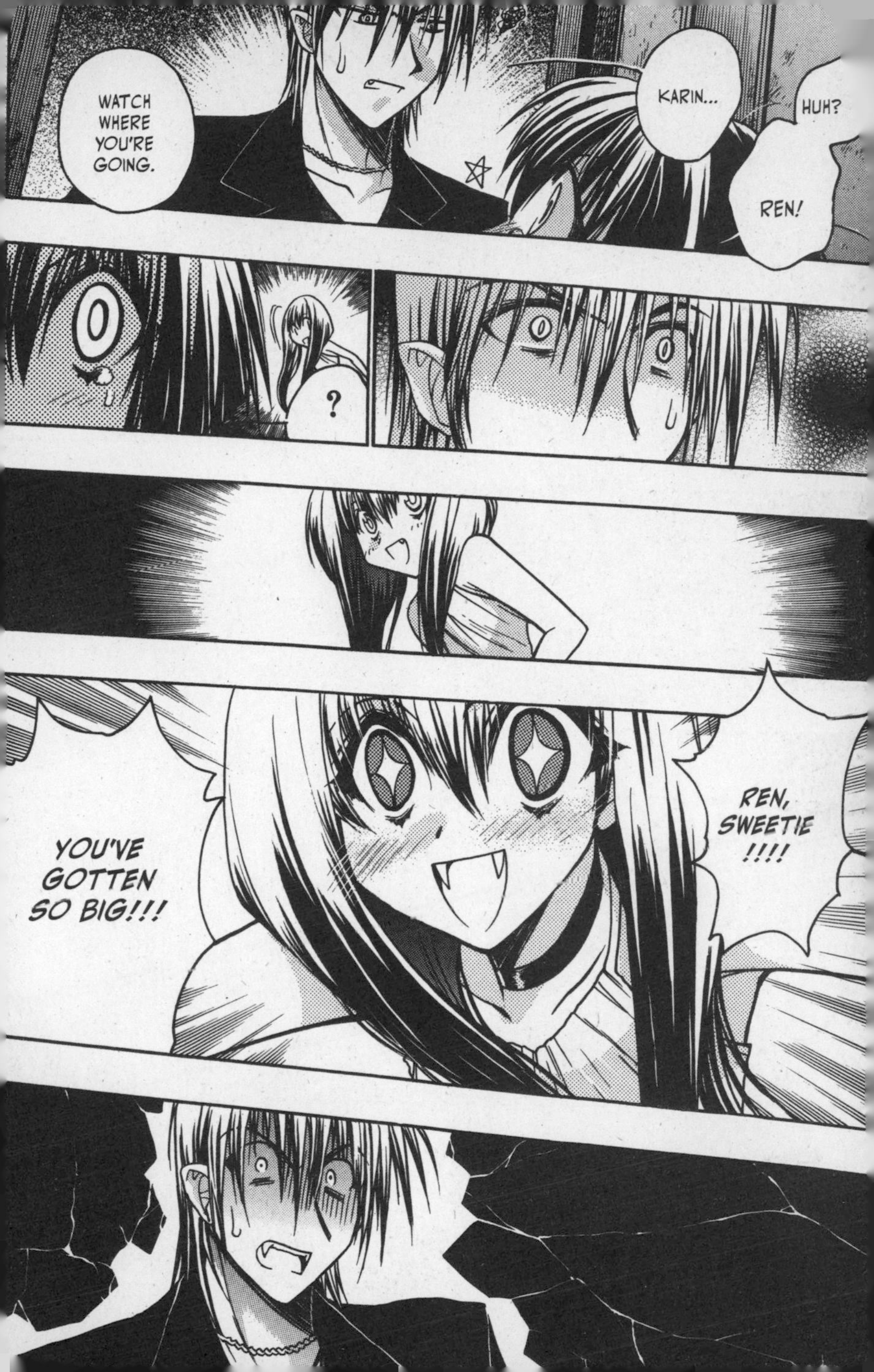
HUH?
REN!
KARIN...
WATCH WHERE YOU'RE GOING.
?
REN, SWEETIE !!!!
YOU'VE GOTTEN SO BIG!!!

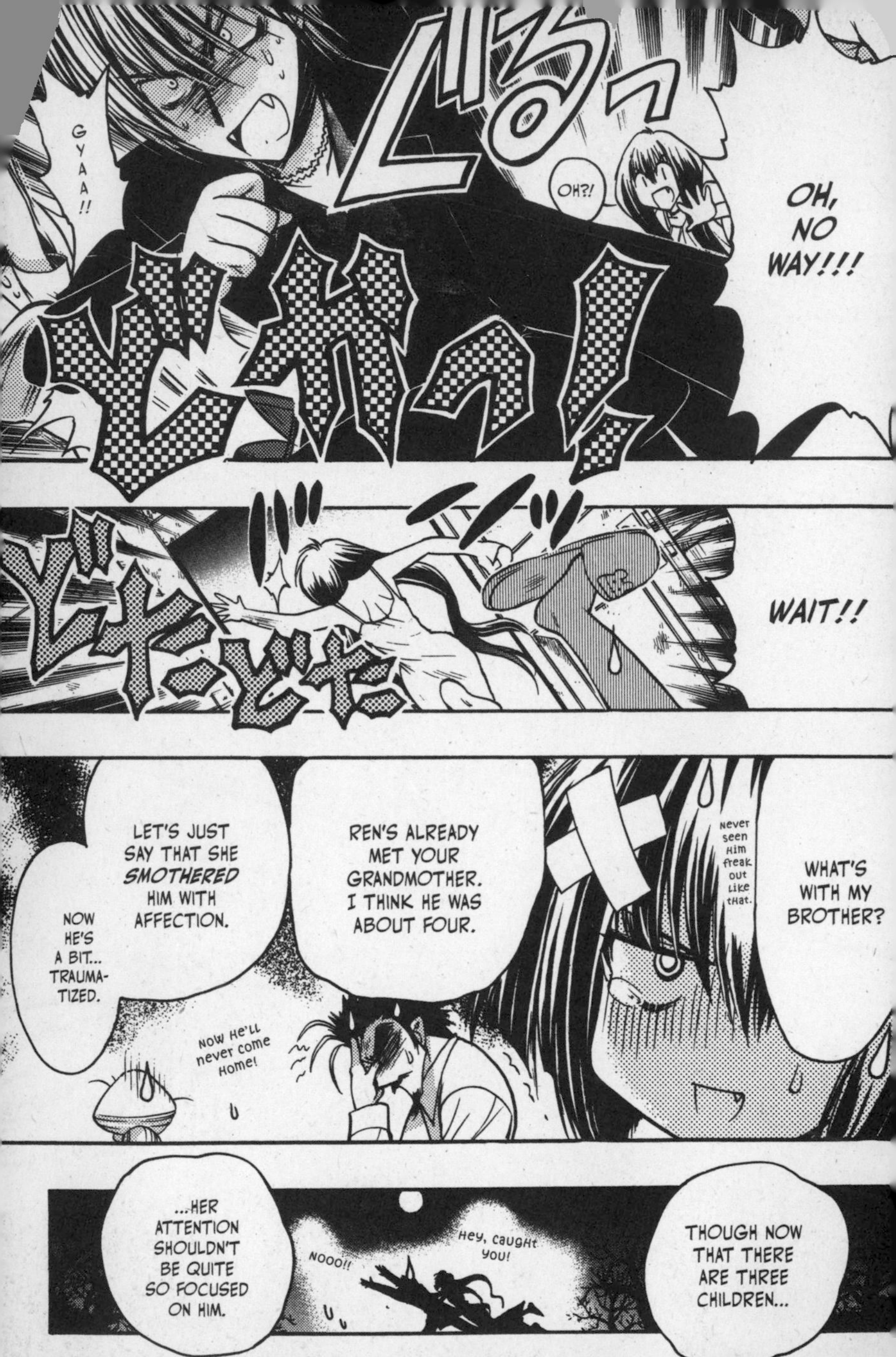
OH, NO WAY!!!
OH?!
GYAA!!
WAIT!!
WHAT'S WITH MY BROTHER?
Never seen him freak out like that.
REN'S ALREADY MET YOUR GRANDMOTHER. I THINK HE WAS ABOUT FOUR.
LET'S JUST SAY THAT SHE *SMOTHERED* HIM WITH AFFECTION.
NOW HE'S A BIT... TRAUMATIZED.
Now he'll never come home!
THOUGH NOW THAT THERE ARE THREE CHILDREN...
Hey, caught you!
NOOO!!
...HER ATTENTION SHOULDN'T BE QUITE SO FOCUSED ON HIM.

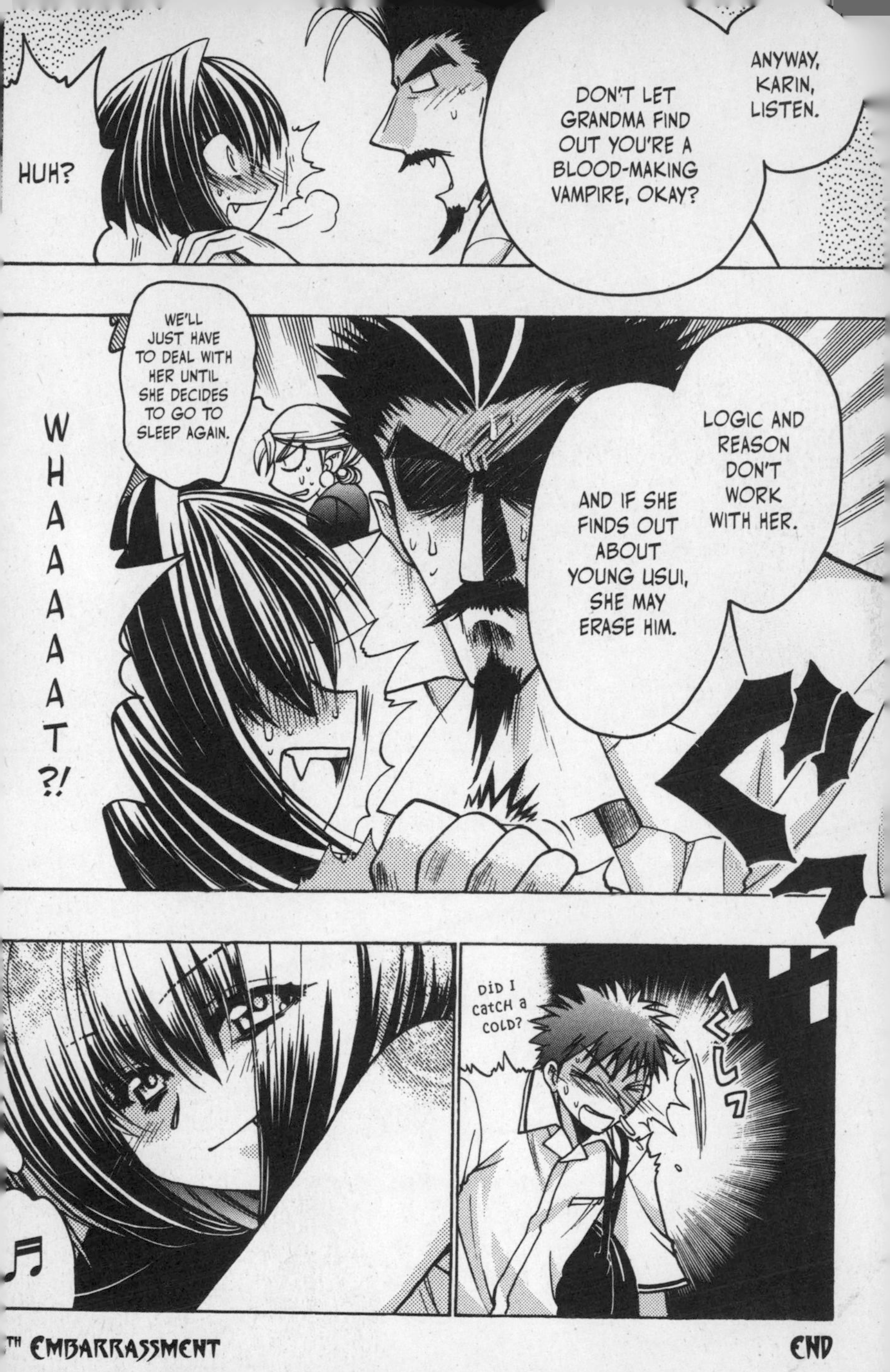
ANYWAY, KARIN, LISTEN.
DON'T LET GRANDMA FIND OUT YOU'RE A BLOOD-MAKING VAMPIRE, OKAY?
HUH?
LOGIC AND REASON DON'T WORK WITH HER.
AND IF SHE FINDS OUT ABOUT YOUNG USUI, SHE MAY ERASE HIM.
WE'LL JUST HAVE TO DEAL WITH HER UNTIL SHE DECIDES TO GO TO SLEEP AGAIN.
WHAAAAAT?!
DID I CATCH A COLD?

TH EMBARRASSMENT END

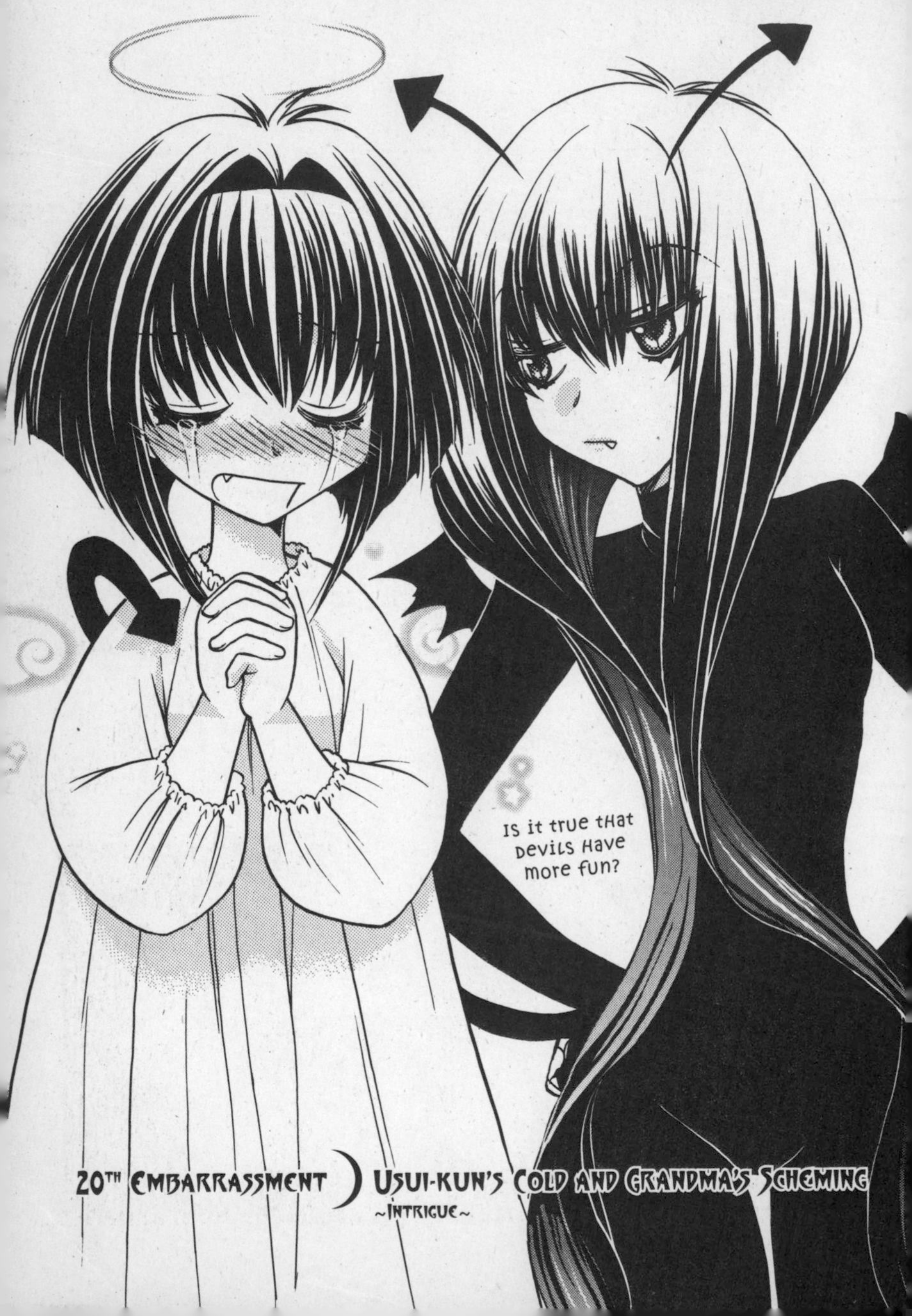
Is it true that devils have more fun?

20th Embarrassment) Usui-kun's Cold and Grandma's Scheming

~Intrigue~

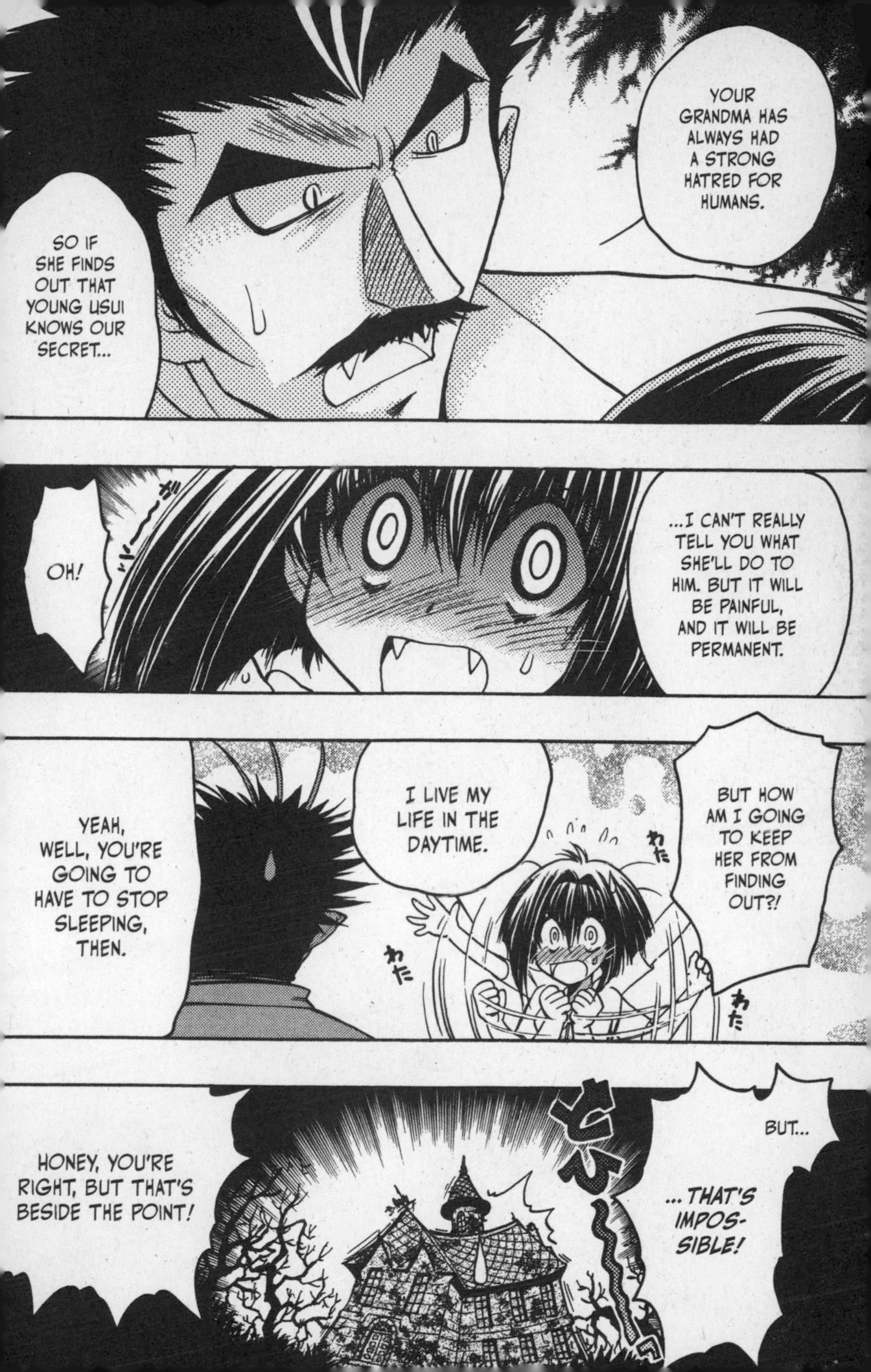
YOUR GRANDMA HAS ALWAYS HAD A STRONG HATRED FOR HUMANS.
SO IF SHE FINDS OUT THAT YOUNG USUI KNOWS OUR SECRET...
...I CAN'T REALLY TELL YOU WHAT SHE'LL DO TO HIM. BUT IT WILL BE PAINFUL, AND IT WILL BE PERMANENT.
OH!
BUT HOW AM I GOING TO KEEP HER FROM FINDING OUT?!
わた
I LIVE MY LIFE IN THE DAYTIME.
わた
わた
YEAH, WELL, YOU'RE GOING TO HAVE TO STOP SLEEPING, THEN.
BUT...
...THAT'S IMPOSSIBLE!
HONEY, YOU'RE RIGHT, BUT THAT'S BESIDE THE POINT!

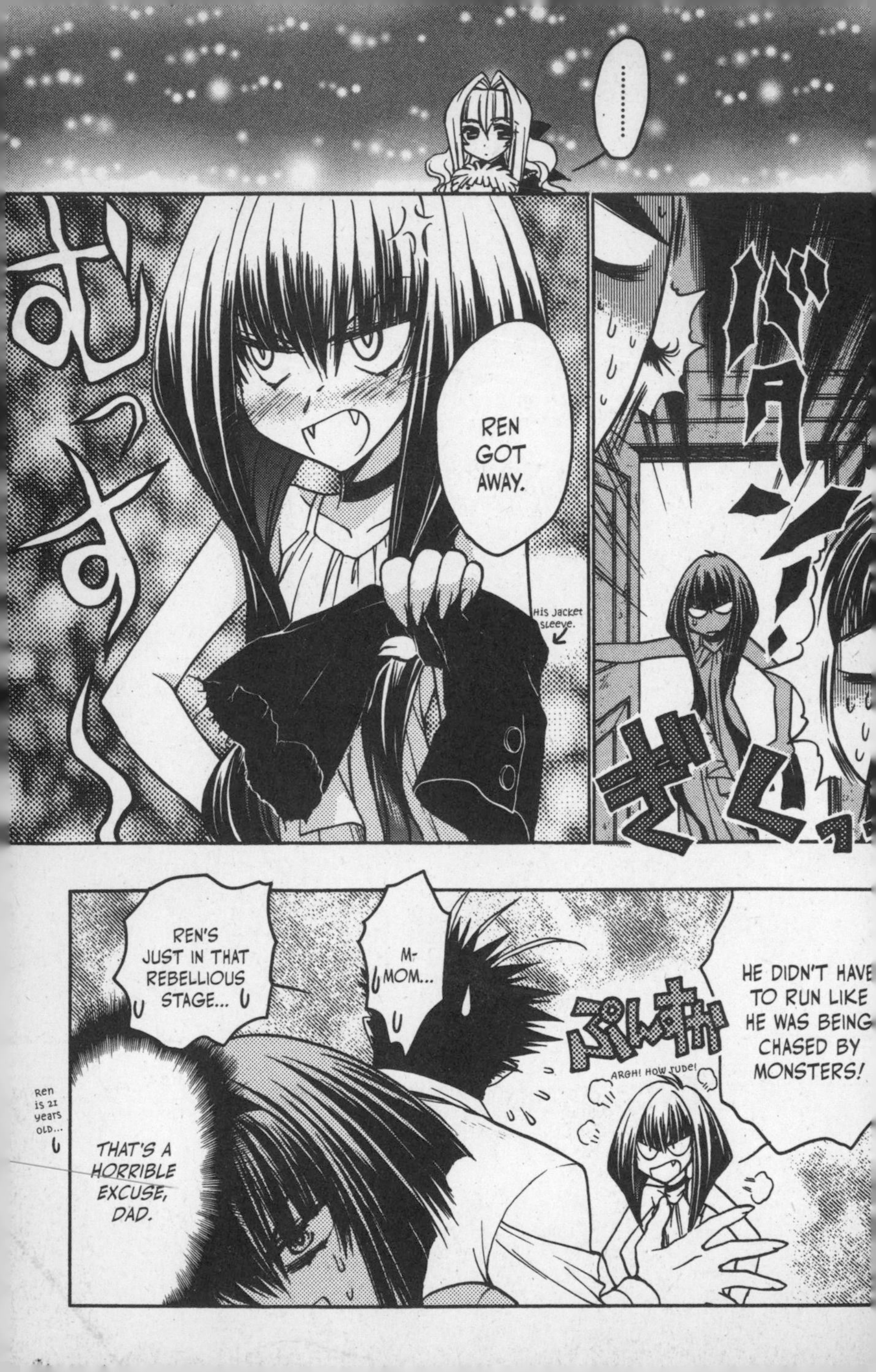
......
バタン!
ぎくっ
REN GOT AWAY.
むっす
His Jacket sleeve.
HE DIDN'T HAVE TO RUN LIKE HE WAS BEING CHASED BY MONSTERS!
ARGH! HOW RUDE!
ぷんすか
M-MOM...
REN'S JUST IN THAT REBELLIOUS STAGE...
THAT'S A HORRIBLE EXCUSE, DAD.
Ren is 21 years old...

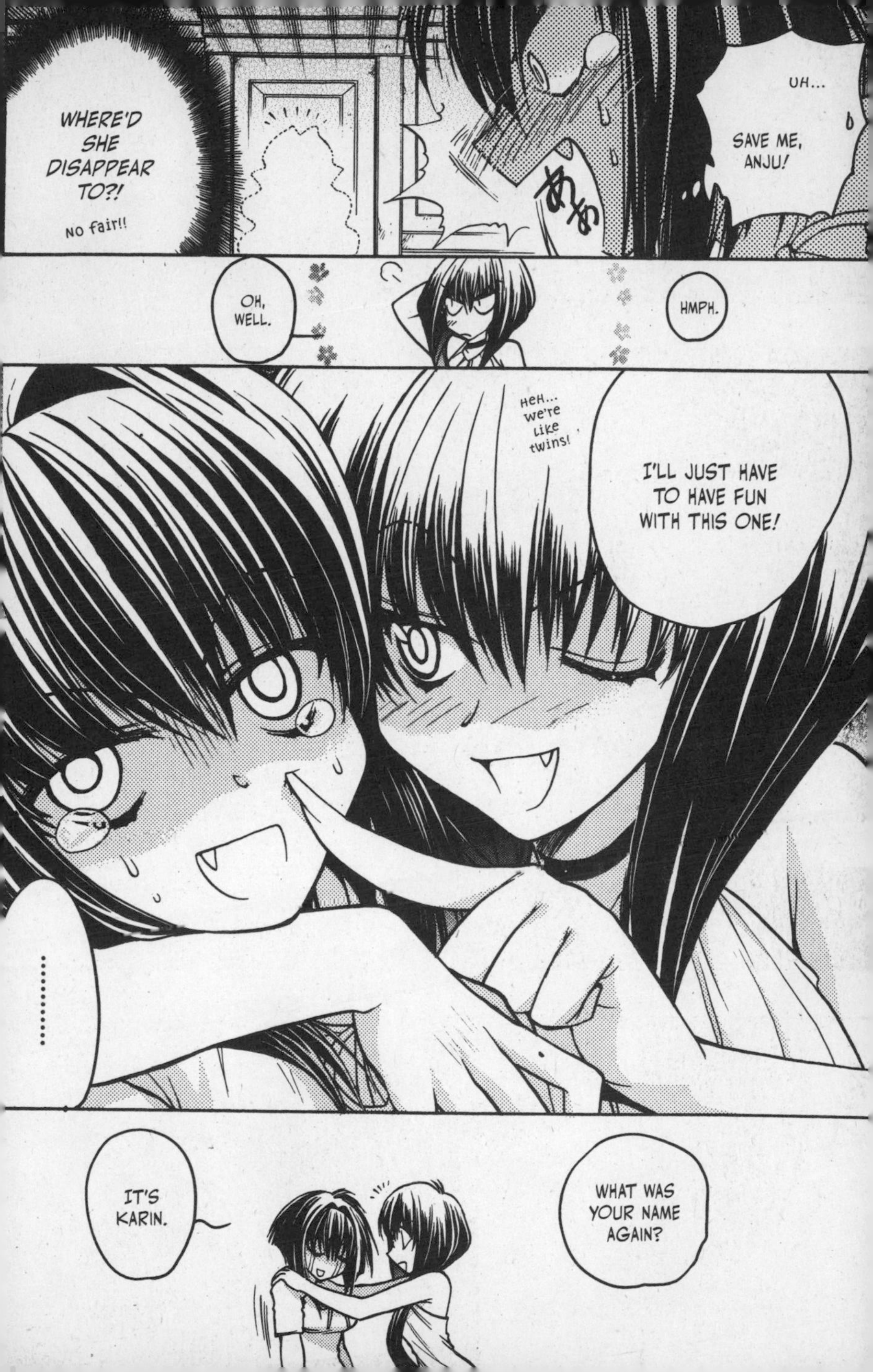
UH...
SAVE ME, ANJU!
あぁ
WHERE'D SHE DISAPPEAR TO?!
No fair!!
HMPH.
OH, WELL.
I'LL JUST HAVE TO HAVE FUN WITH THIS ONE!
Heh... we're like twins!
......
WHAT WAS YOUR NAME AGAIN?
IT'S KARIN.

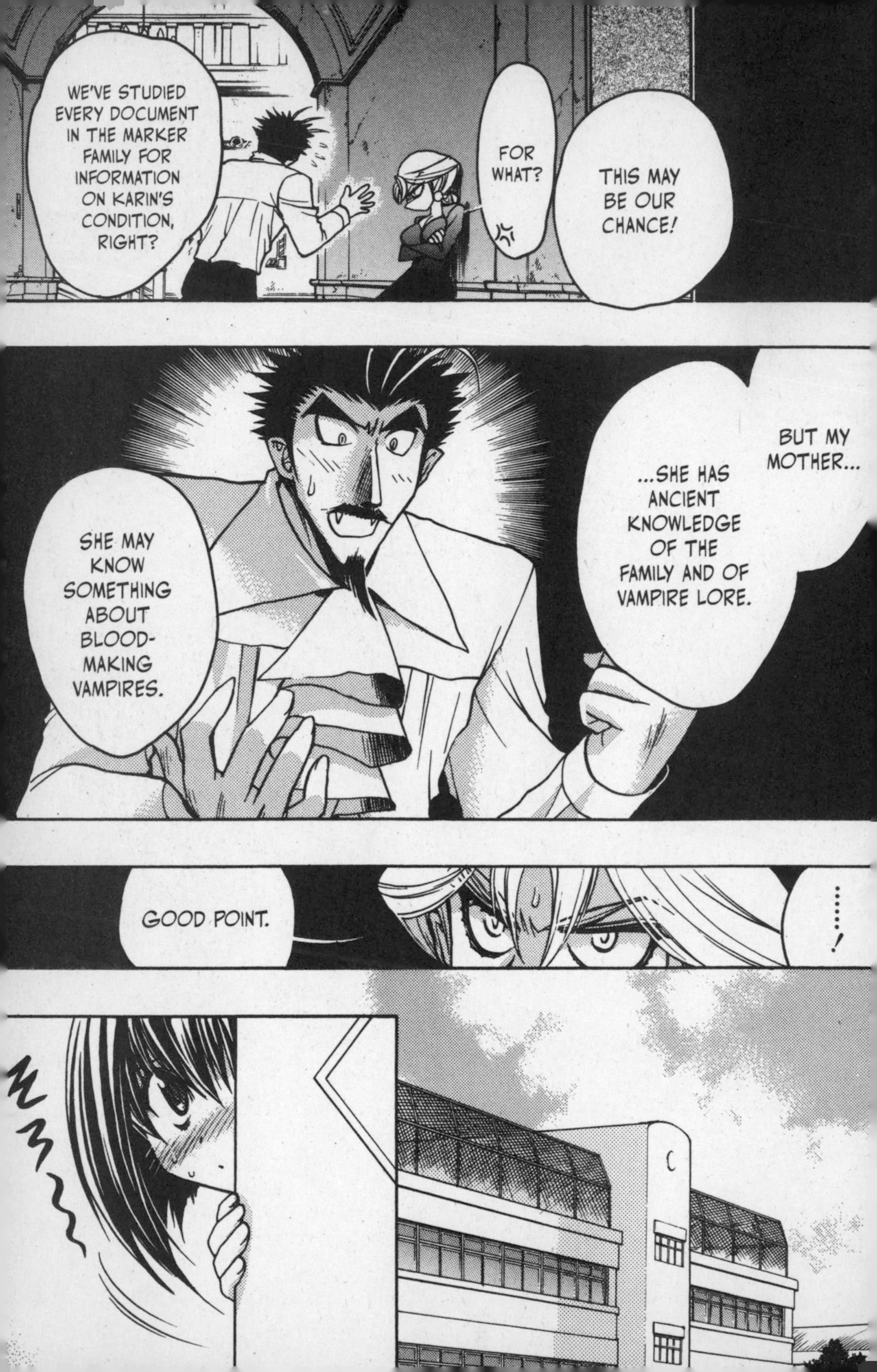
THIS MAY BE OUR CHANCE!
FOR WHAT?
WE'VE STUDIED EVERY DOCUMENT IN THE MARKER FAMILY FOR INFORMATION ON KARIN'S CONDITION, RIGHT?
BUT MY MOTHER...
...SHE HAS ANCIENT KNOWLEDGE OF THE FAMILY AND OF VAMPIRE LORE.
SHE MAY KNOW SOMETHING ABOUT BLOOD-MAKING VAMPIRES.
......!
GOOD POINT.

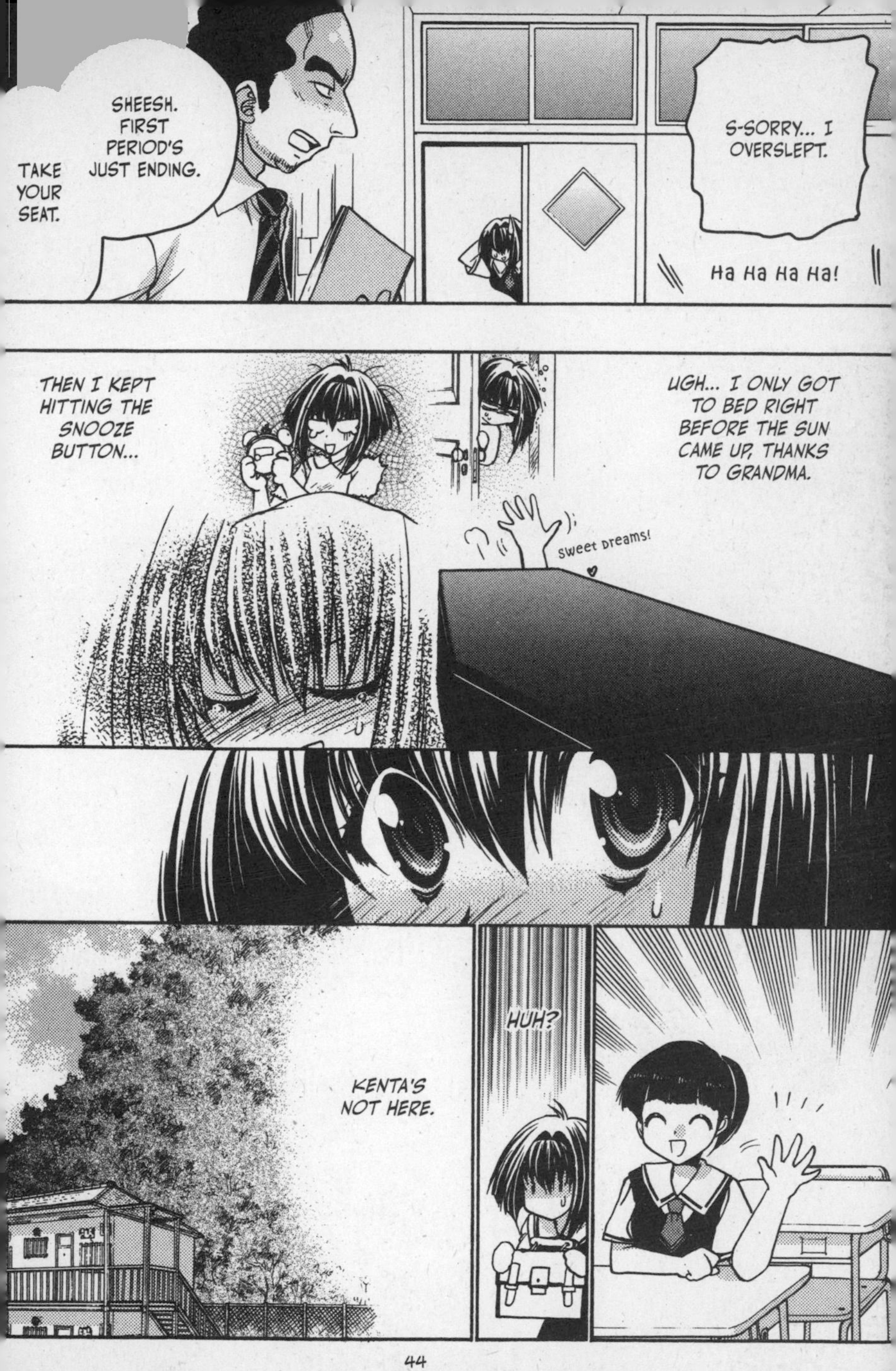
S-SORRY... I OVERSLEPT.
Ha Ha Ha Ha!
SHEESH. FIRST PERIOD'S JUST ENDING.
TAKE YOUR SEAT.
UGH... I ONLY GOT TO BED RIGHT BEFORE THE SUN CAME UP, THANKS TO GRANDMA.
Sweet Dreams!
THEN I KEPT HITTING THE SNOOZE BUTTON...
HUH?
KENTA'S NOT HERE.

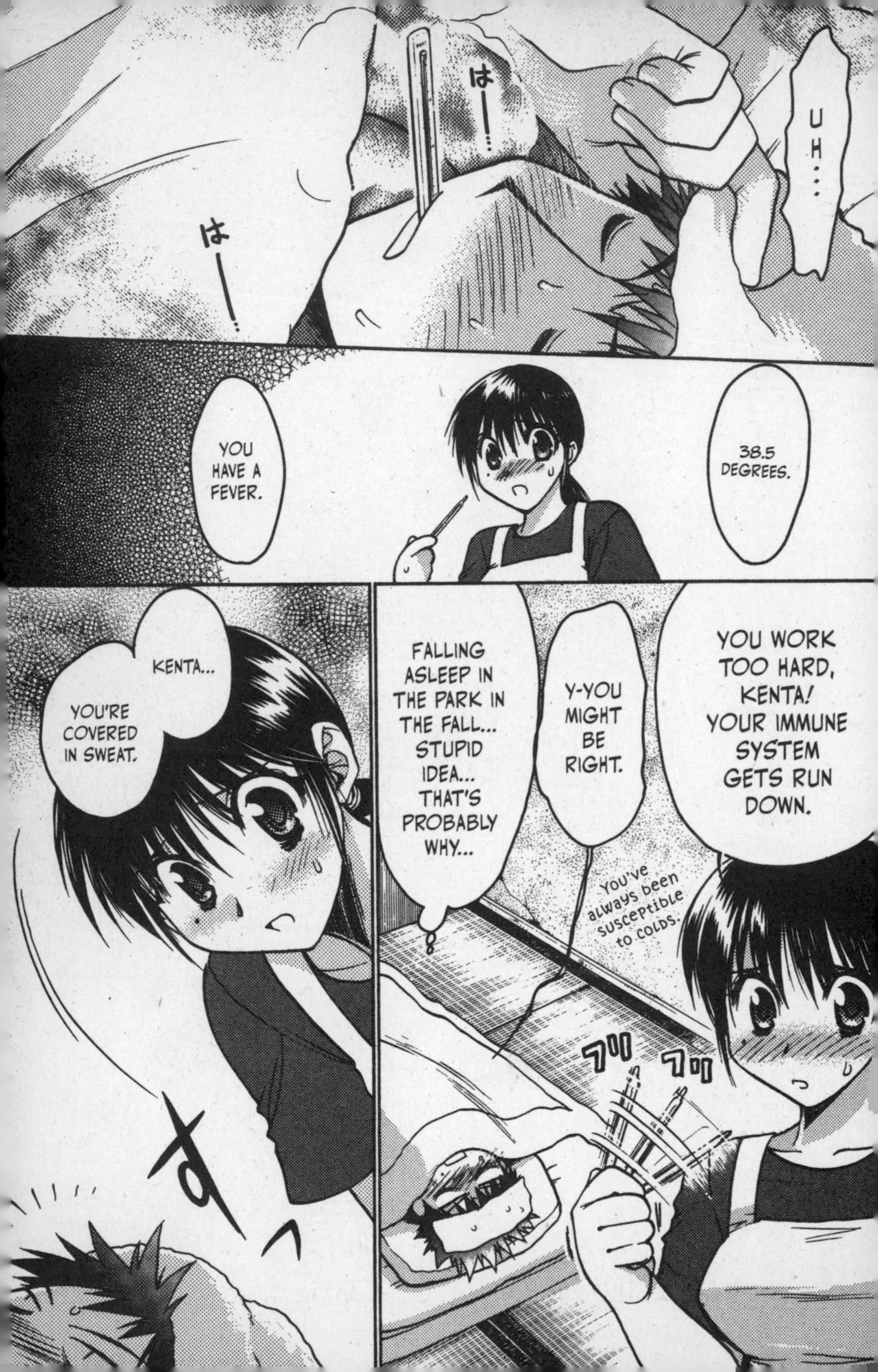
UH...
38.5 DEGREES.
YOU HAVE A FEVER.
YOU WORK TOO HARD, KENTA! YOUR IMMUNE SYSTEM GETS RUN DOWN.
You've always been susceptible to colds.
Y-YOU MIGHT BE RIGHT.
FALLING ASLEEP IN THE PARK IN THE FALL... STUPID IDEA... THAT'S PROBABLY WHY...
KENTA...
YOU'RE COVERED IN SWEAT.

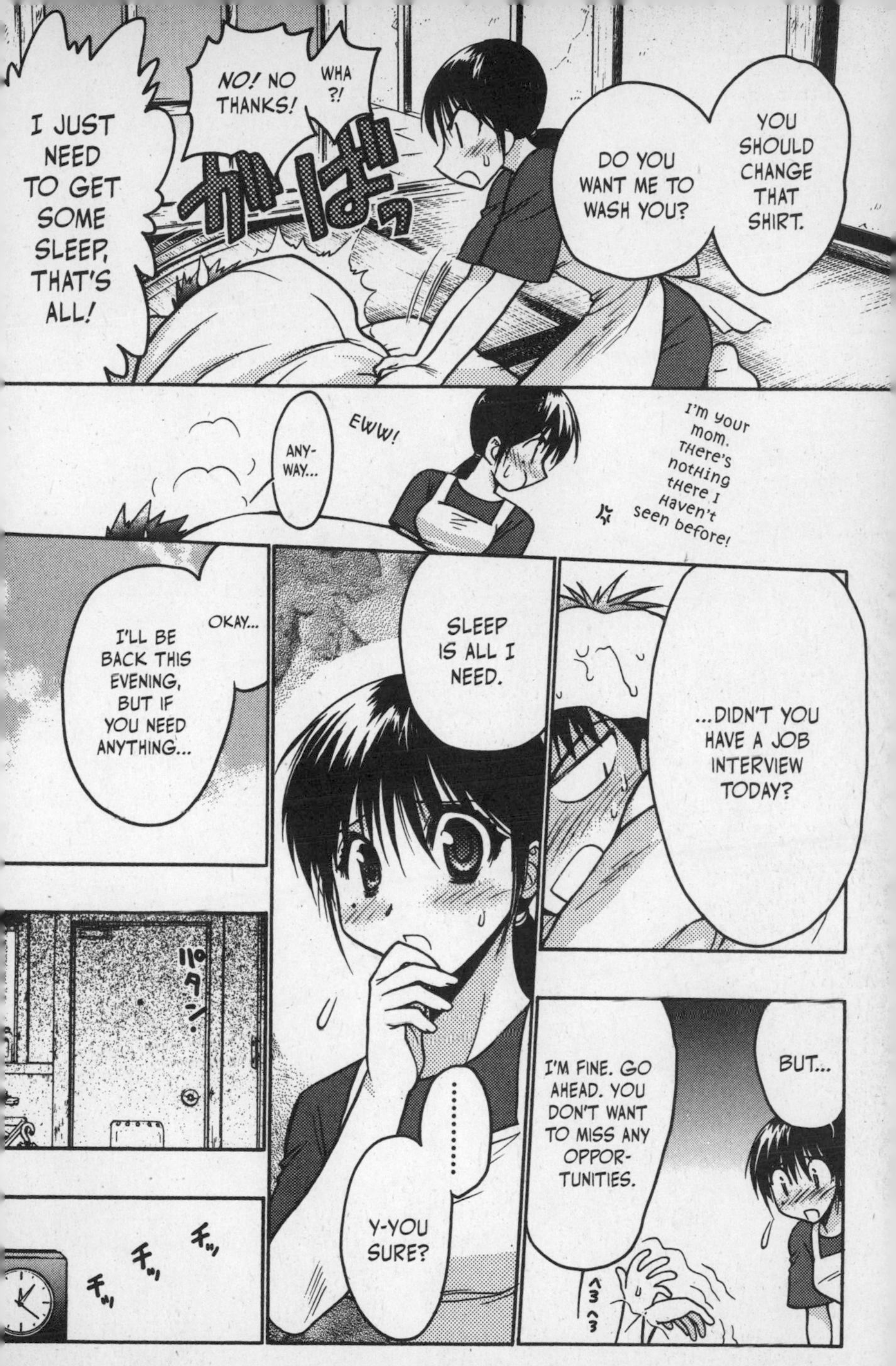
YOU SHOULD CHANGE THAT SHIRT.
DO YOU WANT ME TO WASH YOU?
WHA ?!
NO! NO THANKS!
がばっ
I JUST NEED TO GET SOME SLEEP, THAT'S ALL!
I'm your mom. There's nothing there I haven't seen before!
EWW!
ANY-WAY...
...DIDN'T YOU HAVE A JOB INTERVIEW TODAY?
BUT...
I'M FINE. GO AHEAD. YOU DON'T WANT TO MISS ANY OPPOR-TUNITIES.
SLEEP IS ALL I NEED.
......
Y-YOU SURE?
OKAY...
I'LL BE BACK THIS EVENING, BUT IF YOU NEED ANYTHING...
パタン
チッ
チッ
チッ

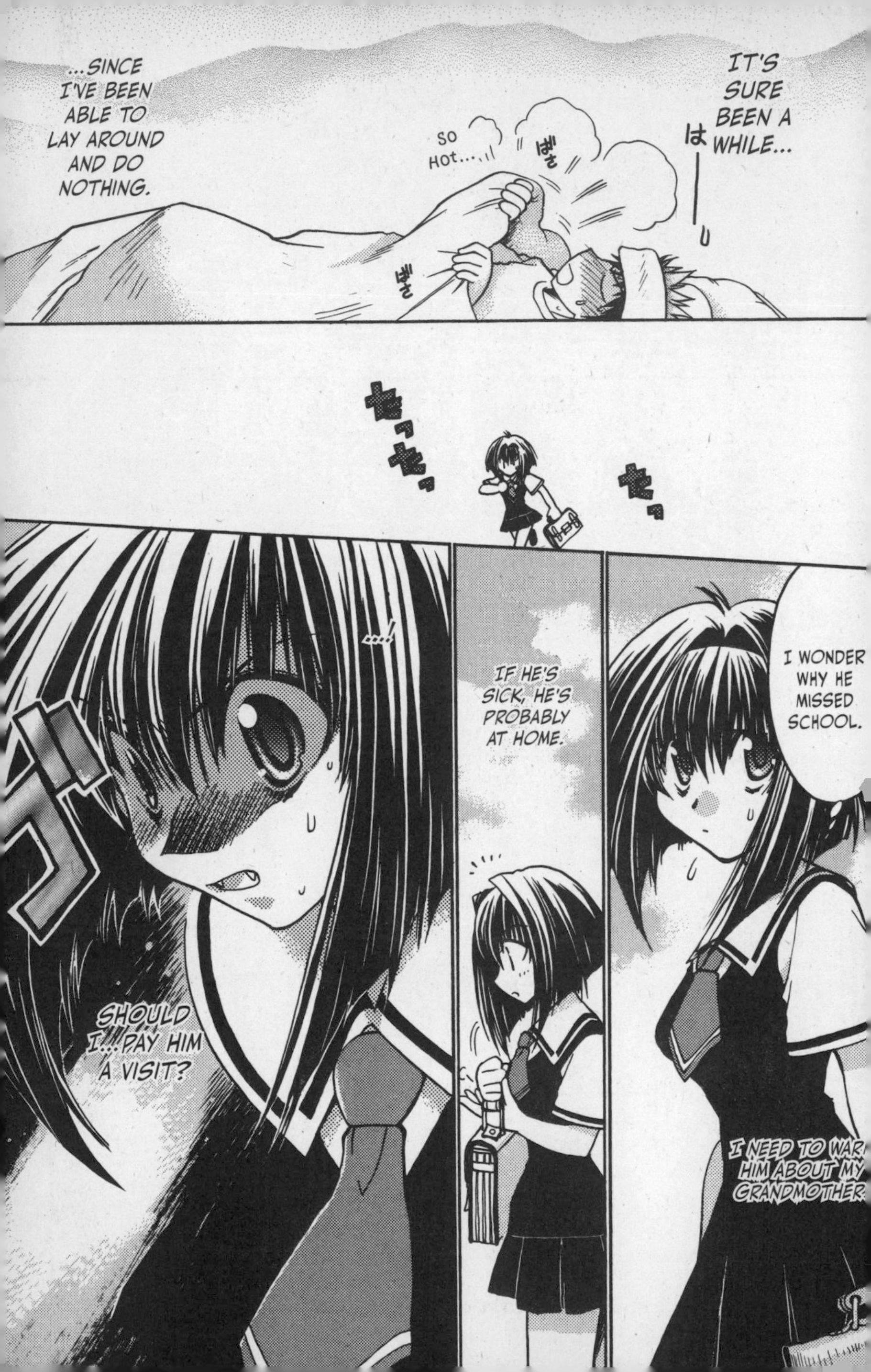
IT'S SURE BEEN A WHILE...
は—
SO HOT...
ばさ
ばさ
...SINCE I'VE BEEN ABLE TO LAY AROUND AND DO NOTHING.
I WONDER WHY HE MISSED SCHOOL.
I NEED TO WAR HIM ABOUT MY GRANDMOTHER
IF HE'S SICK, HE'S PROBABLY AT HOME.
...!
SHOULD I...PAY HIM A VISIT?

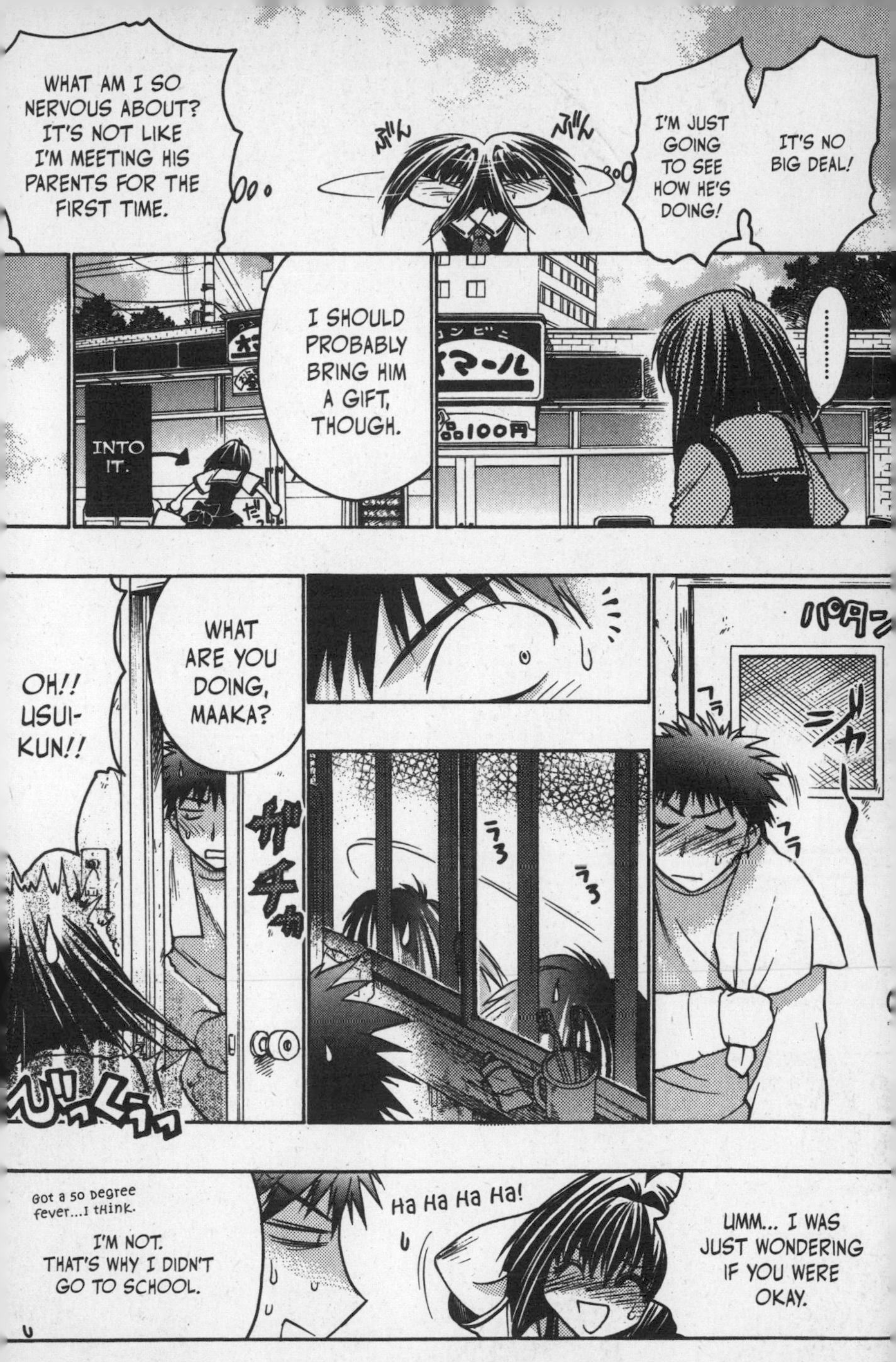
I'M JUST GOING TO SEE HOW HE'S DOING!
IT'S NO BIG DEAL!
WHAT AM I SO NERVOUS ABOUT? IT'S NOT LIKE I'M MEETING HIS PARENTS FOR THE FIRST TIME.
......
I SHOULD PROBABLY BRING HIM A GIFT, THOUGH.
INTO IT.
WHAT ARE YOU DOING, MAAKA?
OH!! USUI-KUN!!
UMM... I WAS JUST WONDERING IF YOU WERE OKAY.
Ha Ha Ha Ha!
I'M NOT. THAT'S WHY I DIDN'T GO TO SCHOOL.
Got a 50 degree fever...I think.

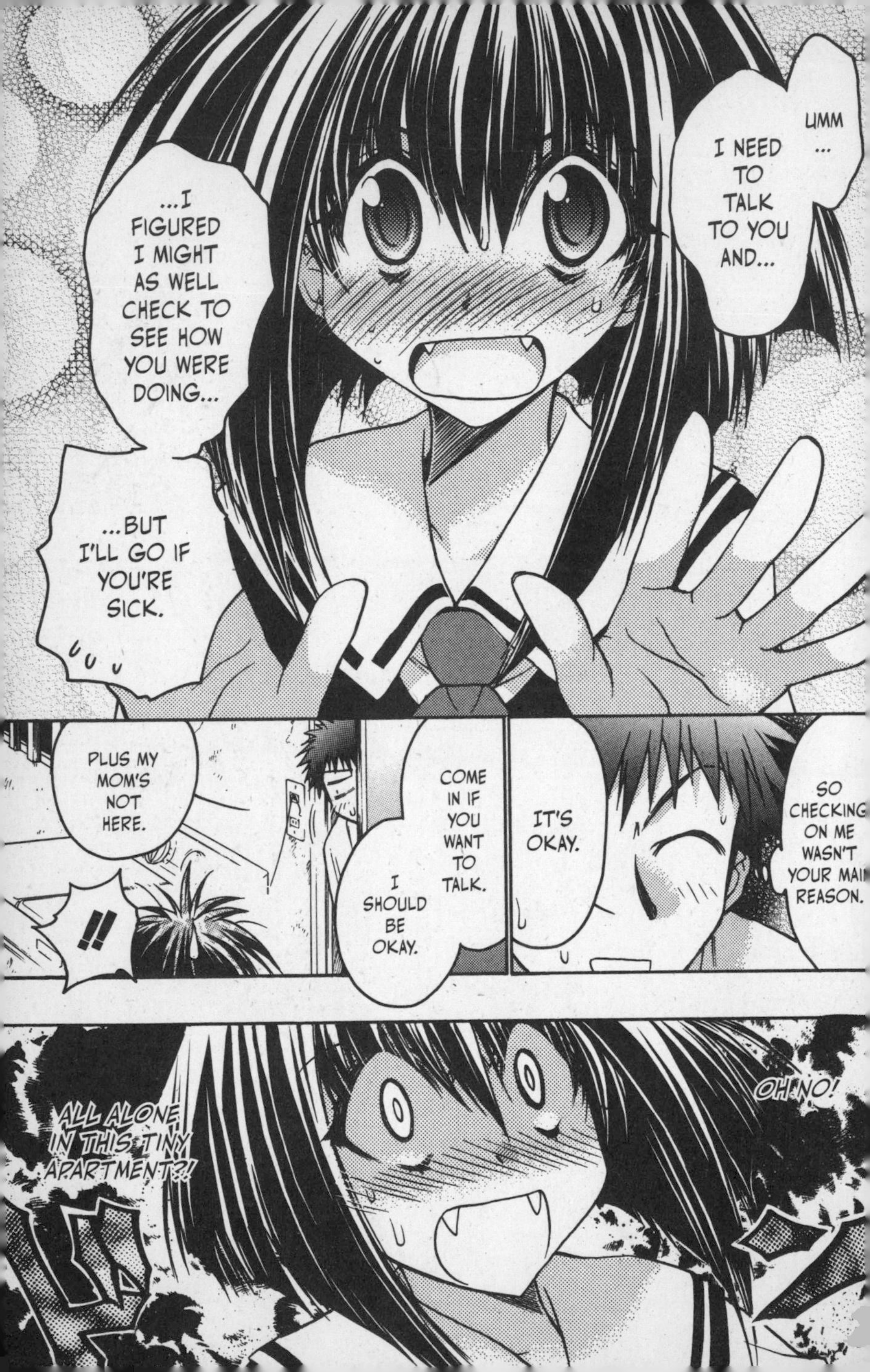
UMM ... I NEED TO TALK TO YOU AND...
...I FIGURED I MIGHT AS WELL CHECK TO SEE HOW YOU WERE DOING...
...BUT I'LL GO IF YOU'RE SICK.
SO CHECKING ON ME WASN'T YOUR MAI REASON.
IT'S OKAY.
COME IN IF YOU WANT TO TALK.
I SHOULD BE OKAY.
PLUS MY MOM'S NOT HERE.
!!
OH NO!
ALL ALONE IN THIS TINY APARTMENT?!

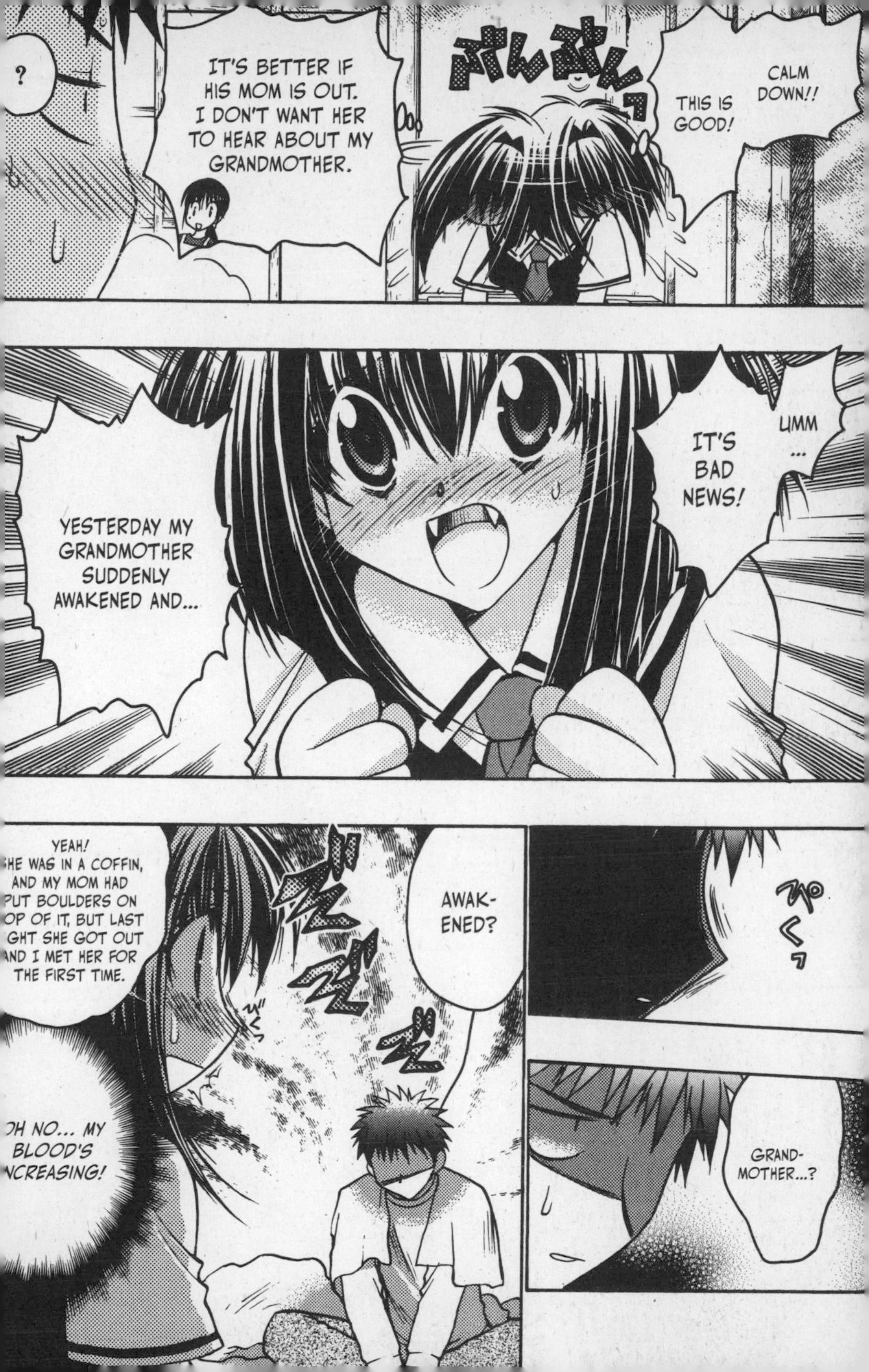
CALM DOWN!!
THIS IS GOOD!
ぷんぷんっ
IT'S BETTER IF HIS MOM IS OUT. I DON'T WANT HER TO HEAR ABOUT MY GRANDMOTHER.
?
UMM ...
IT'S BAD NEWS!
YESTERDAY MY GRANDMOTHER SUDDENLY AWAKENED AND...
ぴくっ
GRAND-MOTHER...?
AWAK-ENED?
YEAH! HE WAS IN A COFFIN, AND MY MOM HAD PUT BOULDERS ON OP OF IT, BUT LAST GHT SHE GOT OUT ND I MET HER FOR THE FIRST TIME.
OH NO... MY BLOOD'S NCREASING!

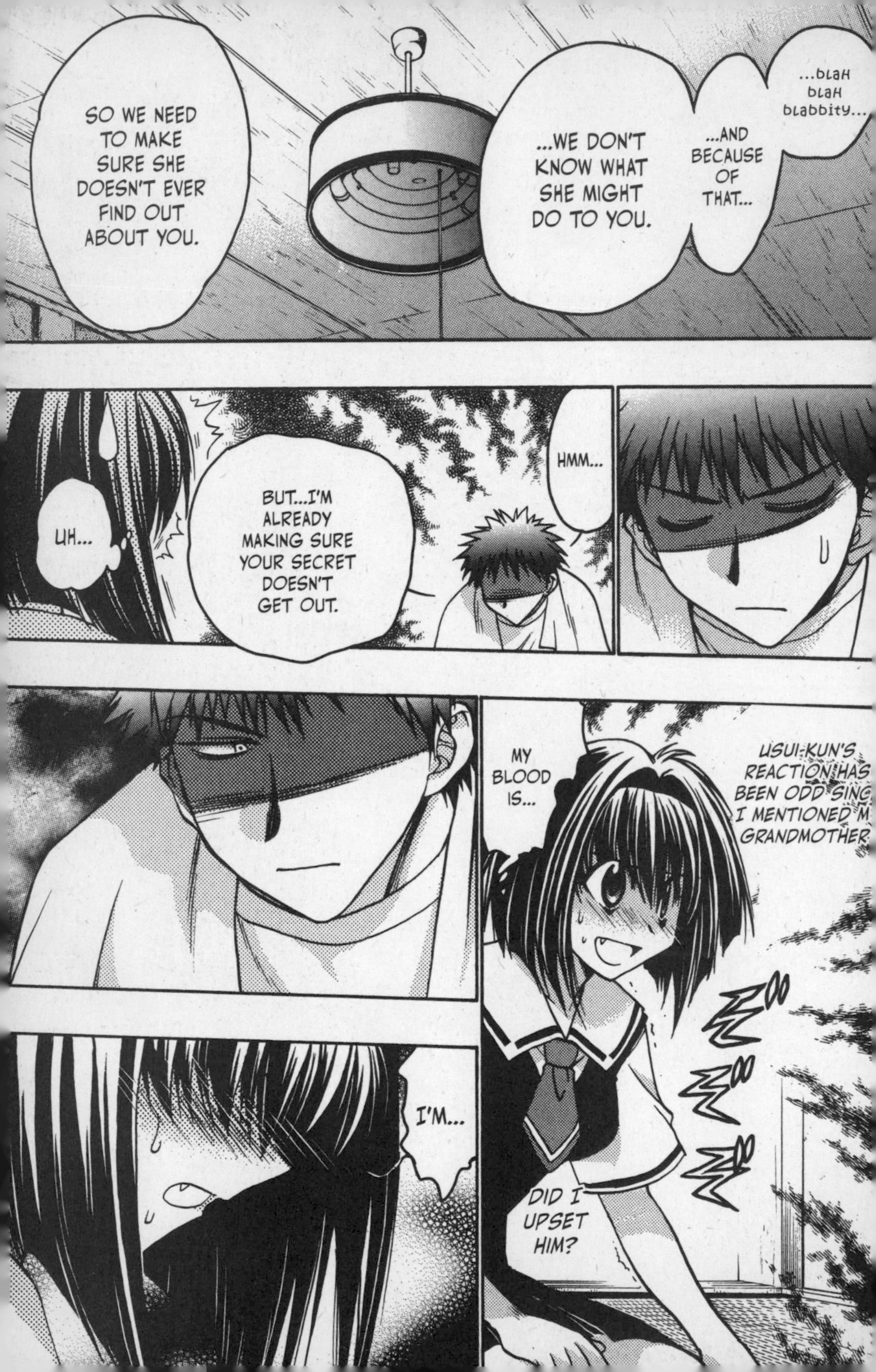
...blah blah blabbity...
...AND BECAUSE OF THAT...
...WE DON'T KNOW WHAT SHE MIGHT DO TO YOU.
SO WE NEED TO MAKE SURE SHE DOESN'T EVER FIND OUT ABOUT YOU.
HMM...
BUT...I'M ALREADY MAKING SURE YOUR SECRET DOESN'T GET OUT.
UH...
USUI-KUN'S REACTION HAS BEEN ODD SINC I MENTIONED M GRANDMOTHER
MY BLOOD IS...
ZOO
ZOO
ZOO
DID I UPSET HIM?
I'M...

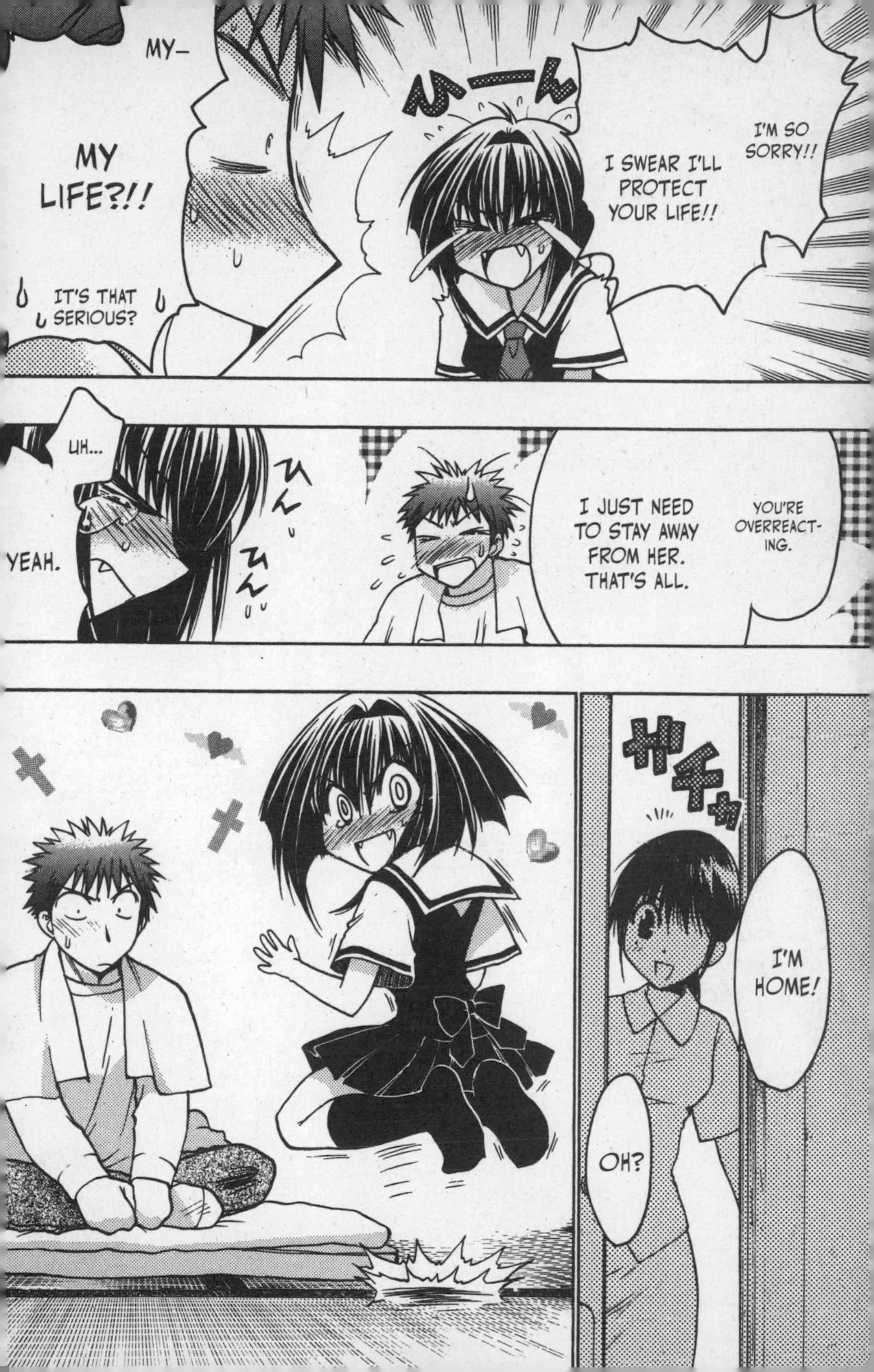
I'M SO SORRY!!
I SWEAR I'LL PROTECT YOUR LIFE!!
ふーん
MY—
MY LIFE?!!
IT'S THAT SERIOUS?
YOU'RE OVERREACT-ING.
I JUST NEED TO STAY AWAY FROM HER. THAT'S ALL.
ひんひん
UH...
YEAH.
ガチャ
I'M HOME!
OH?

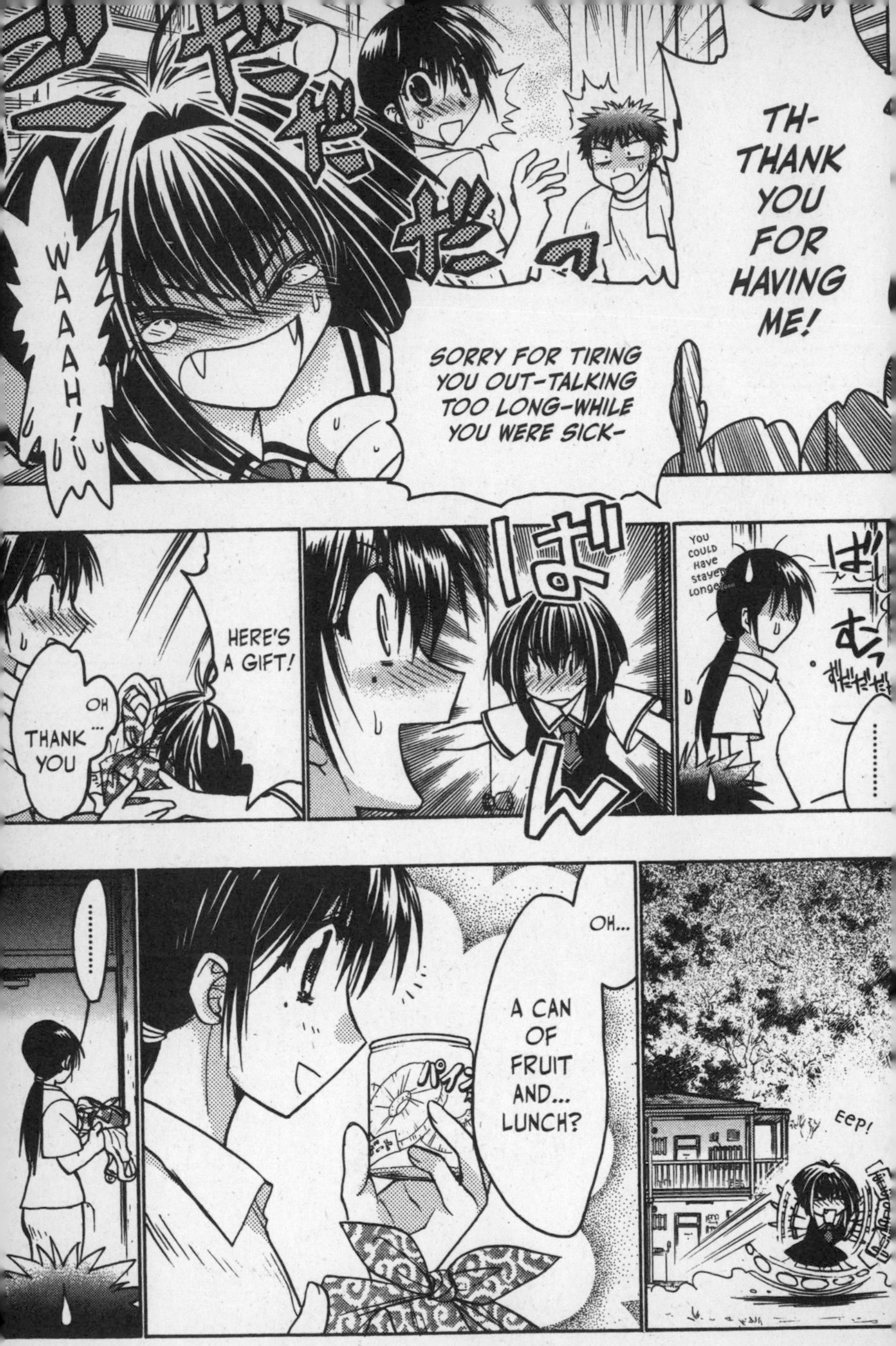
TH-THANK YOU FOR HAVING ME!
SORRY FOR TIRING YOU OUT-TALKING TOO LONG-WHILE YOU WERE SICK-
WAAAAH!
YOU COULD HAVE STAYED LONGER...
......
HERE'S A GIFT!
OH ... THANK YOU
EEP!
OH...
A CAN OF FRUIT AND... LUNCH?
......

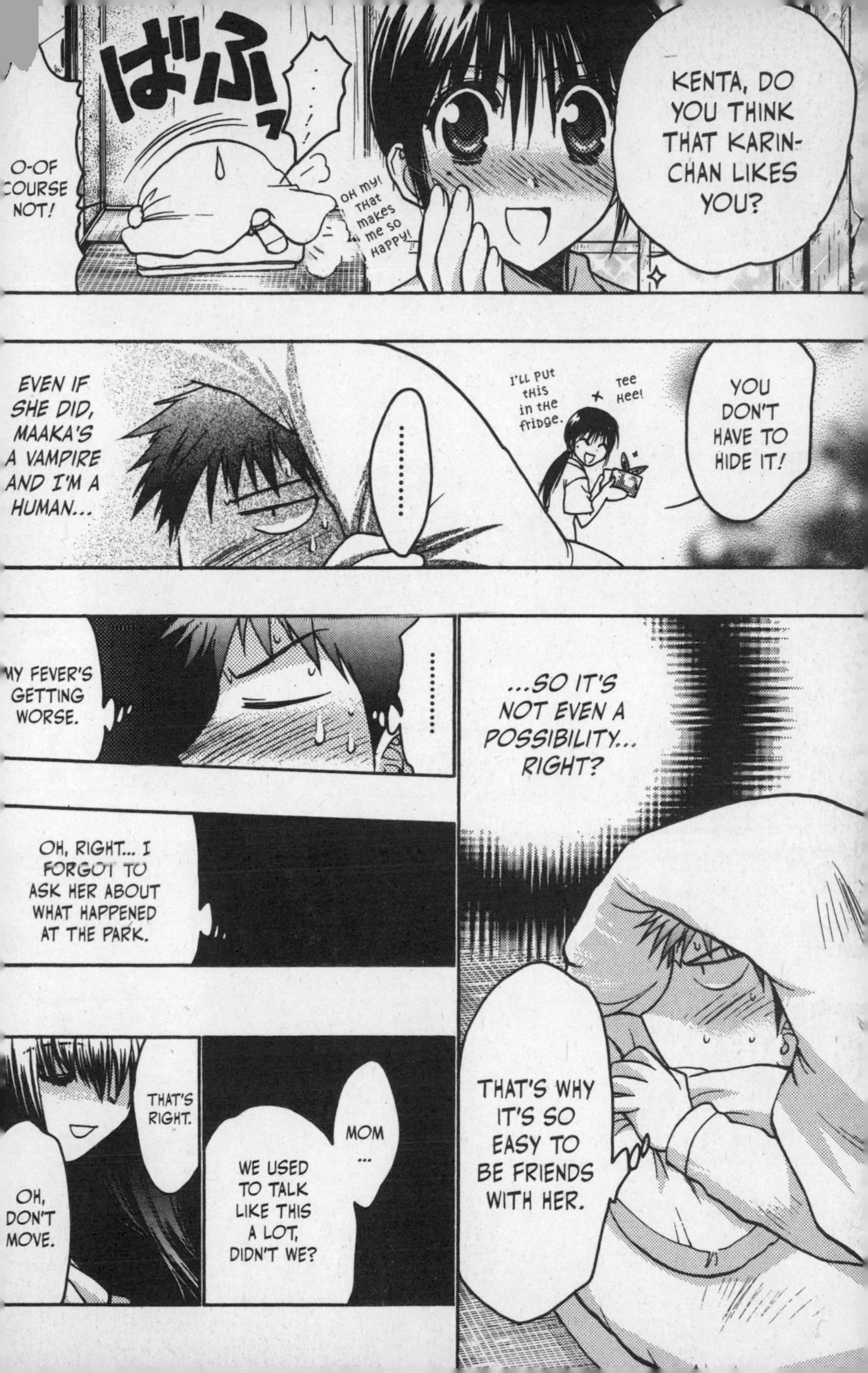
KENTA, DO YOU THINK THAT KARIN-CHAN LIKES YOU?
OH MY! THAT MAKES ME SO HAPPY!
ばふっ
...!
O-OF COURSE NOT!
YOU DON'T HAVE TO HIDE IT!
TEE HEE!
I'LL PUT THIS IN THE FRIDGE.
......
EVEN IF SHE DID, MAAKA'S A VAMPIRE AND I'M A HUMAN...
...SO IT'S NOT EVEN A POSSIBILITY... RIGHT?
THAT'S WHY IT'S SO EASY TO BE FRIENDS WITH HER.
......
MY FEVER'S GETTING WORSE.
OH, RIGHT... I FORGOT TO ASK HER ABOUT WHAT HAPPENED AT THE PARK.
MOM ...
WE USED TO TALK LIKE THIS A LOT, DIDN'T WE?
THAT'S RIGHT.
OH, DON'T MOVE.

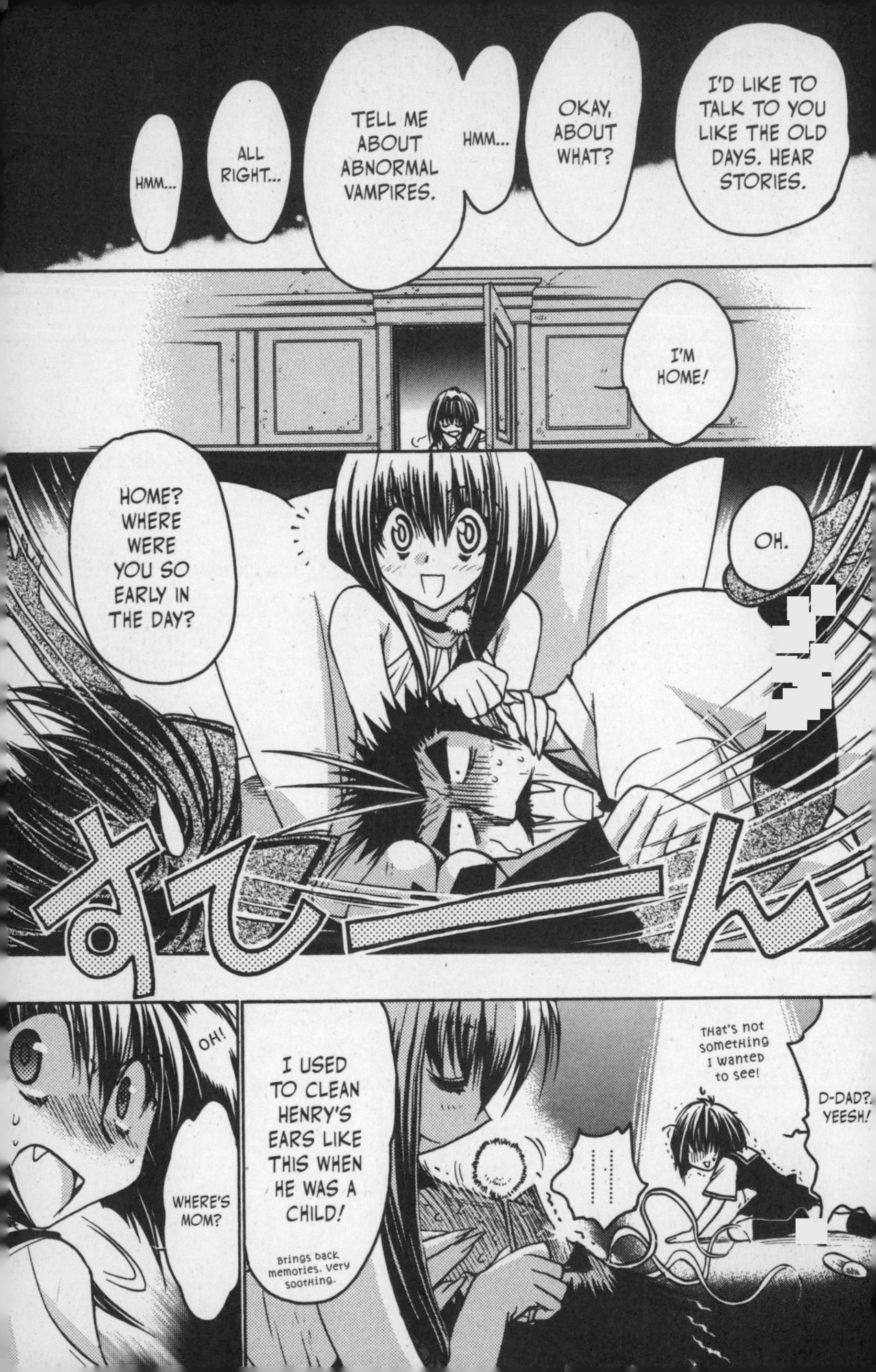

I'D LIKE TO TALK TO YOU LIKE THE OLD DAYS. HEAR STORIES.
OKAY, ABOUT WHAT?
HMM...
TELL ME ABOUT ABNORMAL VAMPIRES.
ALL RIGHT...
HMM...
I'M HOME!
OH.
HOME? WHERE WERE YOU SO EARLY IN THE DAY?
すいーん
D-DAD?. YEESH!
That's not something I wanted to see!
I USED TO CLEAN HENRY'S EARS LIKE THIS WHEN HE WAS A CHILD!
Brings back memories. Very soothing.
OH!
WHERE'S MOM?

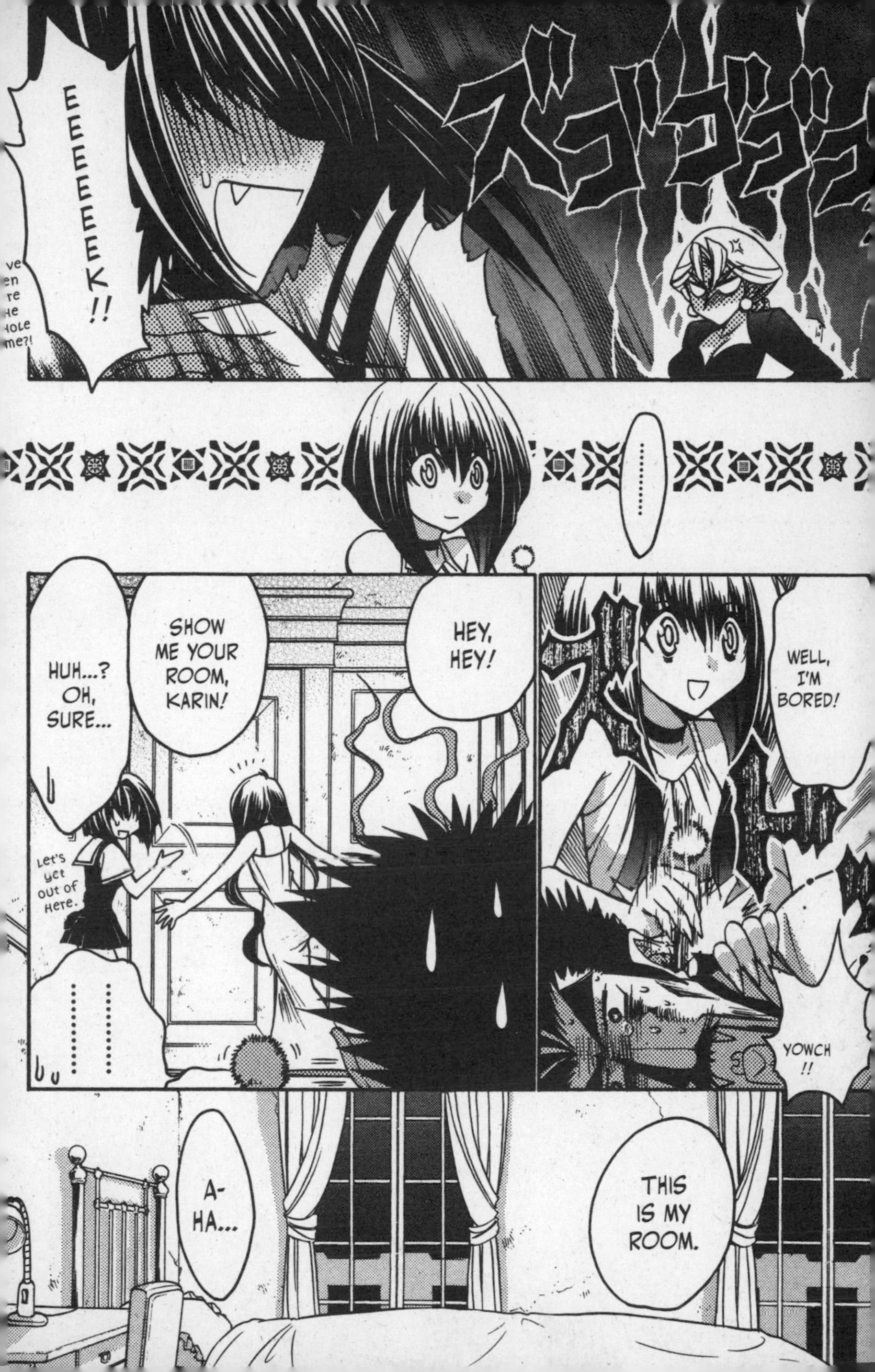
EEEEEEEEK!!
......
WELL, I'M BORED!
YOWCH!!
HEY, HEY!
SHOW ME YOUR ROOM, KARIN!
HUH...? OH, SURE...
Let's get out of Here.
......
THIS IS MY ROOM.
A-HA...

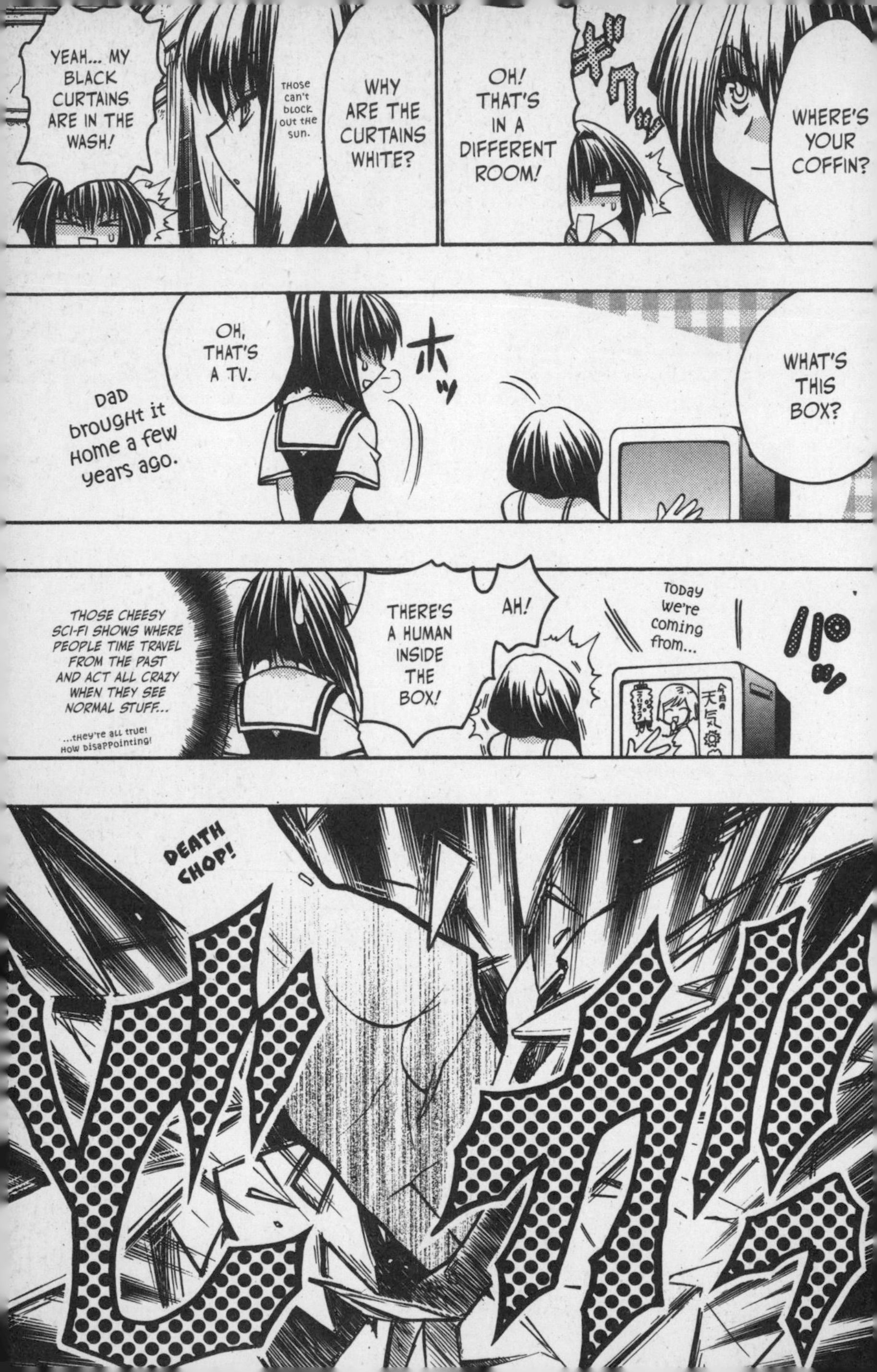
WHERE'S YOUR COFFIN?
OH! THAT'S IN A DIFFERENT ROOM!
WHY ARE THE CURTAINS WHITE?
THOSE can't block out the sun.
YEAH... MY BLACK CURTAINS ARE IN THE WASH!
WHAT'S THIS BOX?
ホッ
OH, THAT'S A TV.
Dad brought it home a few years ago.
パッ
Today we're coming from...
今日の天気
AH!
THERE'S A HUMAN INSIDE THE BOX!
THOSE CHEESY SCI-FI SHOWS WHERE PEOPLE TIME TRAVEL FROM THE PAST AND ACT ALL CRAZY WHEN THEY SEE NORMAL STUFF...
...they're all true! How disappointing!
DEATH CHOP!

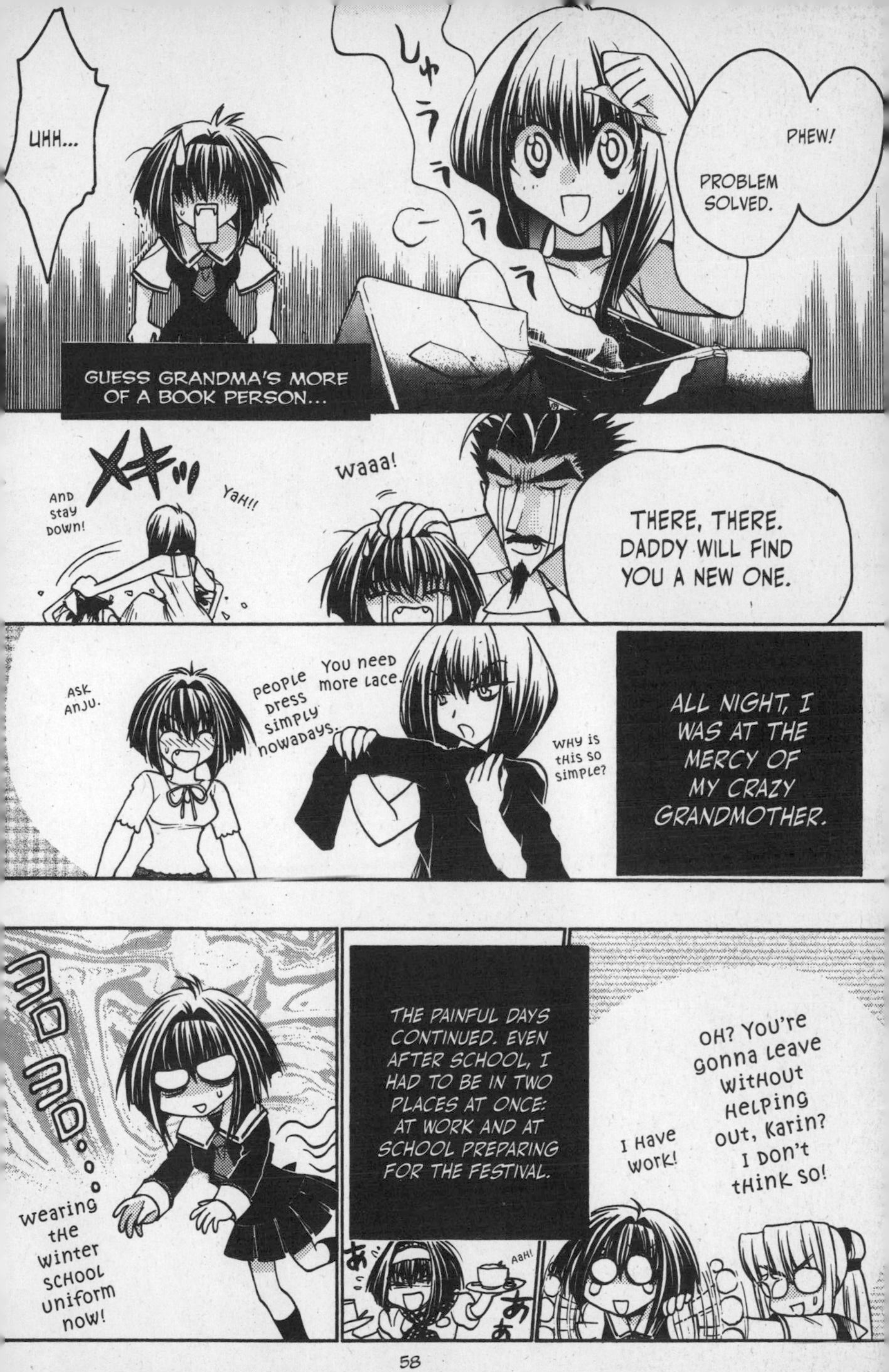

PHEW! PROBLEM SOLVED.
しゅラララ
UHH...
GUESS GRANDMA'S MORE OF A BOOK PERSON...
THERE, THERE. DADDY WILL FIND YOU A NEW ONE.
Waaa!
YaH!!
And stay down!
ALL NIGHT, I WAS AT THE MERCY OF MY CRAZY GRANDMOTHER.
Why is this so simple?
You need more lace.
People dress simply nowadays.
Ask Anju.
Oh? You're gonna leave without helping out, Karin? I don't think so!
I have work!
THE PAINFUL DAYS CONTINUED. EVEN AFTER SCHOOL, I HAD TO BE IN TWO PLACES AT ONCE: AT WORK AND AT SCHOOL PREPARING FOR THE FESTIVAL.
AAH!
wearing the winter school uniform now!

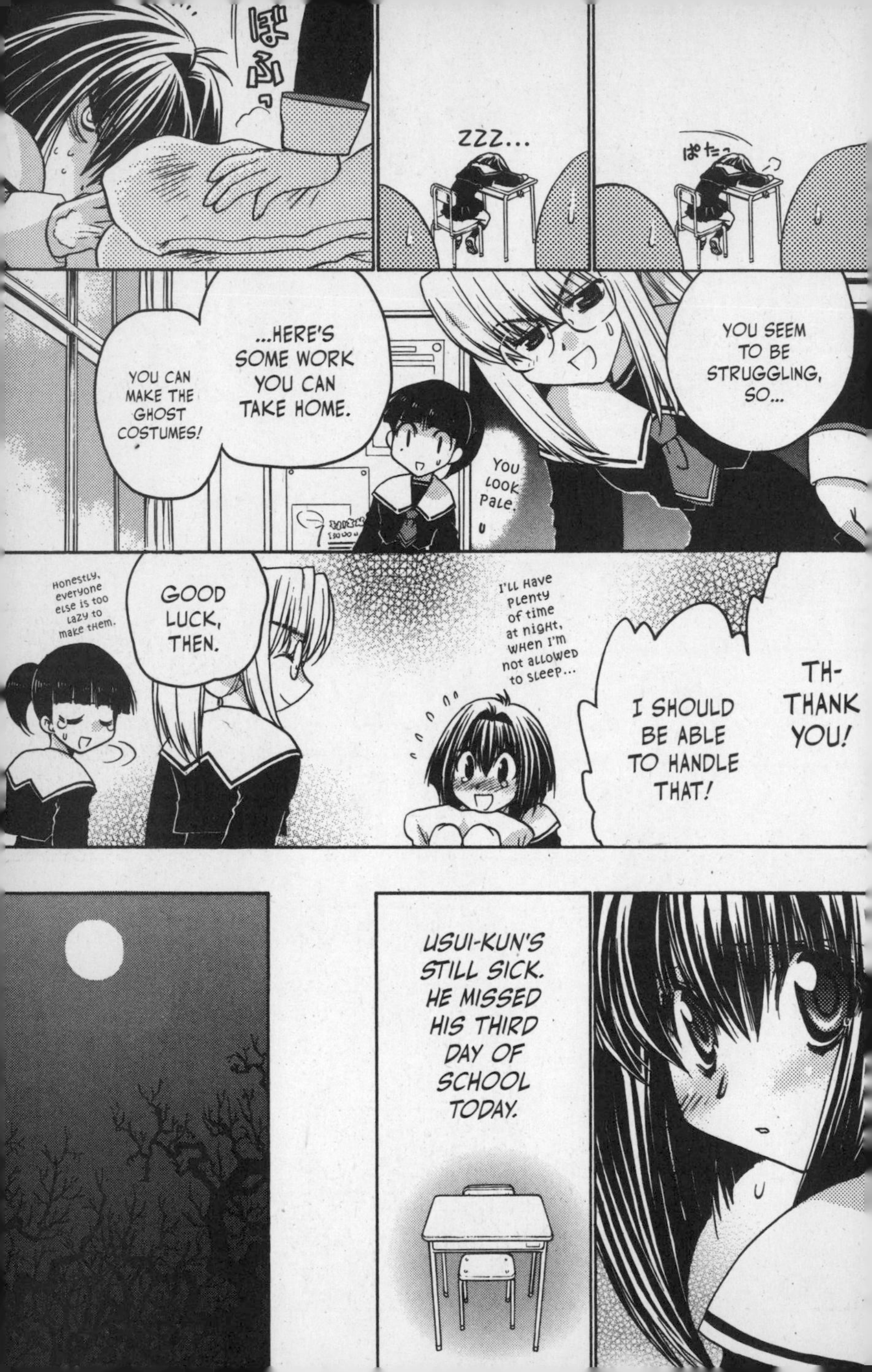
ぱたっ
ZZZ...
ぽふっ
YOU SEEM TO BE STRUGGLING, SO...
You look pale.
...HERE'S SOME WORK YOU CAN TAKE HOME.
YOU CAN MAKE THE GHOST COSTUMES!
TH-THANK YOU!
I SHOULD BE ABLE TO HANDLE THAT!
I'll have plenty of time at night, when I'm not allowed to sleep...
GOOD LUCK, THEN.
Honestly, everyone else is too lazy to make them.
USUI-KUN'S STILL SICK. HE MISSED HIS THIRD DAY OF SCHOOL TODAY.

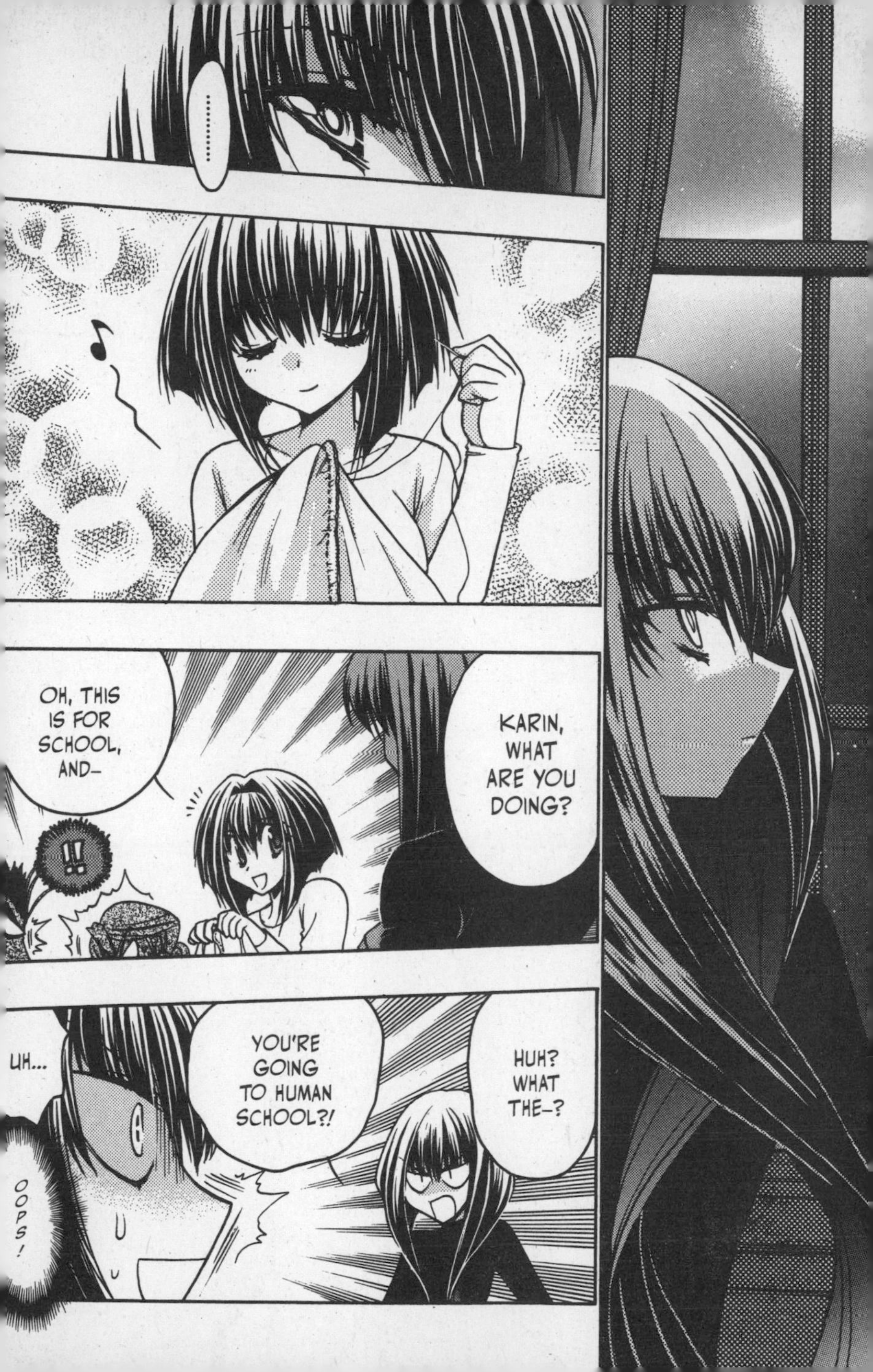
......
KARIN, WHAT ARE YOU DOING?
OH, THIS IS FOR SCHOOL, AND-
!!
HUH? WHAT THE-?
YOU'RE GOING TO HUMAN SCHOOL?!
UH...
OOPS!

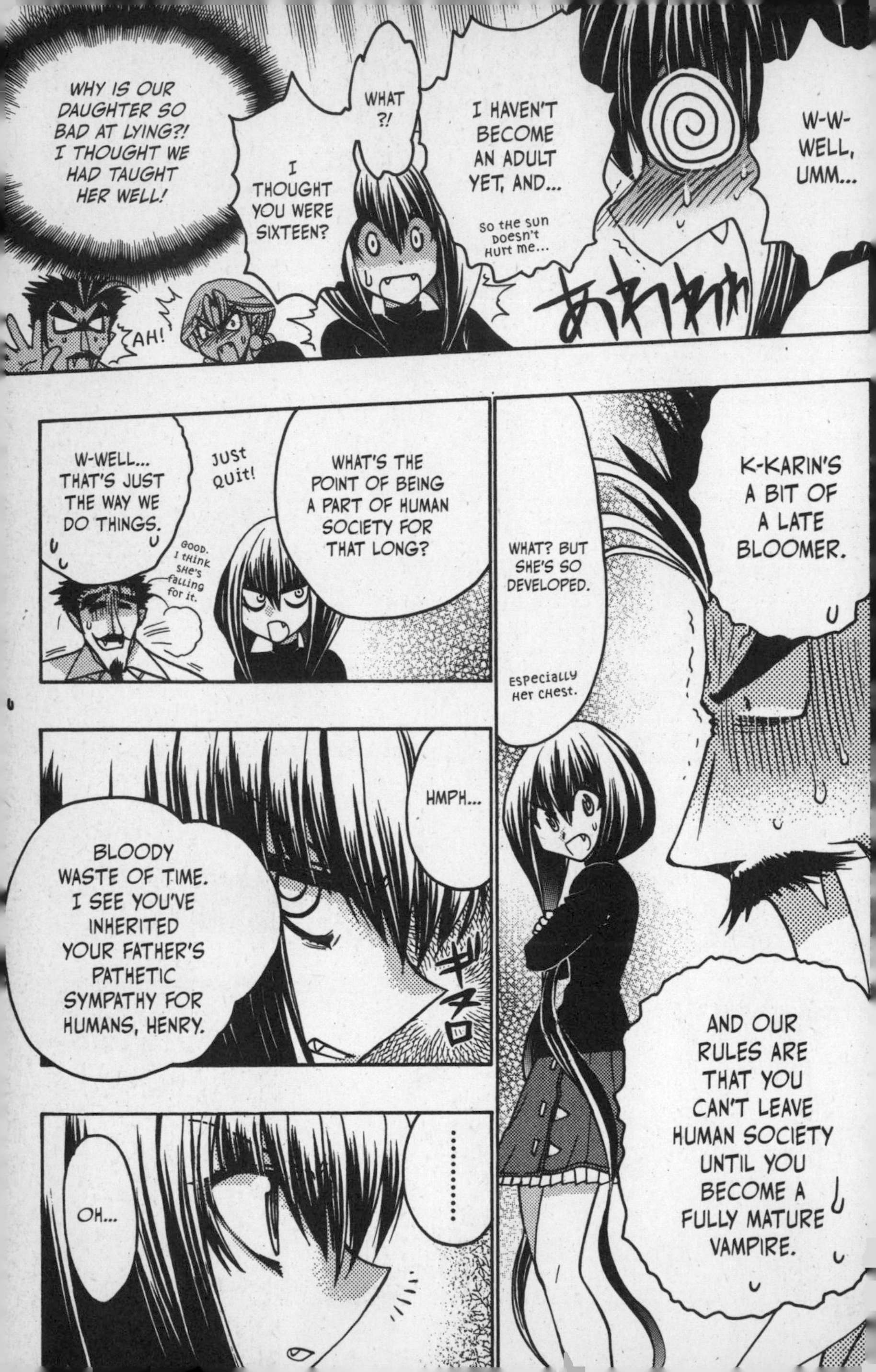
W-W-WELL, UMM...
あわわわ
I HAVEN'T BECOME AN ADULT YET, AND...
So the sun doesn't hurt me...
WHAT?!
I THOUGHT YOU WERE SIXTEEN?
WHY IS OUR DAUGHTER SO BAD AT LYING?! I THOUGHT WE HAD TAUGHT HER WELL!
AH!
K-KARIN'S A BIT OF A LATE BLOOMER.
WHAT? BUT SHE'S SO DEVELOPED.
Especially her chest.
AND OUR RULES ARE THAT YOU CAN'T LEAVE HUMAN SOCIETY UNTIL YOU BECOME A FULLY MATURE VAMPIRE.
WHAT'S THE POINT OF BEING A PART OF HUMAN SOCIETY FOR THAT LONG?
Just quit!
W-WELL... THAT'S JUST THE WAY WE DO THINGS.
Good. I think she's falling for it.
HMPH...
BLOODY WASTE OF TIME. I SEE YOU'VE INHERITED YOUR FATHER'S PATHETIC SYMPATHY FOR HUMANS, HENRY.
ギロ
......
OH...

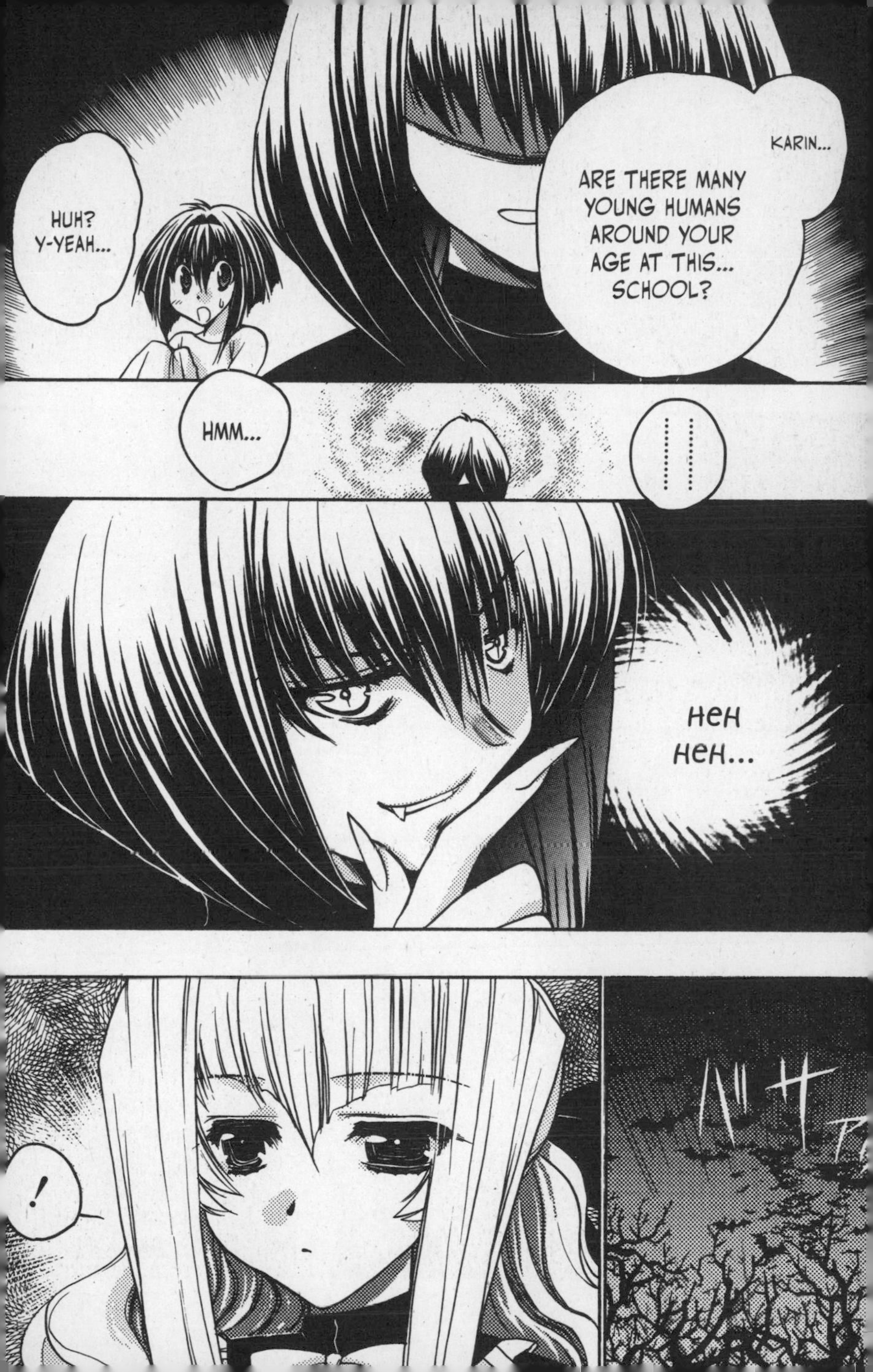
KARIN...
ARE THERE MANY YOUNG HUMANS AROUND YOUR AGE AT THIS... SCHOOL?
HUH? Y-YEAH...
......
HMM...
HEH HEH...
!

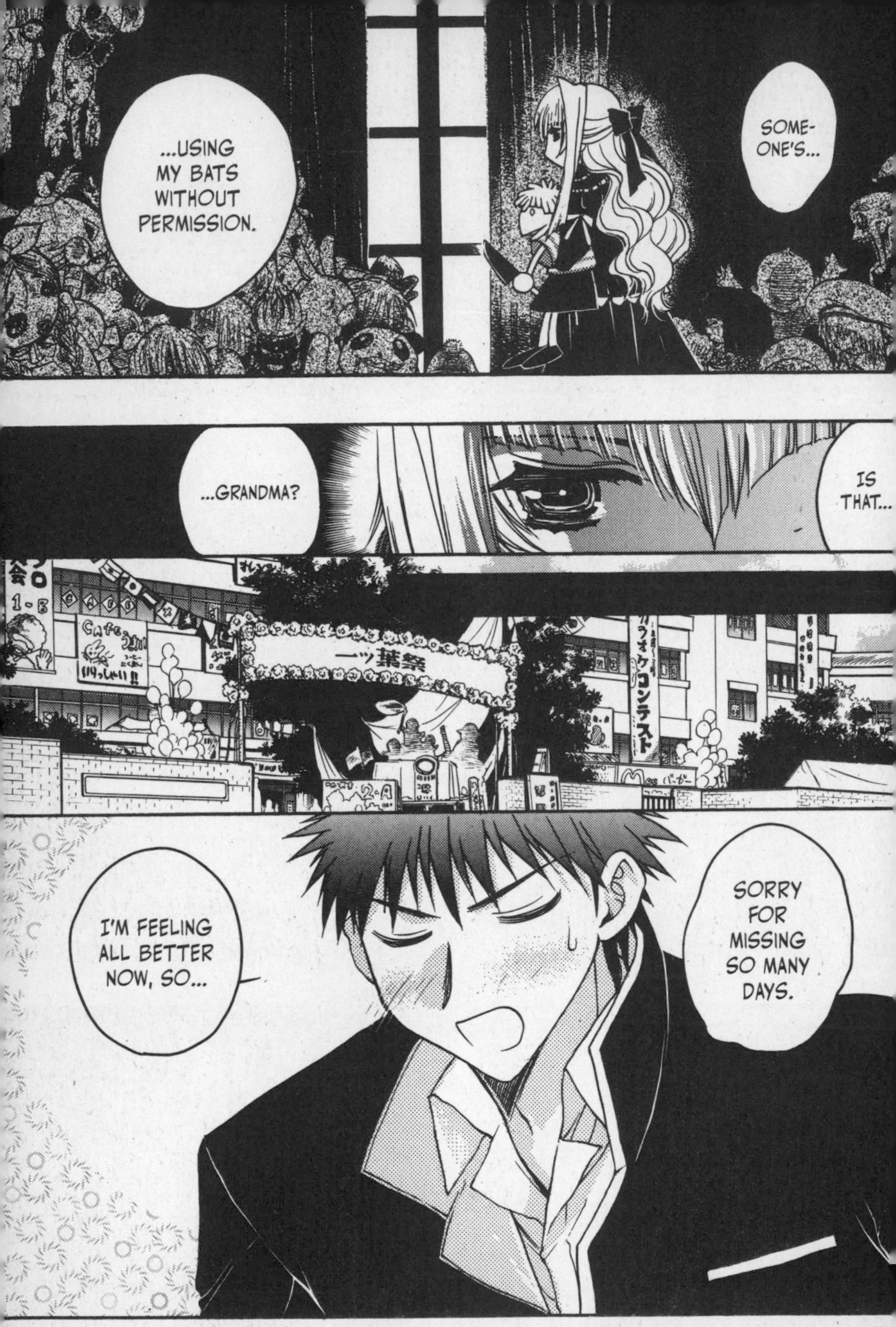
SOME-ONE'S...
...USING MY BATS WITHOUT PERMISSION.
IS THAT...
...GRANDMA?
一ツ葉祭
カラオケコンテスト
SORRY FOR MISSING SO MANY DAYS.
I'M FEELING ALL BETTER NOW, SO...

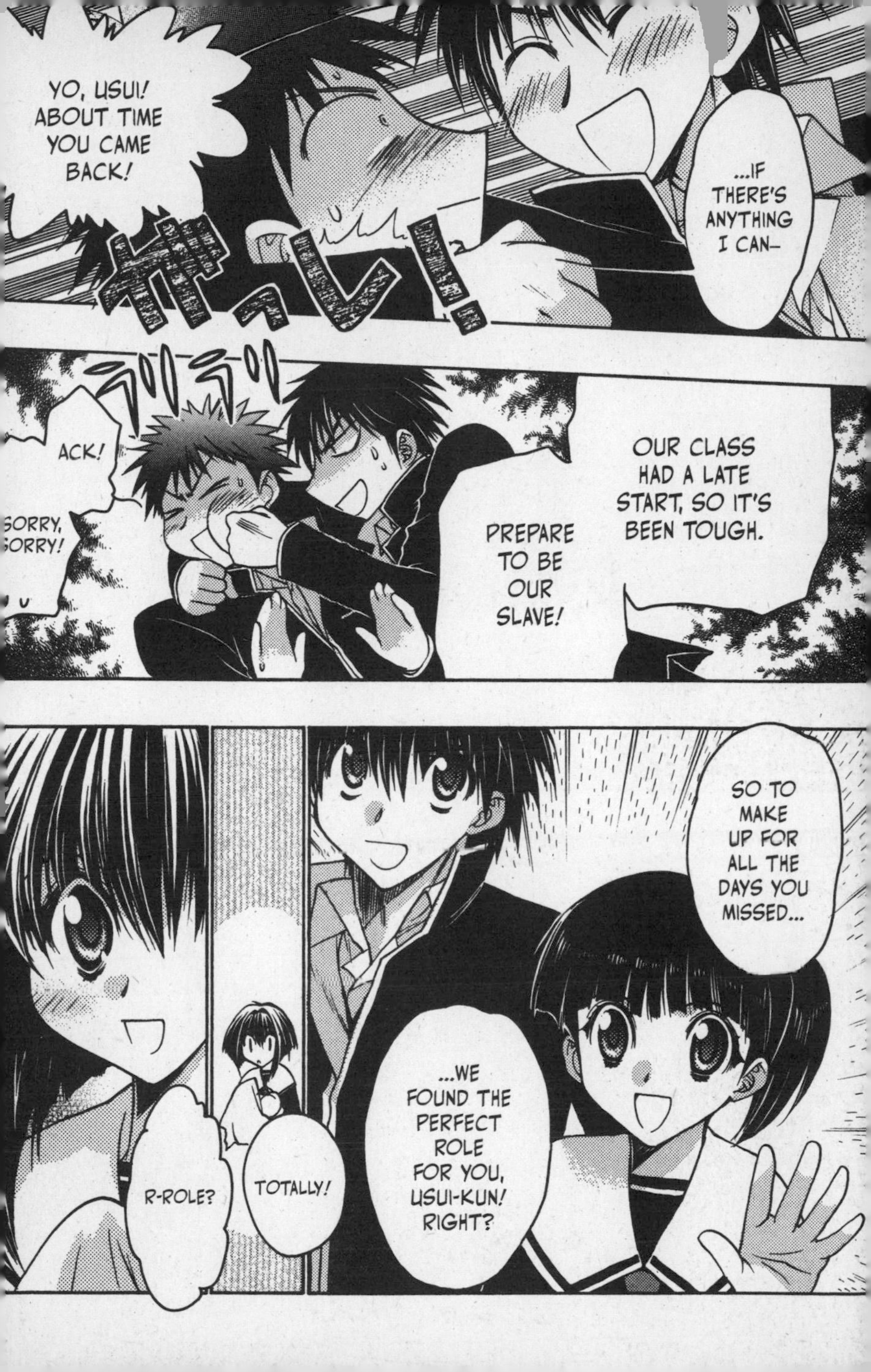
...IF THERE'S ANYTHING I CAN–
YO, USUI! ABOUT TIME YOU CAME BACK!
OUR CLASS HAD A LATE START, SO IT'S BEEN TOUGH.
PREPARE TO BE OUR SLAVE!
ACK!
SORRY, SORRY!
SO TO MAKE UP FOR ALL THE DAYS YOU MISSED...
...WE FOUND THE PERFECT ROLE FOR YOU, USUI-KUN! RIGHT?
TOTALLY!
R-ROLE?

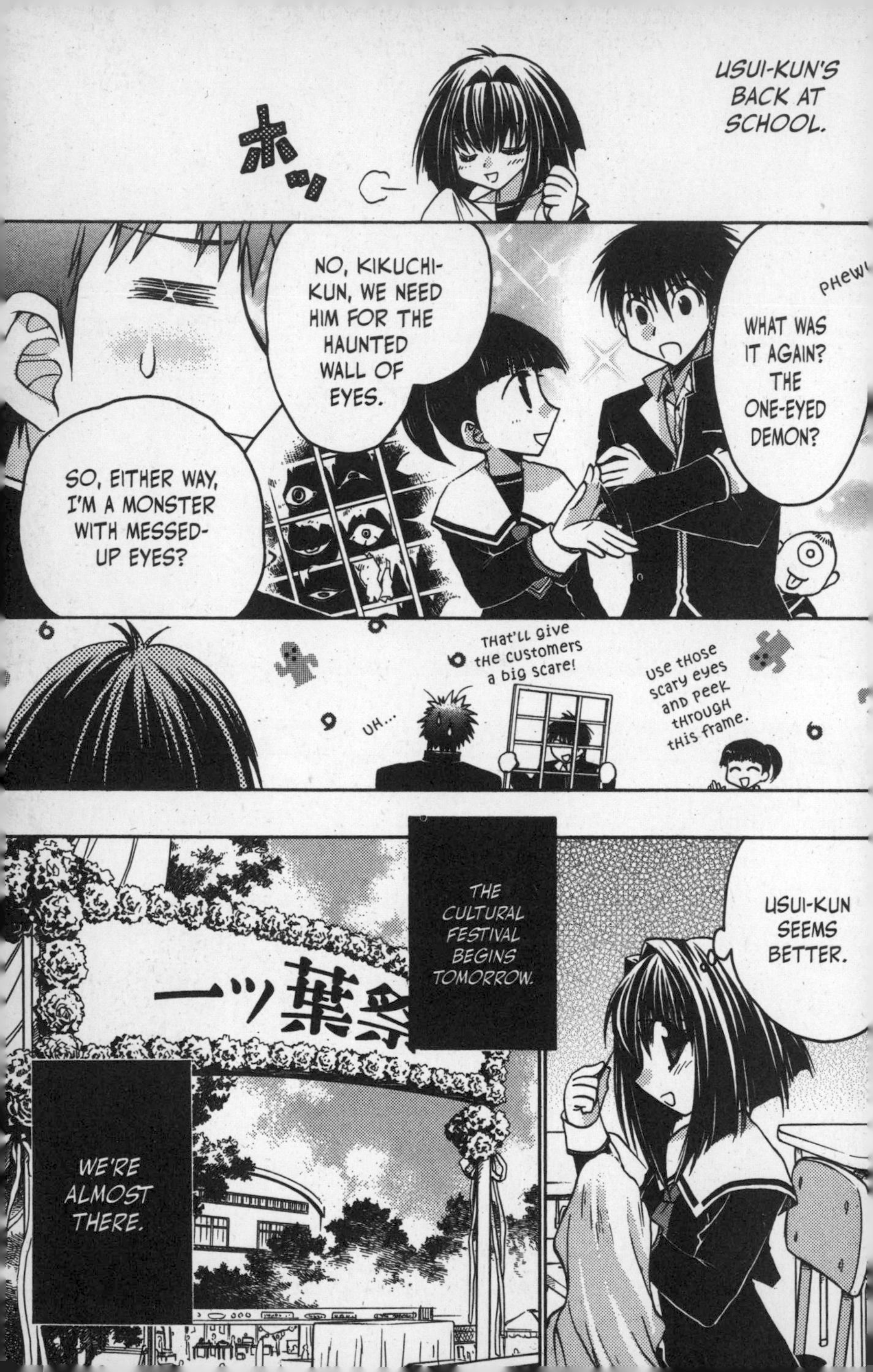
USUI-KUN'S BACK AT SCHOOL.
ホッ
PHEW
WHAT WAS IT AGAIN? THE ONE-EYED DEMON?
NO, KIKUCHI-KUN, WE NEED HIM FOR THE HAUNTED WALL OF EYES.
SO, EITHER WAY, I'M A MONSTER WITH MESSED-UP EYES?
Use those scary eyes and peek through this frame.
That'll give the customers a big scare!
UH...
USUI-KUN SEEMS BETTER.
THE CULTURAL FESTIVAL BEGINS TOMORROW.
一ツ葉
WE'RE ALMOST THERE.

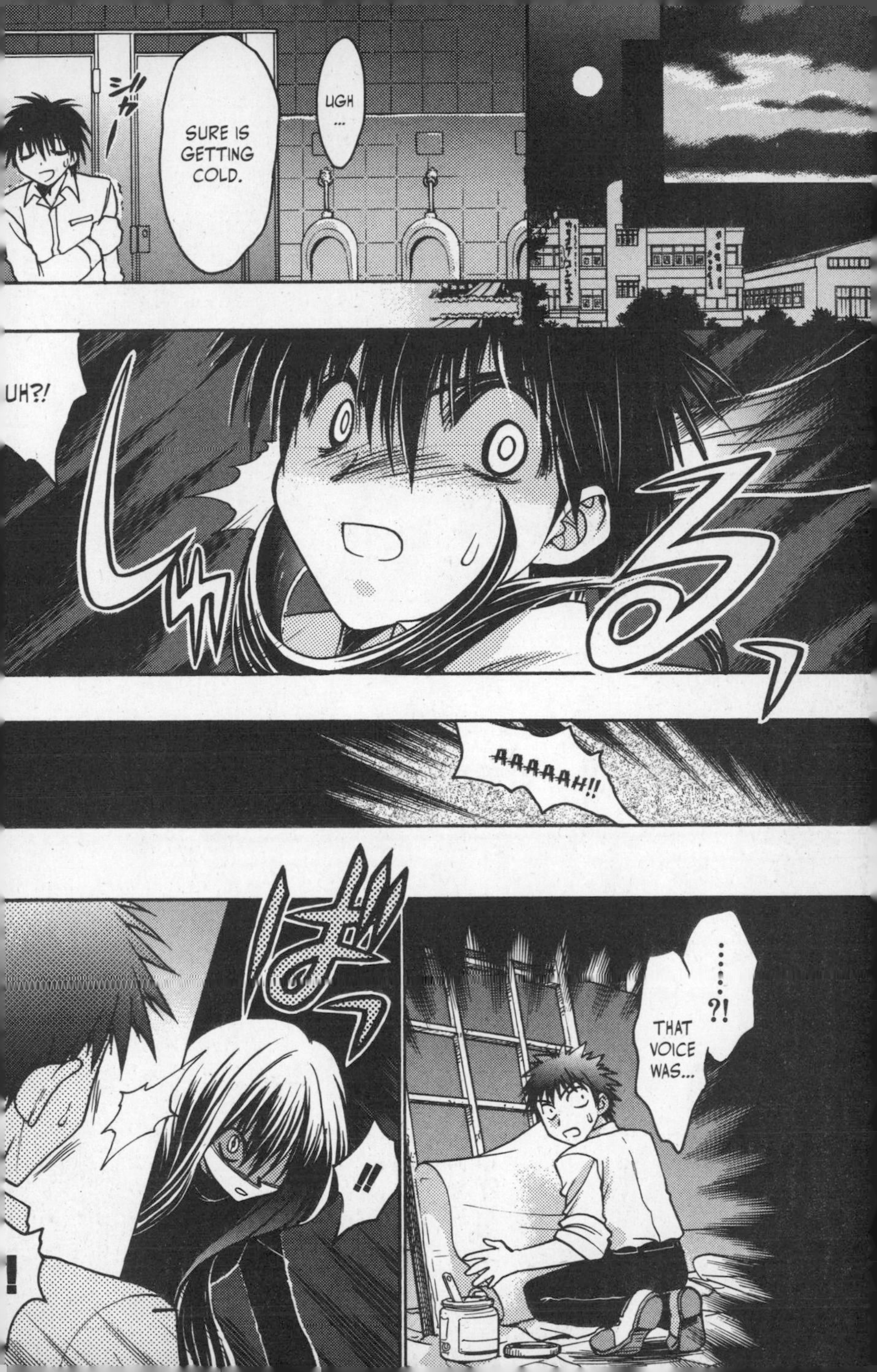
UGH ...
SURE IS GETTING COLD.
UH?!
AAAAAAH!!
......?!
THAT VOICE WAS...
!!
!

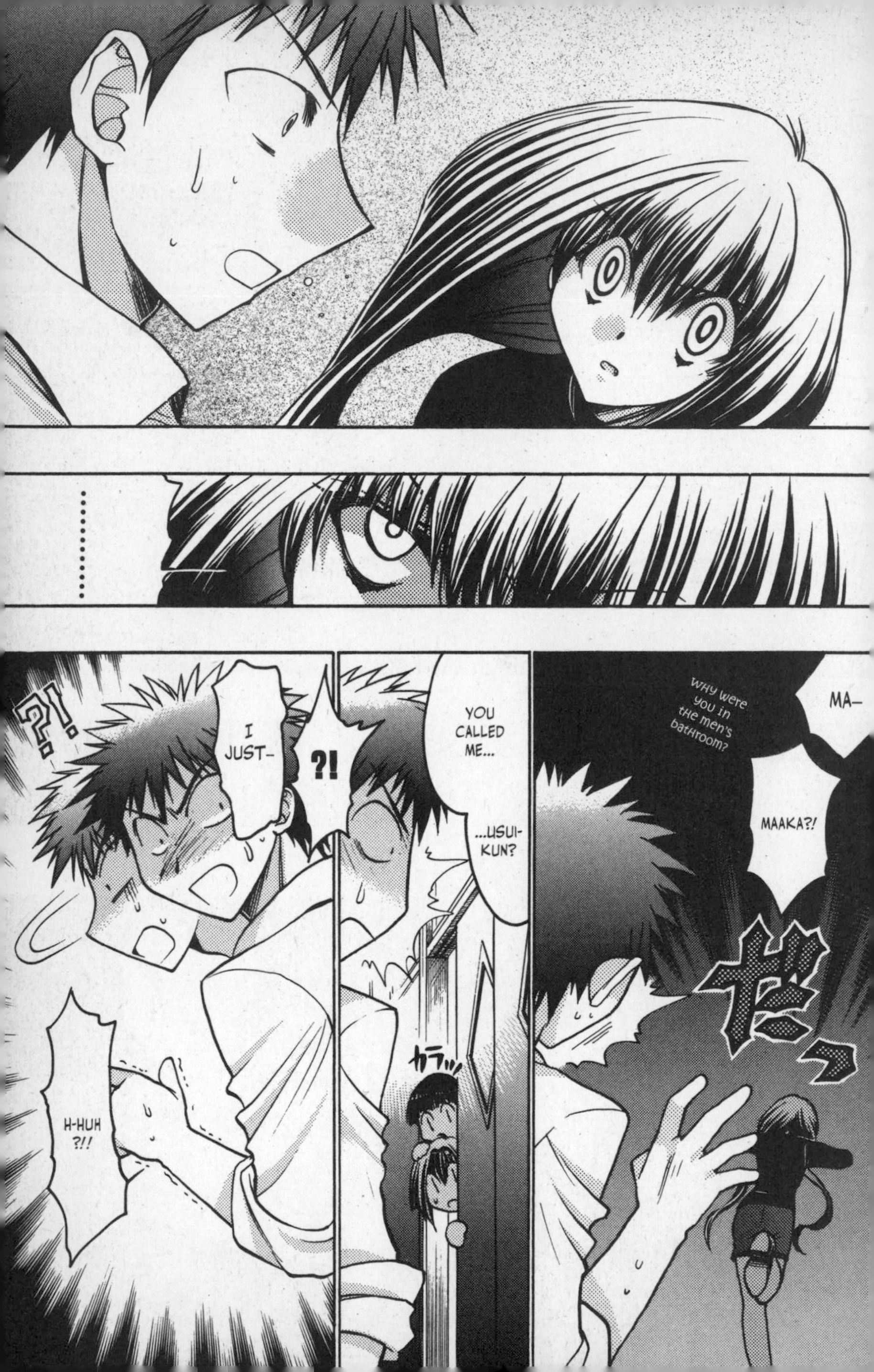

......
MA—
Why were you in the men's bathroom?
MAAKA?!
ダッ
YOU CALLED ME...
...USUI-KUN?
カラッ
I JUST—
?!
?!
H-HUH ?!!

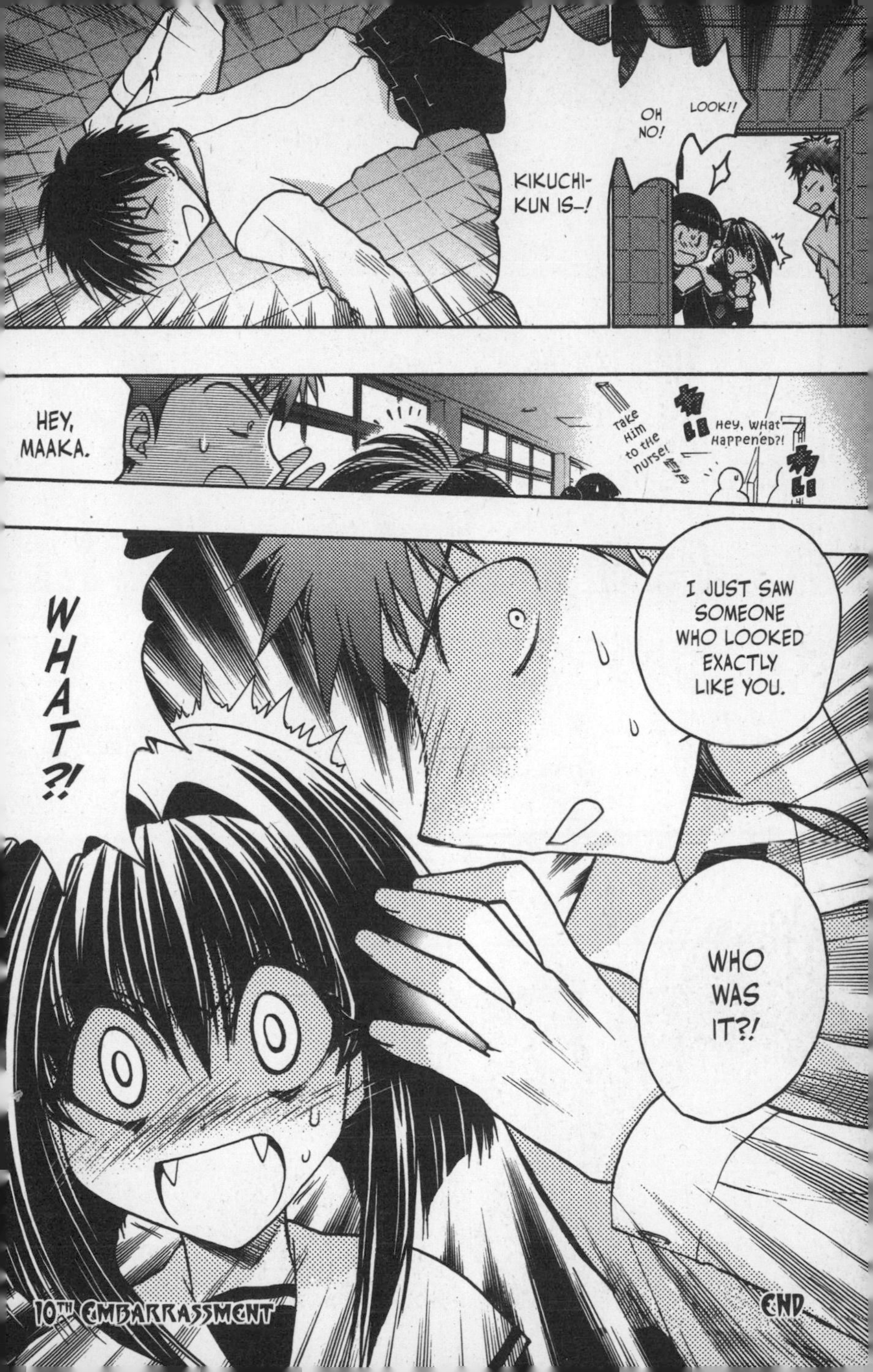

LOOK!!
OH NO!
KIKUCHI-KUN IS–!
Hey, what happened?!
Take him to the nurse!
HEY, MAAKA.
I JUST SAW SOMEONE WHO LOOKED EXACTLY LIKE YOU.
WHO WAS IT?!
WHAT?!
10TH EMBARRASSMENT
END

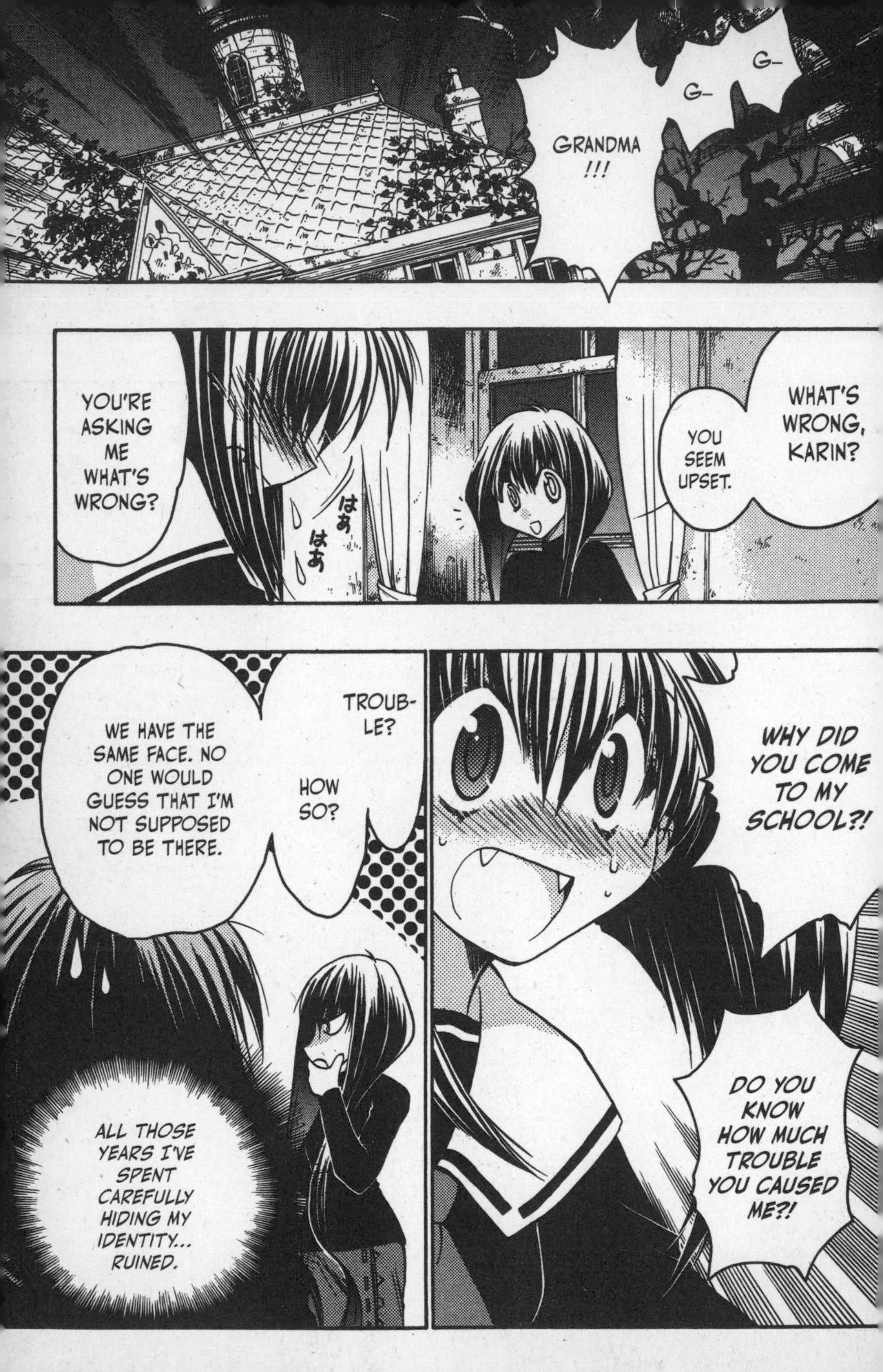
G–
G–
GRANDMA !!!
WHAT'S WRONG, KARIN?
YOU SEEM UPSET.
はあ はあ
YOU'RE ASKING ME WHAT'S WRONG?
WHY DID YOU COME TO MY SCHOOL?!
DO YOU KNOW HOW MUCH TROUBLE YOU CAUSED ME?!
TROUBLE?
HOW SO?
WE HAVE THE SAME FACE. NO ONE WOULD GUESS THAT I'M NOT SUPPOSED TO BE THERE.
ALL THOSE YEARS I'VE SPENT CAREFULLY HIDING MY IDENTITY... RUINED.

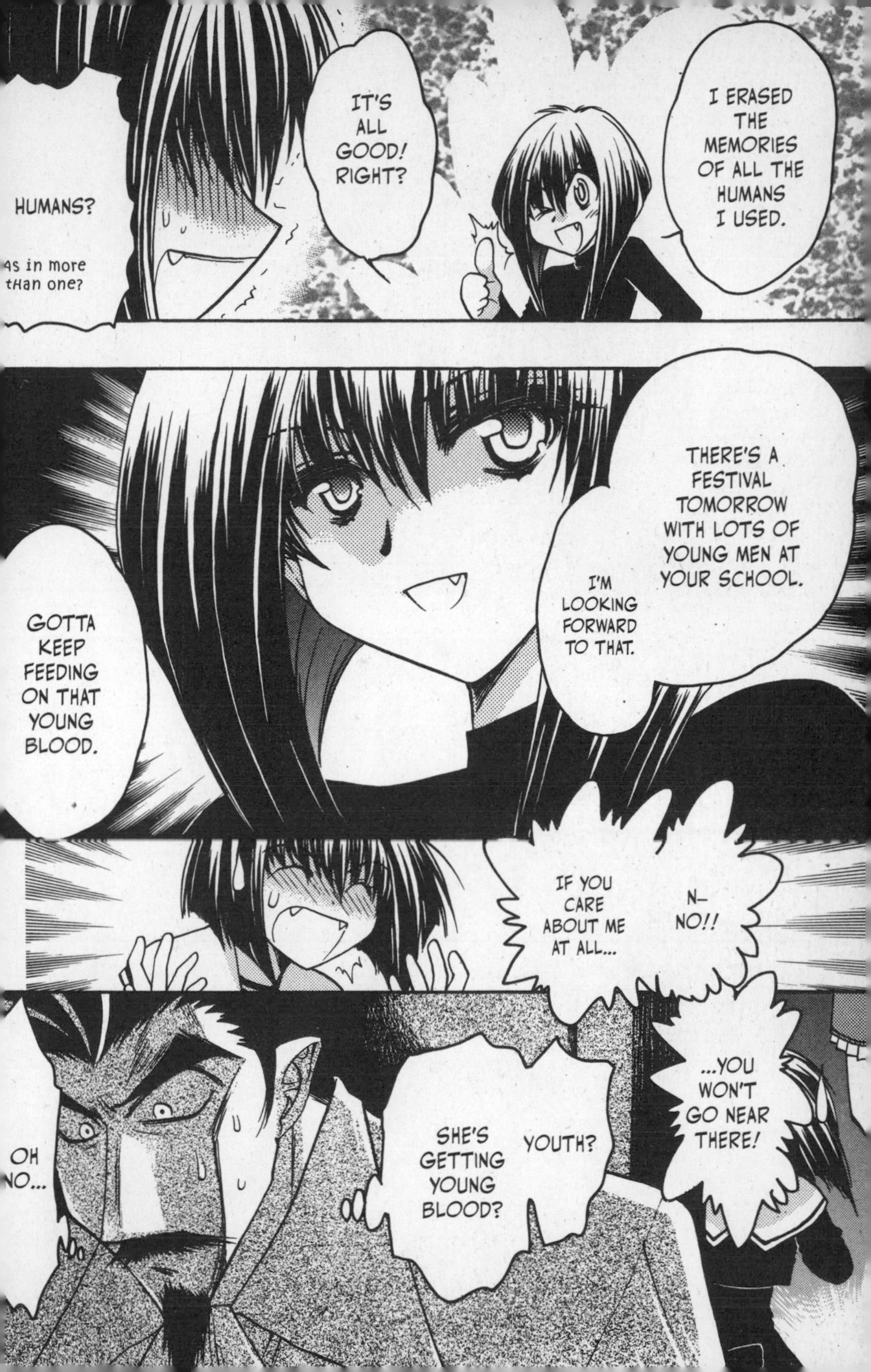
I ERASED THE MEMORIES OF ALL THE HUMANS I USED.
IT'S ALL GOOD! RIGHT?
HUMANS?
As in more than one?
THERE'S A FESTIVAL TOMORROW WITH LOTS OF YOUNG MEN AT YOUR SCHOOL.
I'M LOOKING FORWARD TO THAT.
GOTTA KEEP FEEDING ON THAT YOUNG BLOOD.
N— NO!!
IF YOU CARE ABOUT ME AT ALL...
...YOU WON'T GO NEAR THERE!
YOUTH?
SHE'S GETTING YOUNG BLOOD?
OH NO...

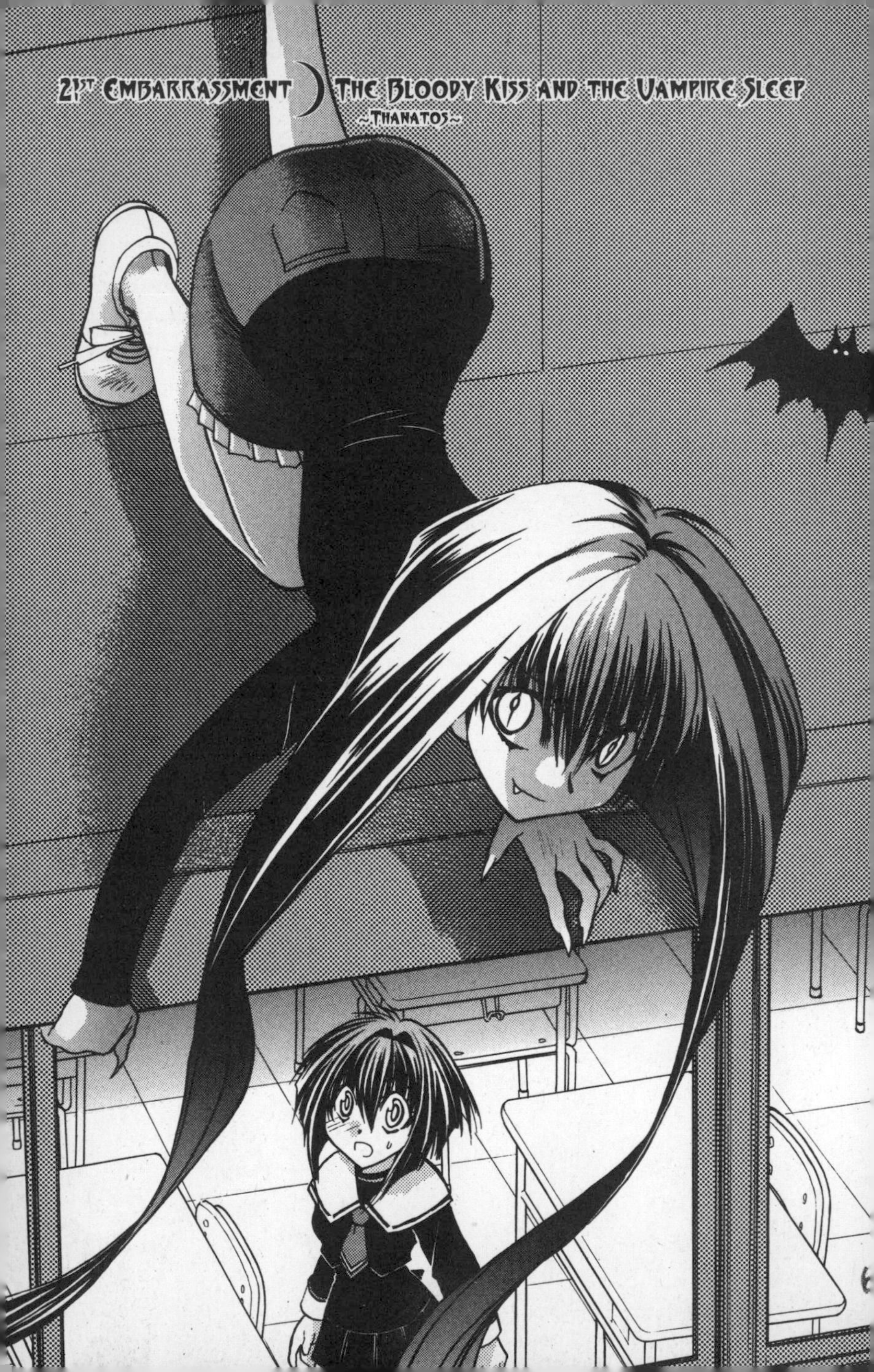
21st Embarrassment The Bloody Kiss and the Vampire Sleep
~Thanatos~

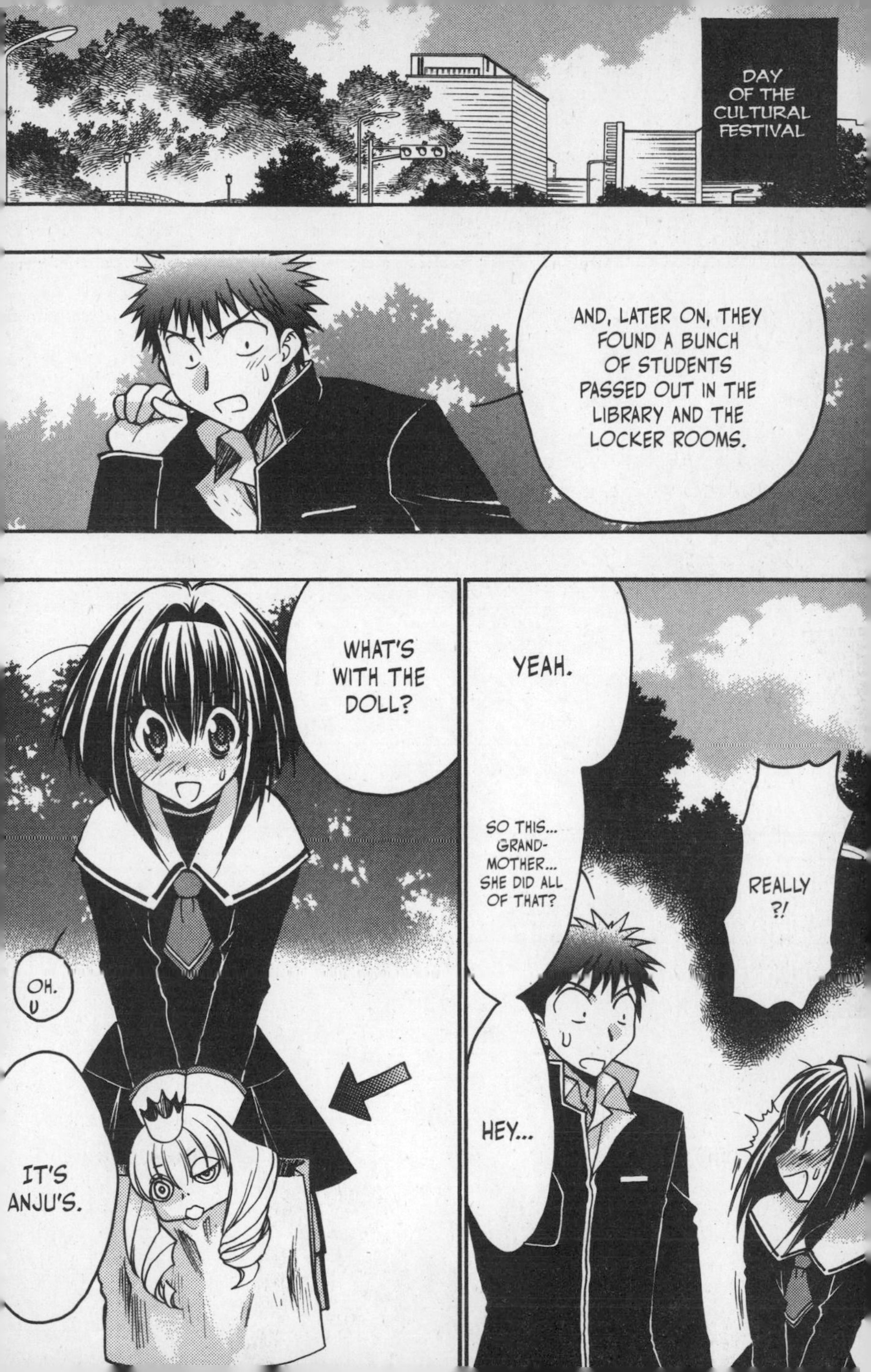
DAY OF THE CULTURAL FESTIVAL
AND, LATER ON, THEY FOUND A BUNCH OF STUDENTS PASSED OUT IN THE LIBRARY AND THE LOCKER ROOMS.
YEAH.
SO THIS... GRAND-MOTHER... SHE DID ALL OF THAT?
REALLY ?!
HEY...
WHAT'S WITH THE DOLL?
OH.
IT'S ANJU'S.

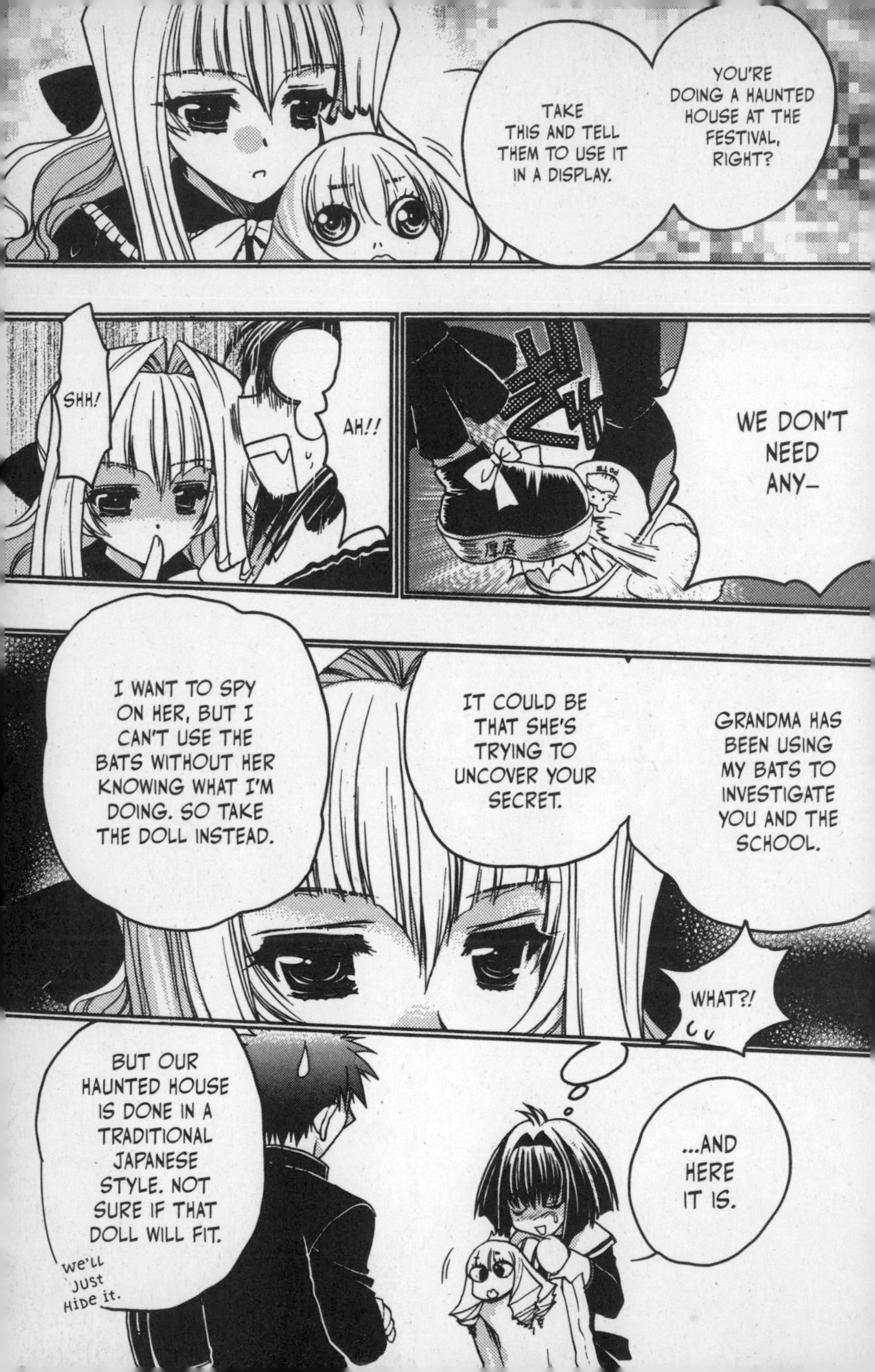
YOU'RE DOING A HAUNTED HOUSE AT THE FESTIVAL, RIGHT?
TAKE THIS AND TELL THEM TO USE IT IN A DISPLAY.
WE DON'T NEED ANY–
AH!!
SHH!
GRANDMA HAS BEEN USING MY BATS TO INVESTIGATE YOU AND THE SCHOOL.
IT COULD BE THAT SHE'S TRYING TO UNCOVER YOUR SECRET.
I WANT TO SPY ON HER, BUT I CAN'T USE THE BATS WITHOUT HER KNOWING WHAT I'M DOING. SO TAKE THE DOLL INSTEAD.
WHAT?!
...AND HERE IT IS.
BUT OUR HAUNTED HOUSE IS DONE IN A TRADITIONAL JAPANESE STYLE. NOT SURE IF THAT DOLL WILL FIT.
We'll JUST HiDe it.

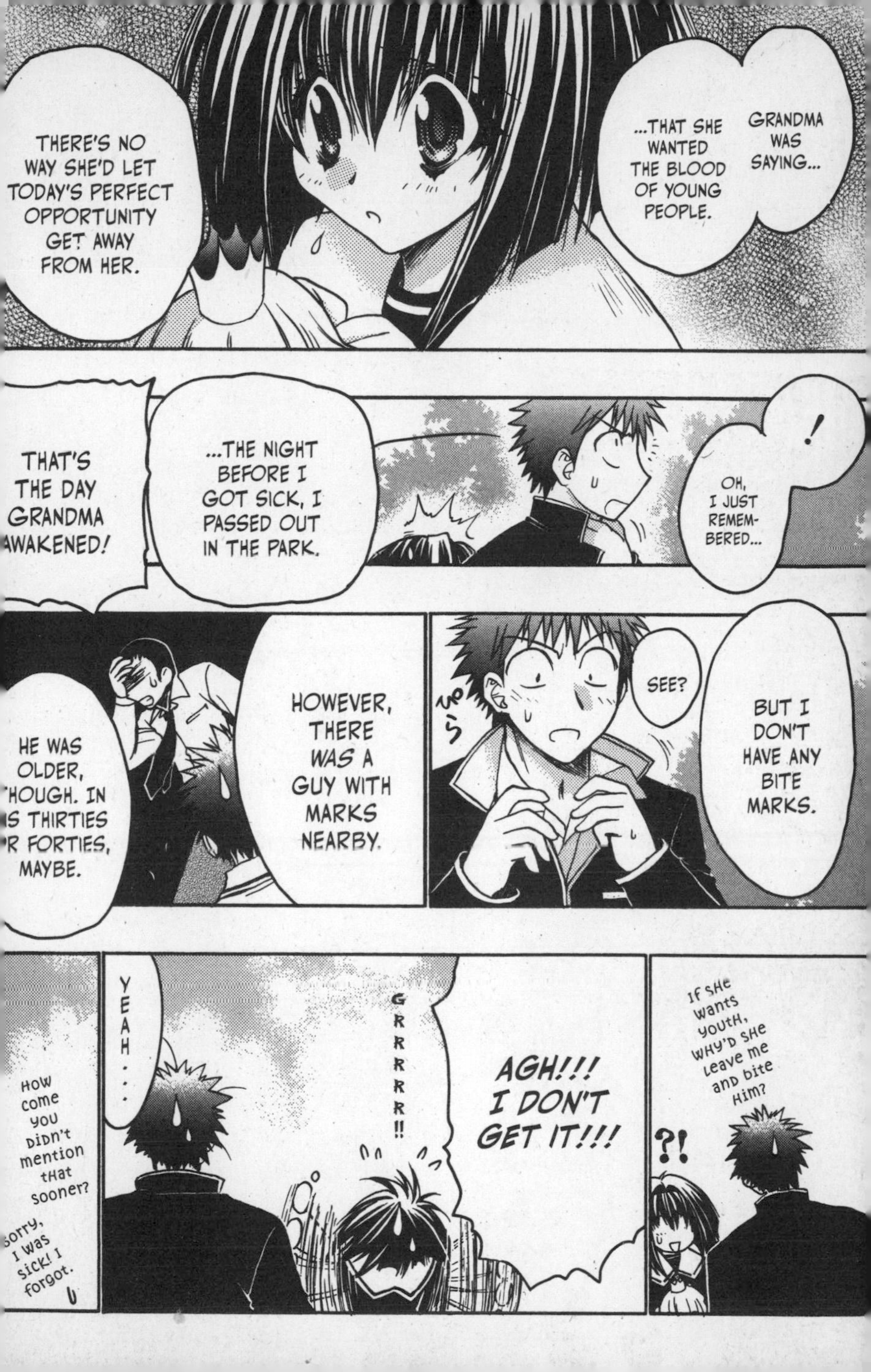
GRANDMA WAS SAYING...
...THAT SHE WANTED THE BLOOD OF YOUNG PEOPLE.
THERE'S NO WAY SHE'D LET TODAY'S PERFECT OPPORTUNITY GET AWAY FROM HER.
!
OH, I JUST REMEMBERED...
...THE NIGHT BEFORE I GOT SICK, I PASSED OUT IN THE PARK.
THAT'S THE DAY GRANDMA AWAKENED!
BUT I DON'T HAVE ANY BITE MARKS.
SEE?
HOWEVER, THERE WAS A GUY WITH MARKS NEARBY.
HE WAS OLDER, THOUGH. IN HIS THIRTIES OR FORTIES, MAYBE.
If SHE wants youtH, WHY'D SHE leave me and bite Him?
?!
AGH!!! I DON'T GET IT!!!
GRRRRR!!
YEAH...
How come you DIDn't mention tHat sooner?
Sorry, I was sick! I forgot.

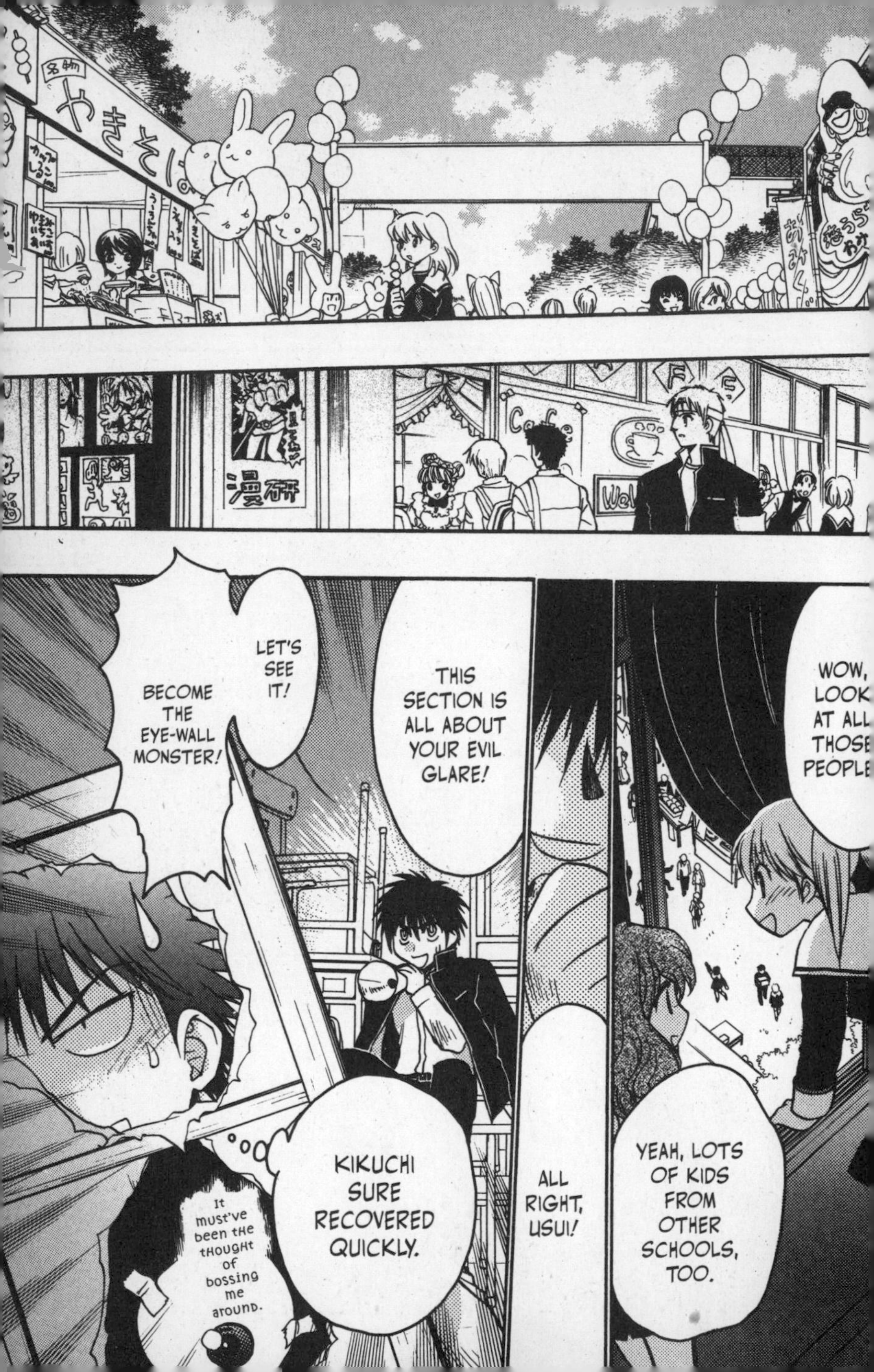

名物
やきそば
Cafe
漫研
WOW, LOOK AT ALL THOSE PEOPLE
YEAH, LOTS OF KIDS FROM OTHER SCHOOLS, TOO.
ALL RIGHT, USUI!
THIS SECTION IS ALL ABOUT YOUR EVIL GLARE!
LET'S SEE IT!
BECOME THE EYE-WALL MONSTER!
KIKUCHI SURE RECOVERED QUICKLY.
It must've been the thought of bossing me around.

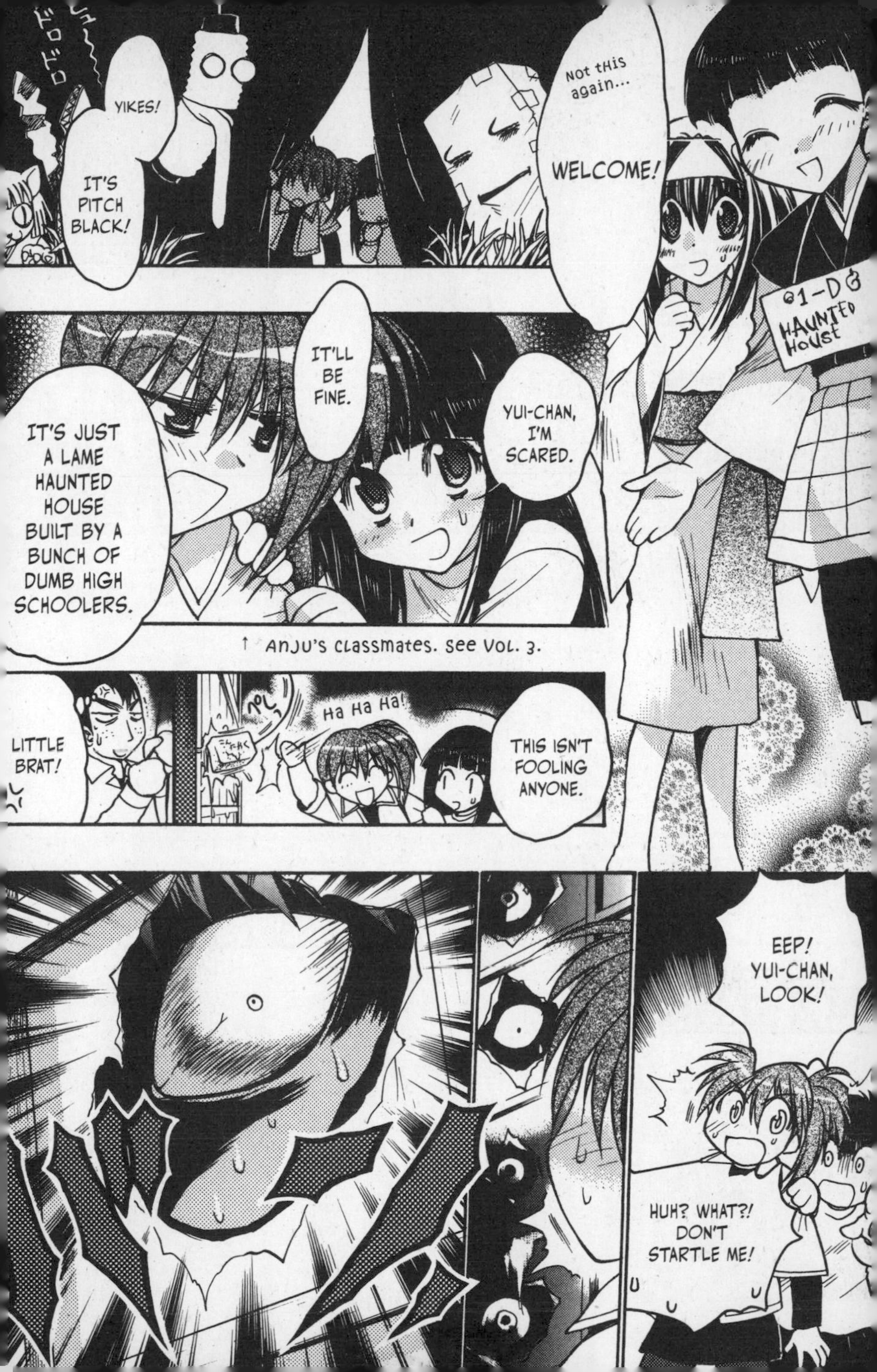
Not this again...
WELCOME!
1-D HAUNTED HOUSE
YIKES!
IT'S PITCH BLACK!
YUI-CHAN, I'M SCARED.
IT'LL BE FINE.
IT'S JUST A LAME HAUNTED HOUSE BUILT BY A BUNCH OF DUMB HIGH SCHOOLERS.
↑ Anju's classmates. See Vol. 3.
THIS ISN'T FOOLING ANYONE.
Ha Ha Ha!
LITTLE BRAT!
EEP! YUI-CHAN, LOOK!
HUH? WHAT?! DON'T STARTLE ME!

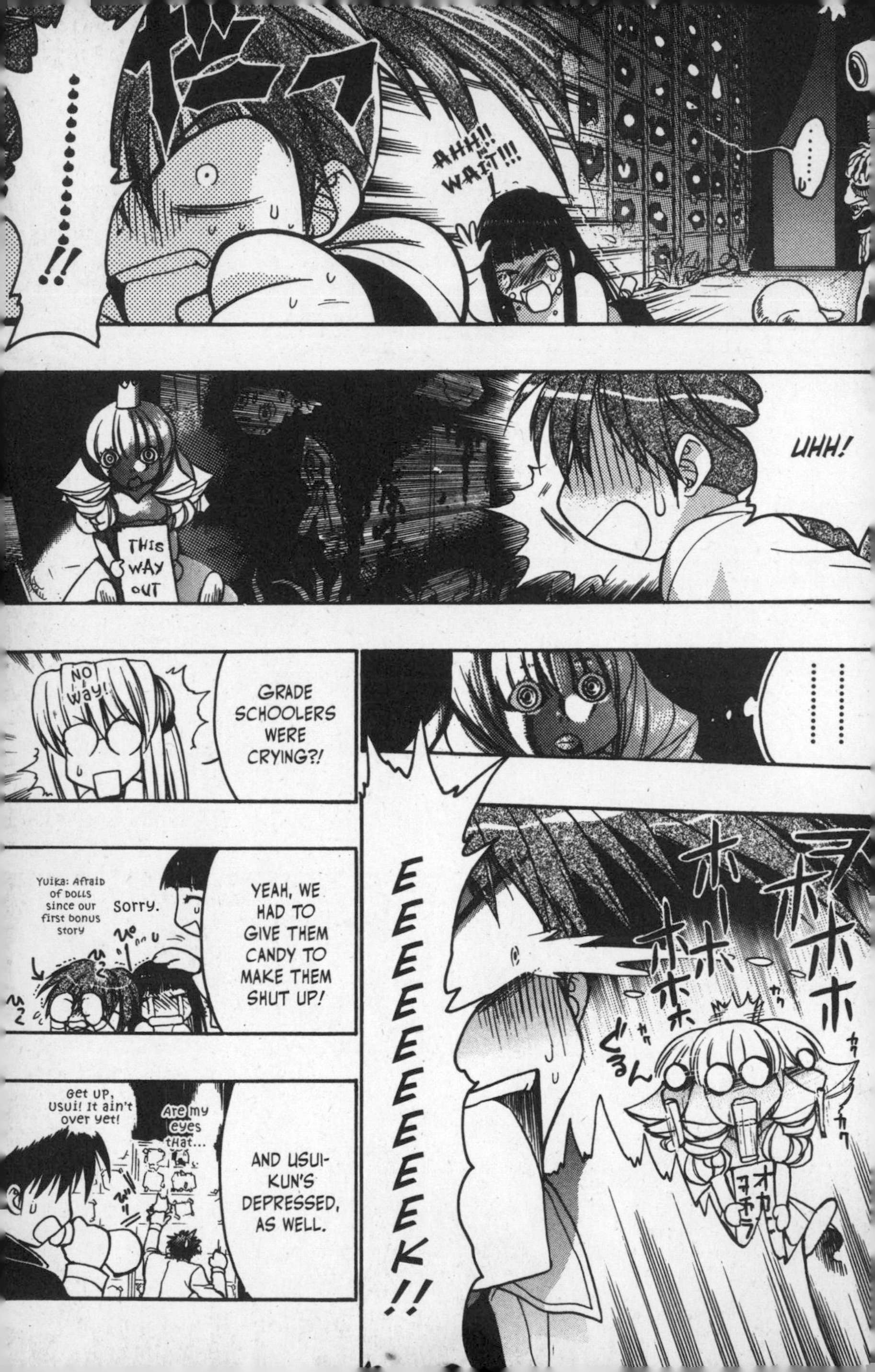
......
AHH!! WAIT!!!
......!!
UHH!
THIS WAY OUT
......
EEEEEEEEEEEEK!!
GRADE SCHOOLERS WERE CRYING?!
NO WAY!
YEAH, WE HAD TO GIVE THEM CANDY TO MAKE THEM SHUT UP!
Sorry.
Yuika: Afraid of dolls since our first bonus story
AND USUI-KUN'S DEPRESSED, AS WELL.
Are my eyes that...
Get up, Usui! It ain't over yet!

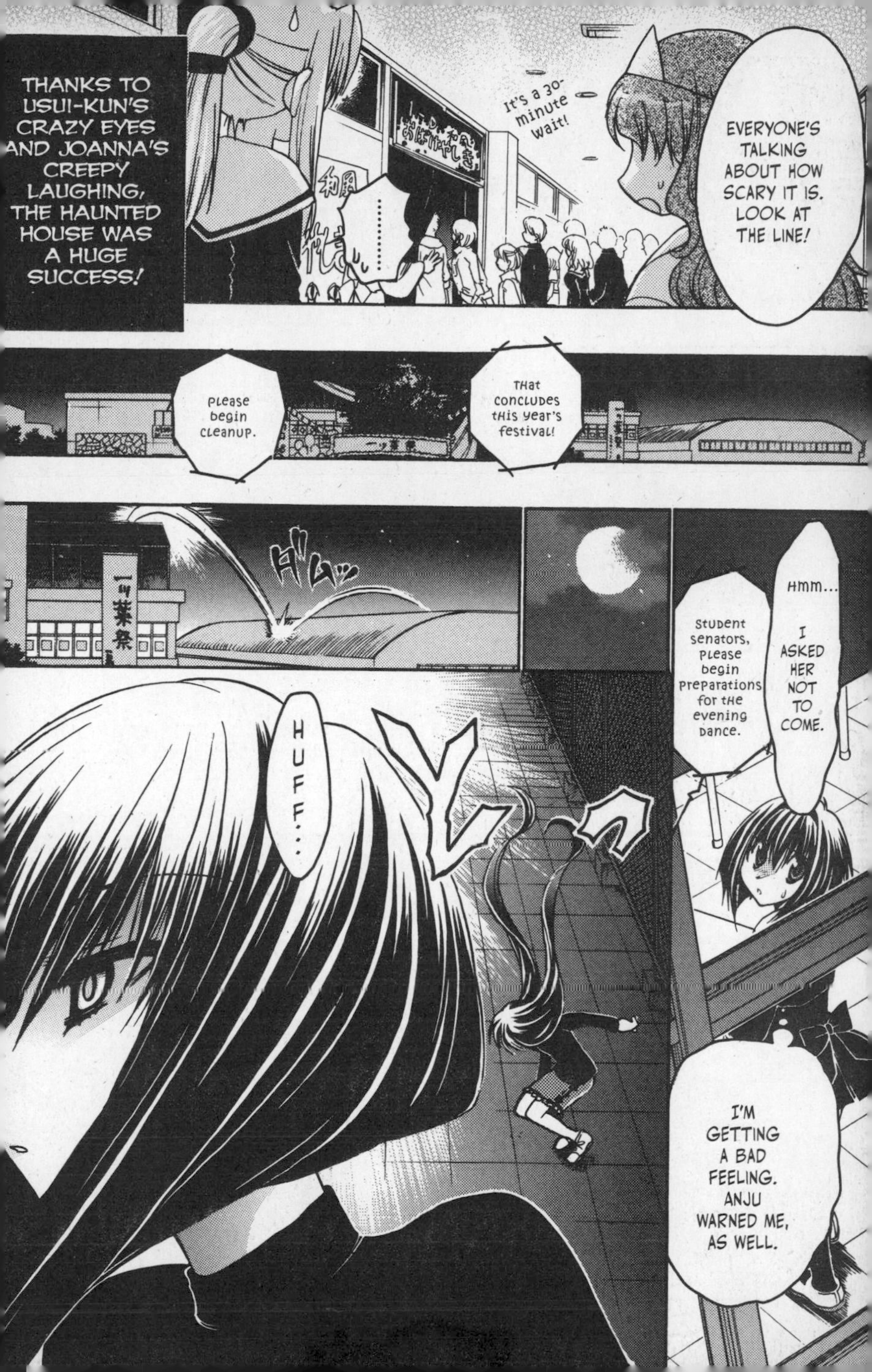
EVERYONE'S TALKING ABOUT HOW SCARY IT IS. LOOK AT THE LINE!
It's a 30-minute wait!
......
THANKS TO USUI-KUN'S CRAZY EYES AND JOANNA'S CREEPY LAUGHING, THE HAUNTED HOUSE WAS A HUGE SUCCESS!
That concludes this year's festival!
Please begin cleanup.
Hmm... I ASKED HER NOT TO COME.
Student senators, please begin preparations for the evening dance.
I'M GETTING A BAD FEELING. ANJU WARNED ME, AS WELL.
HUFF...

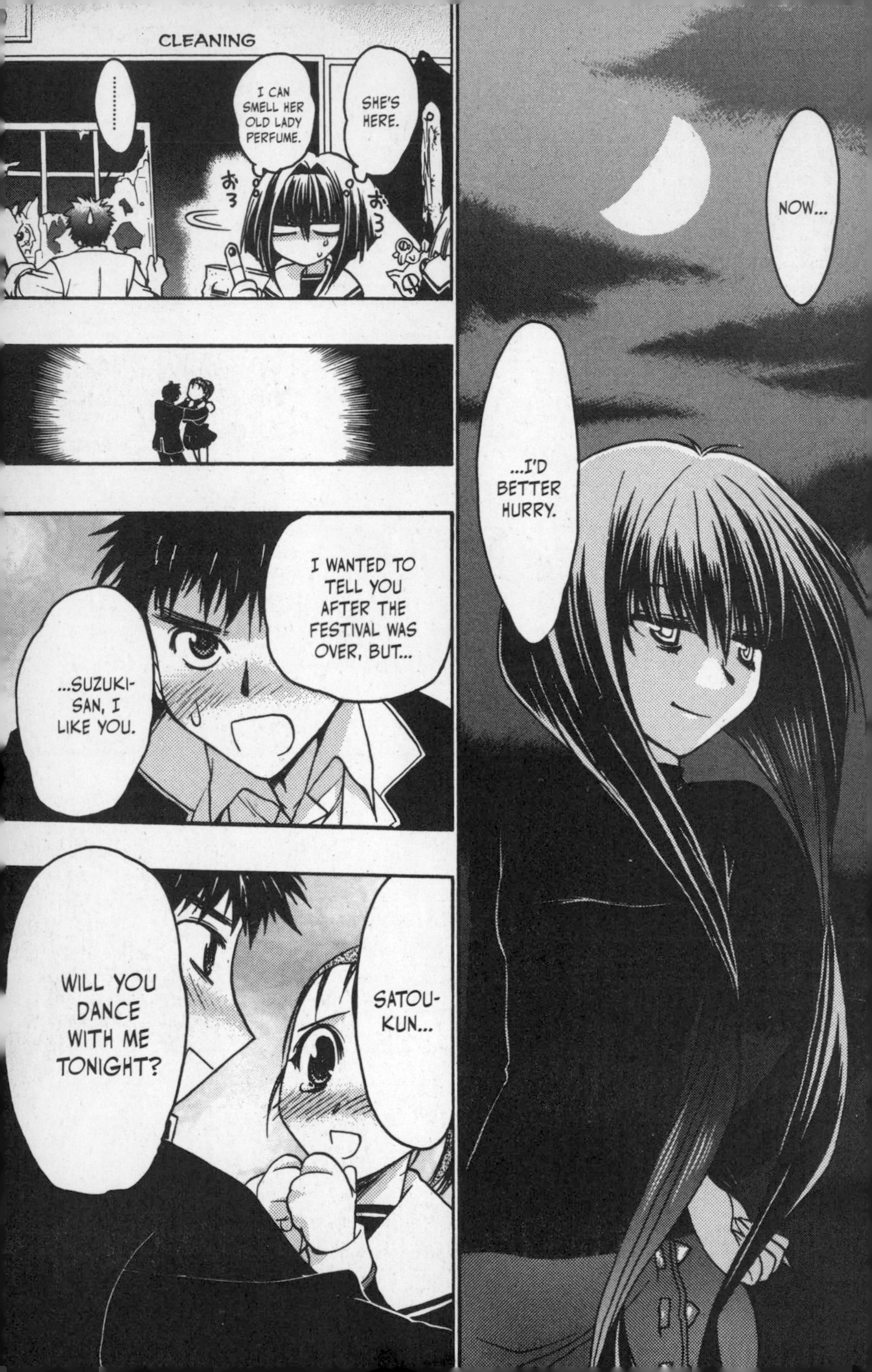
NOW...
...I'D BETTER HURRY.
CLEANING
SHE'S HERE.
I CAN SMELL HER OLD LADY PERFUME.
....
おろ
おろ
I WANTED TO TELL YOU AFTER THE FESTIVAL WAS OVER, BUT...
...SUZUKI-SAN, I LIKE YOU.
SATOU-KUN...
WILL YOU DANCE WITH ME TONIGHT?

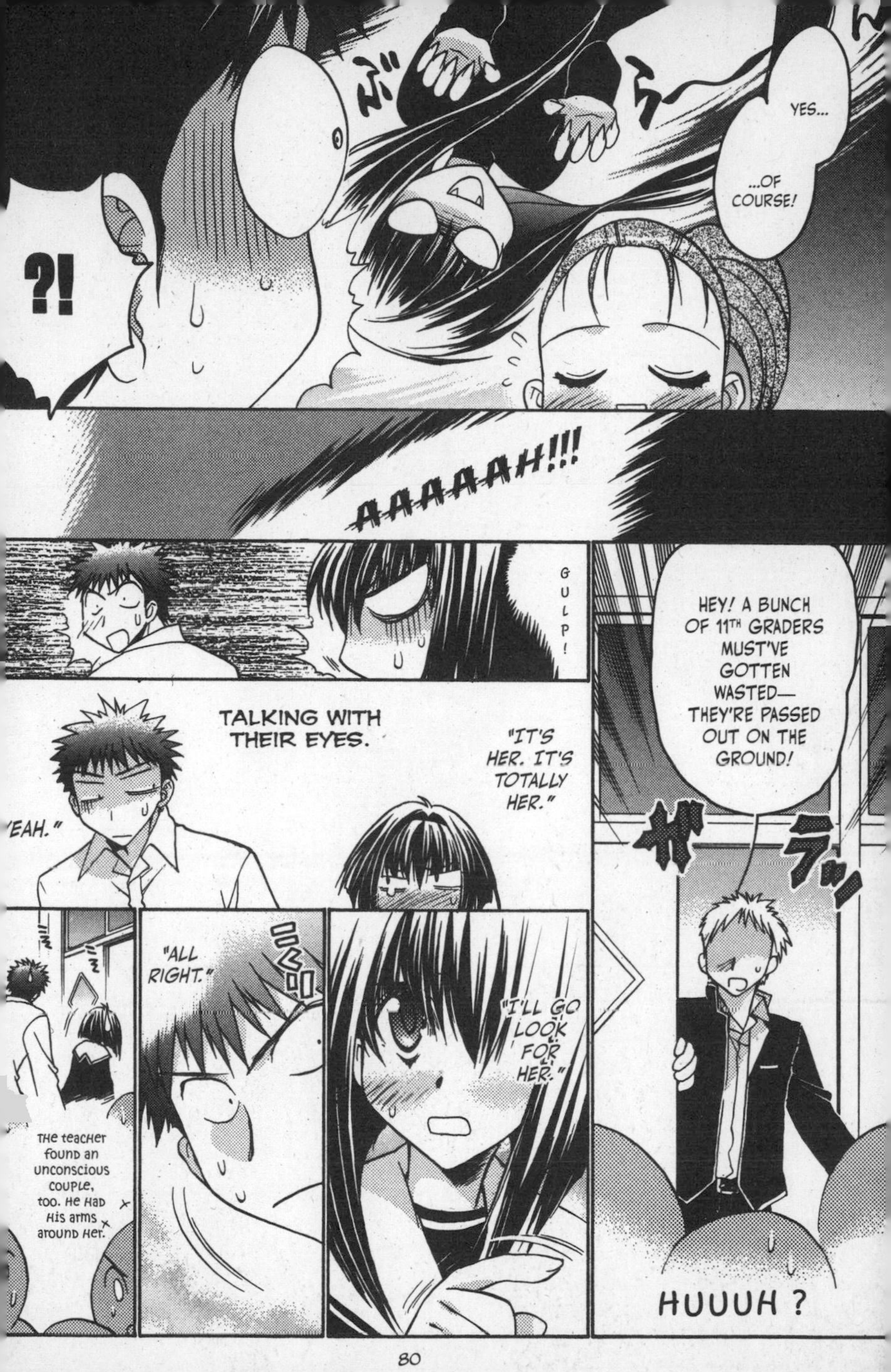
YES...
...OF COURSE!
?!
AAAAAAH!!!
HEY! A BUNCH OF 11TH GRADERS MUST'VE GOTTEN WASTED— THEY'RE PASSED OUT ON THE GROUND!
HUUUH ?
GULP!
"IT'S HER. IT'S TOTALLY HER."
TALKING WITH THEIR EYES.
"YEAH."
"I'LL GO LOOK FOR HER."
"ALL RIGHT."
The teacher found an unconscious couple, too. He had his arms around her.

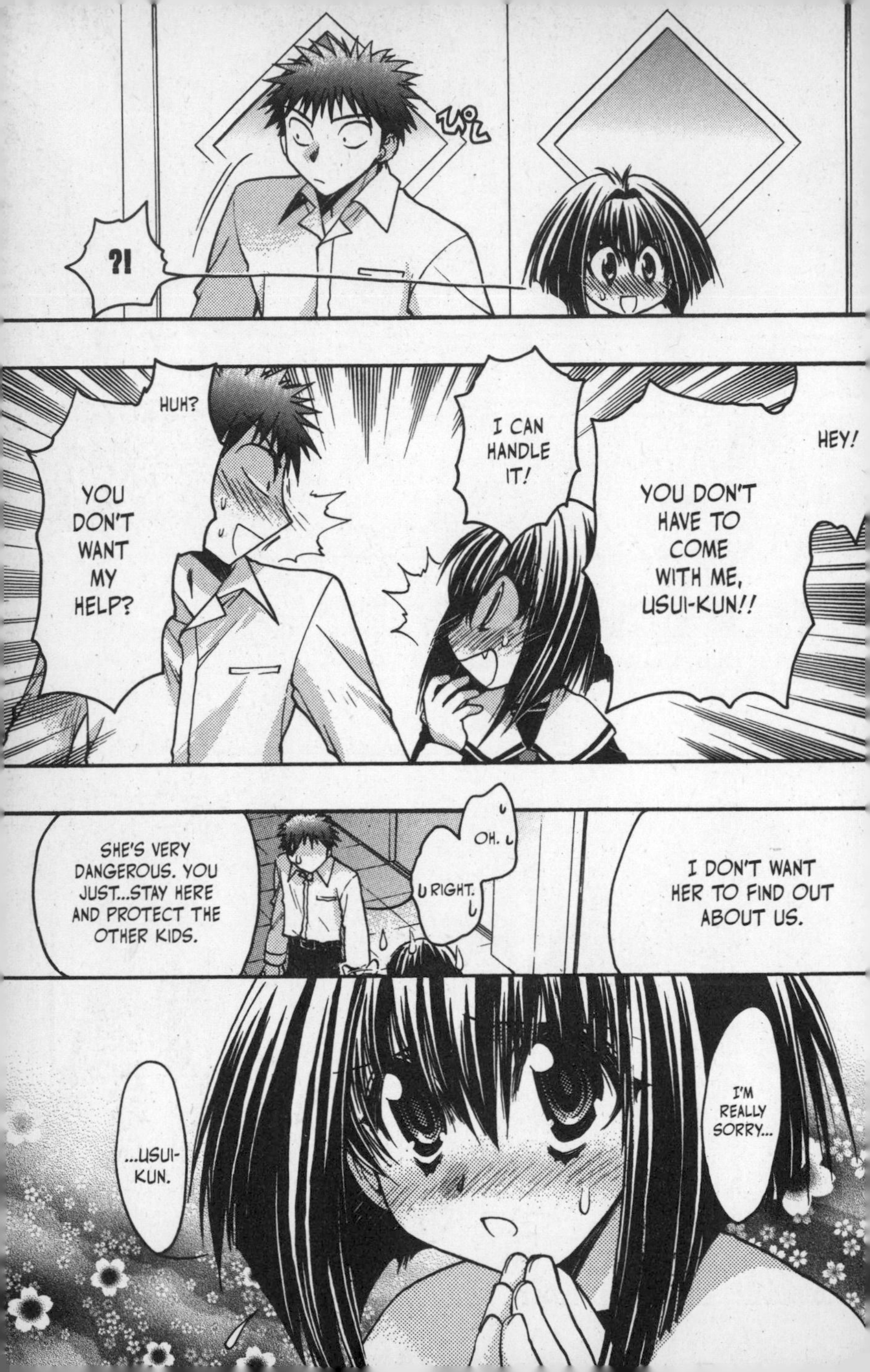
?!
HEY!
YOU DON'T HAVE TO COME WITH ME, USUI-KUN!!
I CAN HANDLE IT!
HUH?
YOU DON'T WANT MY HELP?
I DON'T WANT HER TO FIND OUT ABOUT US.
OH. RIGHT.
SHE'S VERY DANGEROUS. YOU JUST...STAY HERE AND PROTECT THE OTHER KIDS.
I'M REALLY SORRY...
...USUI-KUN.

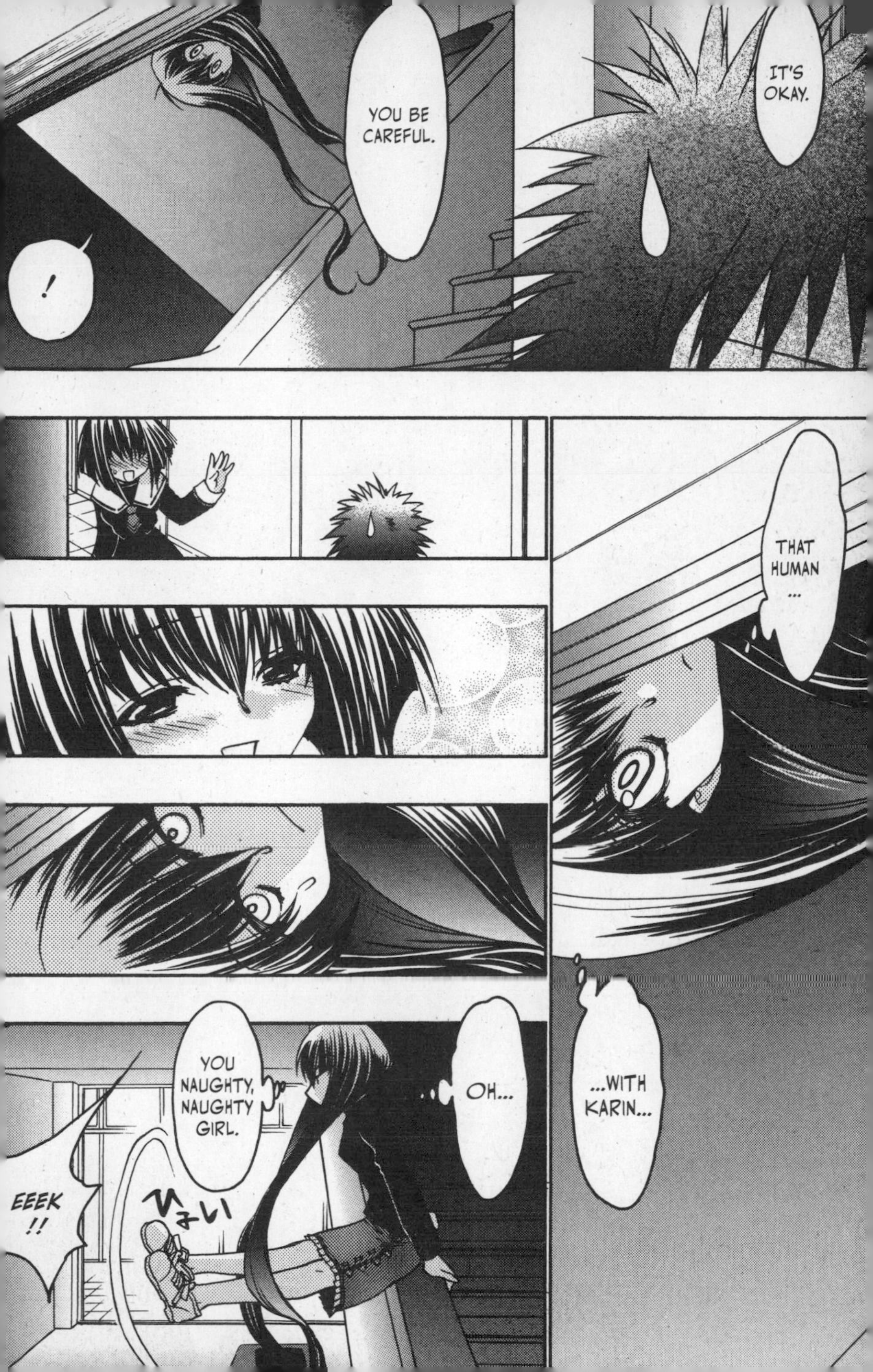
IT'S OKAY.
YOU BE CAREFUL.
!
THAT HUMAN ...
...WITH KARIN...
OH...
YOU NAUGHTY, NAUGHTY GIRL.
ひょい
EEEK !!

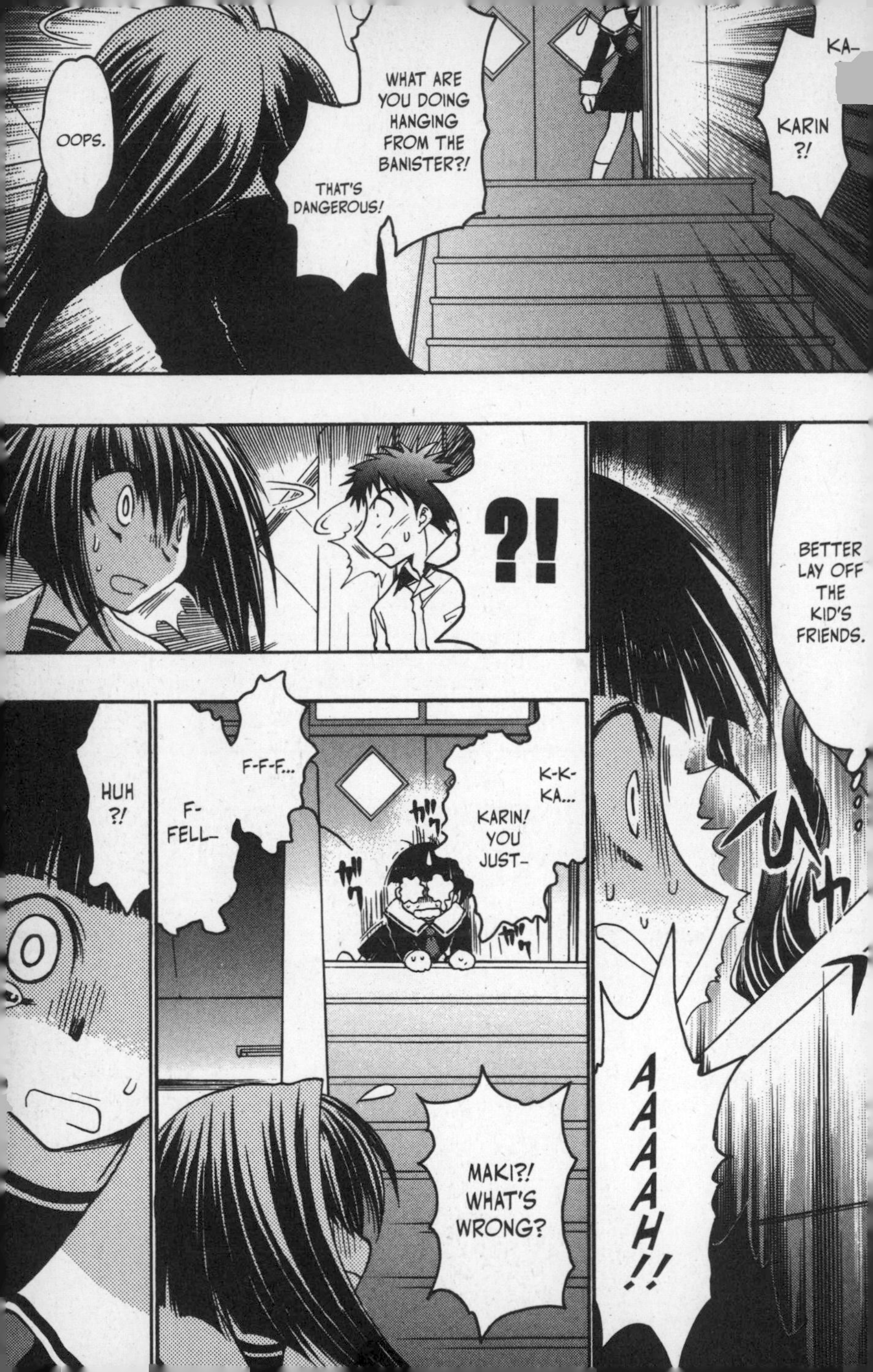
KA-
KARIN ?!
WHAT ARE YOU DOING HANGING FROM THE BANISTER?!
THAT'S DANGEROUS!
OOPS.
BETTER LAY OFF THE KID'S FRIENDS.
AAAAH!!
?!
K-K-KA...
KARIN! YOU JUST-
F-F-F...
F-FELL-
MAKI?! WHAT'S WRONG?
HUH ?!

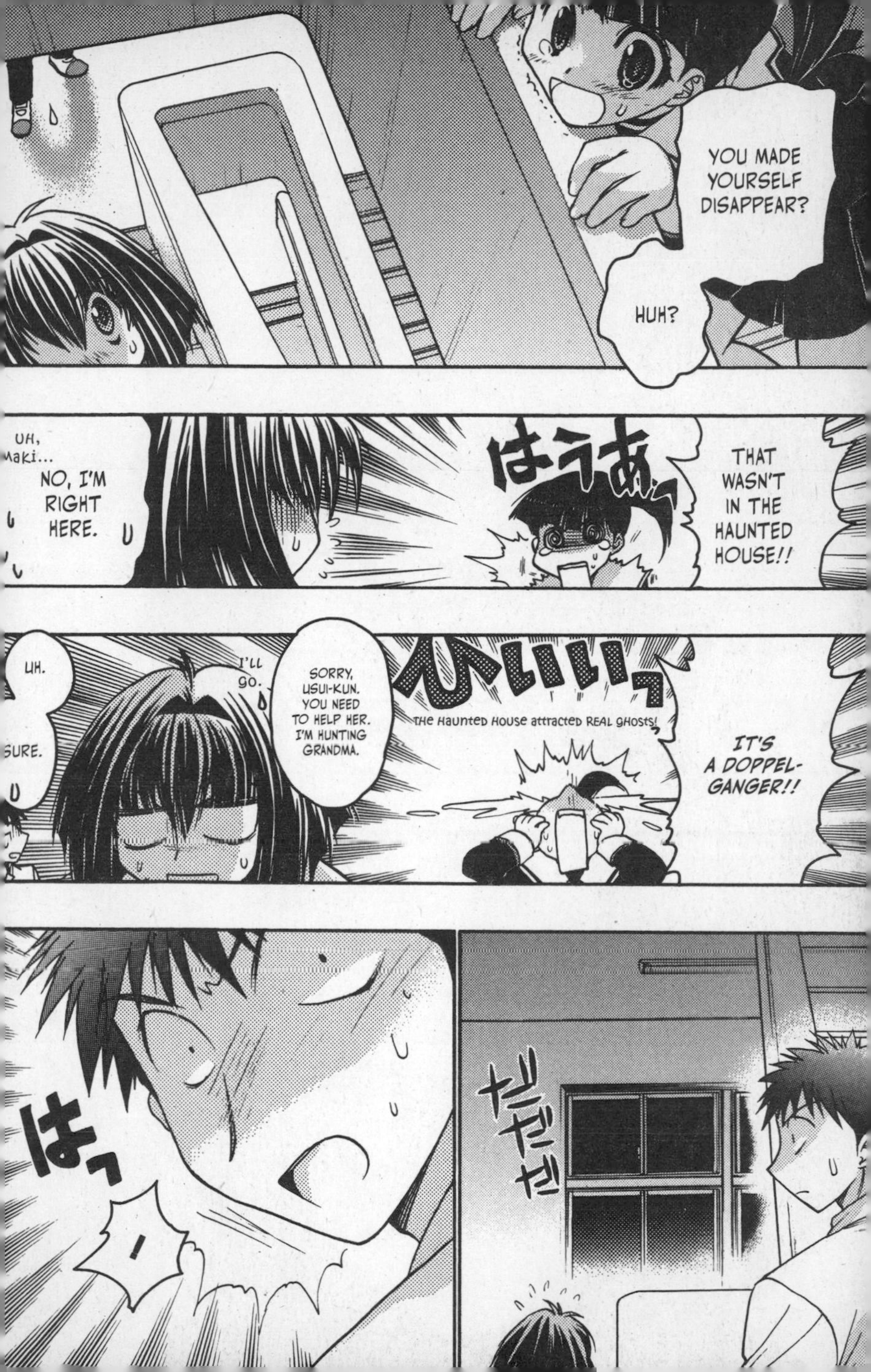
YOU MADE YOURSELF DISAPPEAR?
HUH?
THAT WASN'T IN THE HAUNTED HOUSE!!
はうあっ
UH, MAKI...
NO, I'M RIGHT HERE.
IT'S A DOPPEL-GANGER!!
ひぃぃぃっ
THE HAUNTED HOUSE attracted REAL GHOSTS!
SORRY, USUI-KUN. YOU NEED TO HELP HER. I'M HUNTING GRANDMA.
I'LL GO.
UH.
SURE.
だだだ
はっ

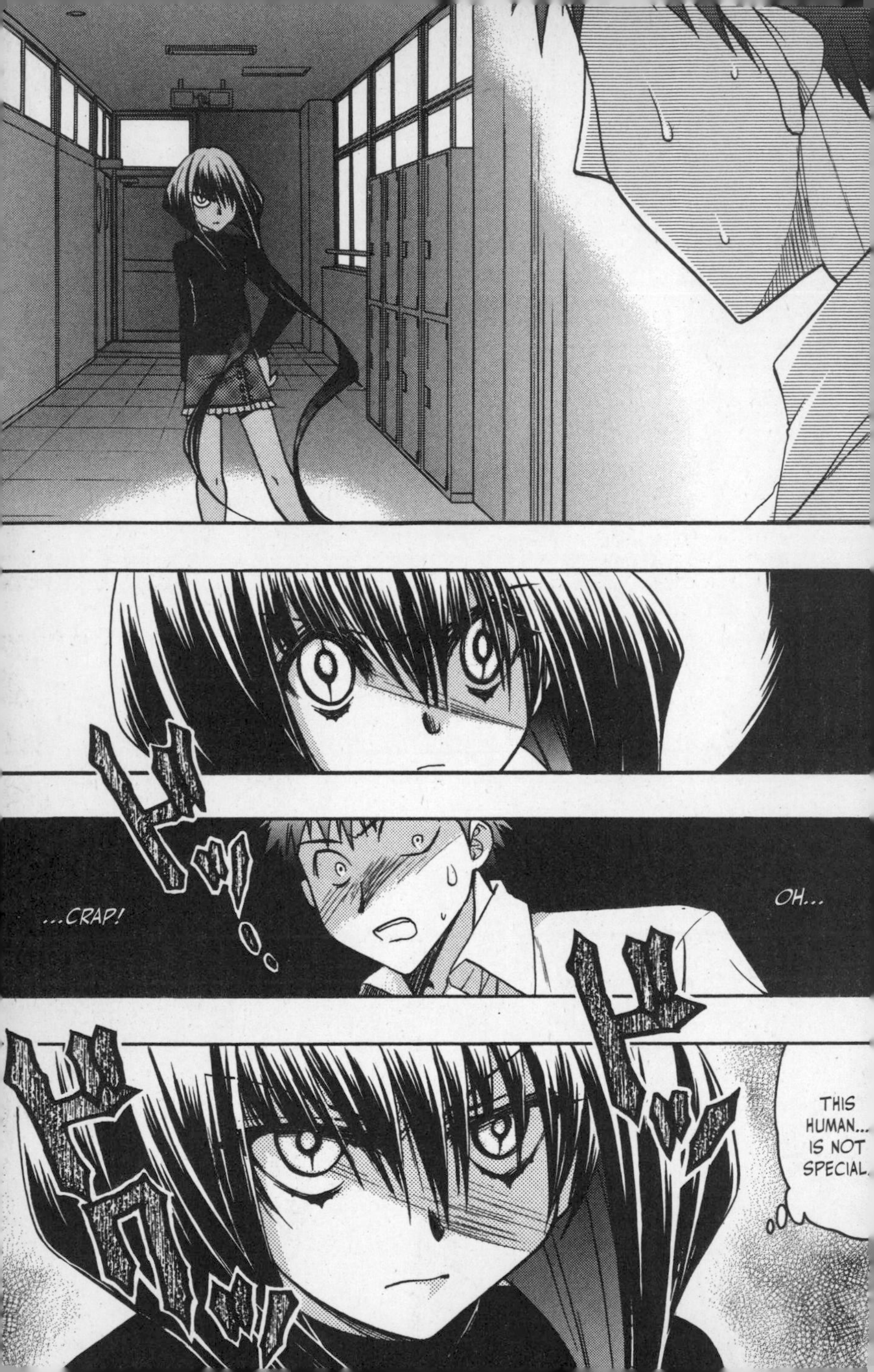
OH...
...CRAP!
THIS HUMAN... IS NOT SPECIAL.

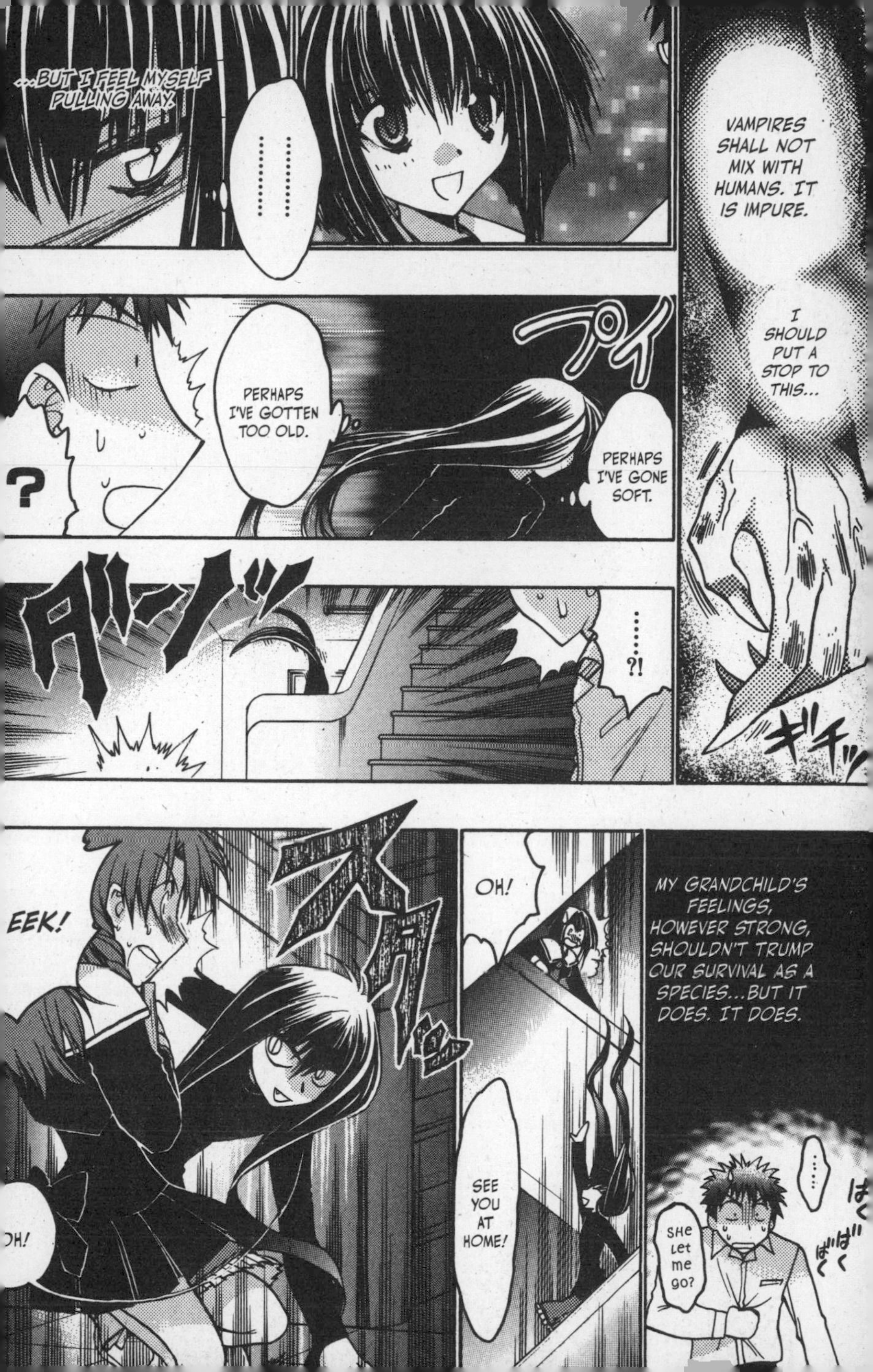
VAMPIRES SHALL NOT MIX WITH HUMANS. IT IS IMPURE.
I SHOULD PUT A STOP TO THIS...
ギチッ
......
...BUT I FEEL MYSELF PULLING AWAY.
プイ
PERHAPS I'VE GONE SOFT.
PERHAPS I'VE GOTTEN TOO OLD.
?
......?!
ダーッ
MY GRANDCHILD'S FEELINGS, HOWEVER STRONG, SHOULDN'T TRUMP OUR SURVIVAL AS A SPECIES...BUT IT DOES. IT DOES.
......
SHE LET ME GO?
OH!
SEE YOU AT HOME!
EEK!

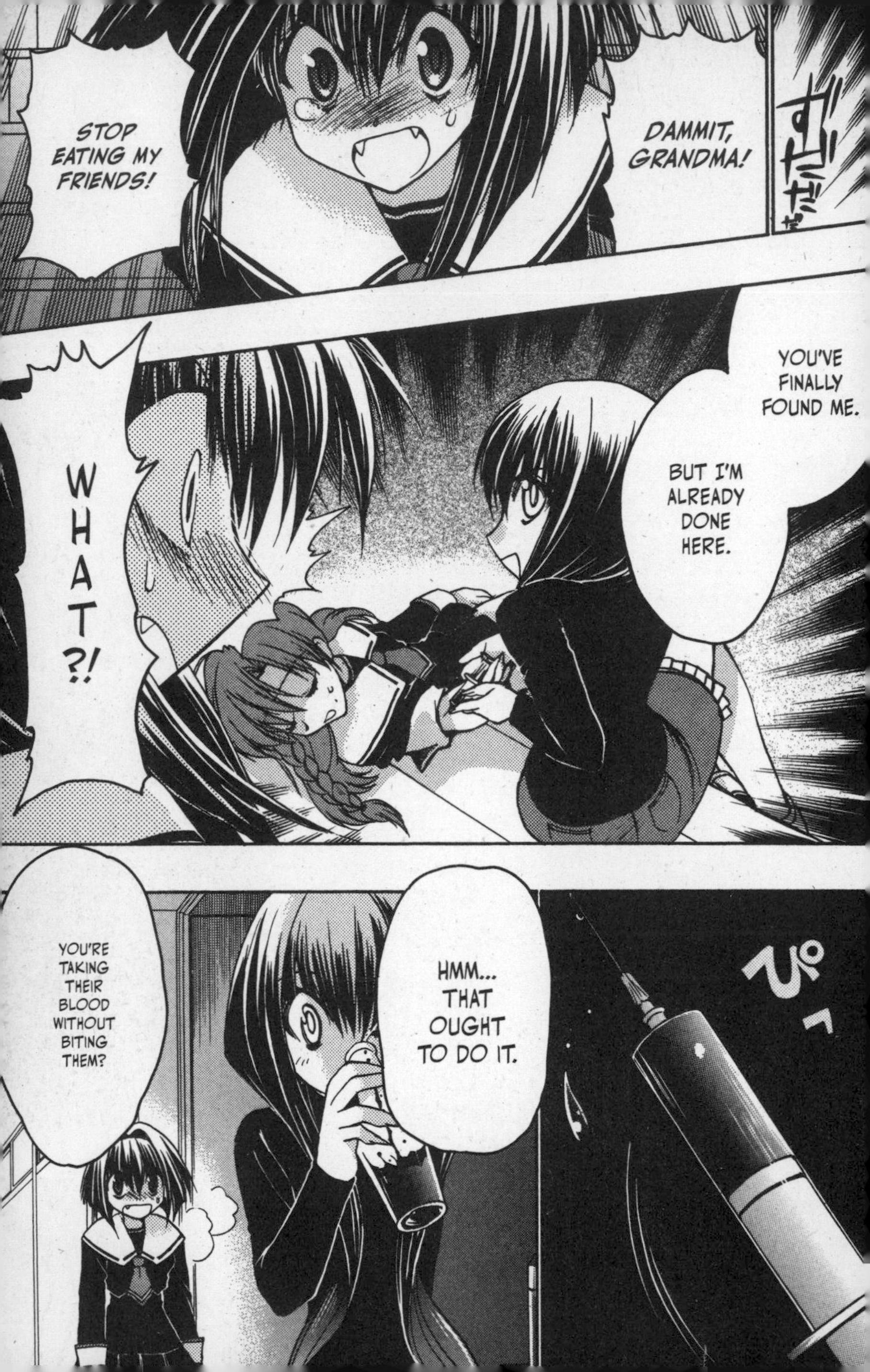
DAMMIT, GRANDMA!
STOP EATING MY FRIENDS!
YOU'VE FINALLY FOUND ME.
BUT I'M ALREADY DONE HERE.
WHAT?!
ぷ
HMM... THAT OUGHT TO DO IT.
YOU'RE TAKING THEIR BLOOD WITHOUT BITING THEM?

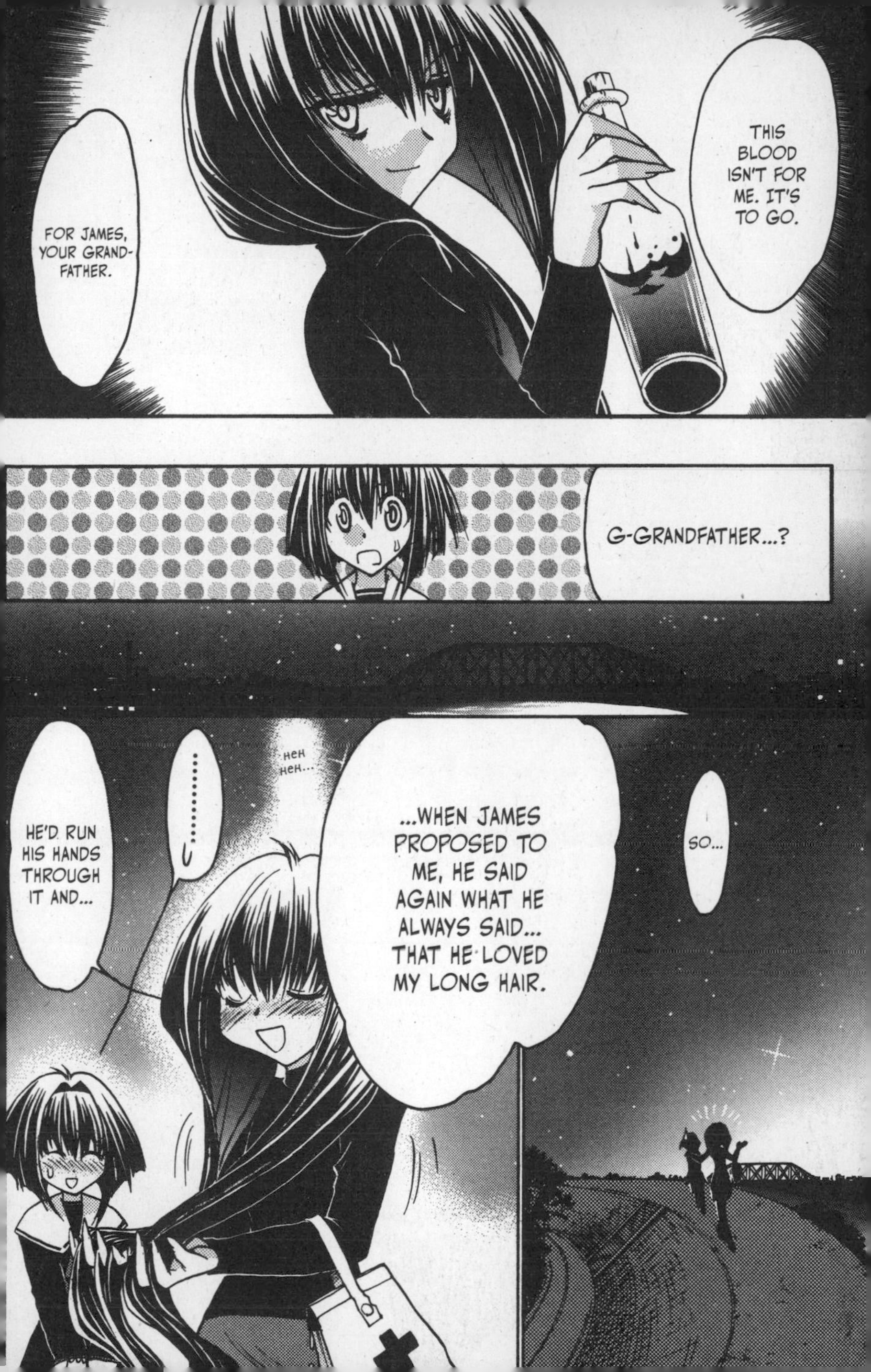
THIS BLOOD ISN'T FOR ME. IT'S TO GO.
FOR JAMES, YOUR GRAND-FATHER.
G-GRANDFATHER...?
SO...
...WHEN JAMES PROPOSED TO ME, HE SAID AGAIN WHAT HE ALWAYS SAID... THAT HE LOVED MY LONG HAIR.
HEH HEH...
......
HE'D RUN HIS HANDS THROUGH IT AND...

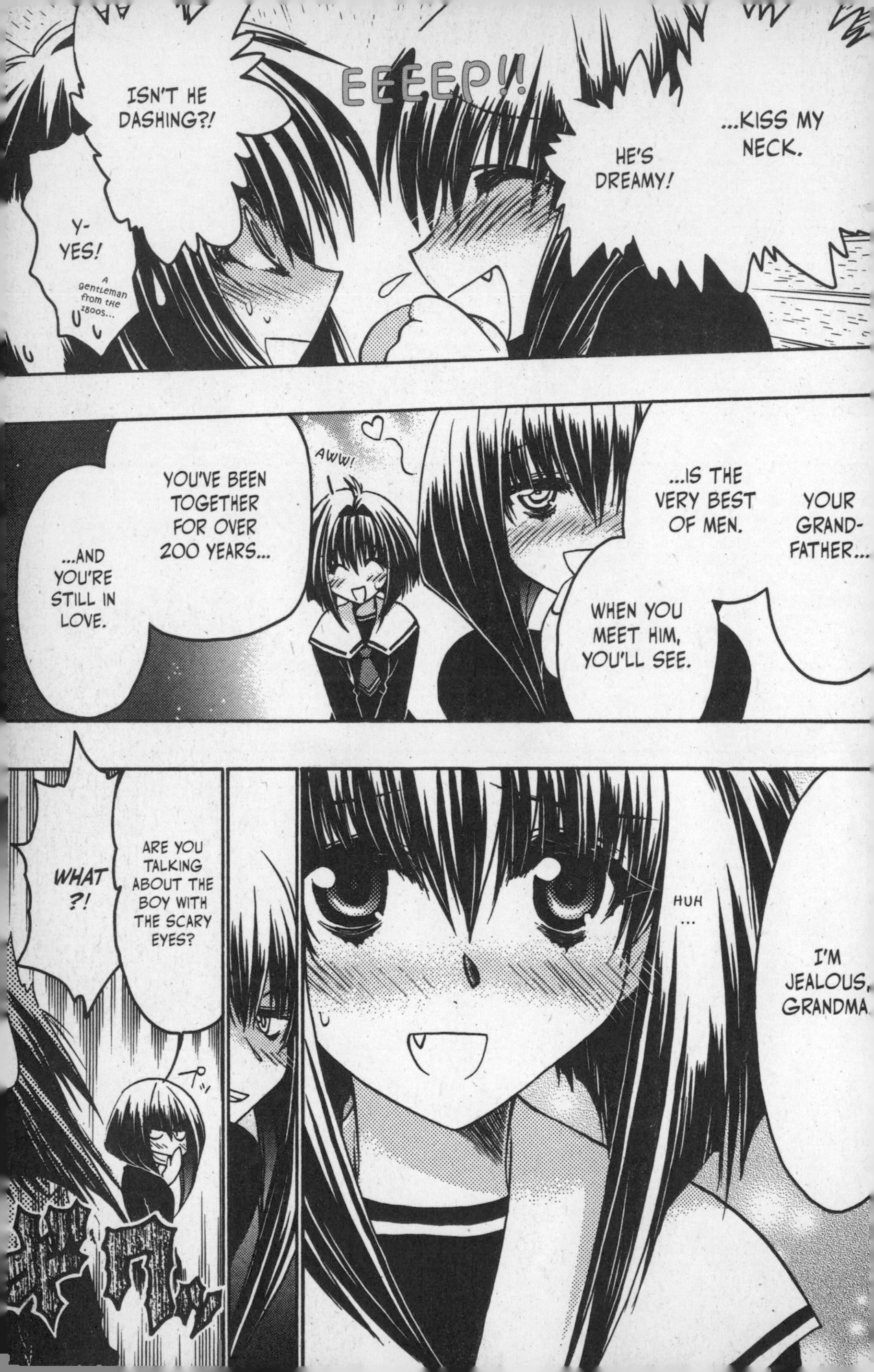
...KISS MY NECK.
HE'S DREAMY!
EEEEP!!
ISN'T HE DASHING?!
Y- YES!
A gentleman from the 1800s...
YOUR GRANDFATHER...
...IS THE VERY BEST OF MEN.
WHEN YOU MEET HIM, YOU'LL SEE.
AWW!
YOU'VE BEEN TOGETHER FOR OVER 200 YEARS...
...AND YOU'RE STILL IN LOVE.
I'M JEALOUS, GRANDMA.
HUH ...
ARE YOU TALKING ABOUT THE BOY WITH THE SCARY EYES?
WHAT ?!

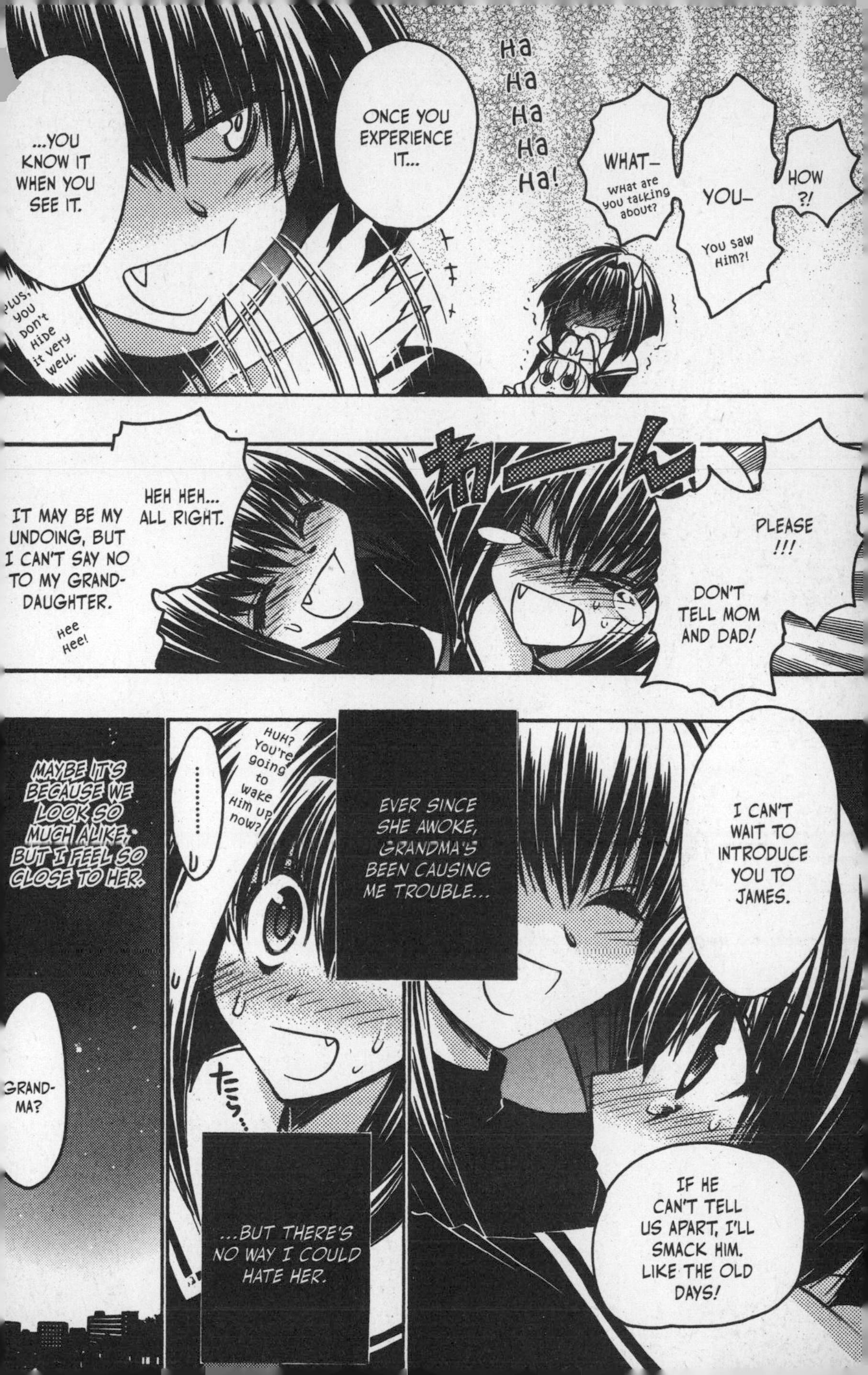
ONCE YOU EXPERIENCE IT...
...YOU KNOW IT WHEN YOU SEE IT.
PLUS, YOU DON'T HIDE IT VERY WELL.
Ha Ha Ha Ha Ha!
WHAT— What are you talking about?
YOU— You saw Him?!
HOW ?!
PLEASE !!!
DON'T TELL MOM AND DAD!
HEH HEH... ALL RIGHT.
IT MAY BE MY UNDOING, BUT I CAN'T SAY NO TO MY GRAND-DAUGHTER.
Hee Hee!
I CAN'T WAIT TO INTRODUCE YOU TO JAMES.
IF HE CAN'T TELL US APART, I'LL SMACK HIM. LIKE THE OLD DAYS!
EVER SINCE SHE AWOKE, GRANDMA'S BEEN CAUSING ME TROUBLE...
....
HUH? You're going to wake Him up now?
...BUT THERE'S NO WAY I COULD HATE HER.
MAYBE IT'S BECAUSE WE LOOK SO MUCH ALIKE, BUT I FEEL SO CLOSE TO HER.
GRAND-MA?

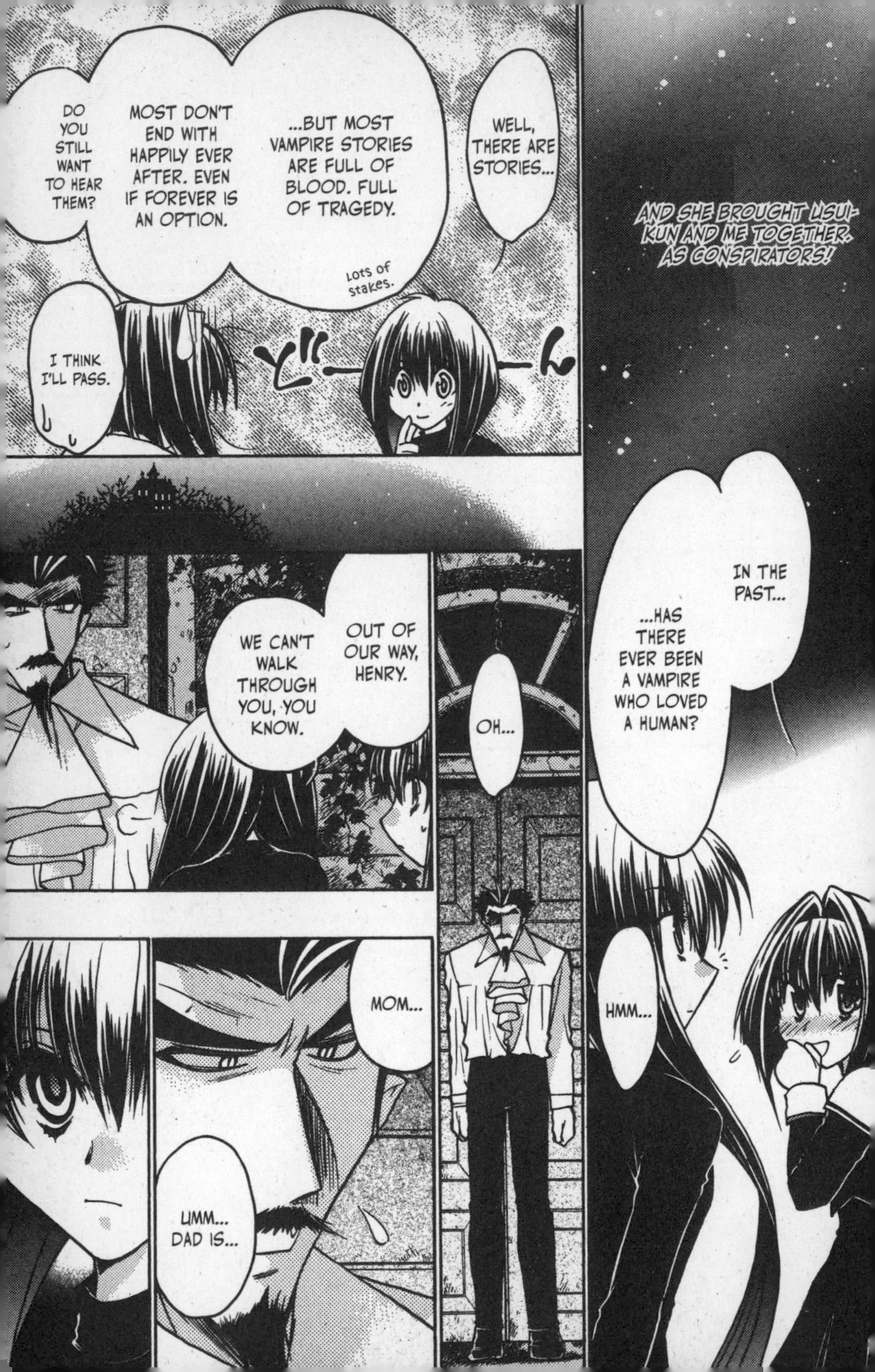
AND SHE BROUGHT USUI-KUN AND ME TOGETHER. AS CONSPIRATORS!
IN THE PAST...
...HAS THERE EVER BEEN A VAMPIRE WHO LOVED A HUMAN?
HMM...
WELL, THERE ARE STORIES...
...BUT MOST VAMPIRE STORIES ARE FULL OF BLOOD. FULL OF TRAGEDY.
MOST DON'T END WITH HAPPILY EVER AFTER. EVEN IF FOREVER IS AN OPTION.
DO YOU STILL WANT TO HEAR THEM?
Lots of stakes.
I THINK I'LL PASS.
OH...
OUT OF OUR WAY, HENRY.
WE CAN'T WALK THROUGH YOU, YOU KNOW.
MOM...
UMM... DAD IS...

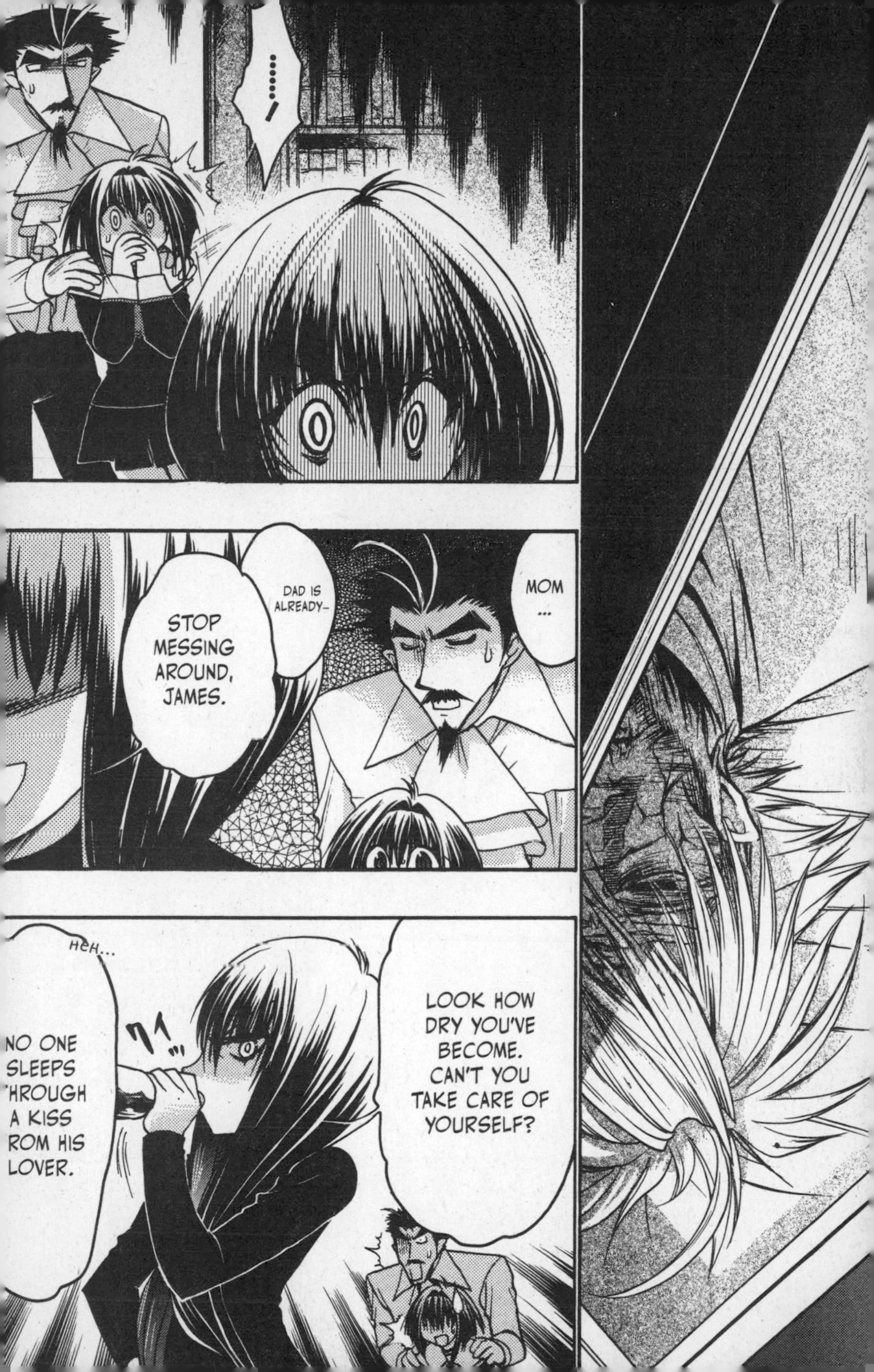
......!
MOM ...
DAD IS ALREADY—
STOP MESSING AROUND, JAMES.
LOOK HOW DRY YOU'VE BECOME. CAN'T YOU TAKE CARE OF YOURSELF?
HEH...
NO ONE SLEEPS HROUGH A KISS ROM HIS LOVER.

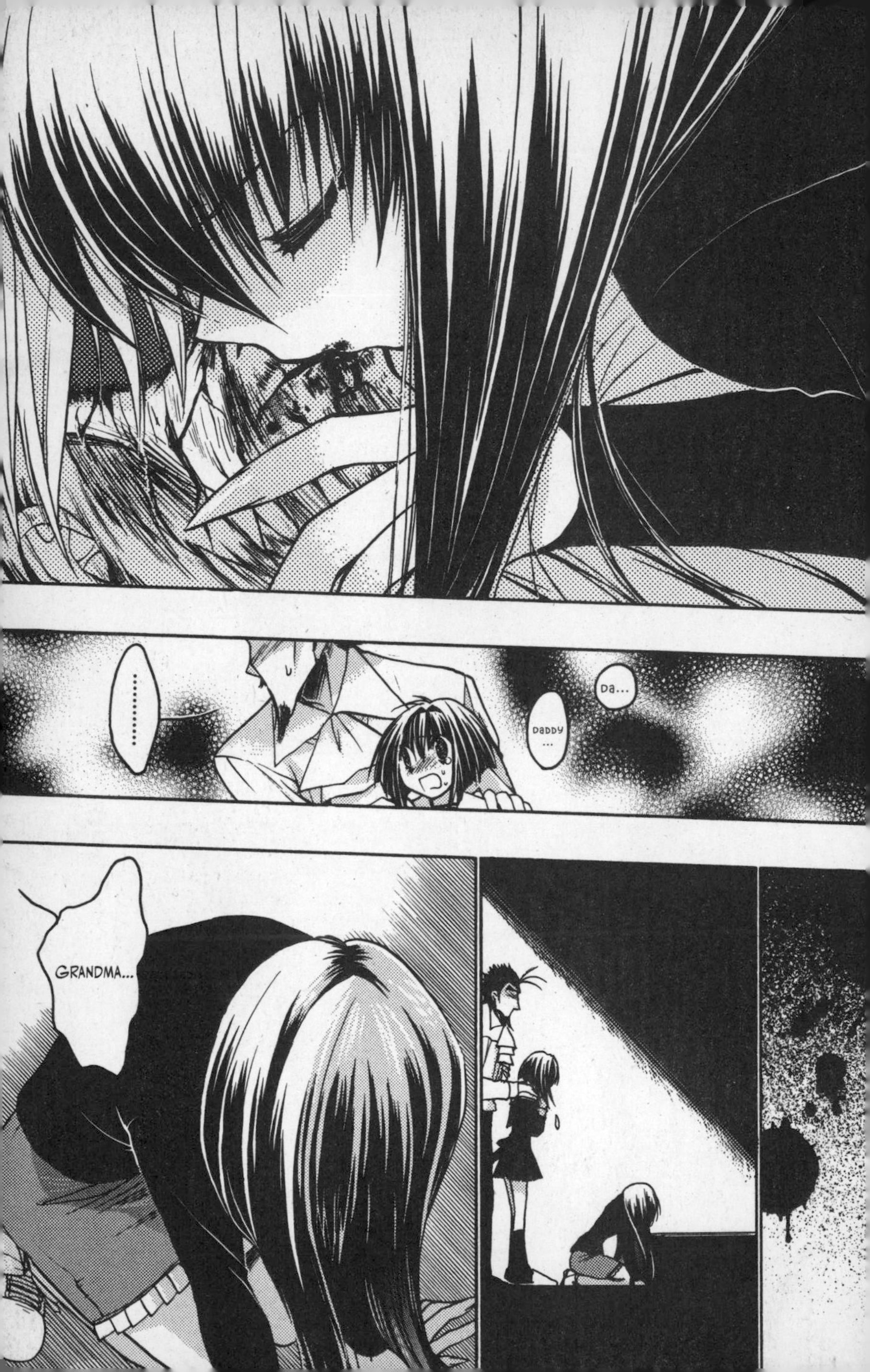
DA...
DADDY ...
....
GRANDMA...

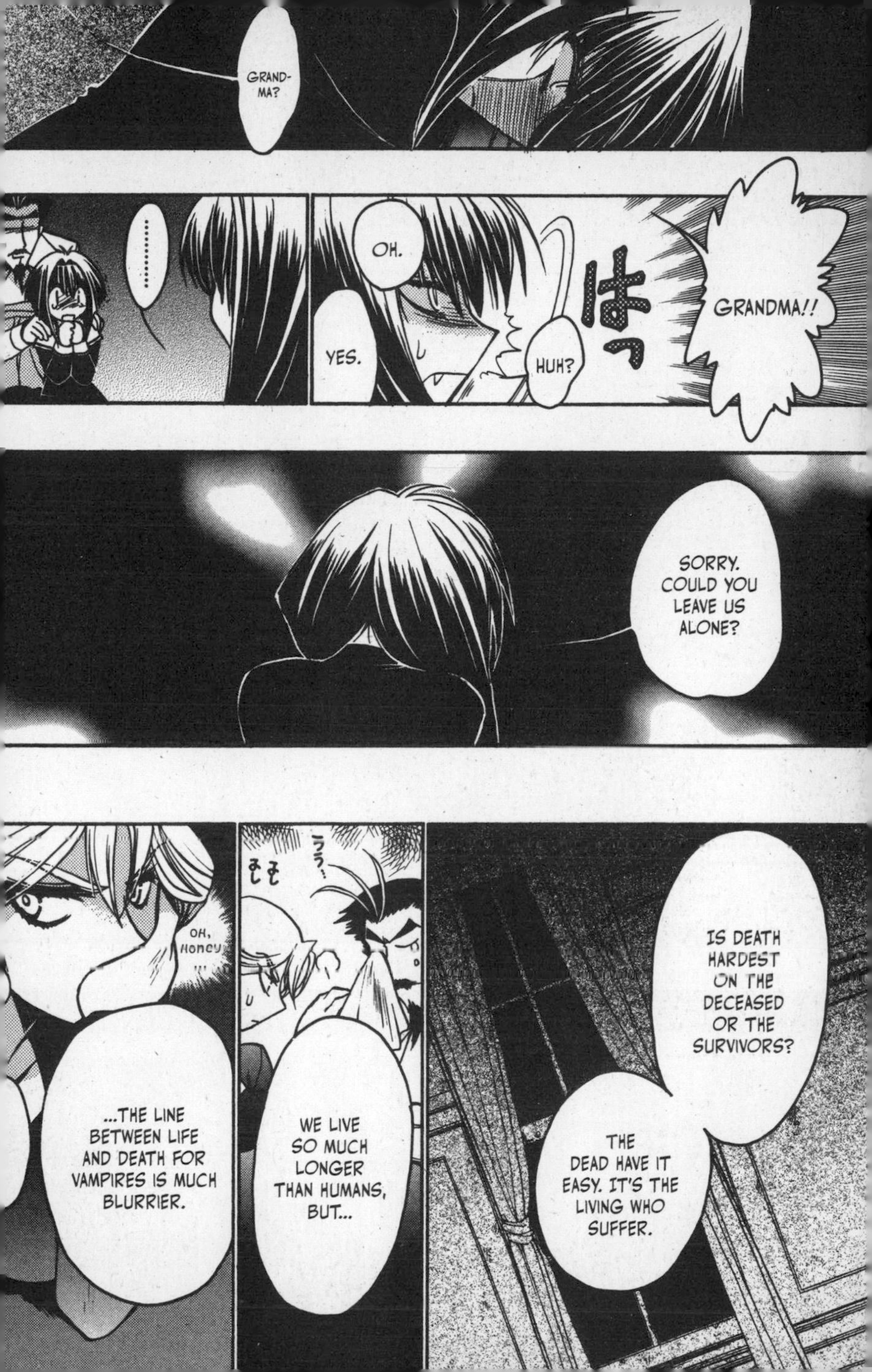
GRAND-MA?
GRANDMA!!
はっ
HUH?
OH.
YES.
....
SORRY. COULD YOU LEAVE US ALONE?
IS DEATH HARDEST ON THE DECEASED OR THE SURVIVORS?
THE DEAD HAVE IT EASY. IT'S THE LIVING WHO SUFFER.
うう…
WE LIVE SO MUCH LONGER THAN HUMANS, BUT...
OH, Honey...
...THE LINE BETWEEN LIFE AND DEATH FOR VAMPIRES IS MUCH BLURRIER.

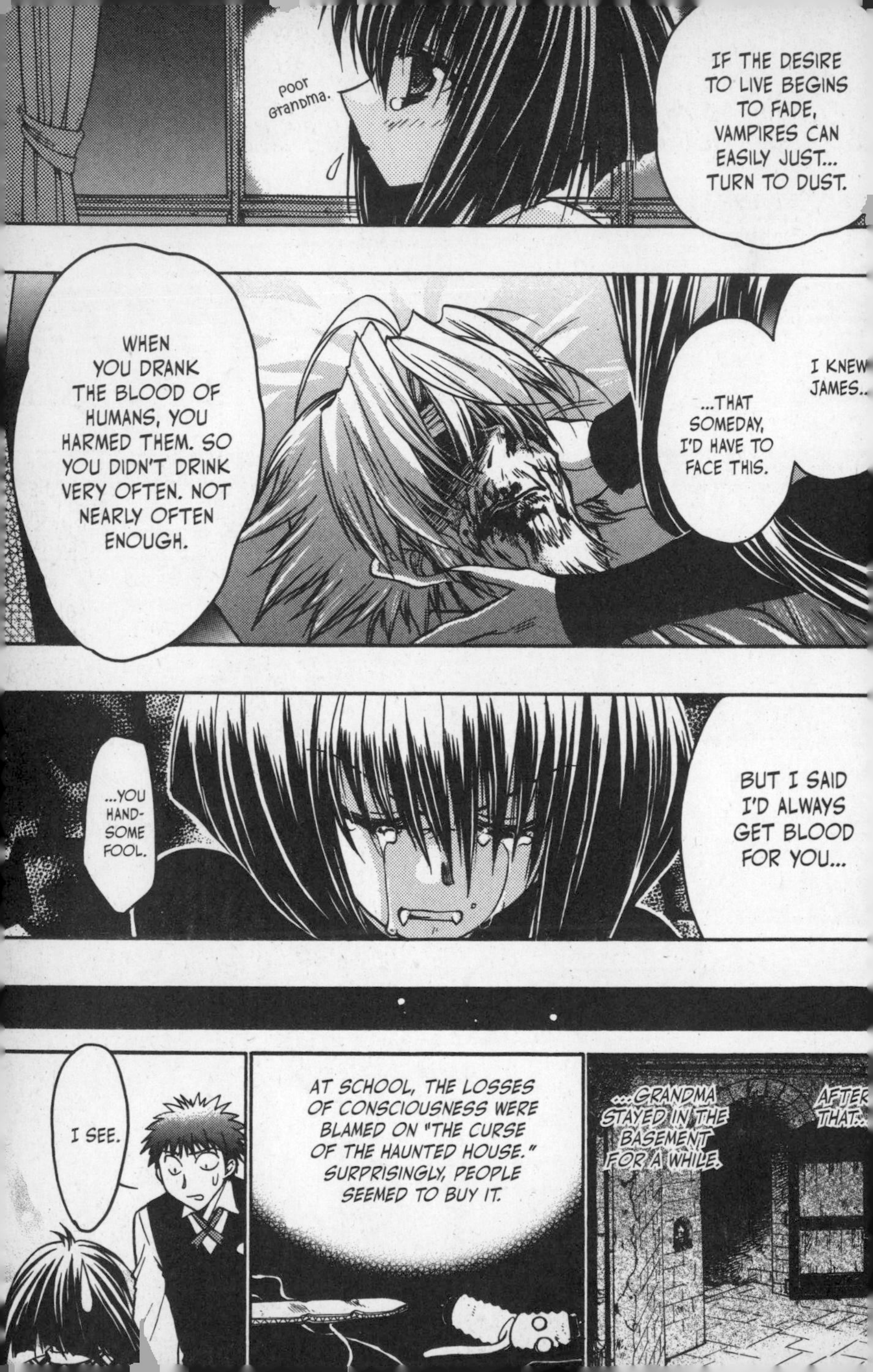
IF THE DESIRE TO LIVE BEGINS TO FADE, VAMPIRES CAN EASILY JUST... TURN TO DUST.
Poor Grandma.
I KNEW JAMES...
...THAT SOMEDAY, I'D HAVE TO FACE THIS.
WHEN YOU DRANK THE BLOOD OF HUMANS, YOU HARMED THEM. SO YOU DIDN'T DRINK VERY OFTEN. NOT NEARLY OFTEN ENOUGH.
BUT I SAID I'D ALWAYS GET BLOOD FOR YOU...
...YOU HAND-SOME FOOL.
AFTER THAT...
...GRANDMA STAYED IN THE BASEMENT FOR A WHILE.
AT SCHOOL, THE LOSSES OF CONSCIOUSNESS WERE BLAMED ON "THE CURSE OF THE HAUNTED HOUSE." SURPRISINGLY, PEOPLE SEEMED TO BUY IT.
I SEE.

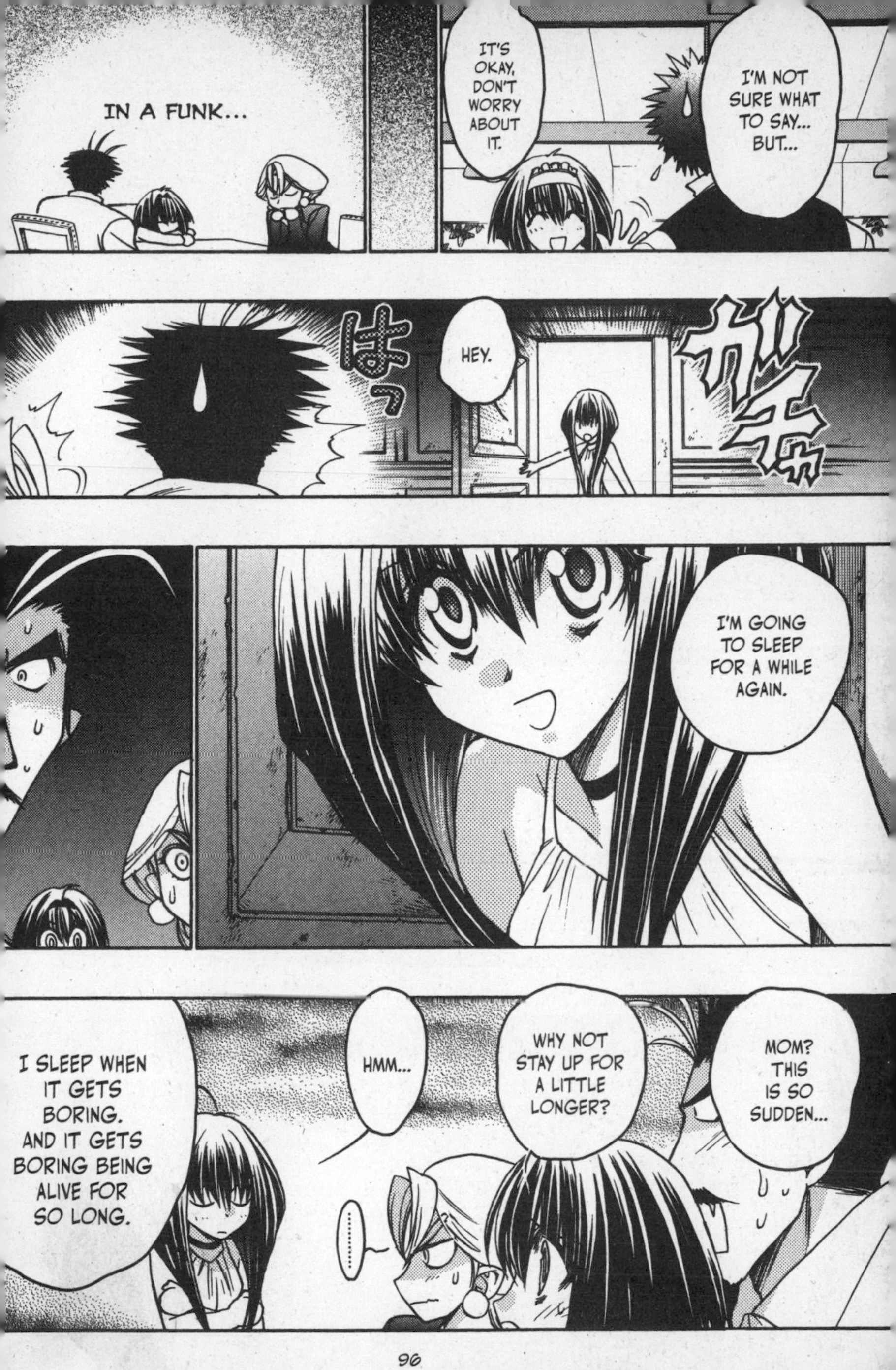
I'M NOT SURE WHAT TO SAY... BUT...
IT'S OKAY, DON'T WORRY ABOUT IT.
IN A FUNK...
カチャ
HEY.
はっ
I'M GOING TO SLEEP FOR A WHILE AGAIN.
MOM? THIS IS SO SUDDEN...
WHY NOT STAY UP FOR A LITTLE LONGER?
HMM...
......
I SLEEP WHEN IT GETS BORING. AND IT GETS BORING BEING ALIVE FOR SO LONG.

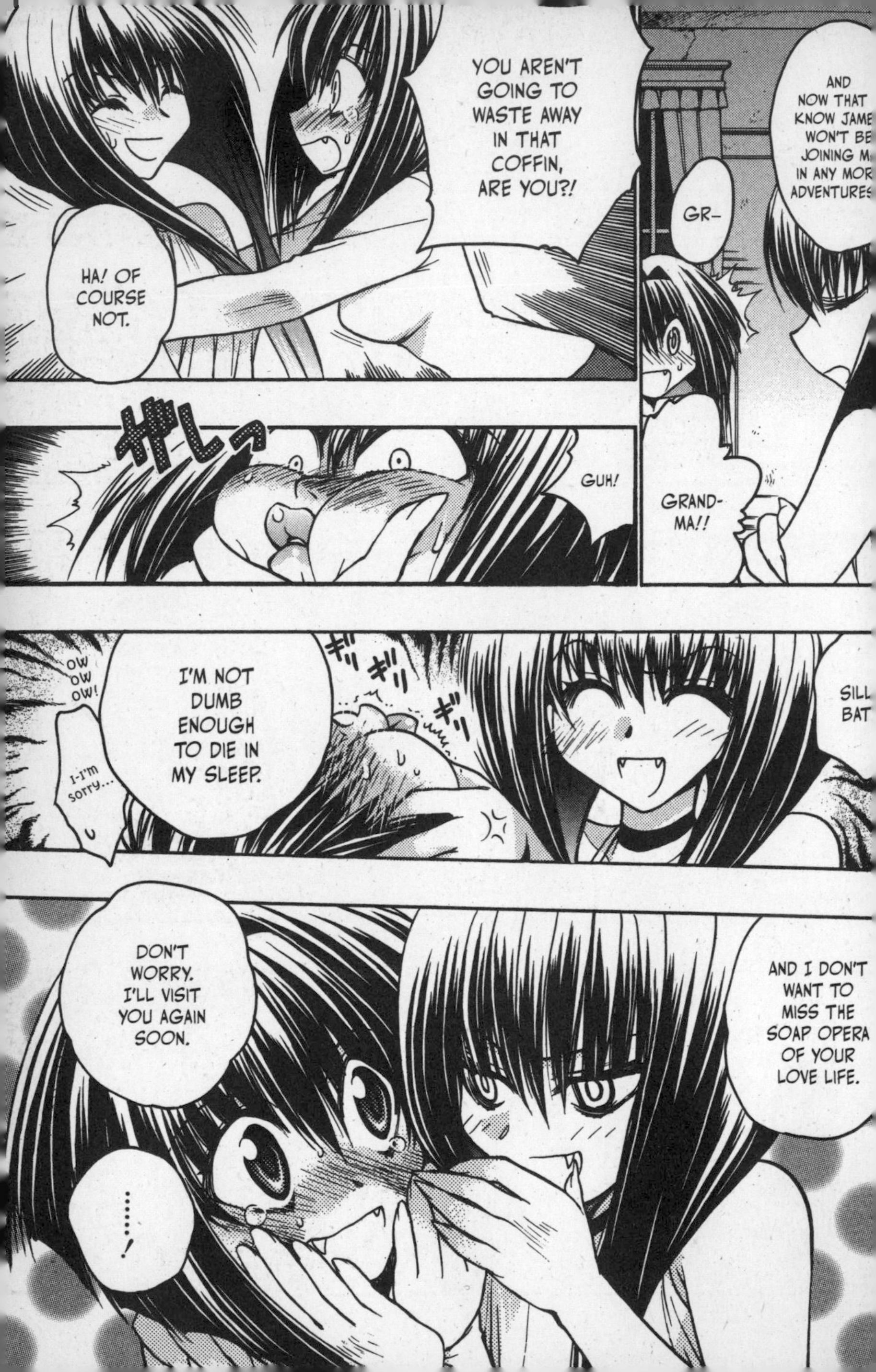
AND NOW THAT KNOW JAME WON'T BE JOINING M IN ANY MOR ADVENTURES
GR-
GRAND-MA!!
YOU AREN'T GOING TO WASTE AWAY IN THAT COFFIN, ARE YOU?!
HA! OF COURSE NOT.
GUH!
SILL BAT
I'M NOT DUMB ENOUGH TO DIE IN MY SLEEP.
OW OW OW!
I-I'm sorry...
AND I DON'T WANT TO MISS THE SOAP OPERA OF YOUR LOVE LIFE.
DON'T WORRY. I'LL VISIT YOU AGAIN SOON.
......!

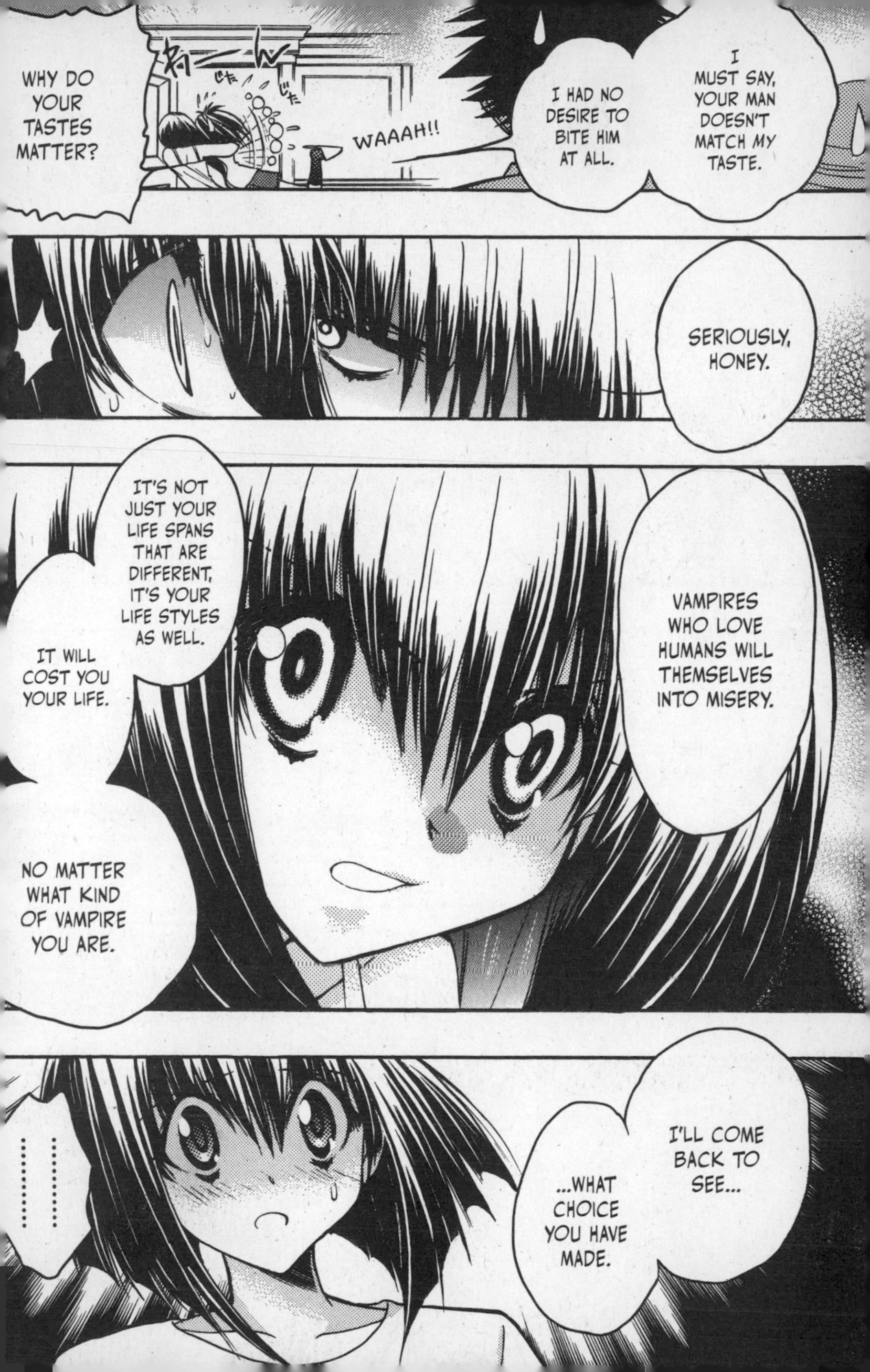
I MUST SAY, YOUR MAN DOESN'T MATCH MY TASTE.
I HAD NO DESIRE TO BITE HIM AT ALL.
WAAAH!!
WHY DO YOUR TASTES MATTER?
SERIOUSLY, HONEY.
VAMPIRES WHO LOVE HUMANS WILL THEMSELVES INTO MISERY.
IT'S NOT JUST YOUR LIFE SPANS THAT ARE DIFFERENT, IT'S YOUR LIFE STYLES AS WELL.
IT WILL COST YOU YOUR LIFE.
NO MATTER WHAT KIND OF VAMPIRE YOU ARE.
I'LL COME BACK TO SEE...
...WHAT CHOICE YOU HAVE MADE.
......
......

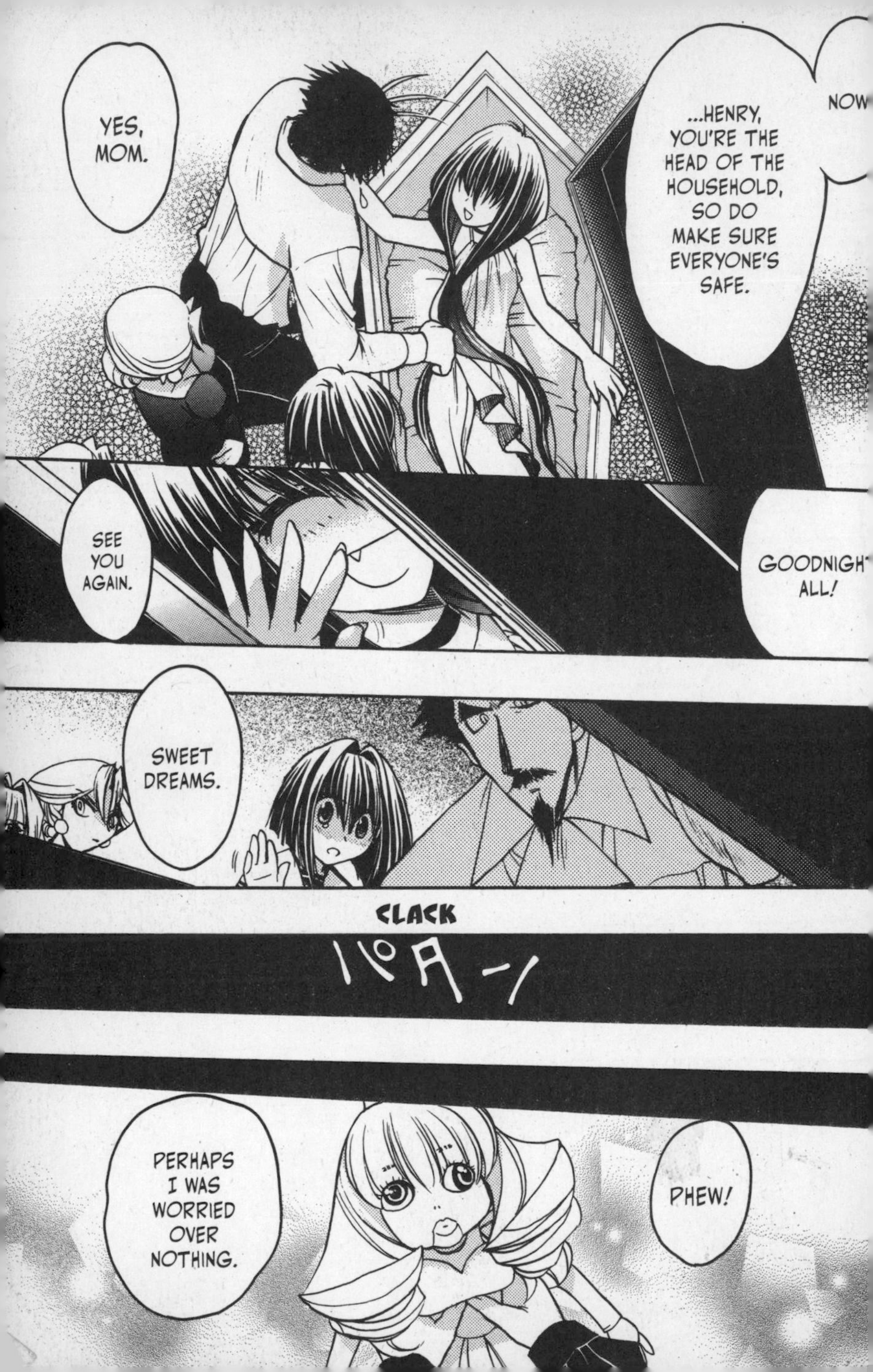
NOW
...HENRY, YOU'RE THE HEAD OF THE HOUSEHOLD, SO DO MAKE SURE EVERYONE'S SAFE.
YES, MOM.
GOODNIGHT ALL!
SEE YOU AGAIN.
SWEET DREAMS.
CLACK
パターン
PHEW!
PERHAPS I WAS WORRIED OVER NOTHING.

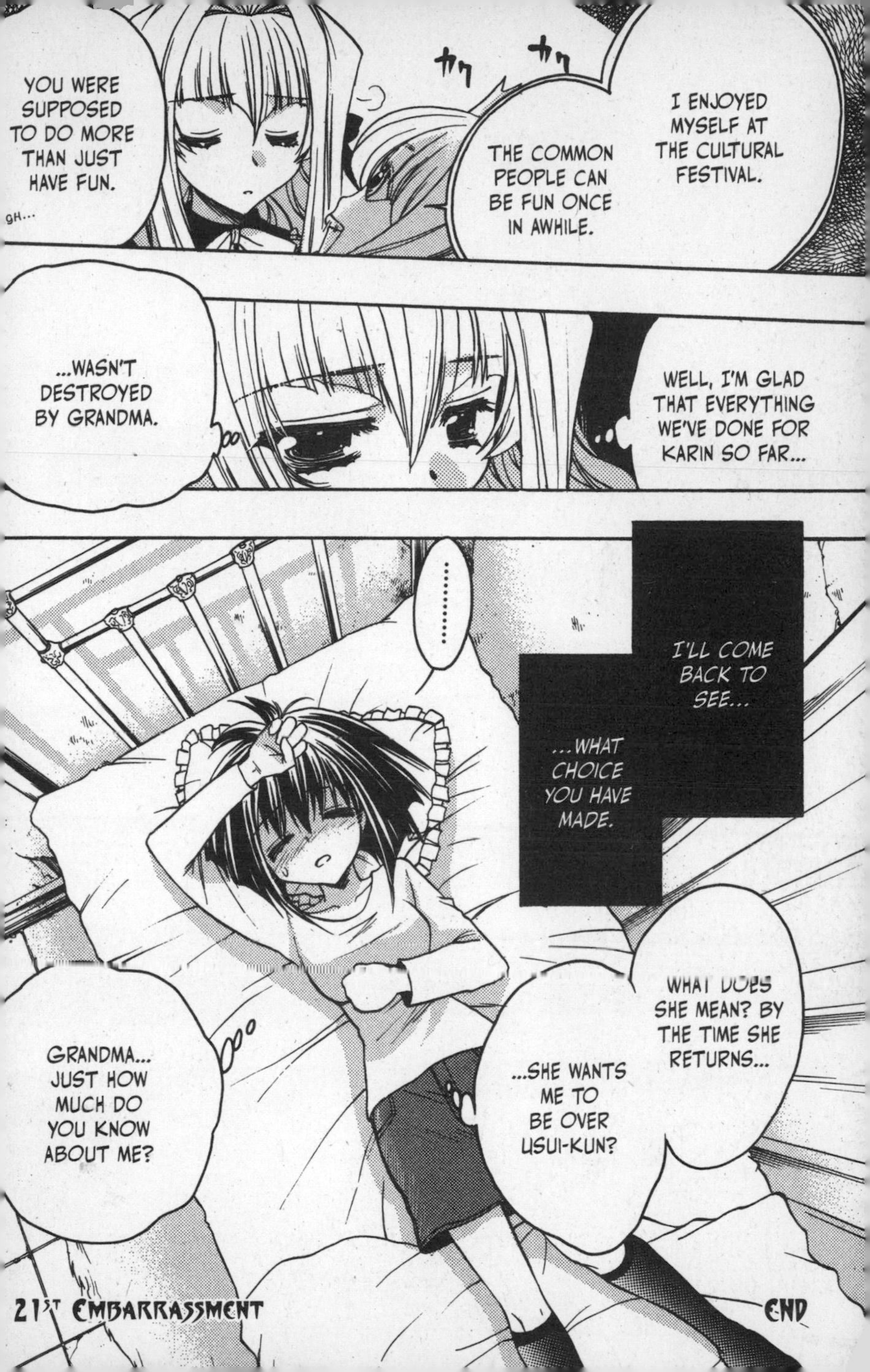
I ENJOYED MYSELF AT THE CULTURAL FESTIVAL.
THE COMMON PEOPLE CAN BE FUN ONCE IN AWHILE.
YOU WERE SUPPOSED TO DO MORE THAN JUST HAVE FUN.
GH...
WELL, I'M GLAD THAT EVERYTHING WE'VE DONE FOR KARIN SO FAR...
...WASN'T DESTROYED BY GRANDMA.
I'LL COME BACK TO SEE...
...WHAT CHOICE YOU HAVE MADE.
WHAT DOES SHE MEAN? BY THE TIME SHE RETURNS...
...SHE WANTS ME TO BE OVER USUI-KUN?
GRANDMA... JUST HOW MUCH DO YOU KNOW ABOUT ME?
21ST EMBARRASSMENT
END

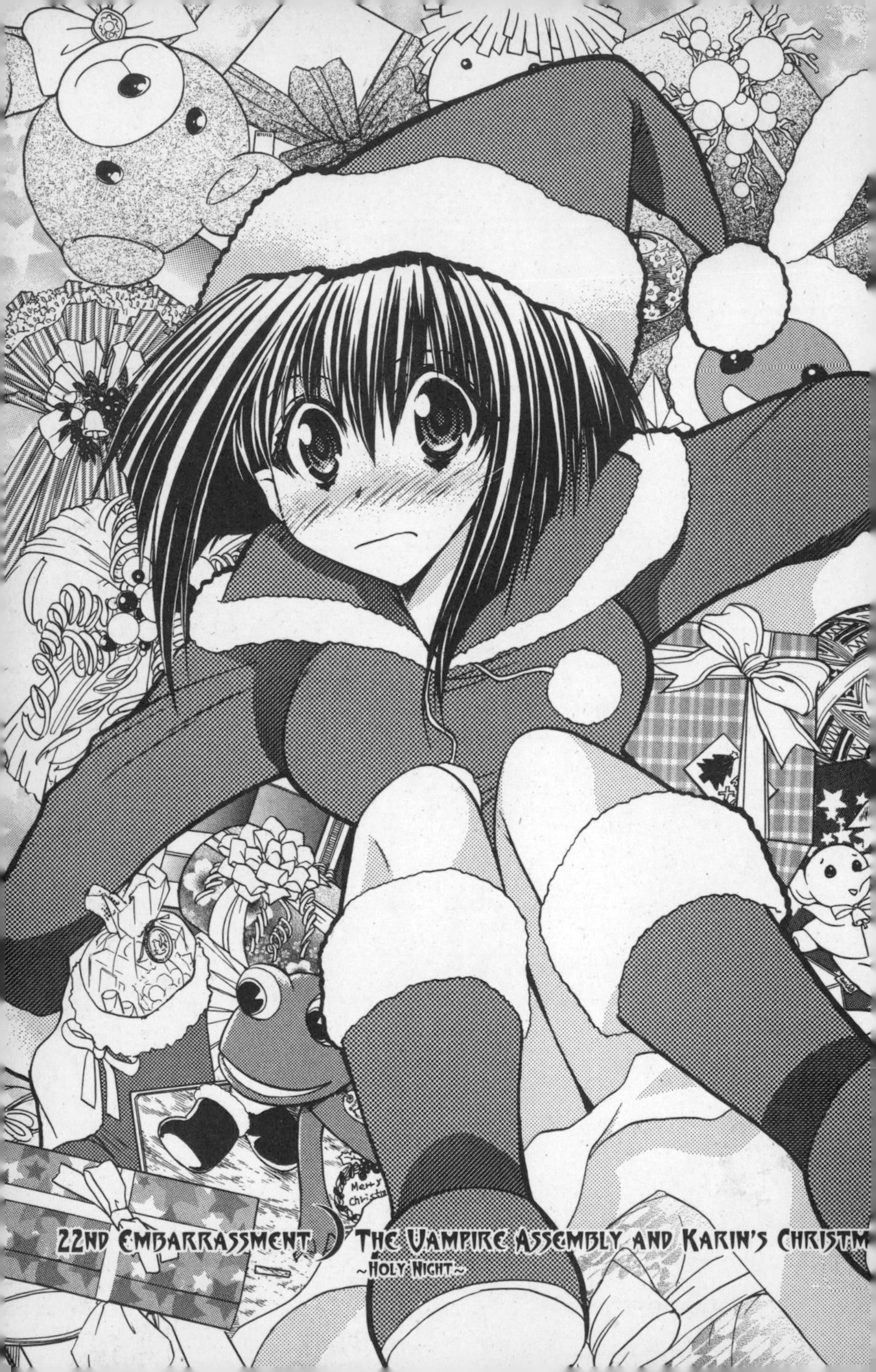
22nd Embarrassment The Vampire Assembly and Karin's Christm
~Holy Night~

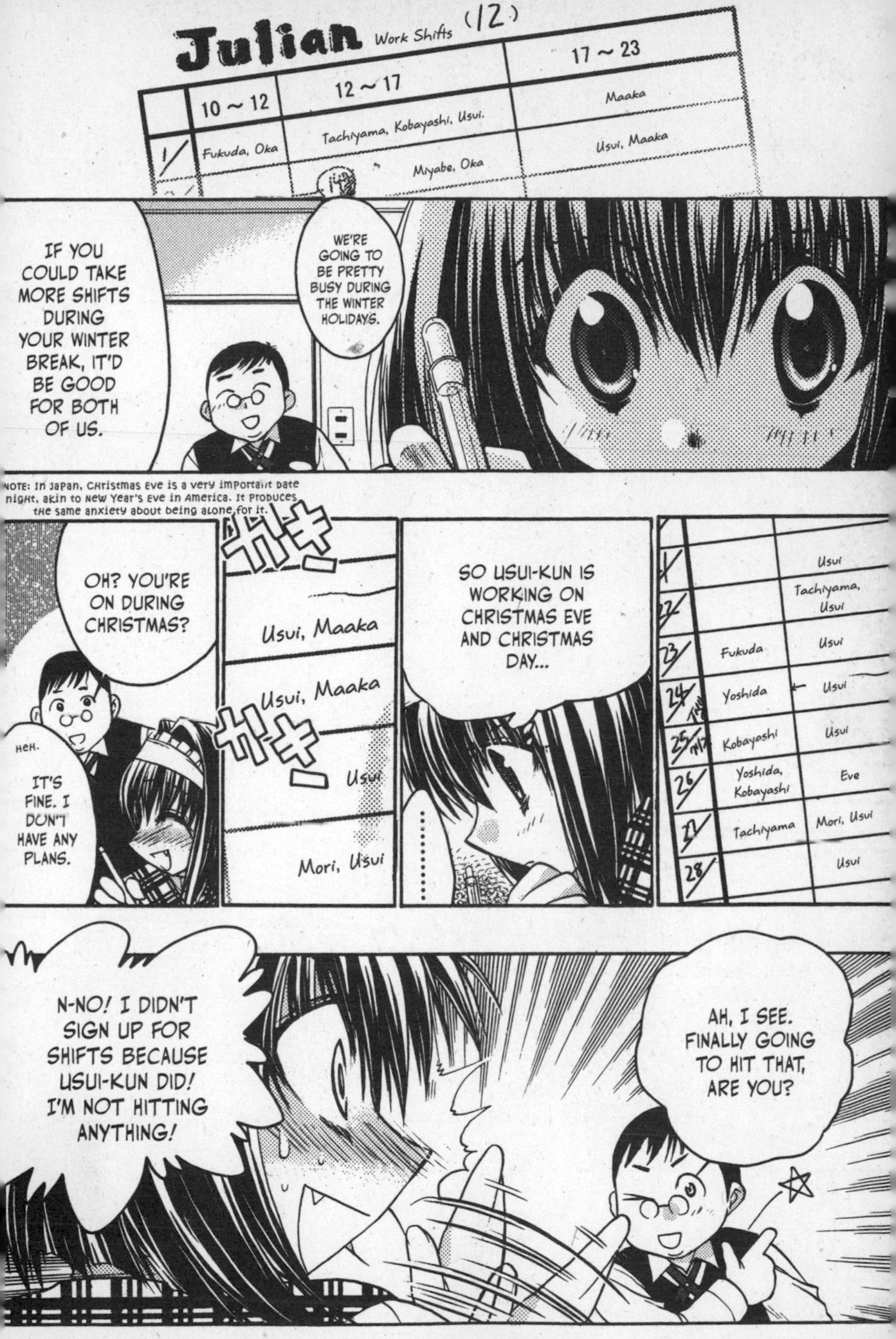
Julian Work Shifts (12)
10 ~ 12
12 ~ 17
17 ~ 23
Fukuda, Oka
Tachiyama, Kobayashi, Usui.
Maaka
Miyabe, Oka
Usui, Maaka
WE'RE GOING TO BE PRETTY BUSY DURING THE WINTER HOLIDAYS.
IF YOU COULD TAKE MORE SHIFTS DURING YOUR WINTER BREAK, IT'D BE GOOD FOR BOTH OF US.
NOTE: In Japan, Christmas Eve is a very important date night, akin to New Year's Eve in America. It produces the same anxiety about being alone for it.
Usui
Tachiyama, Usui
Fukuda
Usui
Yoshida
Usui
Kobayashi
Usui
Yoshida, Kobayashi
Eve
Tachiyama
Mori, Usui
Usui
SO USUI-KUN IS WORKING ON CHRISTMAS EVE AND CHRISTMAS DAY...
Usui, Maaka
Usui, Maaka
Usui
Mori, Usui
OH? YOU'RE ON DURING CHRISTMAS?
HEH.
IT'S FINE. I DON'T HAVE ANY PLANS.
AH, I SEE. FINALLY GOING TO HIT THAT, ARE YOU?
N-NO! I DIDN'T SIGN UP FOR SHIFTS BECAUSE USUI-KUN DID! I'M NOT HITTING ANYTHING!

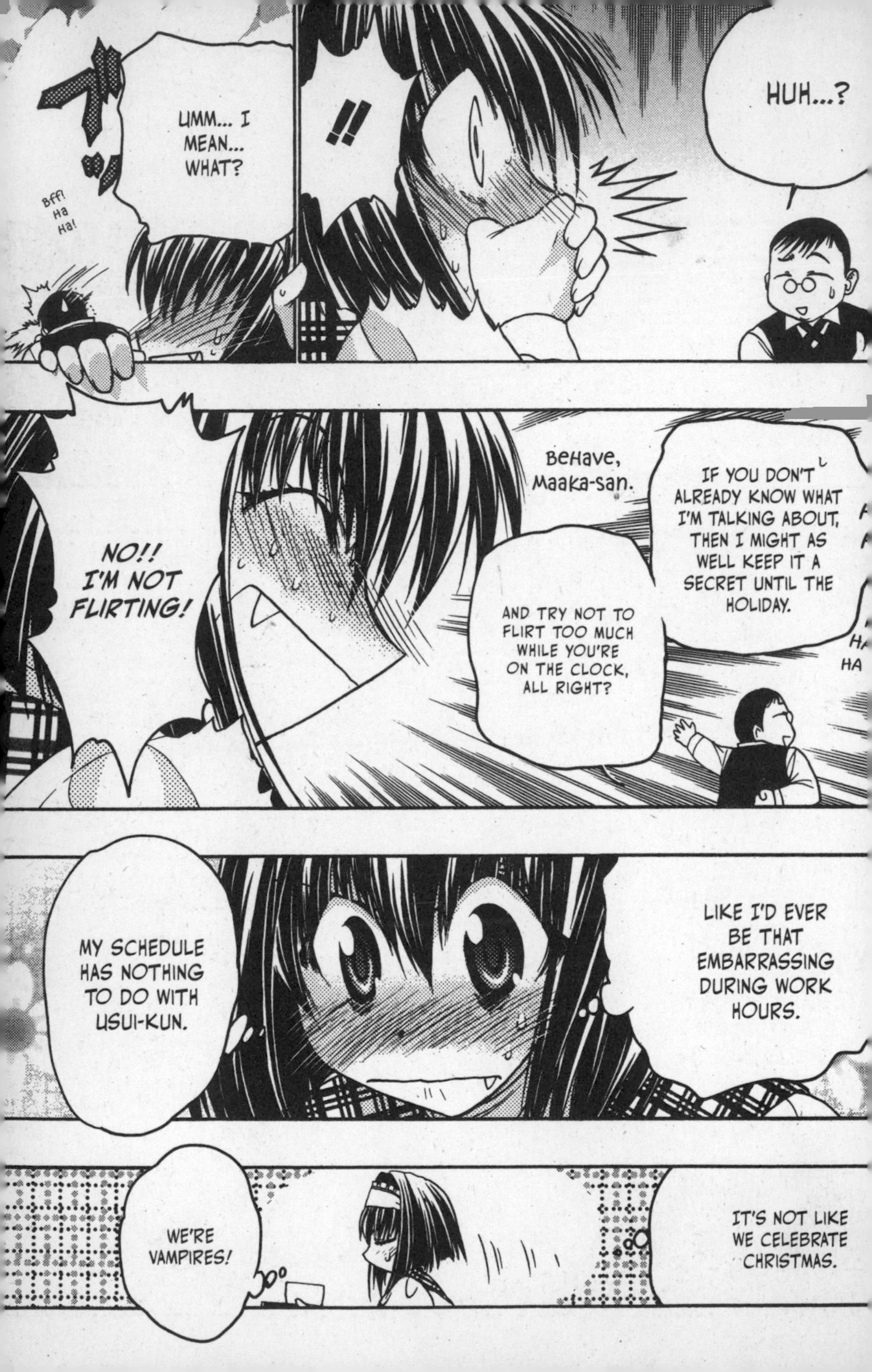
HUH...?
!!
UMM... I MEAN... WHAT?
Bff! Ha Ha!
IF YOU DON'T ALREADY KNOW WHAT I'M TALKING ABOUT, THEN I MIGHT AS WELL KEEP IT A SECRET UNTIL THE HOLIDAY.
Behave, Maaka-san.
AND TRY NOT TO FLIRT TOO MUCH WHILE YOU'RE ON THE CLOCK, ALL RIGHT?
HA
NO!! I'M NOT FLIRTING!
LIKE I'D EVER BE THAT EMBARRASSING DURING WORK HOURS.
MY SCHEDULE HAS NOTHING TO DO WITH USUI-KUN.
IT'S NOT LIKE WE CELEBRATE CHRISTMAS.
WE'RE VAMPIRES!

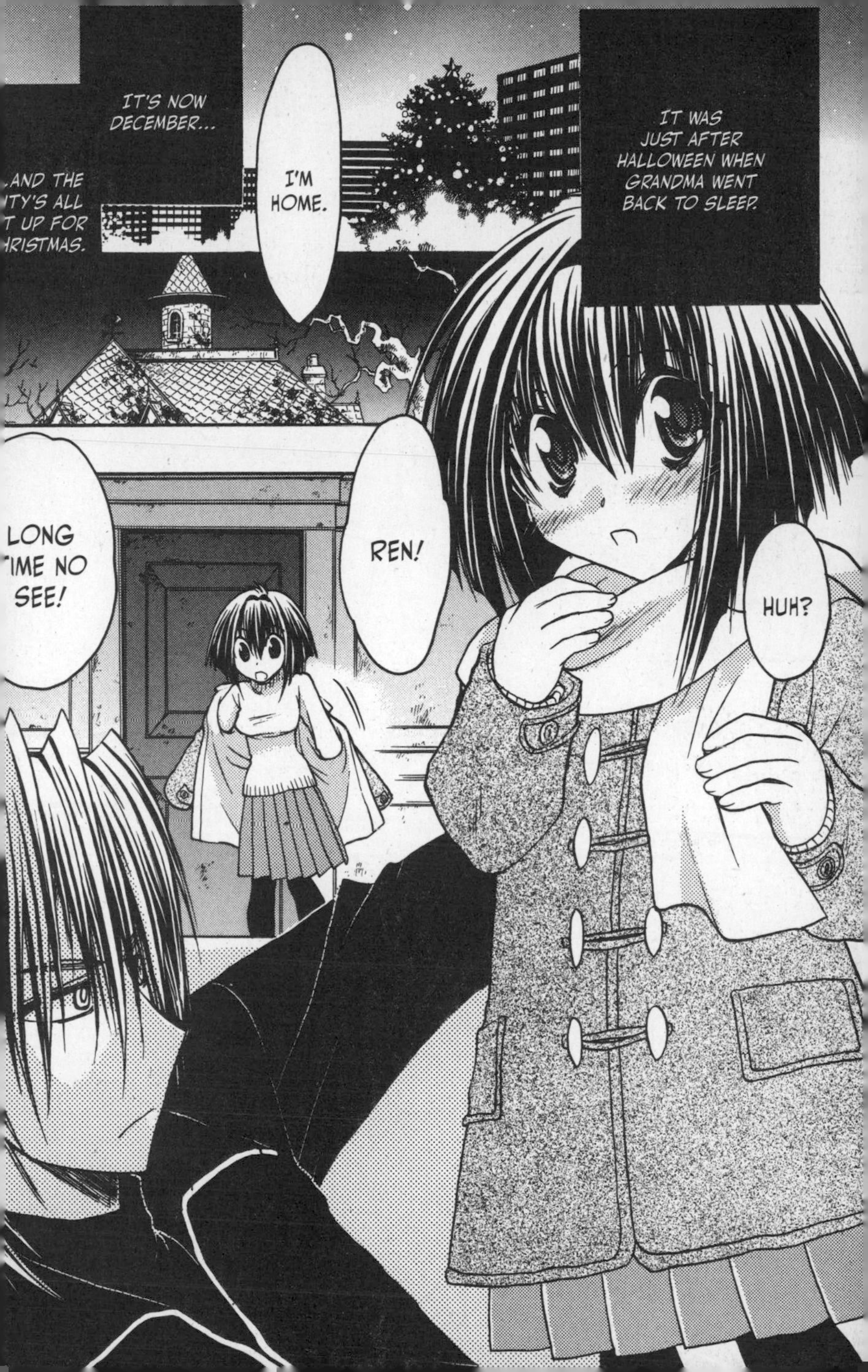

IT WAS JUST AFTER HALLOWEEN WHEN GRANDMA WENT BACK TO SLEEP.
I'M HOME.
IT'S NOW DECEMBER...
.AND THE ITY'S ALL T UP FOR IRISTMAS.
HUH?
REN!
LONG IME NO SEE!

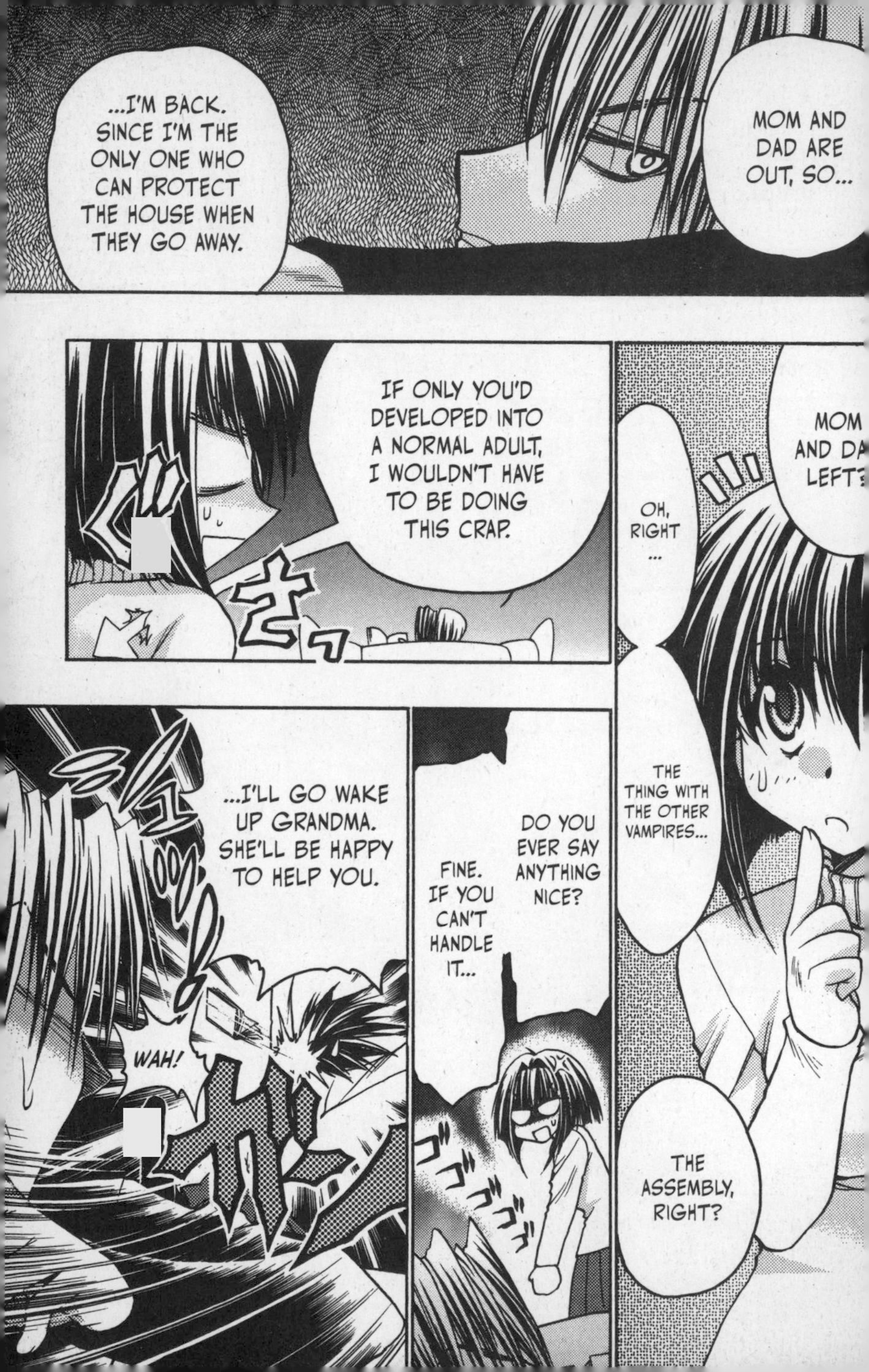
MOM AND DAD ARE OUT, SO...
...I'M BACK. SINCE I'M THE ONLY ONE WHO CAN PROTECT THE HOUSE WHEN THEY GO AWAY.
MOM AND DA LEFT?
OH, RIGHT ...
THE THING WITH THE OTHER VAMPIRES...
THE ASSEMBLY, RIGHT?
IF ONLY YOU'D DEVELOPED INTO A NORMAL ADULT, I WOULDN'T HAVE TO BE DOING THIS CRAP.
DO YOU EVER SAY ANYTHING NICE?
FINE. IF YOU CAN'T HANDLE IT...
...I'LL GO WAKE UP GRANDMA. SHE'LL BE HAPPY TO HELP YOU.
WAH!

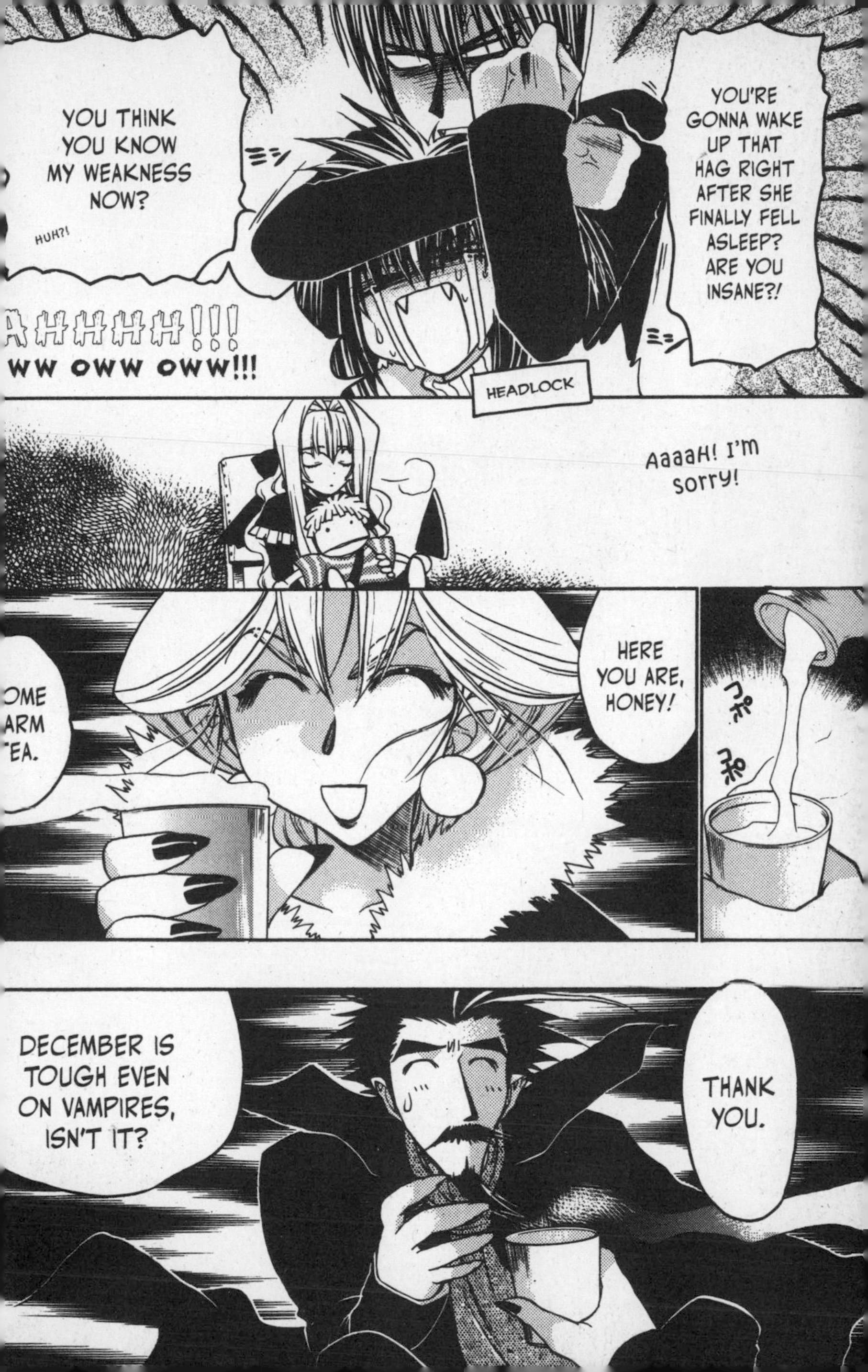
YOU'RE GONNA WAKE UP THAT HAG RIGHT AFTER SHE FINALLY FELL ASLEEP? ARE YOU INSANE?!
ミシ
YOU THINK YOU KNOW MY WEAKNESS NOW?
ミシ
HUH?!
AHHHHH!!!
WW OWW OWW!!!
HEADLOCK
AaaaH! I'm sorry!
コポ
コポ
HERE YOU ARE, HONEY!
OME ARM EA.
THANK YOU.
DECEMBER IS TOUGH EVEN ON VAMPIRES, ISN'T IT?

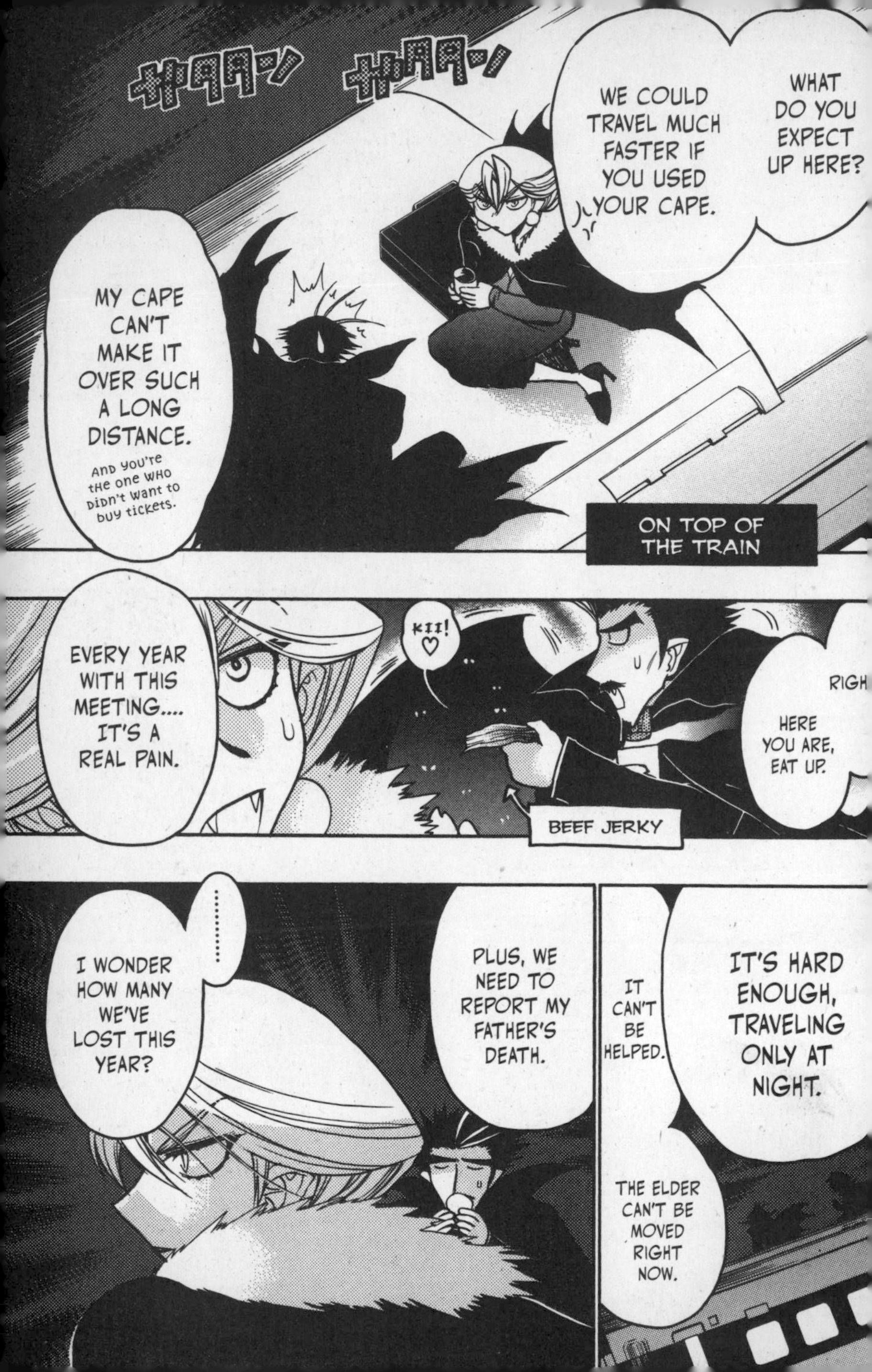
WHAT DO YOU EXPECT UP HERE?
WE COULD TRAVEL MUCH FASTER IF YOU USED YOUR CAPE.
MY CAPE CAN'T MAKE IT OVER SUCH A LONG DISTANCE.
And you're the one who didn't want to buy tickets.
ON TOP OF THE TRAIN
RIGH
HERE YOU ARE, EAT UP.
BEEF JERKY
KII! ♡
EVERY YEAR WITH THIS MEETING.... IT'S A REAL PAIN.
IT'S HARD ENOUGH, TRAVELING ONLY AT NIGHT.
IT CAN'T BE HELPED.
THE ELDER CAN'T BE MOVED RIGHT NOW.
PLUS, WE NEED TO REPORT MY FATHER'S DEATH.
....
I WONDER HOW MANY WE'VE LOST THIS YEAR?

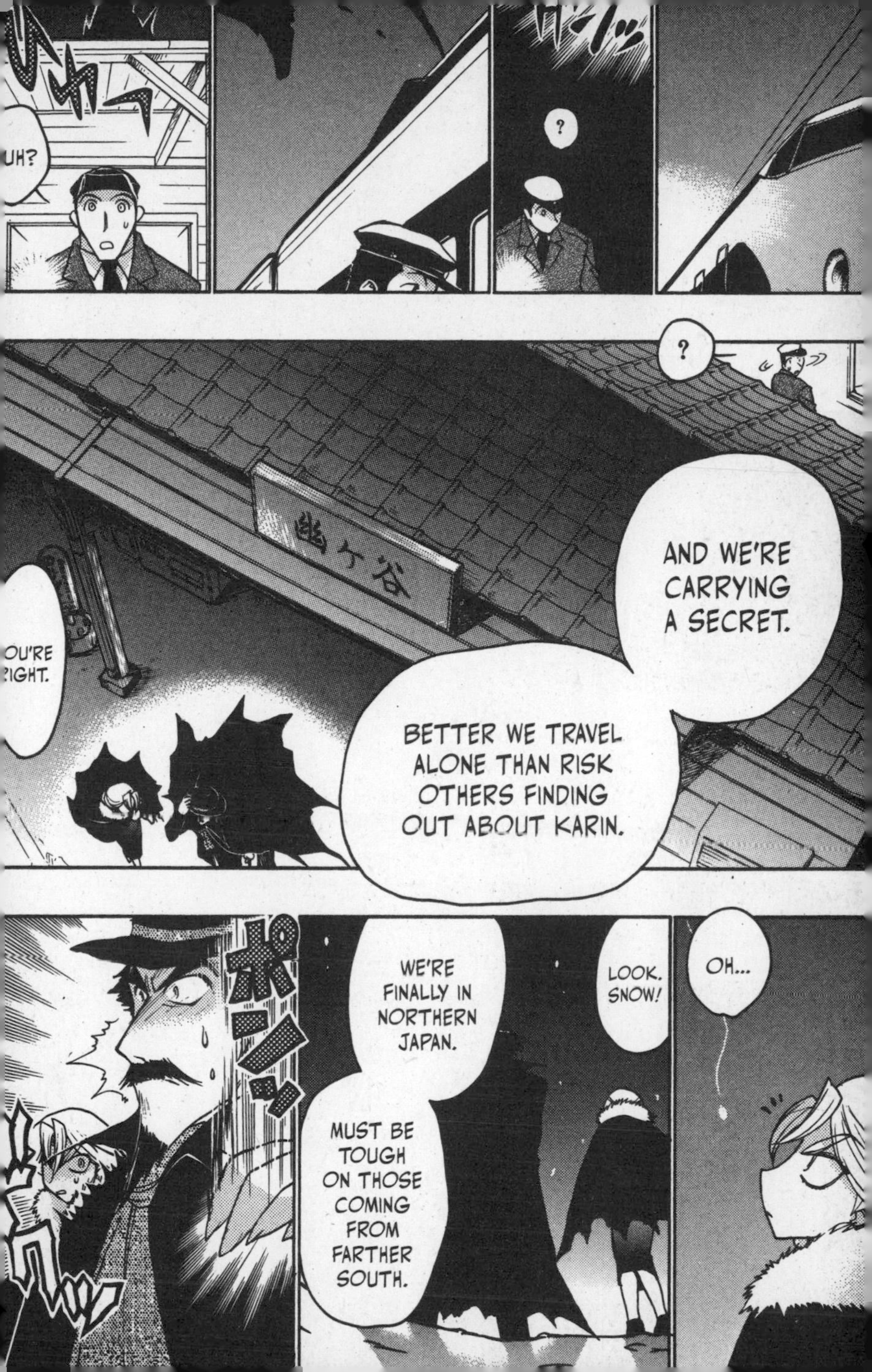
?
UH?
?
AND WE'RE CARRYING A SECRET.
BETTER WE TRAVEL ALONE THAN RISK OTHERS FINDING OUT ABOUT KARIN.
幽ケ谷
OU'RE RIGHT.
OH...
LOOK. SNOW!
WE'RE FINALLY IN NORTHERN JAPAN.
MUST BE TOUGH ON THOSE COMING FROM FARTHER SOUTH.

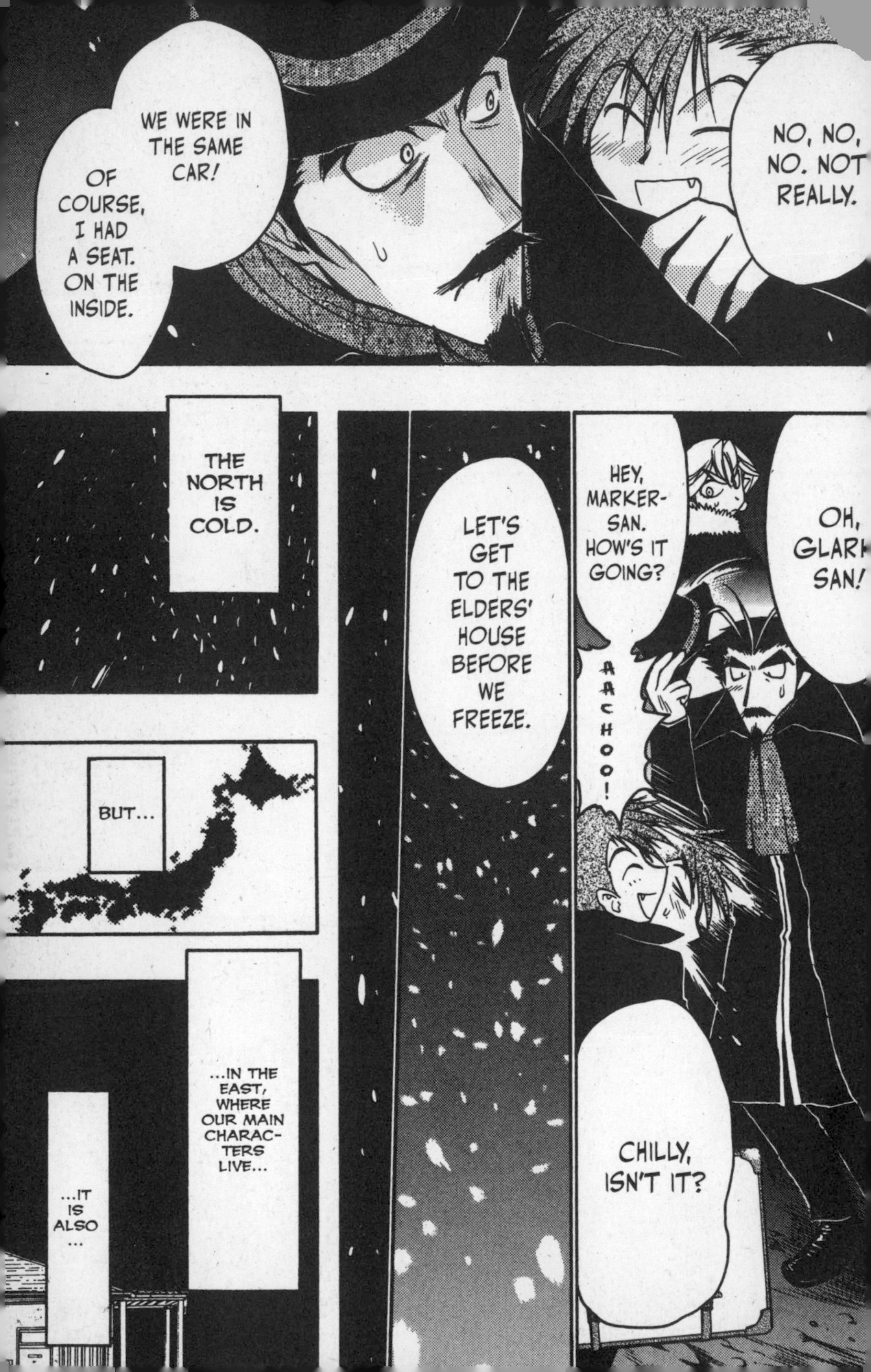
NO, NO, NO. NOT REALLY.
WE WERE IN THE SAME CAR!
OF COURSE, I HAD A SEAT. ON THE INSIDE.
OH, GLARK SAN!
HEY, MARKER-SAN. HOW'S IT GOING?
AACHOO!
CHILLY, ISN'T IT?
LET'S GET TO THE ELDERS' HOUSE BEFORE WE FREEZE.
THE NORTH IS COLD.
BUT...
...IN THE EAST, WHERE OUR MAIN CHARACTERS LIVE...
...IT IS ALSO ...

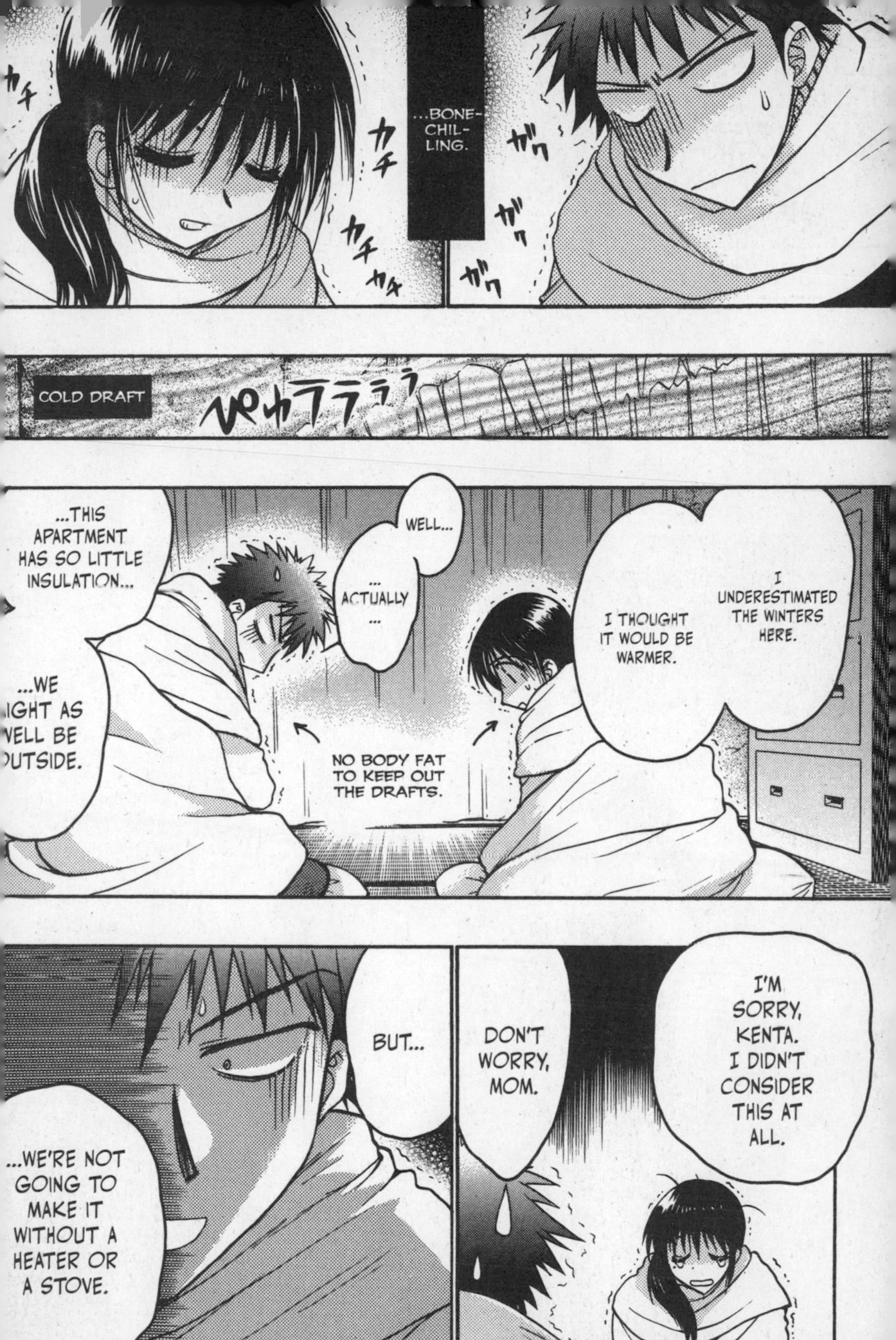

ガク
ガク
ガク
...BONE-CHIL-LING.
カチ
カチ
カチカチ
COLD DRAFT
ぴゅララララ
I UNDERESTIMATED THE WINTERS HERE.
I THOUGHT IT WOULD BE WARMER.
NO BODY FAT TO KEEP OUT THE DRAFTS.
WELL...
...ACTUALLY...
...THIS APARTMENT HAS SO LITTLE INSULATION...
...WE IGHT AS ELL BE UTSIDE.
I'M SORRY, KENTA. I DIDN'T CONSIDER THIS AT ALL.
DON'T WORRY, MOM.
BUT...
...WE'RE NOT GOING TO MAKE IT WITHOUT A HEATER OR A STOVE.

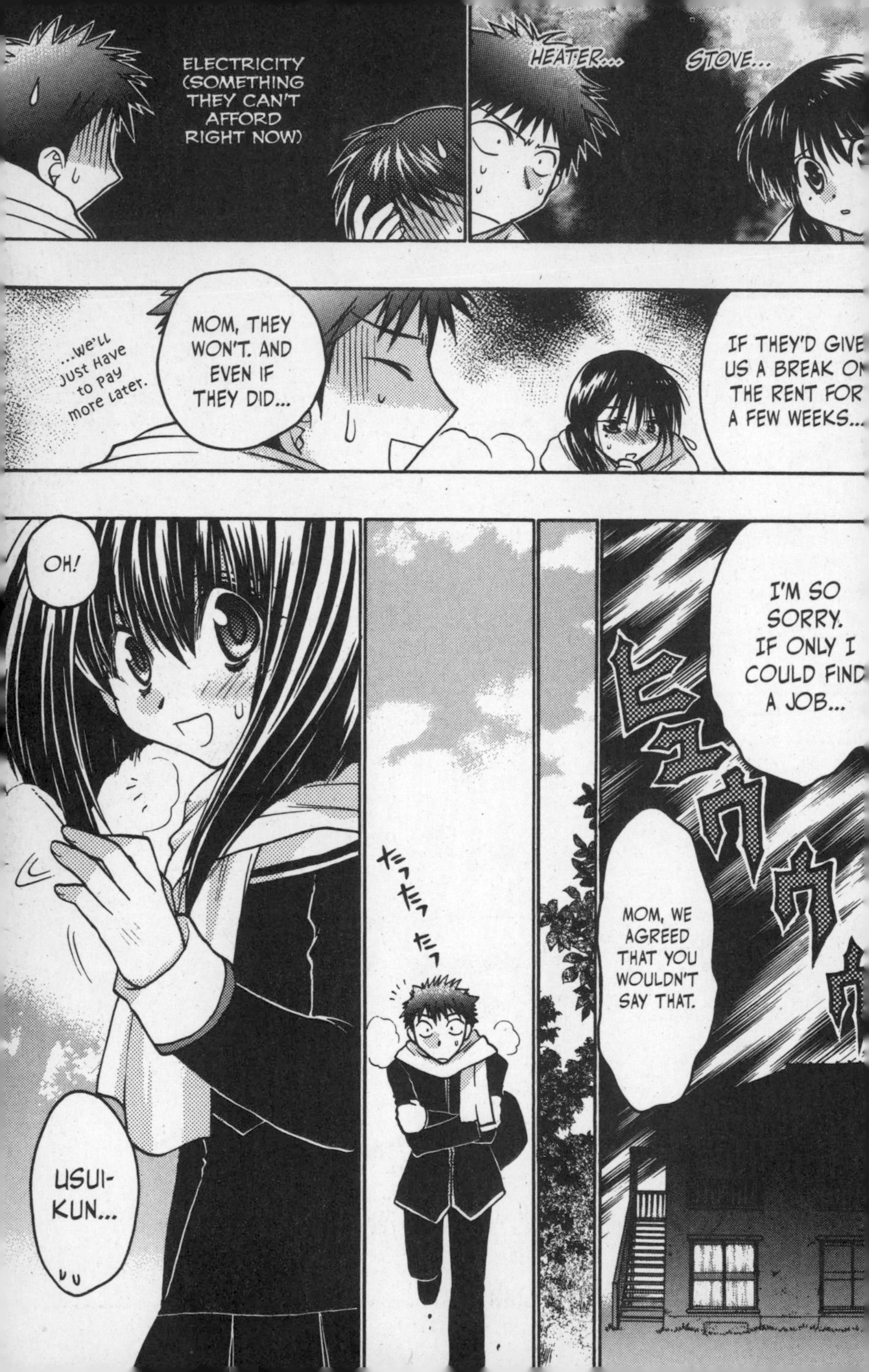
STOVE...
HEATER...
ELECTRICITY (SOMETHING THEY CAN'T AFFORD RIGHT NOW)
IF THEY'D GIVE US A BREAK ON THE RENT FOR A FEW WEEKS...
MOM, THEY WON'T. AND EVEN IF THEY DID...
...we'll just have to pay more later.
I'M SO SORRY. IF ONLY I COULD FIND A JOB...
ヒュウウ
MOM, WE AGREED THAT YOU WOULDN'T SAY THAT.
たっ たっ たっ
OH!
USUI-KUN...

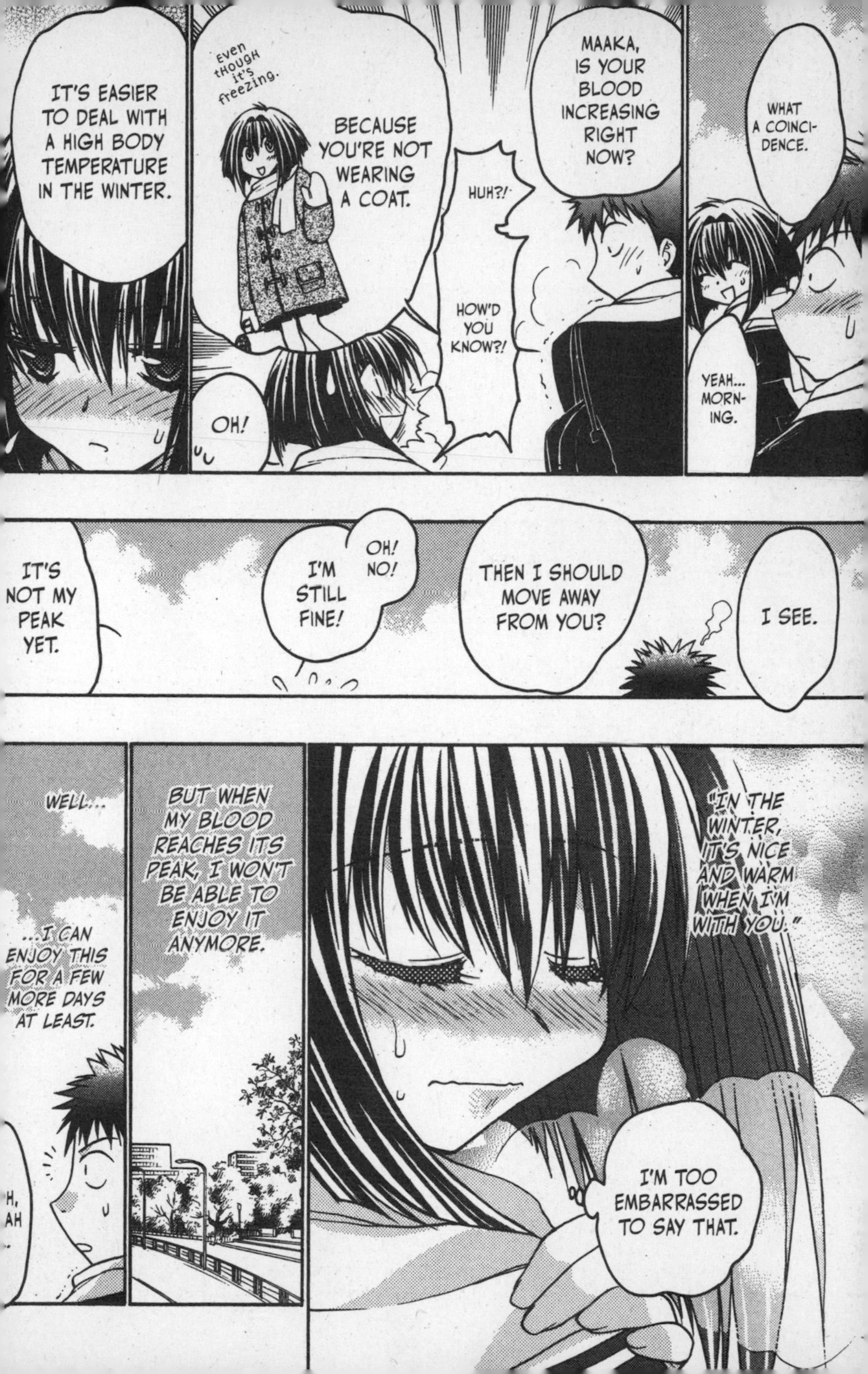
WHAT A COINCIDENCE.
YEAH... MORNING.
MAAKA, IS YOUR BLOOD INCREASING RIGHT NOW?
HUH?!
HOW'D YOU KNOW?!
BECAUSE YOU'RE NOT WEARING A COAT.
Even though it's freezing.
OH!
IT'S EASIER TO DEAL WITH A HIGH BODY TEMPERATURE IN THE WINTER.
I SEE.
THEN I SHOULD MOVE AWAY FROM YOU?
OH! NO!
I'M STILL FINE!
IT'S NOT MY PEAK YET.
"IN THE WINTER, IT'S NICE AND WARM WHEN I'M WITH YOU."
I'M TOO EMBARRASSED TO SAY THAT.
BUT WHEN MY BLOOD REACHES ITS PEAK, I WON'T BE ABLE TO ENJOY IT ANYMORE.
WELL...
...I CAN ENJOY THIS FOR A FEW MORE DAYS AT LEAST.

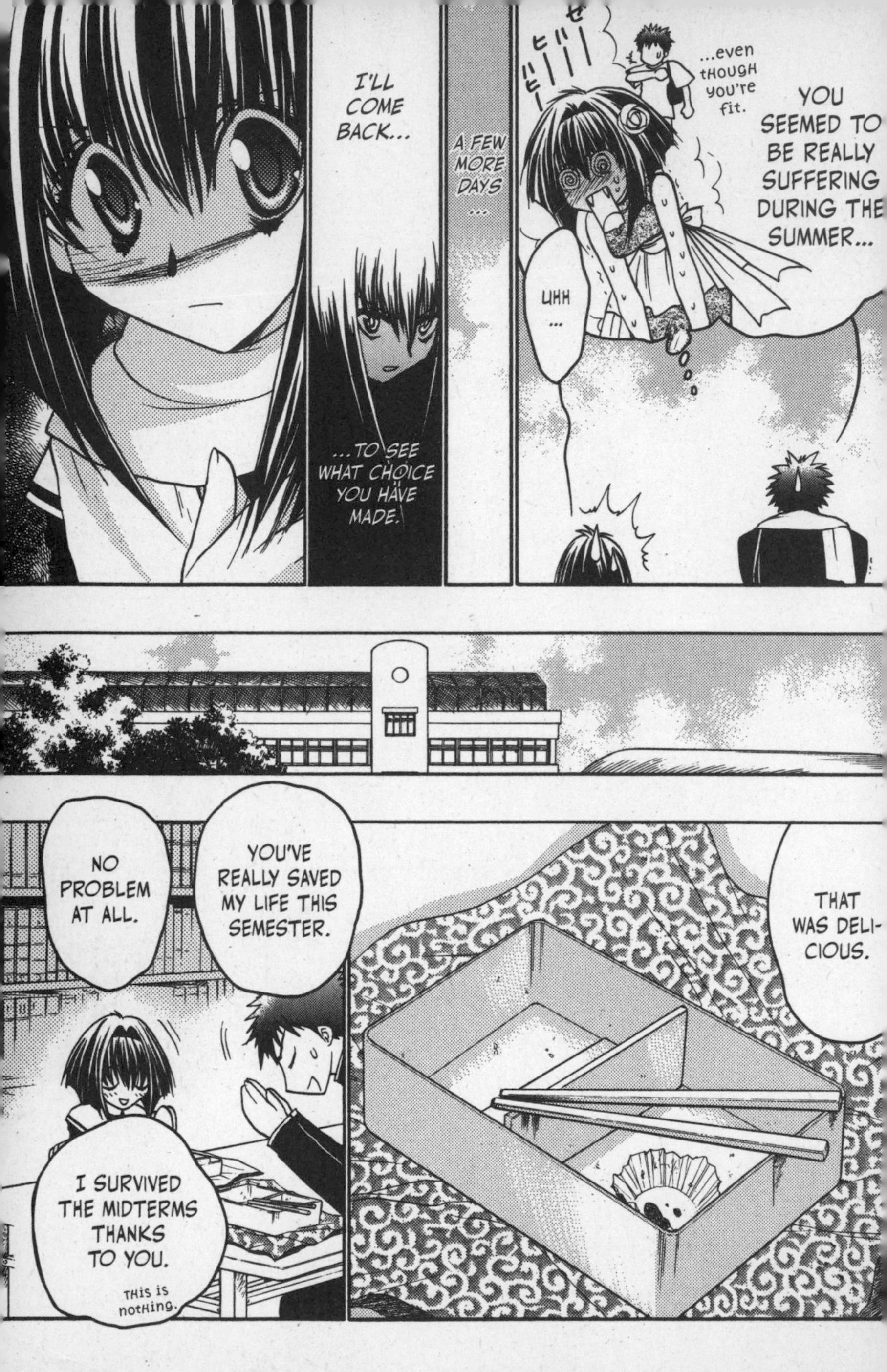
YOU SEEMED TO BE REALLY SUFFERING DURING THE SUMMER...
...even though you're fit.
ゼーハーヒーハヒー
UHH ...
A FEW MORE DAYS ...
I'LL COME BACK...
...TO SEE WHAT CHOICE YOU HAVE MADE.
THAT WAS DELICIOUS.
YOU'VE REALLY SAVED MY LIFE THIS SEMESTER.
NO PROBLEM AT ALL.
I SURVIVED THE MIDTERMS THANKS TO YOU.
This is nothing.

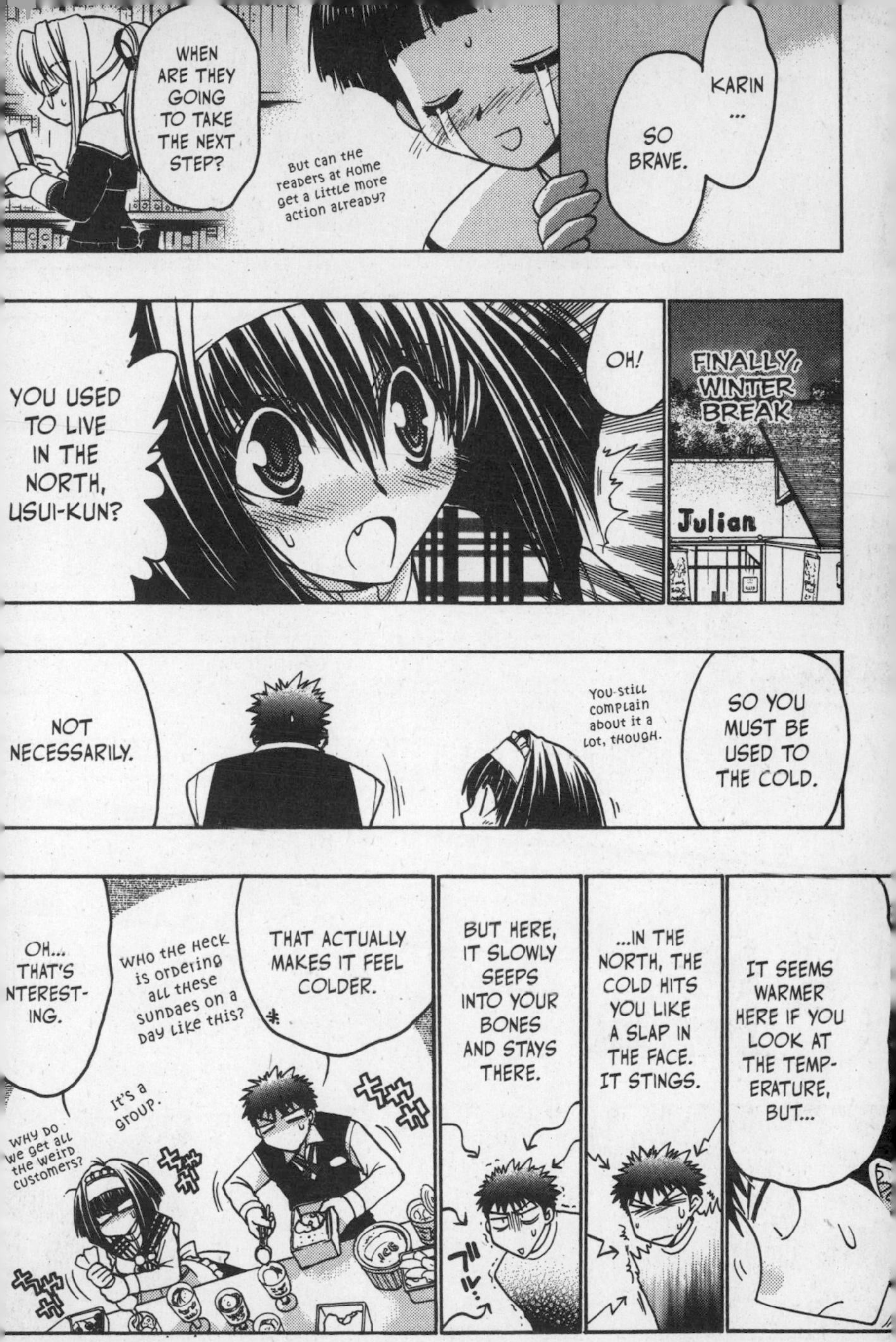
KARIN ...
SO BRAVE.
WHEN ARE THEY GOING TO TAKE THE NEXT STEP?
But can the readers at home get a little more action already?
FINALLY, WINTER BREAK
Julian
OH!
YOU USED TO LIVE IN THE NORTH, USUI-KUN?
SO YOU MUST BE USED TO THE COLD.
You still complain about it a lot, though.
NOT NECESSARILY.
IT SEEMS WARMER HERE IF YOU LOOK AT THE TEMP-ERATURE, BUT...
...IN THE NORTH, THE COLD HITS YOU LIKE A SLAP IN THE FACE. IT STINGS.
BUT HERE, IT SLOWLY SEEPS INTO YOUR BONES AND STAYS THERE.
THAT ACTUALLY MAKES IT FEEL COLDER.
*
Who the heck is ordering all these sundaes on a day like this?
OH... THAT'S NTEREST-ING.
It's a group.
Why do we get all the weird customers?

*This is what my friend from Hokkaido told me.

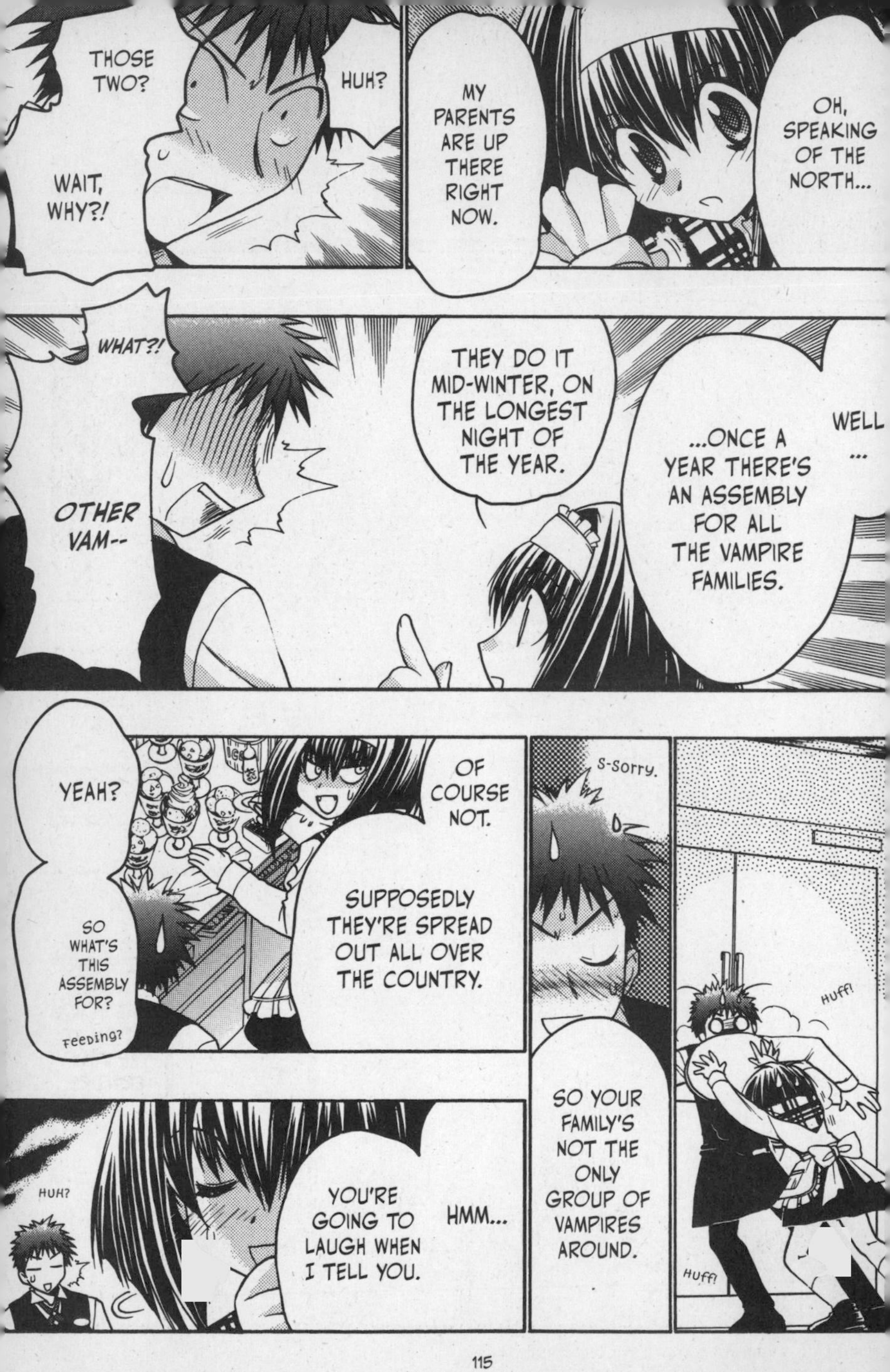
OH, SPEAKING OF THE NORTH...
MY PARENTS ARE UP THERE RIGHT NOW.
HUH?
THOSE TWO?
WAIT, WHY?!
WELL...
...ONCE A YEAR THERE'S AN ASSEMBLY FOR ALL THE VAMPIRE FAMILIES.
THEY DO IT MID-WINTER, ON THE LONGEST NIGHT OF THE YEAR.
WHAT?!
OTHER VAM--
Huff!
Huff!
S-Sorry.
SO YOUR FAMILY'S NOT THE ONLY GROUP OF VAMPIRES AROUND.
OF COURSE NOT.
SUPPOSEDLY THEY'RE SPREAD OUT ALL OVER THE COUNTRY.
YEAH?
SO WHAT'S THIS ASSEMBLY FOR?
Feeding?
HMM...
YOU'RE GOING TO LAUGH WHEN I TELL YOU.
HUH?

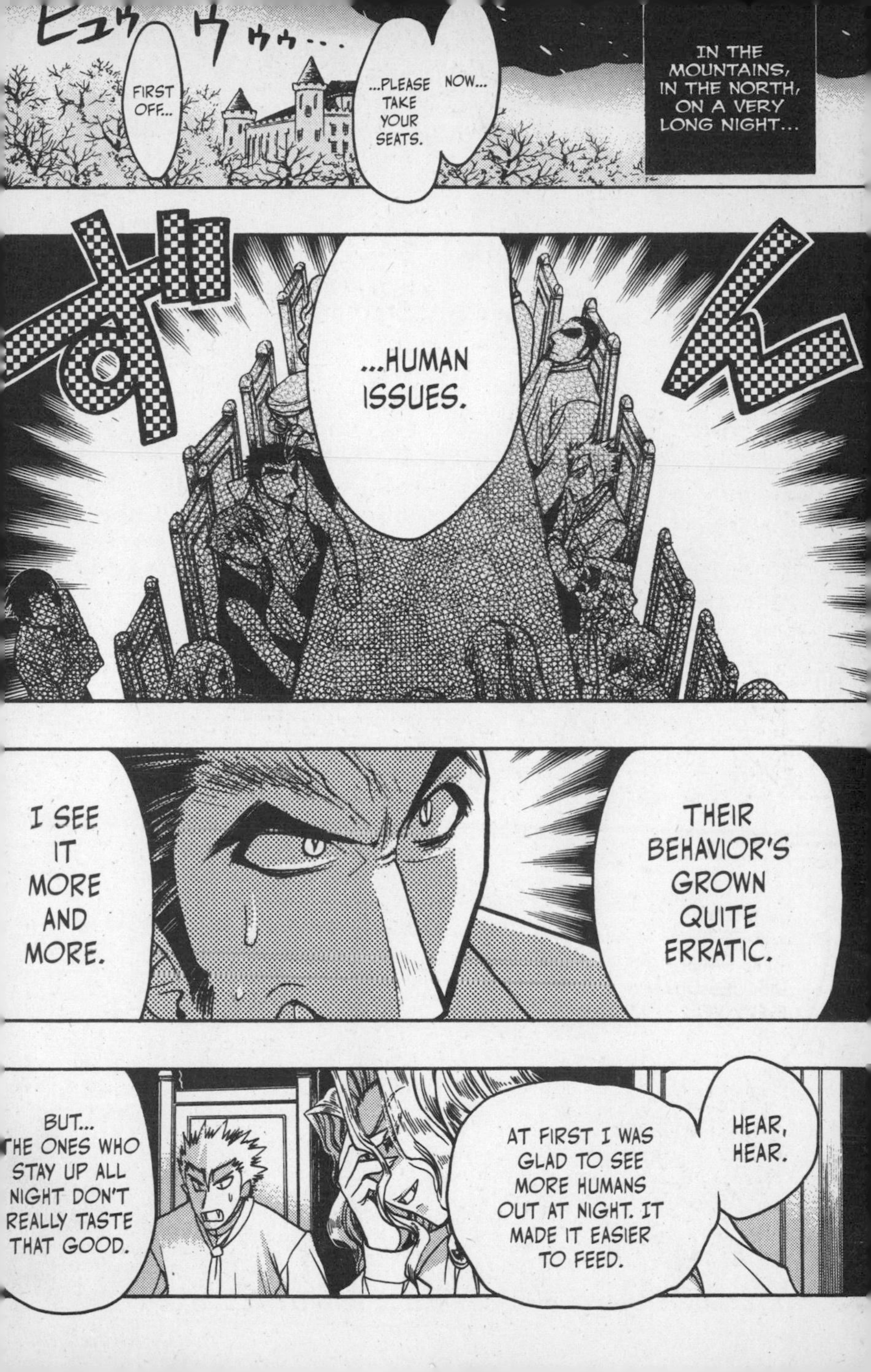
IN THE MOUNTAINS, IN THE NORTH, ON A VERY LONG NIGHT...
NOW...
...PLEASE TAKE YOUR SEATS.
FIRST OFF...
ヒュゥ ウゥゥ...
...HUMAN ISSUES.
THEIR BEHAVIOR'S GROWN QUITE ERRATIC.
I SEE IT MORE AND MORE.
HEAR, HEAR.
AT FIRST I WAS GLAD TO SEE MORE HUMANS OUT AT NIGHT. IT MADE IT EASIER TO FEED.
BUT... THE ONES WHO STAY UP ALL NIGHT DON'T REALLY TASTE THAT GOOD.

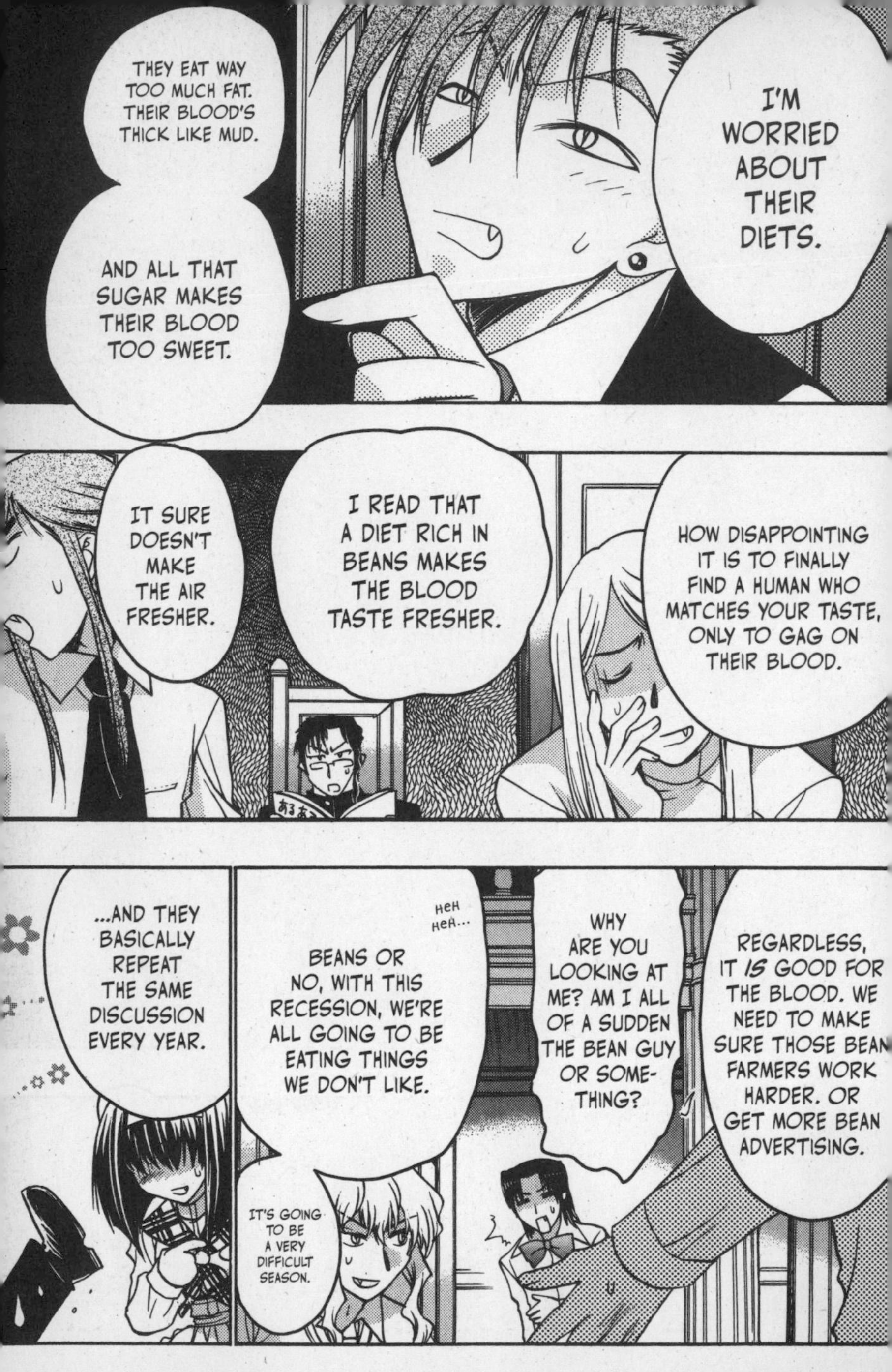
I'M WORRIED ABOUT THEIR DIETS.
THEY EAT WAY TOO MUCH FAT. THEIR BLOOD'S THICK LIKE MUD.
AND ALL THAT SUGAR MAKES THEIR BLOOD TOO SWEET.
HOW DISAPPOINTING IT IS TO FINALLY FIND A HUMAN WHO MATCHES YOUR TASTE, ONLY TO GAG ON THEIR BLOOD.
I READ THAT A DIET RICH IN BEANS MAKES THE BLOOD TASTE FRESHER.
IT SURE DOESN'T MAKE THE AIR FRESHER.
REGARDLESS, IT *IS* GOOD FOR THE BLOOD. WE NEED TO MAKE SURE THOSE BEAN FARMERS WORK HARDER. OR GET MORE BEAN ADVERTISING.
WHY ARE YOU LOOKING AT ME? AM I ALL OF A SUDDEN THE BEAN GUY OR SOME-THING?
HEH HEH...
BEANS OR NO, WITH THIS RECESSION, WE'RE ALL GOING TO BE EATING THINGS WE DON'T LIKE.
IT'S GOING TO BE A VERY DIFFICULT SEASON.
...AND THEY BASICALLY REPEAT THE SAME DISCUSSION EVERY YEAR.

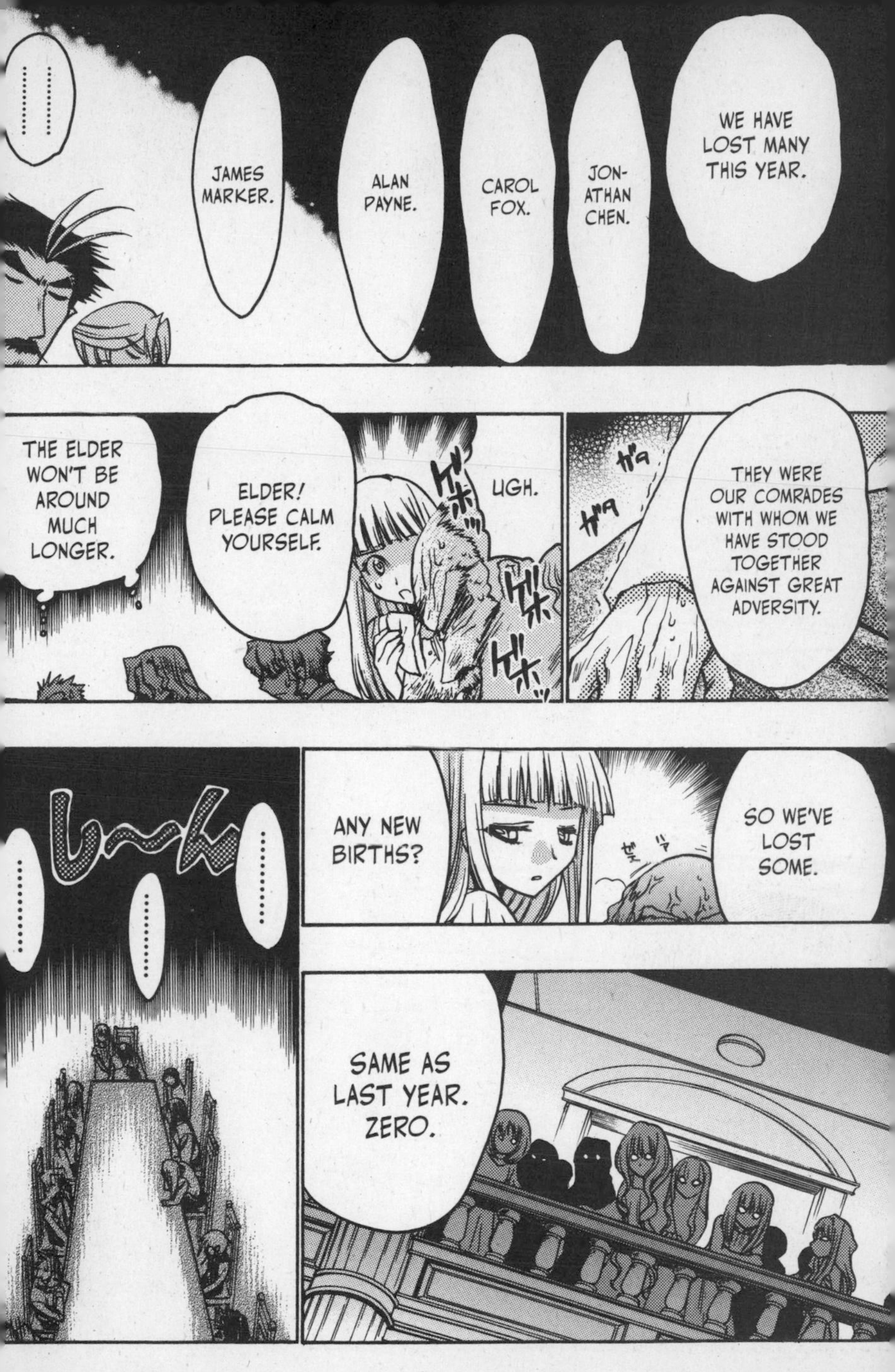
WE HAVE LOST MANY THIS YEAR.
JON-ATHAN CHEN.
CAROL FOX.
ALAN PAYNE.
JAMES MARKER.
......
THEY WERE OUR COMRADES WITH WHOM WE HAVE STOOD TOGETHER AGAINST GREAT ADVERSITY.
UGH.
ELDER! PLEASE CALM YOURSELF.
THE ELDER WON'T BE AROUND MUCH LONGER.
SO WE'VE LOST SOME.
ANY NEW BIRTHS?
SAME AS LAST YEAR. ZERO.
......
......
......

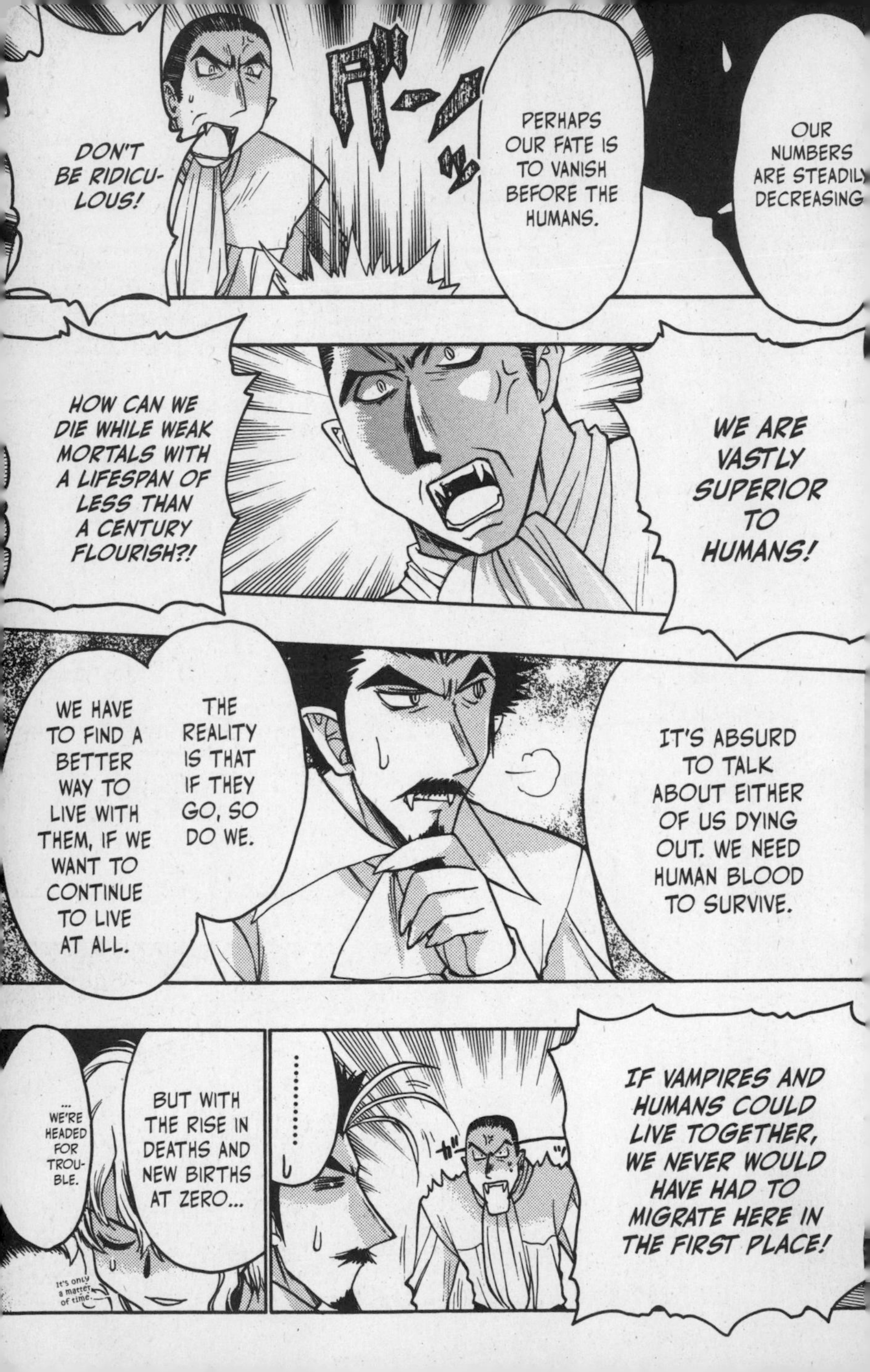
OUR NUMBERS ARE STEADILY DECREASING
PERHAPS OUR FATE IS TO VANISH BEFORE THE HUMANS.
DON'T BE RIDICU-LOUS!
WE ARE VASTLY SUPERIOR TO HUMANS!
HOW CAN WE DIE WHILE WEAK MORTALS WITH A LIFESPAN OF LESS THAN A CENTURY FLOURISH?!
IT'S ABSURD TO TALK ABOUT EITHER OF US DYING OUT. WE NEED HUMAN BLOOD TO SURVIVE.
THE REALITY IS THAT IF THEY GO, SO DO WE.
WE HAVE TO FIND A BETTER WAY TO LIVE WITH THEM, IF WE WANT TO CONTINUE TO LIVE AT ALL.
IF VAMPIRES AND HUMANS COULD LIVE TOGETHER, WE NEVER WOULD HAVE HAD TO MIGRATE HERE IN THE FIRST PLACE!
....
BUT WITH THE RISE IN DEATHS AND NEW BIRTHS AT ZERO...
...WE'RE HEADED FOR TROU-BLE.
It's only a matter of time.

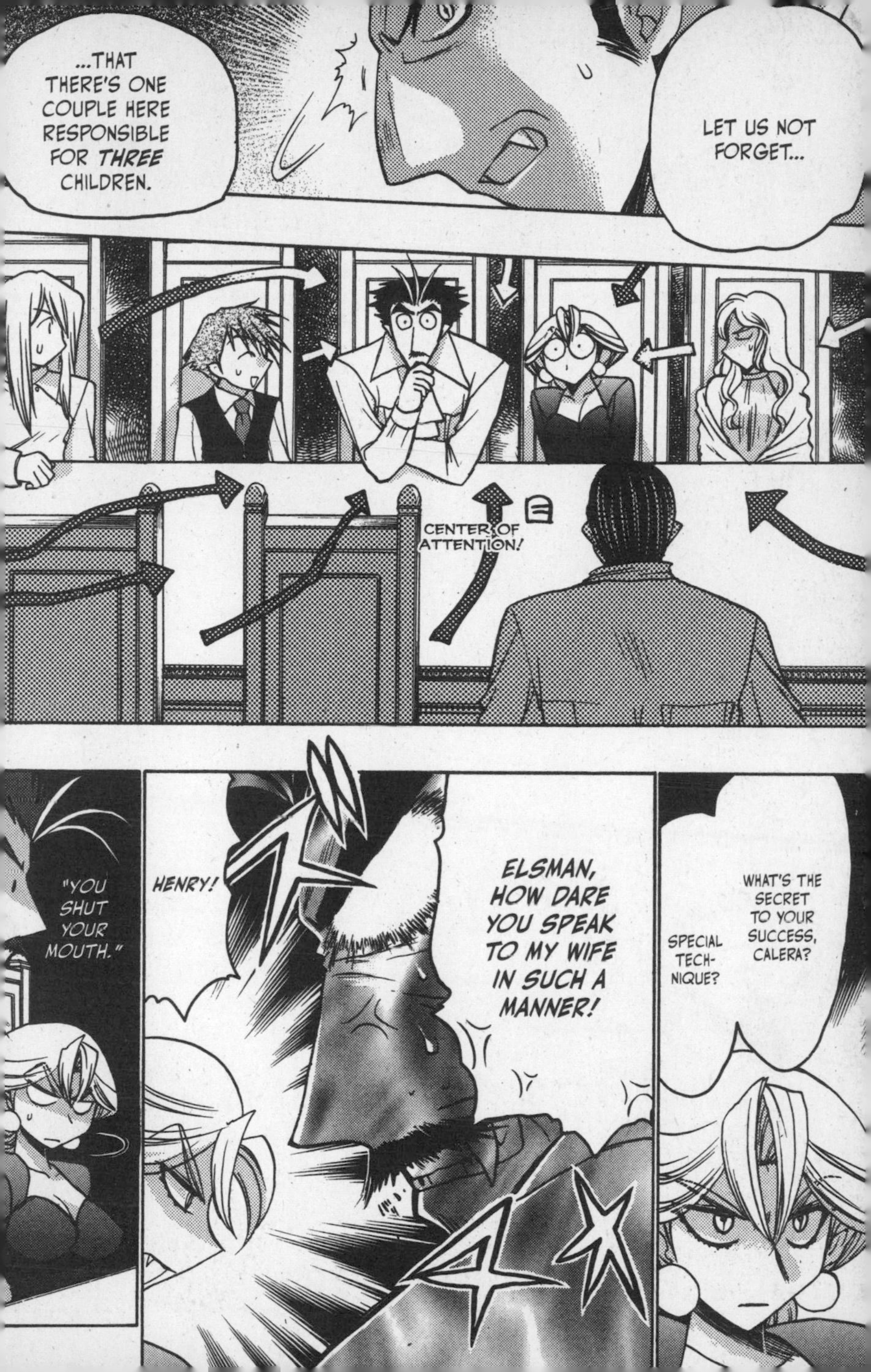
LET US NOT FORGET...
...THAT THERE'S ONE COUPLE HERE RESPONSIBLE FOR *THREE* CHILDREN.
CENTER OF ATTENTION!
WHAT'S THE SECRET TO YOUR SUCCESS, CALERA?
SPECIAL TECH-NIQUE?
ELSMAN, HOW DARE YOU SPEAK TO MY WIFE IN SUCH A MANNER!
HENRY!
"YOU SHUT YOUR MOUTH."

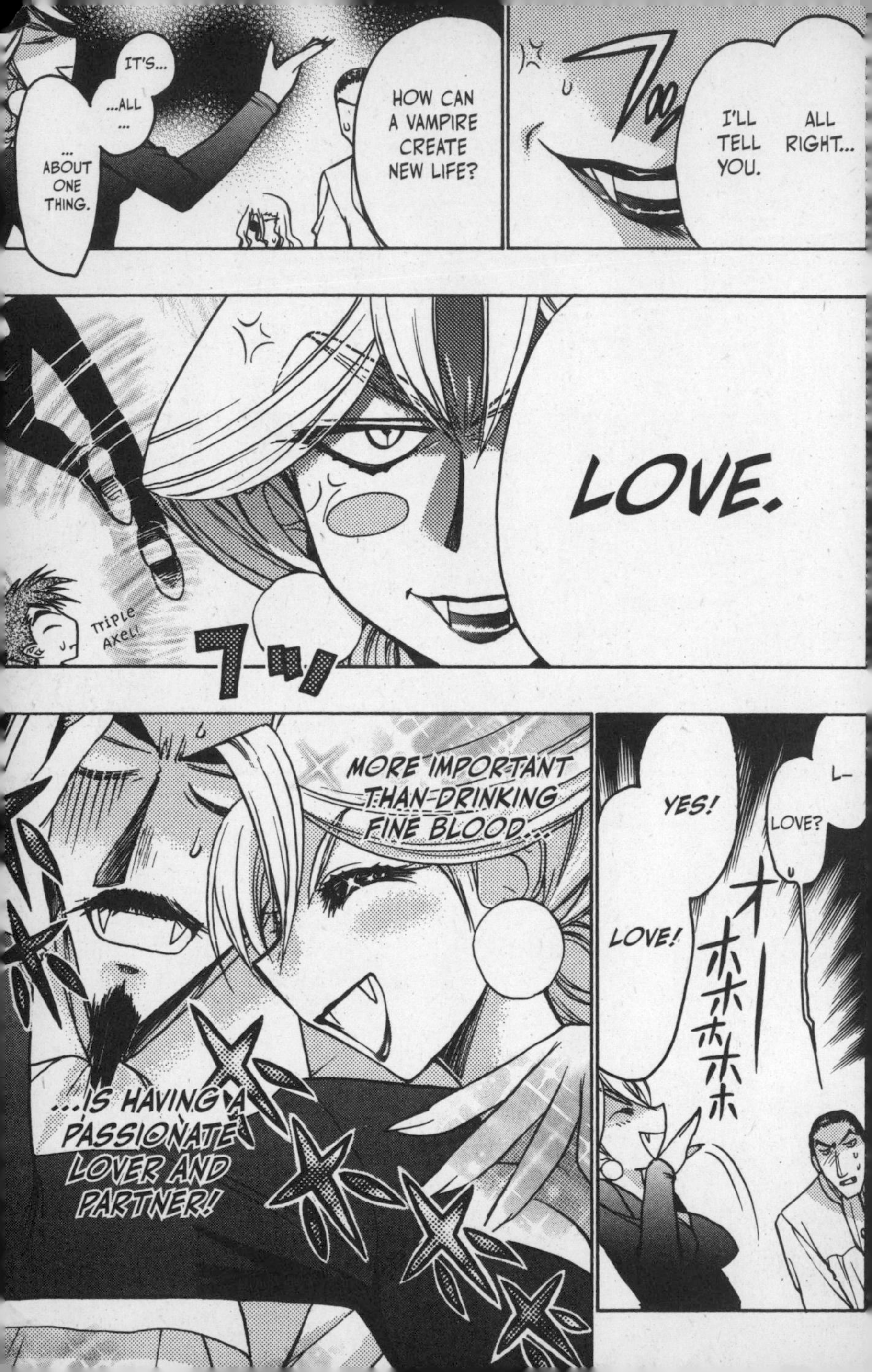
ALL RIGHT... I'LL TELL YOU.
HOW CAN A VAMPIRE CREATE NEW LIFE?
IT'S...
...ALL...
...ABOUT ONE THING.
LOVE.
フッ
TRIPLE AXEL!
L— LOVE?
YES! LOVE!
オーホホホホホ
MORE IMPORTANT THAN DRINKING FINE BLOOD...
...IS HAVING A PASSIONATE LOVER AND PARTNER!

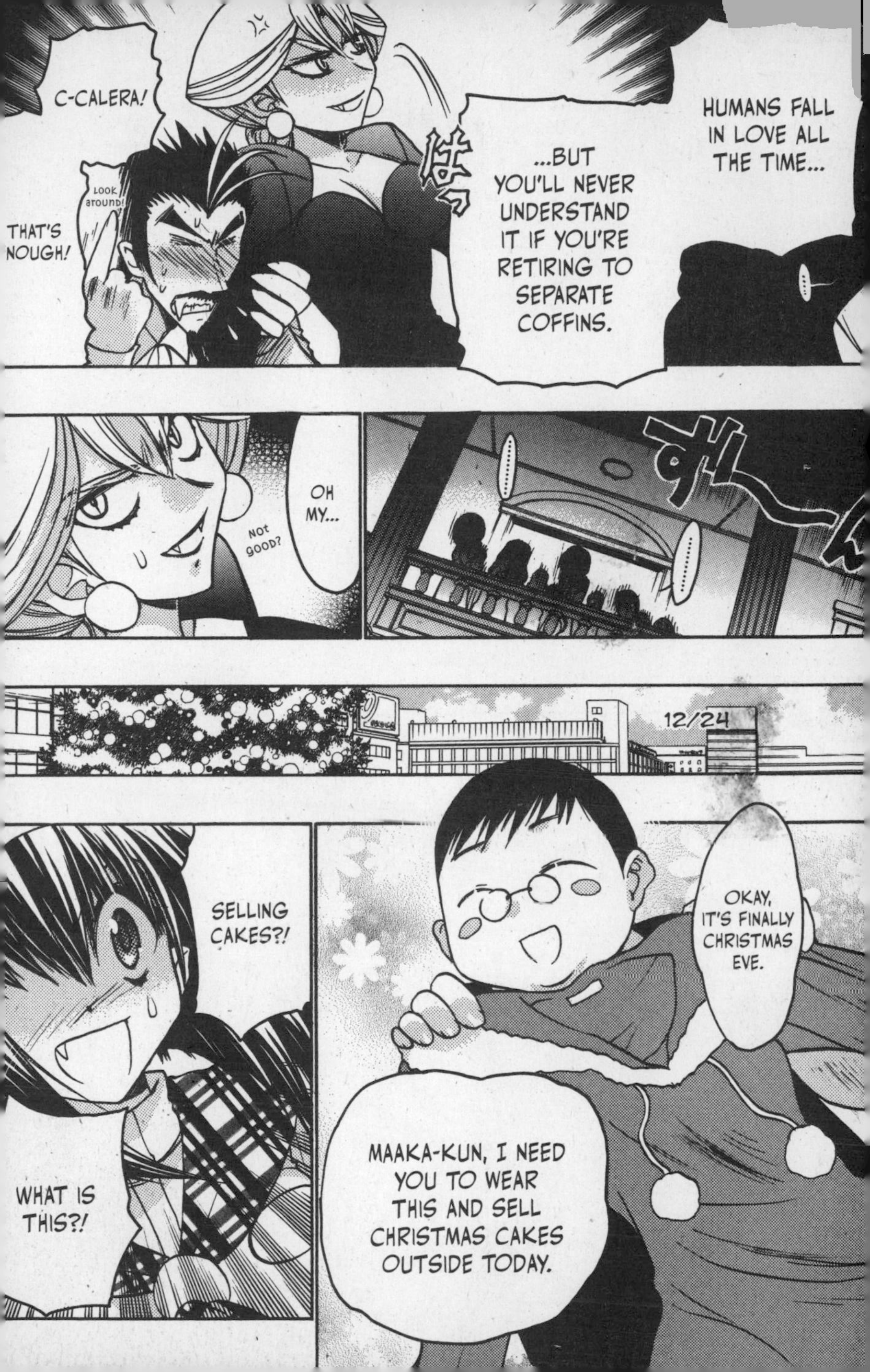
HUMANS FALL IN LOVE ALL THE TIME...
...BUT YOU'LL NEVER UNDERSTAND IT IF YOU'RE RETIRING TO SEPARATE COFFINS.
はっ
C-CALERA!
LOOK AROUND!
THAT'S NOUGH!
すーん
OH MY...
Not good?
12/24
OKAY, IT'S FINALLY CHRISTMAS EVE.
MAAKA-KUN, I NEED YOU TO WEAR THIS AND SELL CHRISTMAS CAKES OUTSIDE TODAY.
SELLING CAKES?!
WHAT IS THIS?!

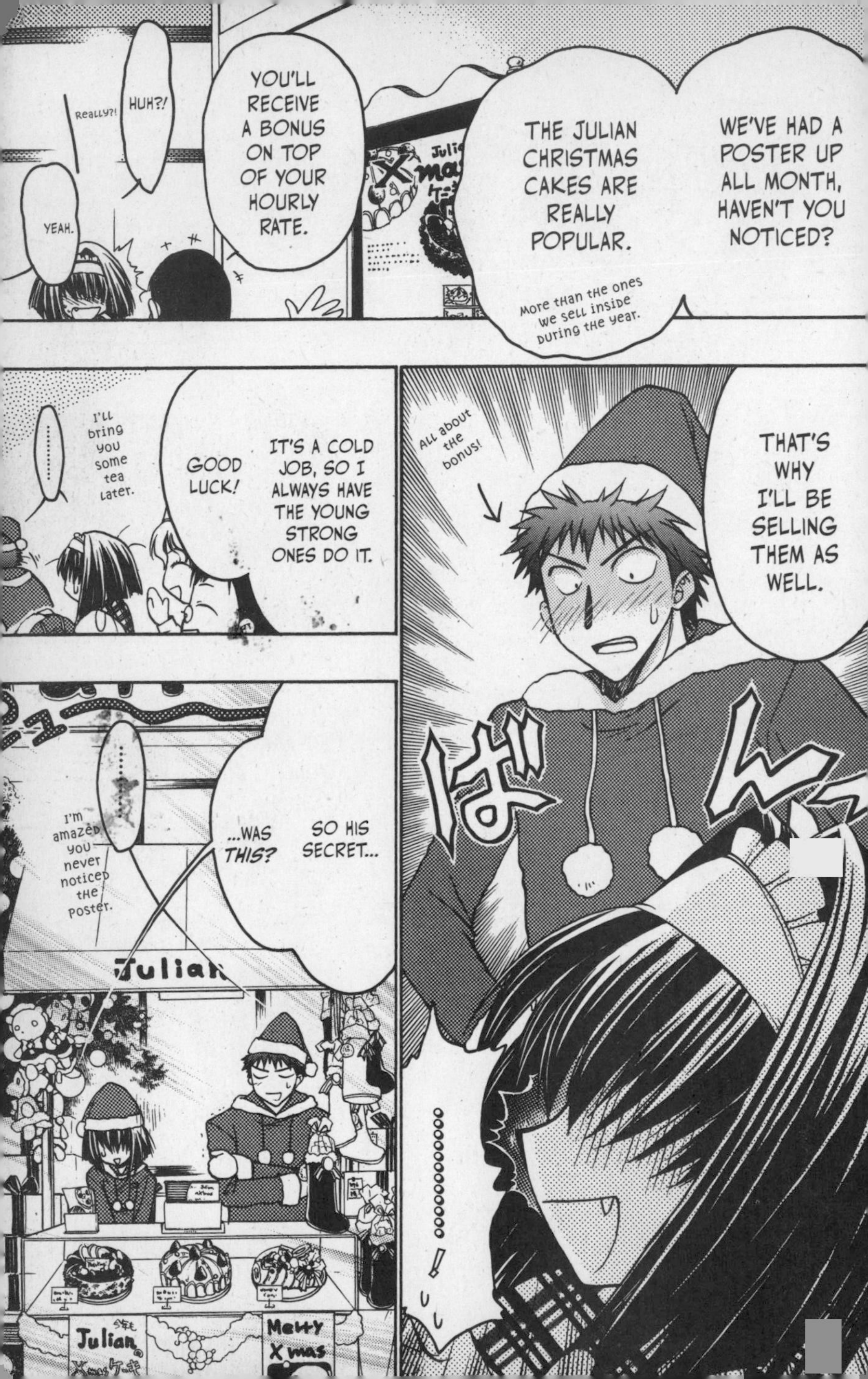
WE'VE HAD A POSTER UP ALL MONTH, HAVEN'T YOU NOTICED?
THE JULIAN CHRISTMAS CAKES ARE REALLY POPULAR.
More than the ones we sell inside during the year.
YOU'LL RECEIVE A BONUS ON TOP OF YOUR HOURLY RATE.
HUH?!
Really?!
YEAH.
THAT'S WHY I'LL BE SELLING THEM AS WELL.
All about the bonus!
ばん
OOOOOOOOOOOOOO!
IT'S A COLD JOB, SO I ALWAYS HAVE THE YOUNG STRONG ONES DO IT.
GOOD LUCK!
I'll bring you some tea later.
......
SO HIS SECRET...
...WAS THIS?
......
I'm amazed you never noticed the poster.
Julian
Julian
Melty X mas

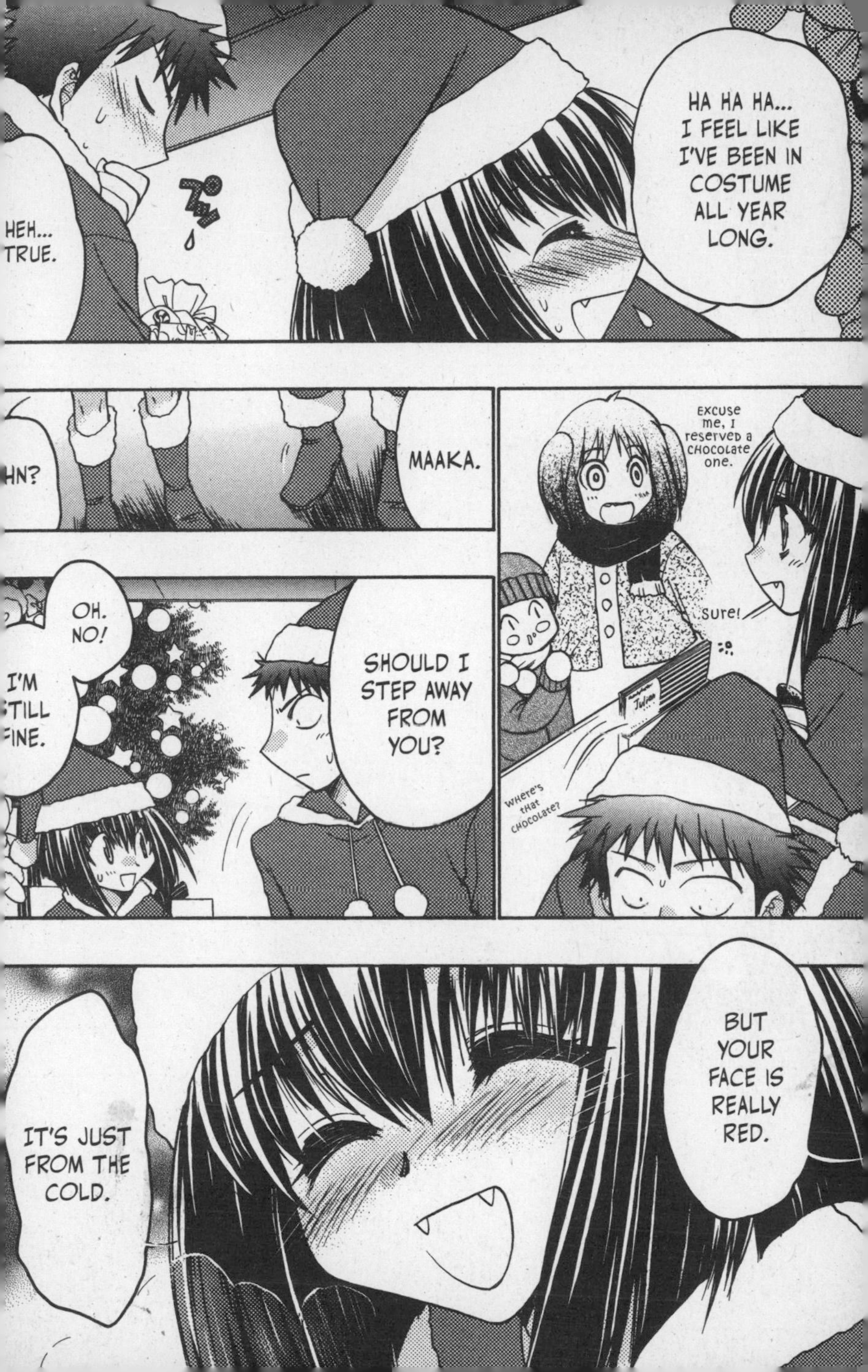
HA HA HA... I FEEL LIKE I'VE BEEN IN COSTUME ALL YEAR LONG.
HEH... TRUE.
Excuse me, I reserved a chocolate one.
Sure!
Where's that chocolate?
MAAKA.
HN?
SHOULD I STEP AWAY FROM YOU?
OH. NO!
I'M TILL INE.
BUT YOUR FACE IS REALLY RED.
IT'S JUST FROM THE COLD.

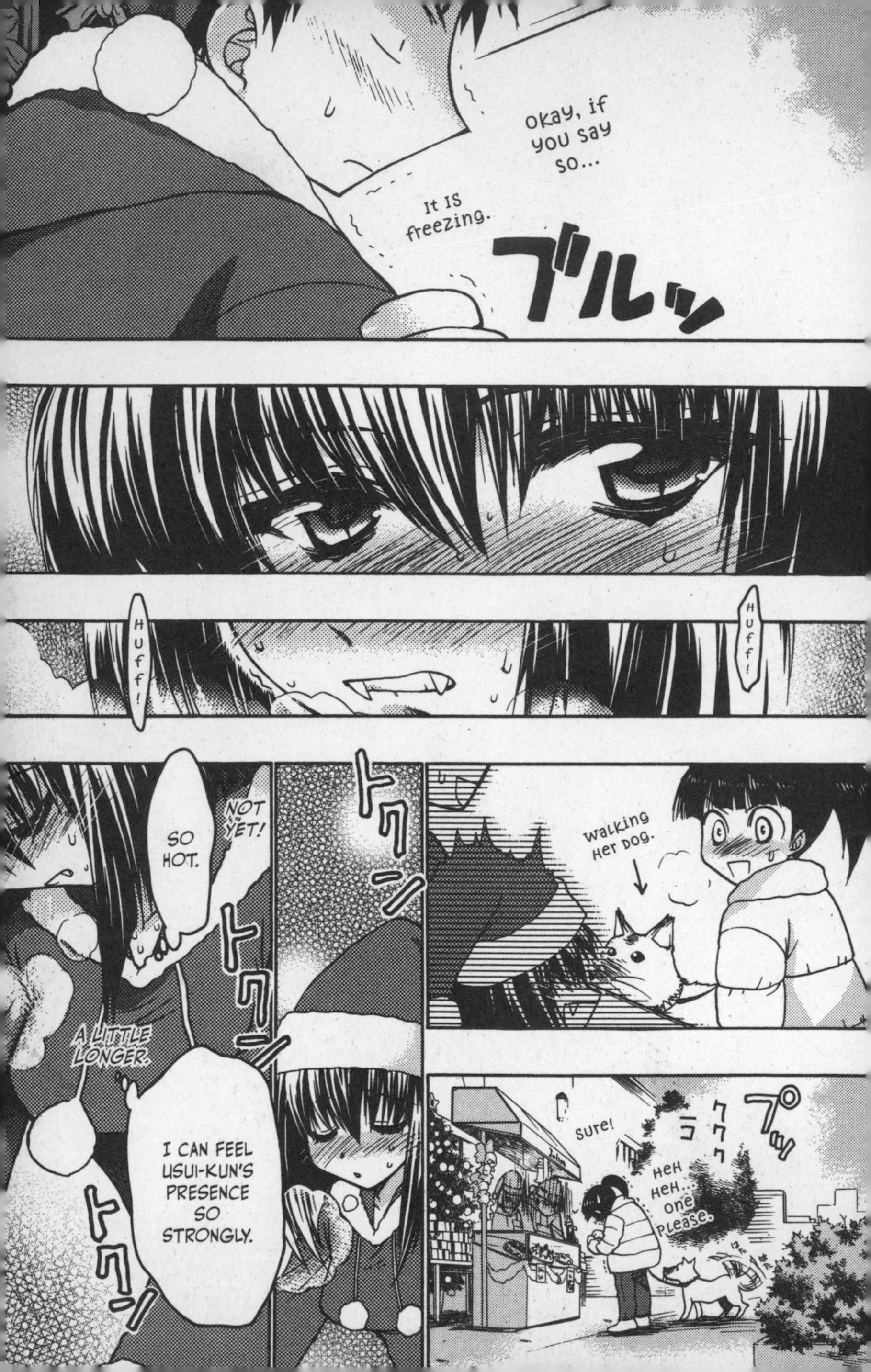

Okay, if you say so...
It IS freezing.
ブルッ
Huff!
Huff!
Walking her dog.
プッ
ククク
Sure!
Heh heh... one please.
トクン
トクン
トクン
I can feel Usui-kun's presence so strongly.
Not yet!
So hot.
A little longer.

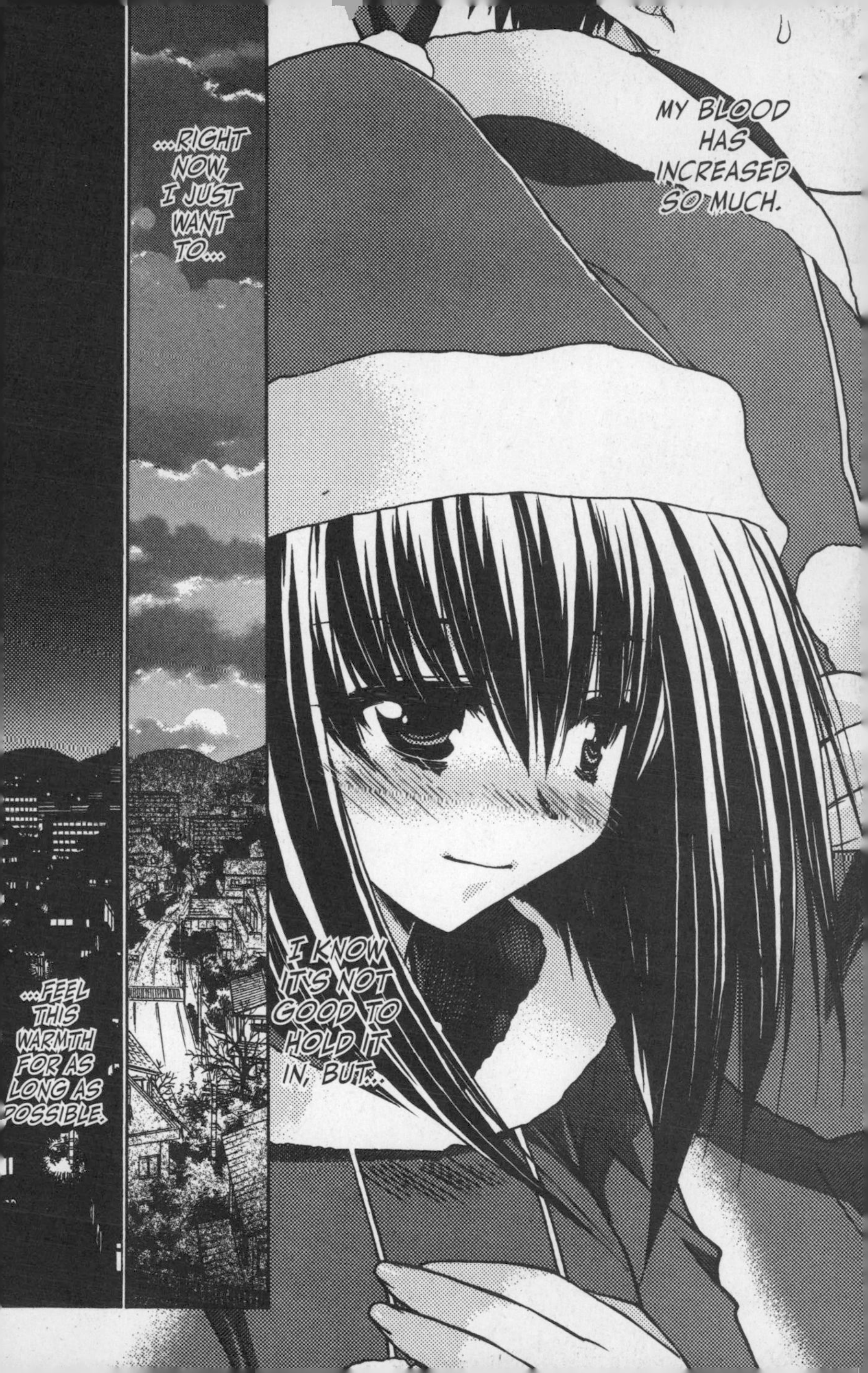
MY BLOOD HAS INCREASED SO MUCH.
I KNOW IT'S NOT GOOD TO HOLD IT IN, BUT...
...RIGHT NOW, I JUST WANT TO...
...FEEL THIS WARMTH FOR AS LONG AS POSSIBLE.

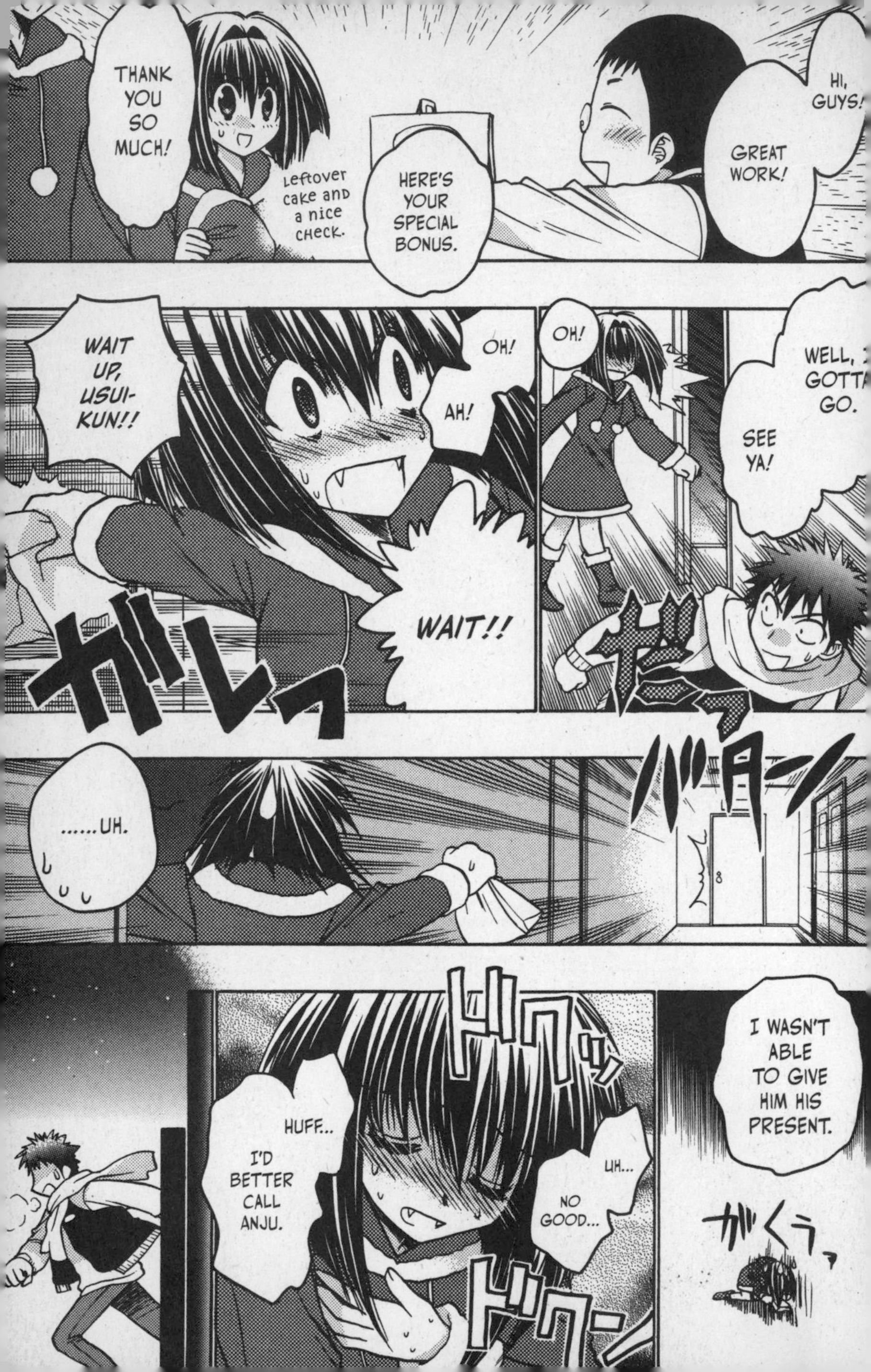
HI, GUYS!
GREAT WORK!
HERE'S YOUR SPECIAL BONUS.
Leftover cake and a nice check.
THANK YOU SO MUCH!
WELL, GOTTA GO.
SEE YA!
OH!
OH!
AH!
WAIT!!
WAIT UP, USUI-KUN!!
......UH.
I WASN'T ABLE TO GIVE HIM HIS PRESENT.
UH...
NO GOOD...
HUFF...
I'D BETTER CALL ANJU.

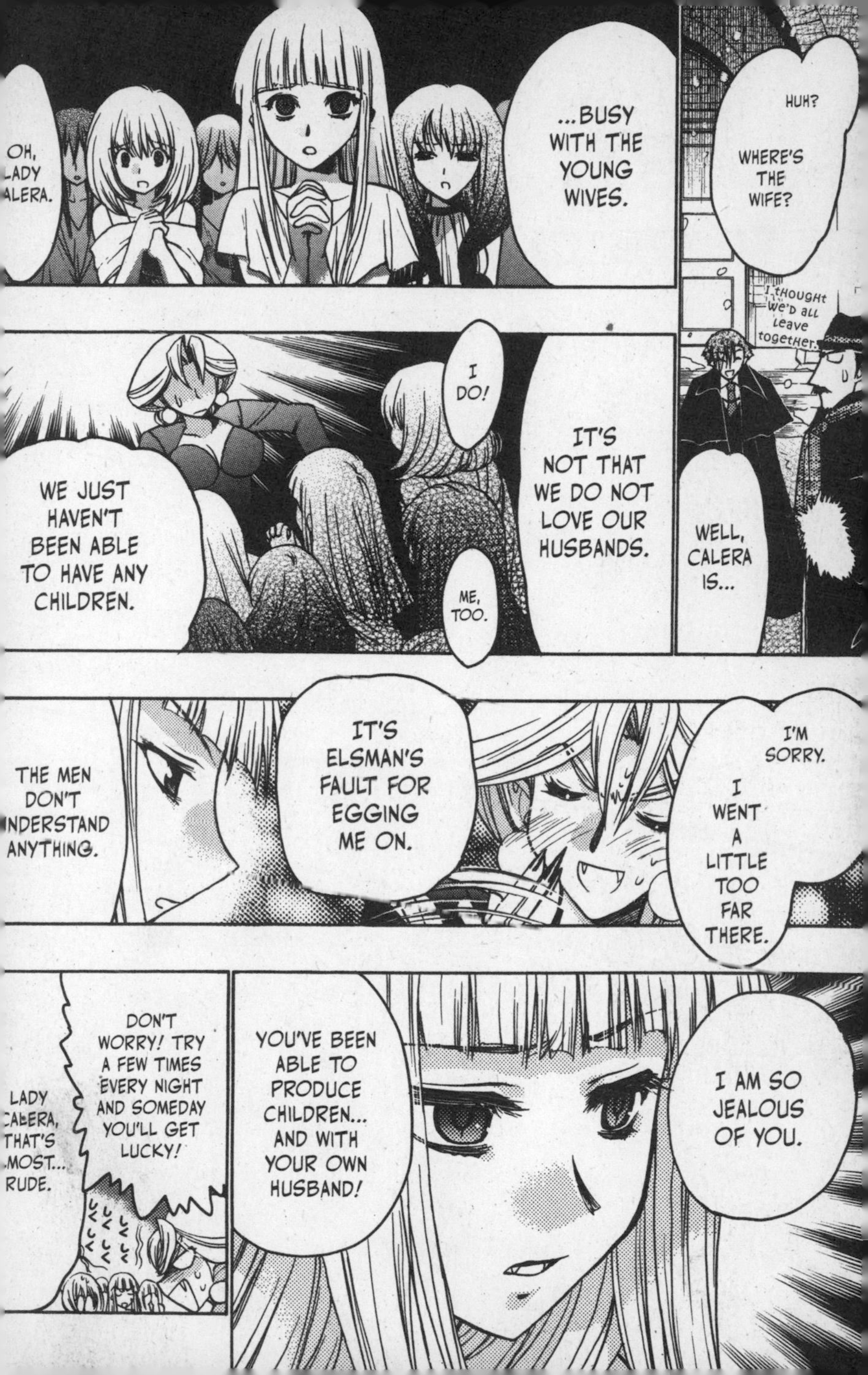
HUH?
WHERE'S THE WIFE?
I thought we'd all leave together.
WELL, CALERA IS...
...BUSY WITH THE YOUNG WIVES.
OH, LADY CALERA.
IT'S NOT THAT WE DO NOT LOVE OUR HUSBANDS.
I DO!
ME, TOO.
WE JUST HAVEN'T BEEN ABLE TO HAVE ANY CHILDREN.
I'M SORRY.
I WENT A LITTLE TOO FAR THERE.
IT'S ELSMAN'S FAULT FOR EGGING ME ON.
THE MEN DON'T UNDERSTAND ANYTHING.
I AM SO JEALOUS OF YOU.
YOU'VE BEEN ABLE TO PRODUCE CHILDREN... AND WITH YOUR OWN HUSBAND!
DON'T WORRY! TRY A FEW TIMES EVERY NIGHT AND SOMEDAY YOU'LL GET LUCKY!
LADY CALERA, THAT'S MOST... RUDE.

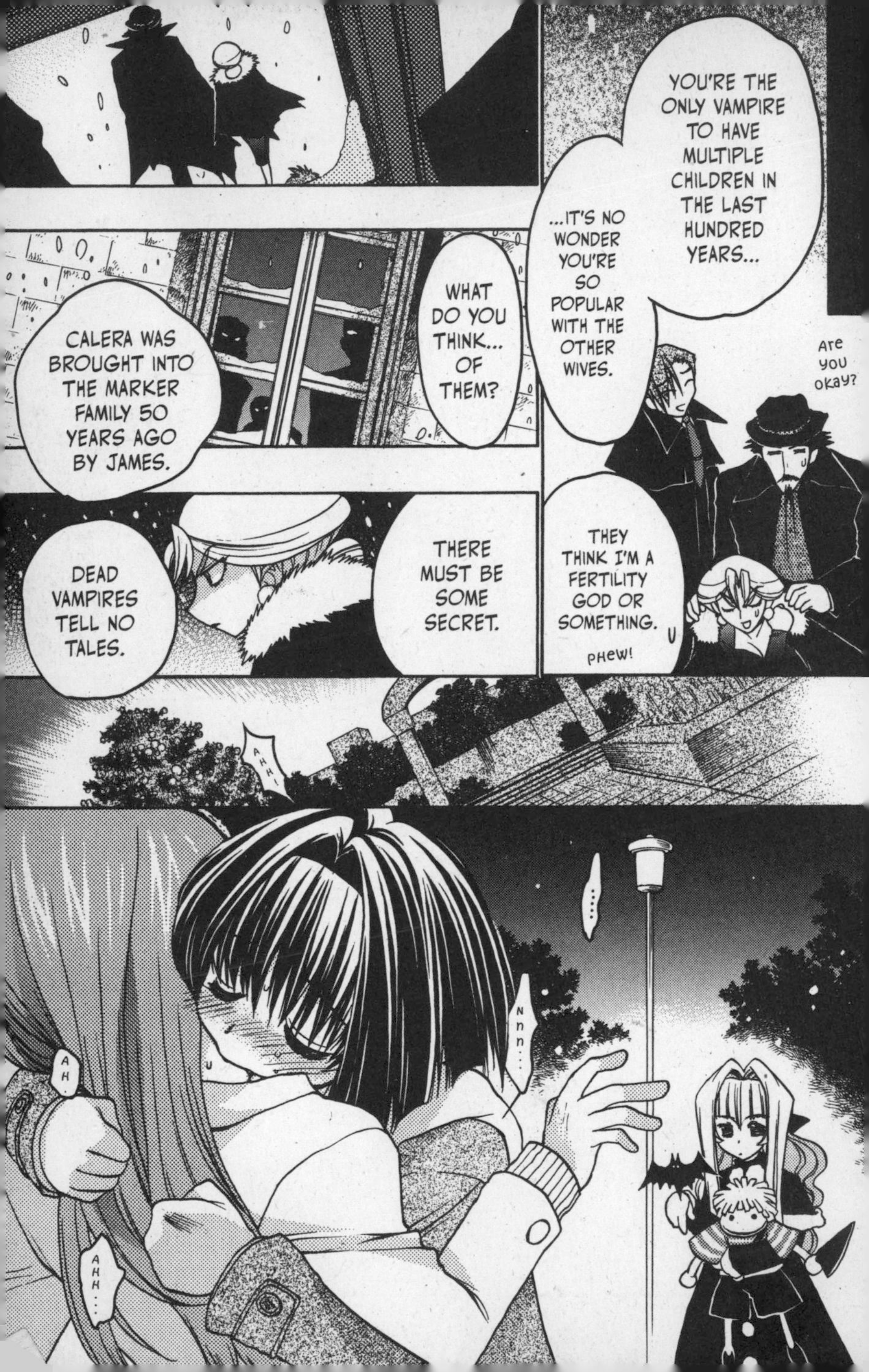
YOU'RE THE ONLY VAMPIRE TO HAVE MULTIPLE CHILDREN IN THE LAST HUNDRED YEARS...
...IT'S NO WONDER YOU'RE SO POPULAR WITH THE OTHER WIVES.
Are you okay?
THEY THINK I'M A FERTILITY GOD OR SOMETHING.
PHEW!
WHAT DO YOU THINK... OF THEM?
CALERA WAS BROUGHT INTO THE MARKER FAMILY 50 YEARS AGO BY JAMES.
THERE MUST BE SOME SECRET.
DEAD VAMPIRES TELL NO TALES.
AHH!
....
Nnn...
AH..
AHH...

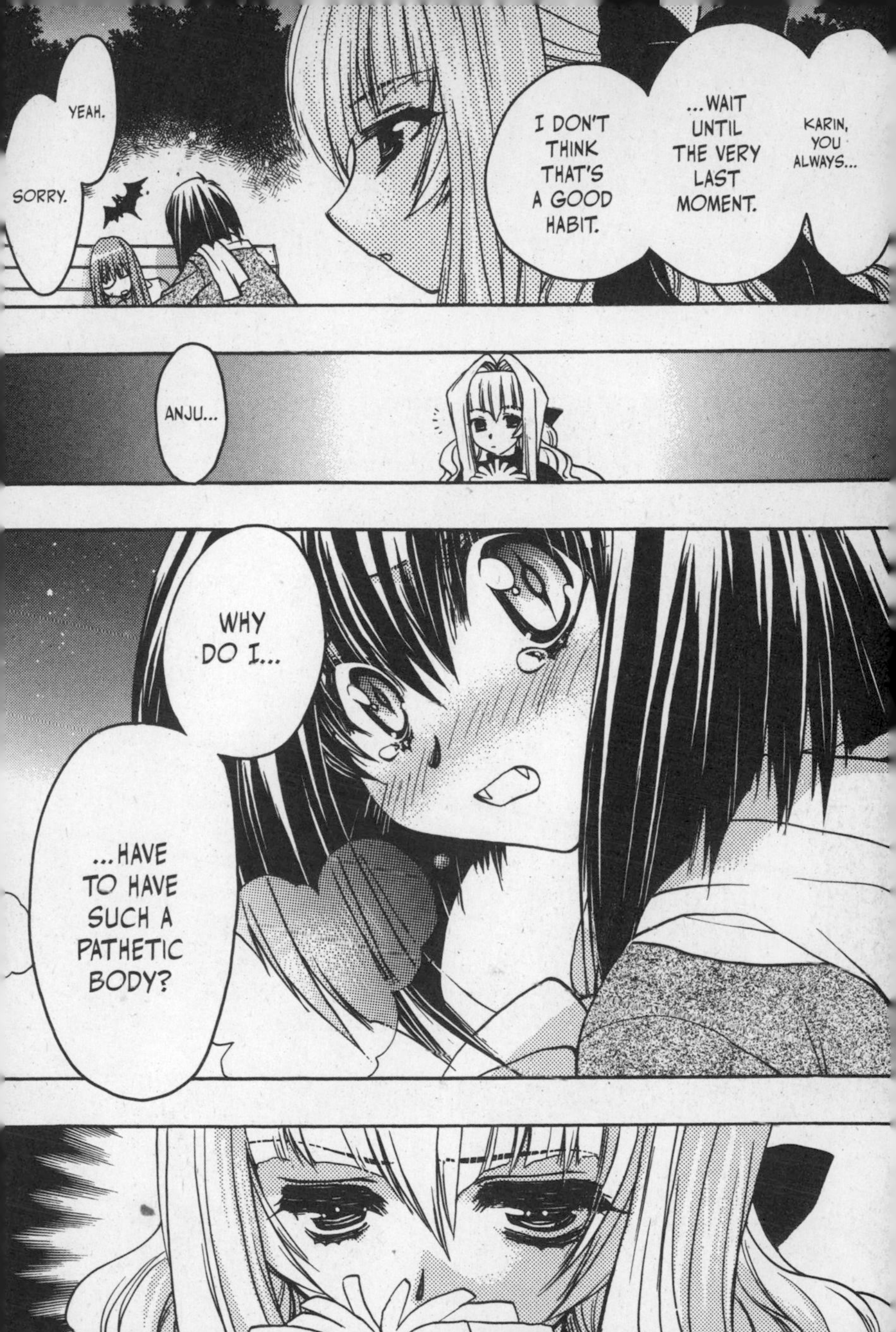
KARIN, YOU ALWAYS...
...WAIT UNTIL THE VERY LAST MOMENT.
I DON'T THINK THAT'S A GOOD HABIT.
YEAH.
SORRY.
ANJU...
WHY DO I...
...HAVE TO HAVE SUCH A PATHETIC BODY?

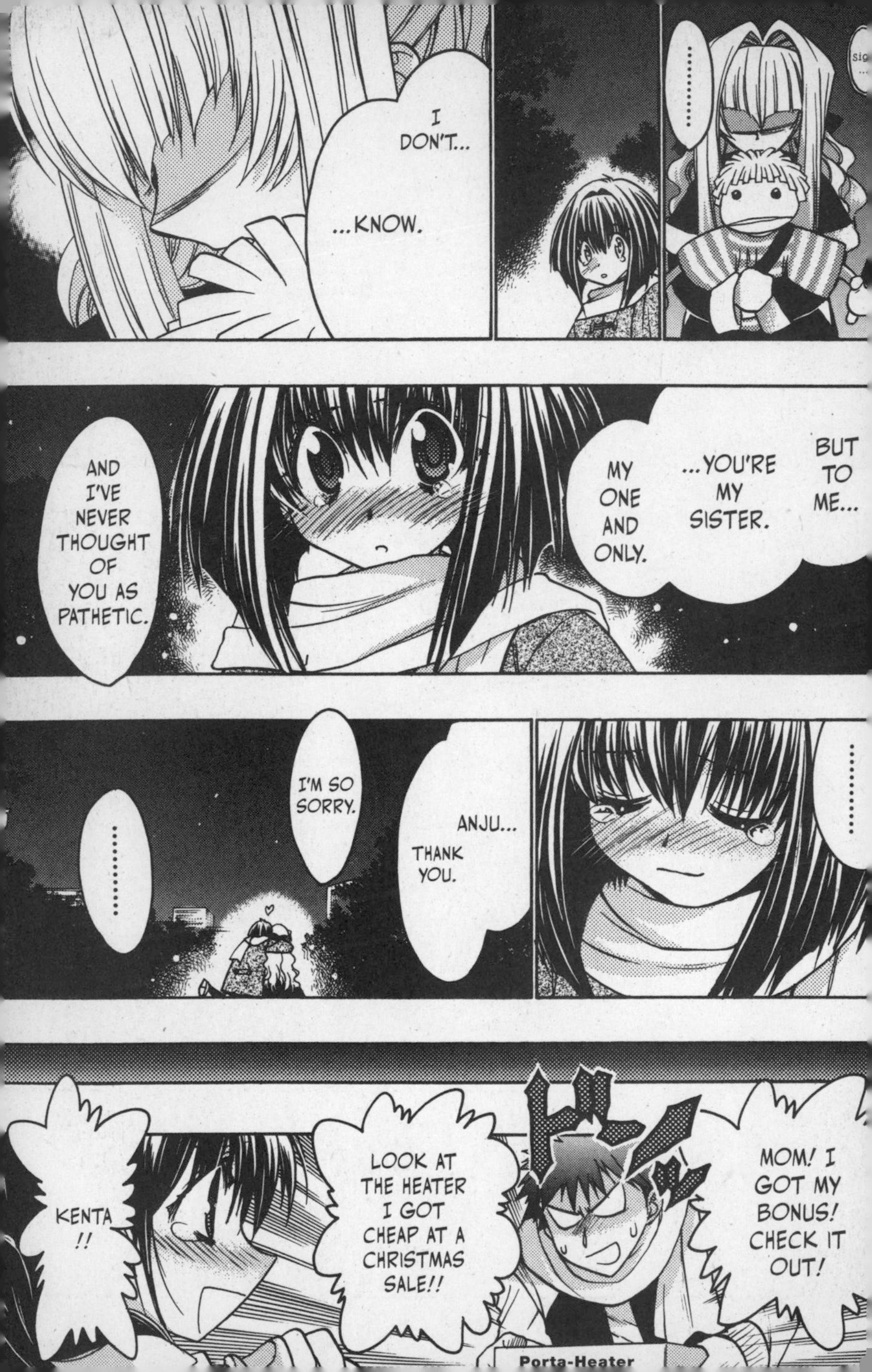
sig
...
......
I DON'T...
...KNOW.
BUT TO ME...
...YOU'RE MY SISTER.
MY ONE AND ONLY.
AND I'VE NEVER THOUGHT OF YOU AS PATHETIC.
......
ANJU...
THANK YOU.
I'M SO SORRY.
......
MOM! I GOT MY BONUS! CHECK IT OUT!
LOOK AT THE HEATER I GOT CHEAP AT A CHRISTMAS SALE!!
KENTA!!
Porta-Heater

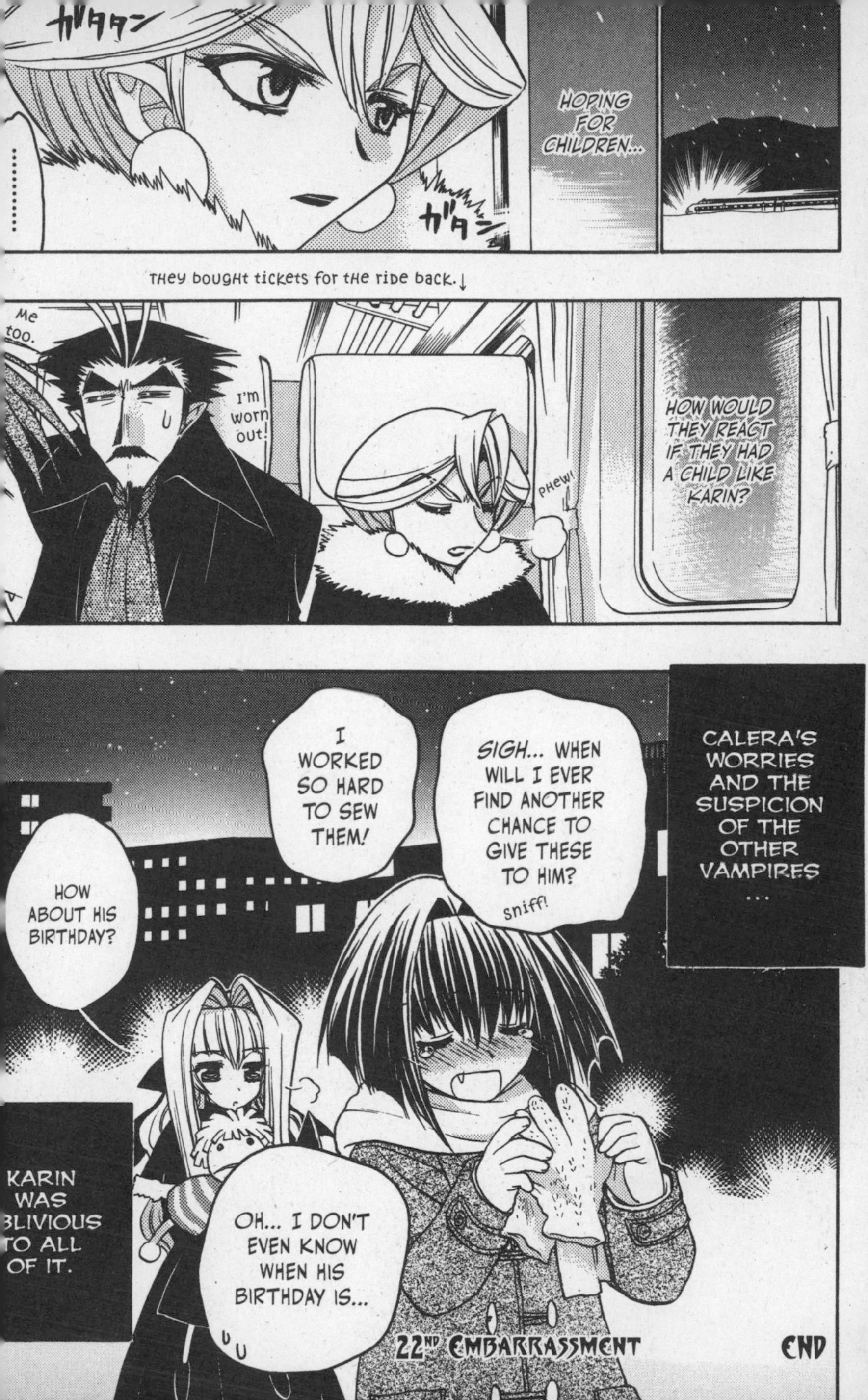
HOPING FOR CHILDREN...
ガタタン
ガタン
......
They bought tickets for the ride back.↓
HOW WOULD THEY REACT IF THEY HAD A CHILD LIKE KARIN?
PHEW!
I'm worn out!
Me too.
CALERA'S WORRIES AND THE SUSPICION OF THE OTHER VAMPIRES ...
SIGH... WHEN WILL I EVER FIND ANOTHER CHANCE TO GIVE THESE TO HIM?
sniff!
I WORKED SO HARD TO SEW THEM!
HOW ABOUT HIS BIRTHDAY?
OH... I DON'T EVEN KNOW WHEN HIS BIRTHDAY IS...
KARIN WAS BLIVIOUS TO ALL OF IT.
22ND EMBARRASSMENT
END

3RD Bonus Story) James' Lie and Calera's Pride

~Henry & Calera Special~

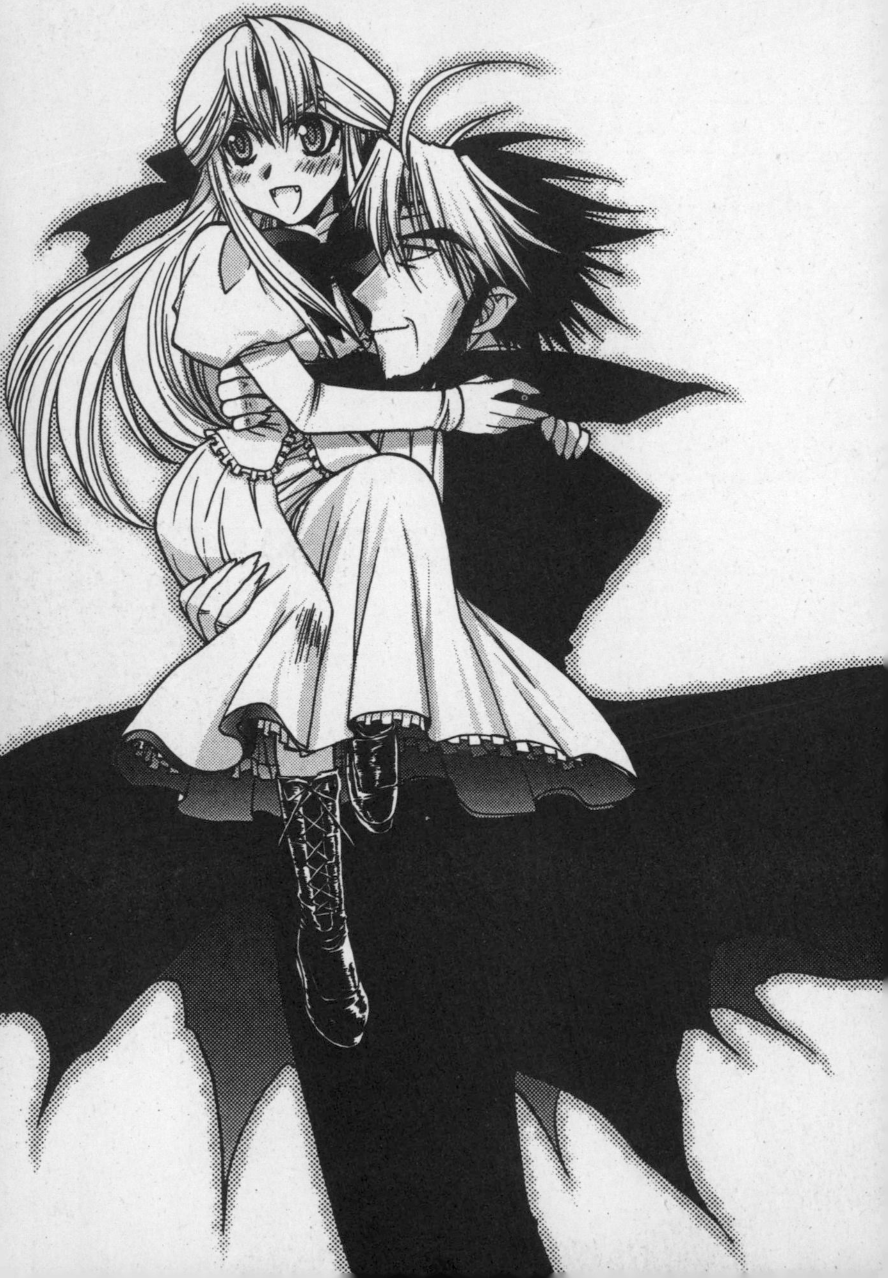

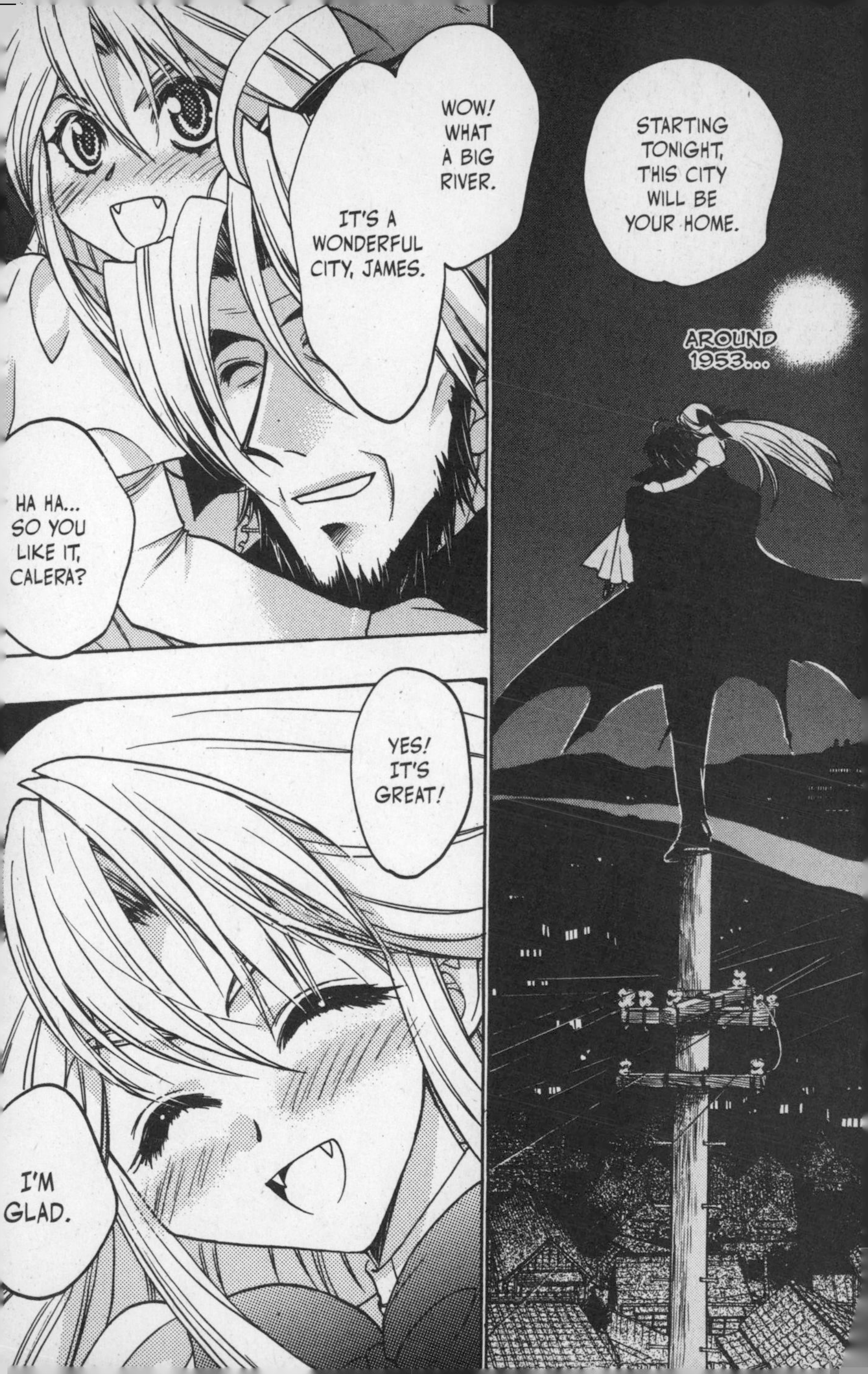
STARTING TONIGHT, THIS CITY WILL BE YOUR HOME.
AROUND 1953...
WOW! WHAT A BIG RIVER.
IT'S A WONDERFUL CITY, JAMES.
HA HA... SO YOU LIKE IT, CALERA?
YES! IT'S GREAT!
I'M GLAD.

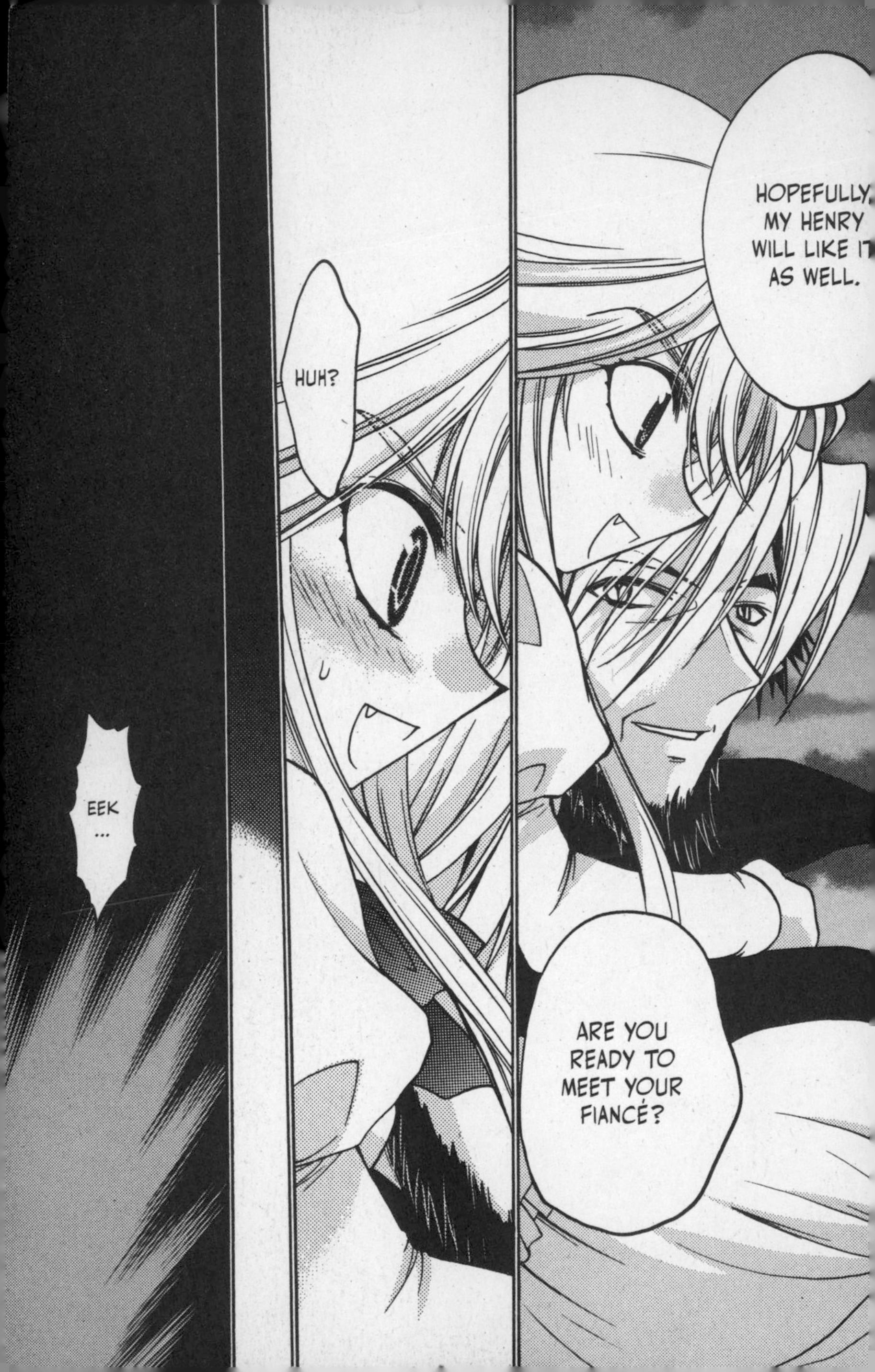
HOPEFULLY, MY HENRY WILL LIKE IT AS WELL.
ARE YOU READY TO MEET YOUR FIANCÉ?
HUH?
EEK ...

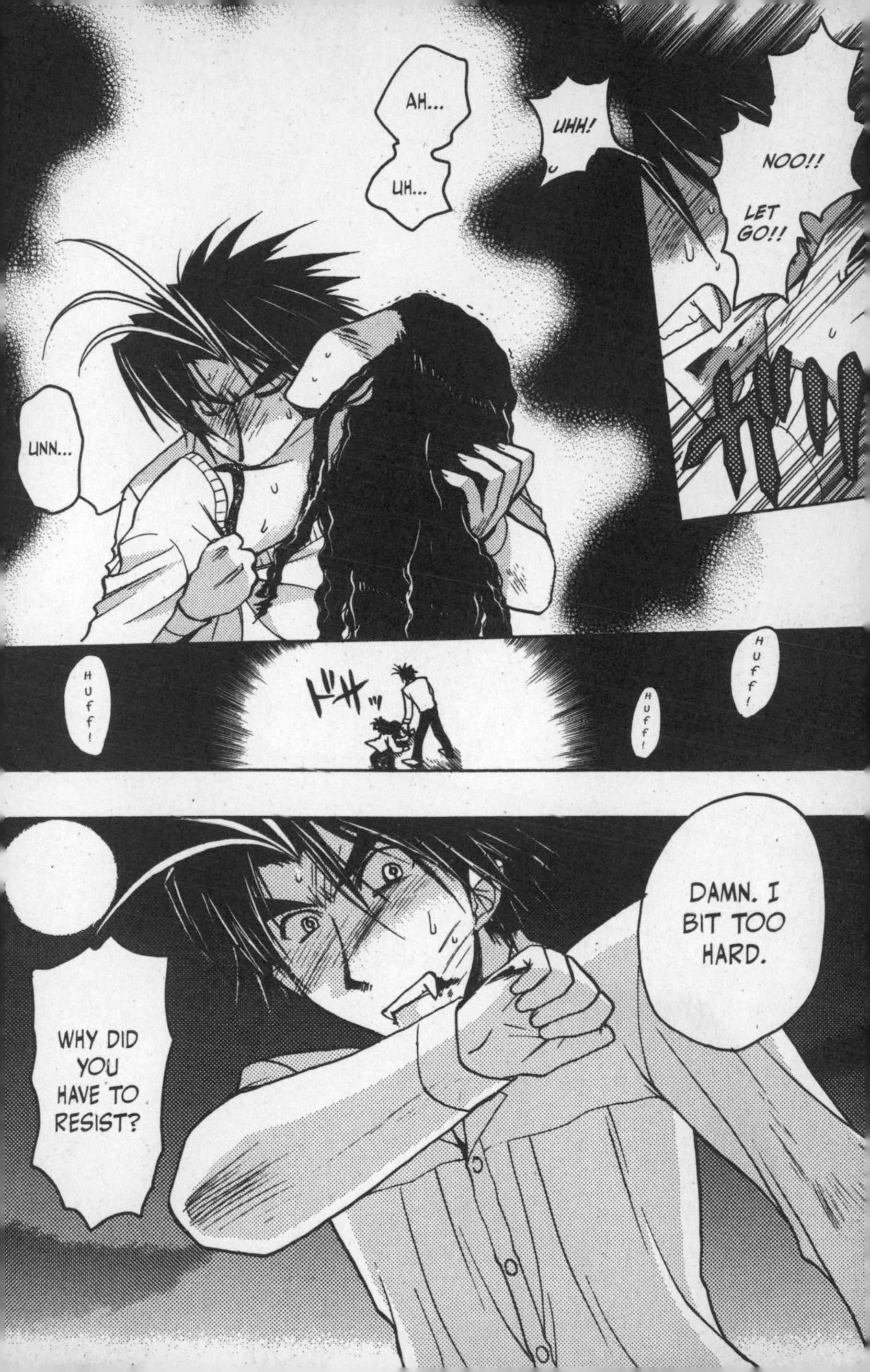
UHH!
NOO!!
LET GO!!
AH...
UH...
UNN...
HUFF!
HUFF!
ドサッ
HUFF!
DAMN. I BIT TOO HARD.
WHY DID YOU HAVE TO RESIST?

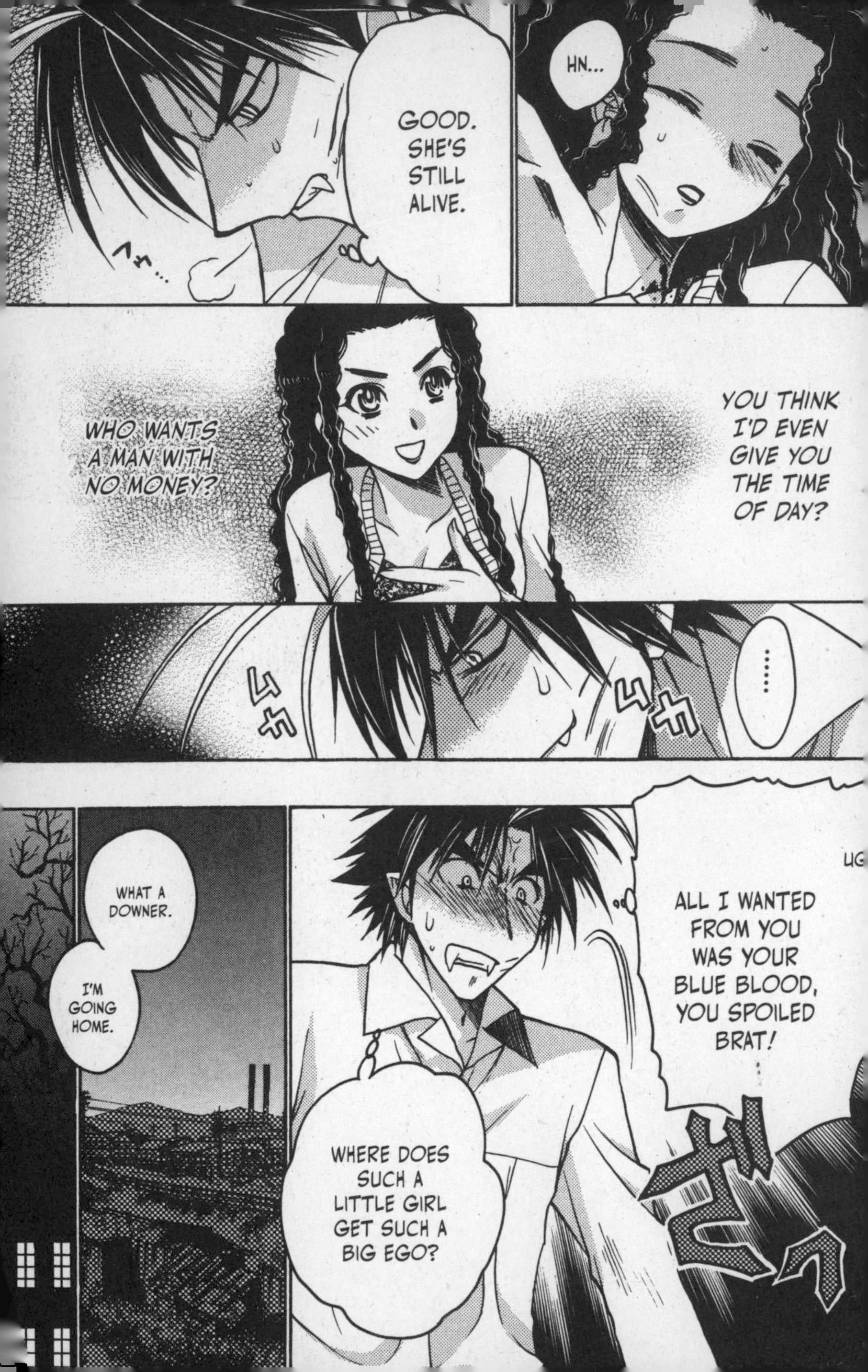
HN...
GOOD. SHE'S STILL ALIVE.
YOU THINK I'D EVEN GIVE YOU THE TIME OF DAY?
WHO WANTS A MAN WITH NO MONEY?
......
ムカ
ムカ
UG
ALL I WANTED FROM YOU WAS YOUR BLUE BLOOD, YOU SPOILED BRAT!
WHERE DOES SUCH A LITTLE GIRL GET SUCH A BIG EGO?
WHAT A DOWNER.
I'M GOING HOME.

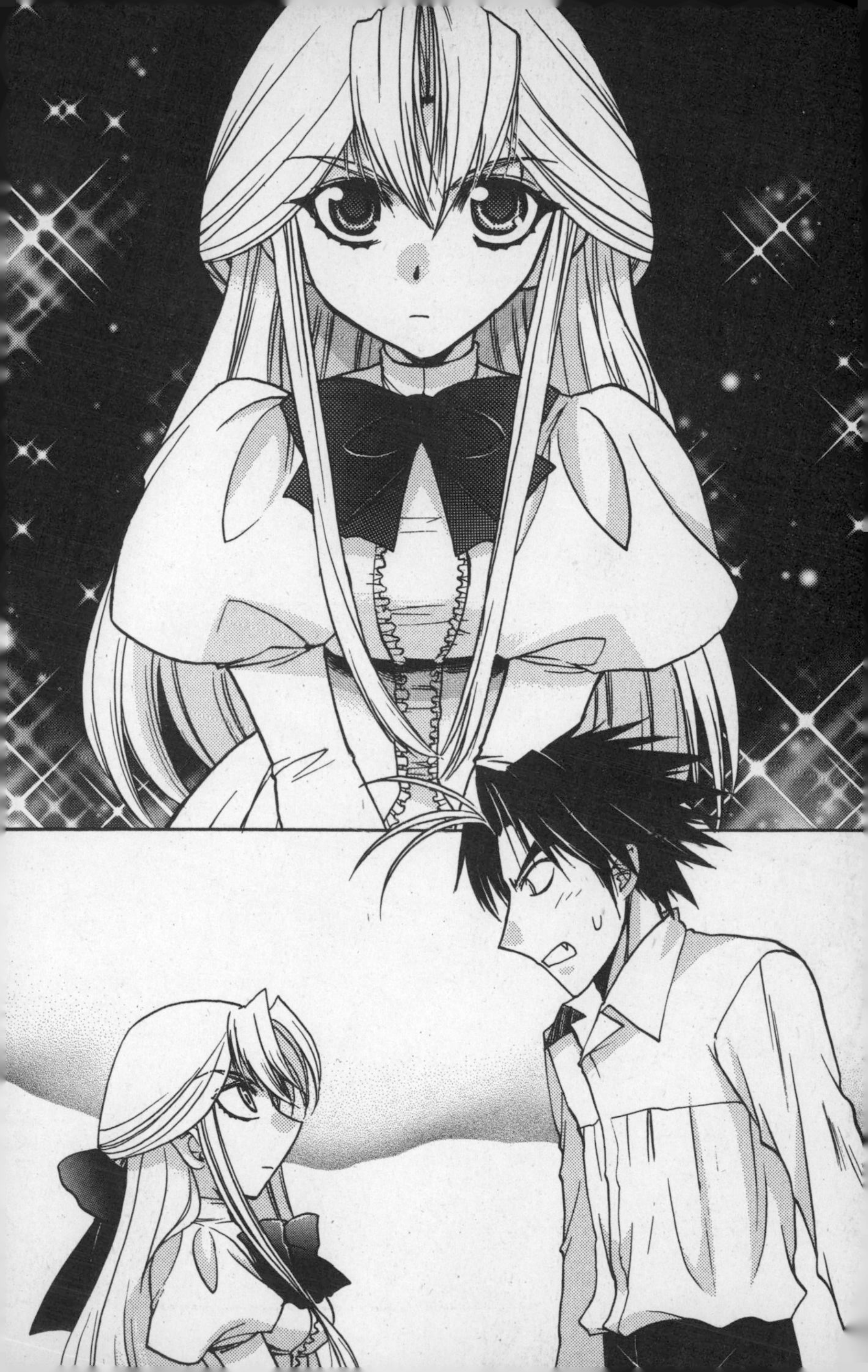

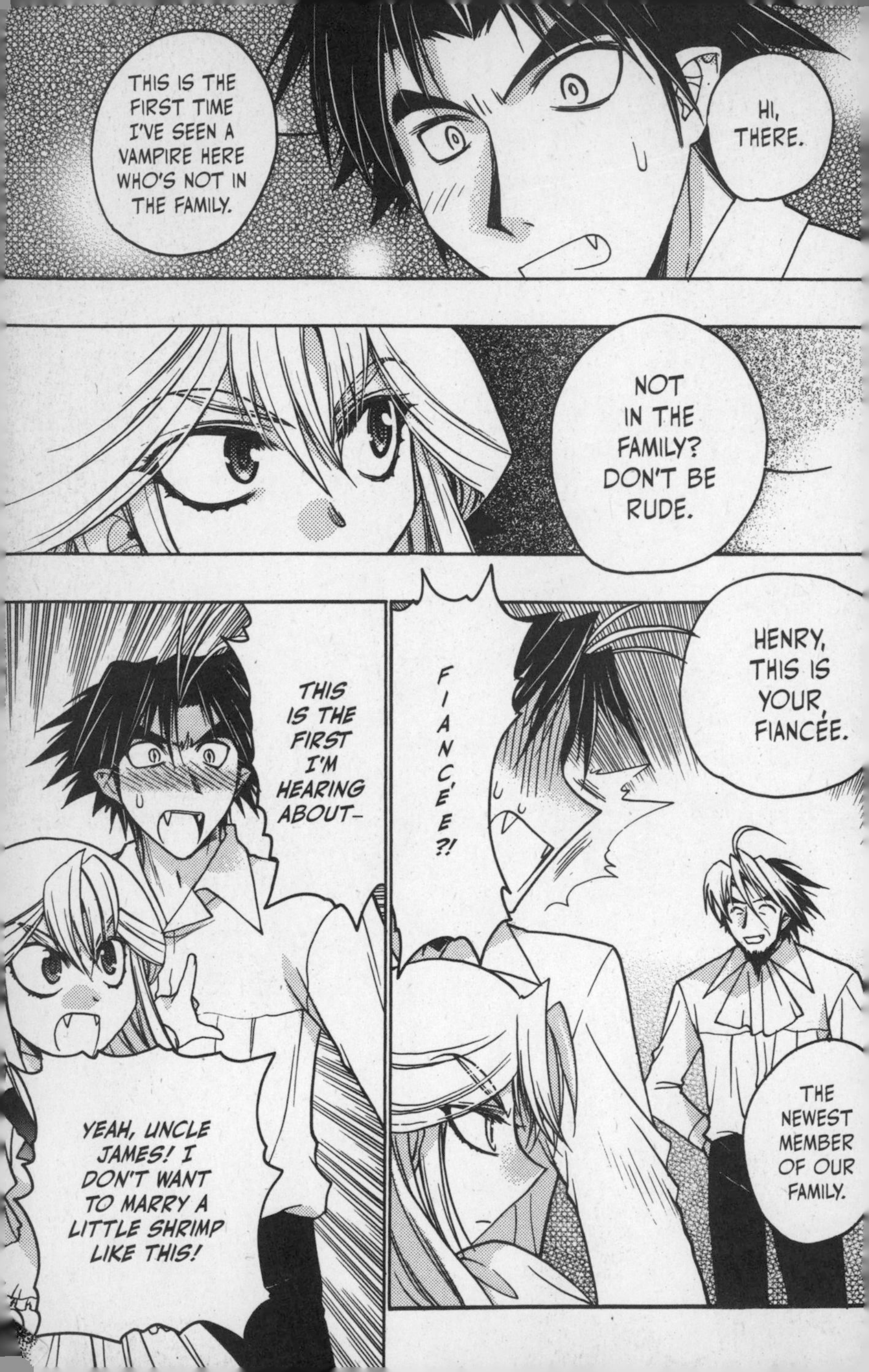
HI, THERE.
THIS IS THE FIRST TIME I'VE SEEN A VAMPIRE HERE WHO'S NOT IN THE FAMILY.
NOT IN THE FAMILY? DON'T BE RUDE.
HENRY, THIS IS YOUR FIANCÉE.
FIANCÉE?!
THE NEWEST MEMBER OF OUR FAMILY.
THIS IS THE FIRST I'M HEARING ABOUT-
YEAH, UNCLE JAMES! I DON'T WANT TO MARRY A LITTLE SHRIMP LIKE THIS!

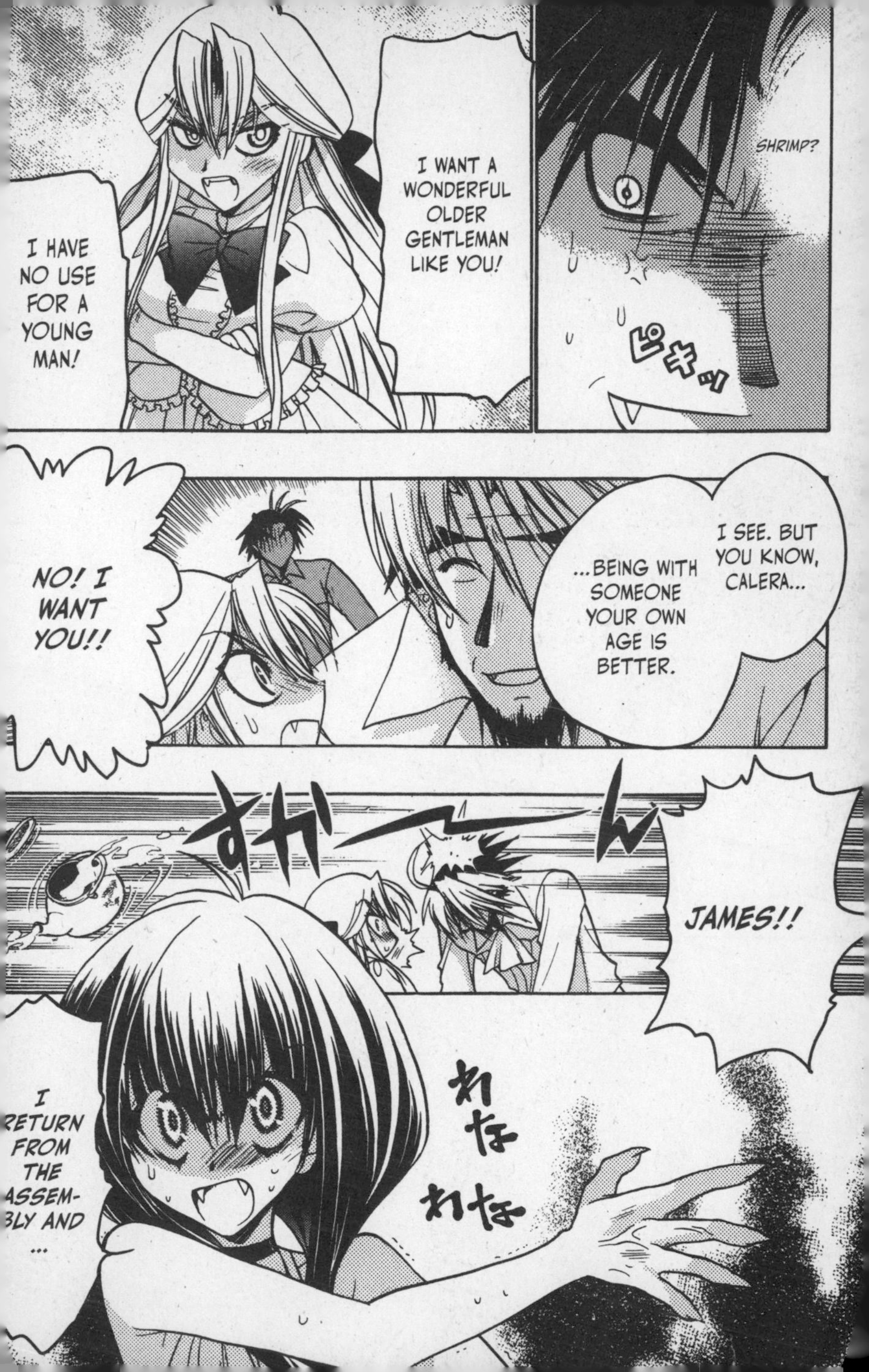
SHRIMP?
ピキッ
I WANT A WONDERFUL OLDER GENTLEMAN LIKE YOU!
I HAVE NO USE FOR A YOUNG MAN!
I SEE. BUT YOU KNOW, CALERA...
...BEING WITH SOMEONE YOUR OWN AGE IS BETTER.
NO! I WANT YOU!!
JAMES!!
I RETURN FROM THE ASSEM-BLY AND ...

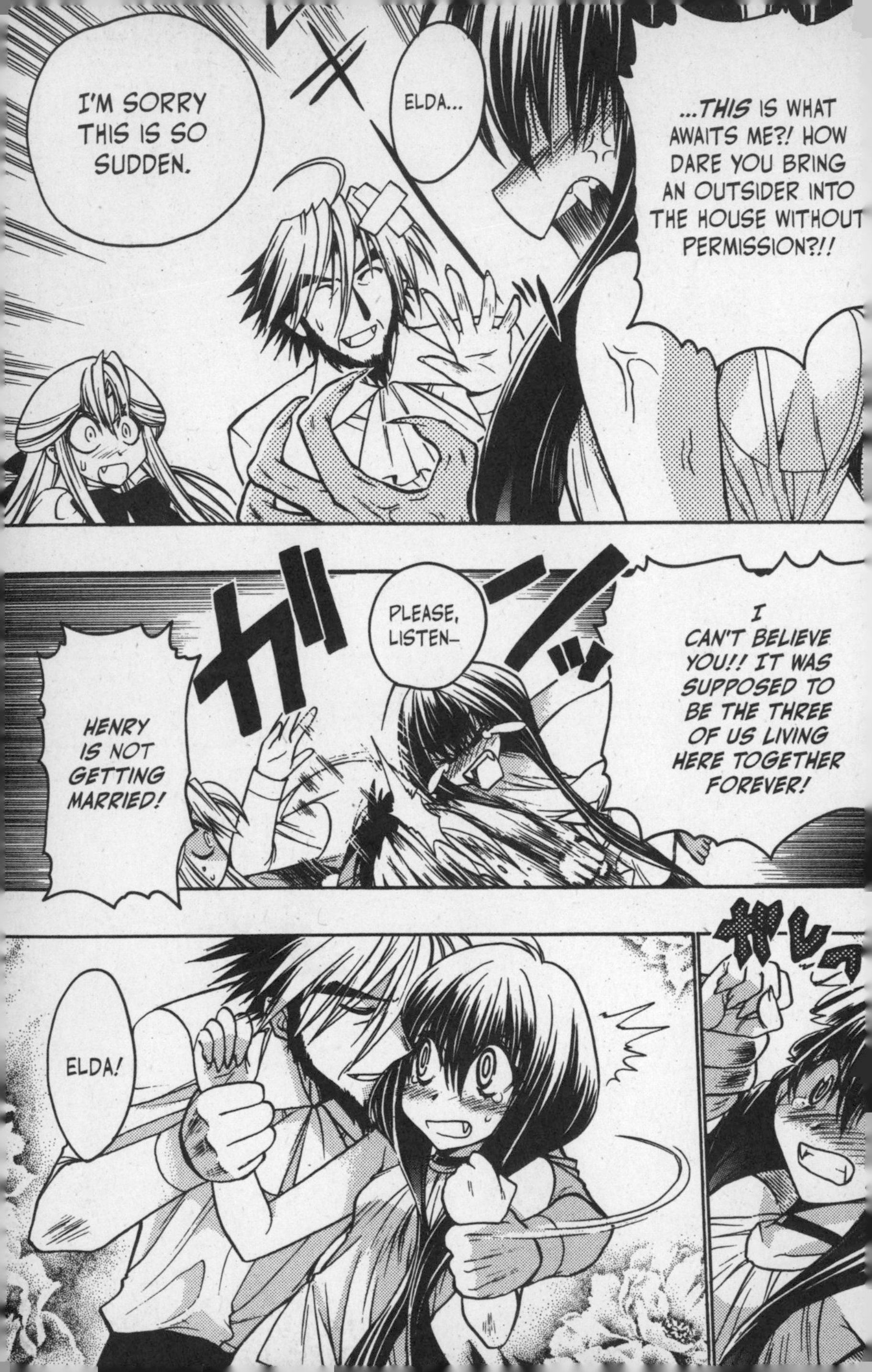
...THIS IS WHAT AWAITS ME?! HOW DARE YOU BRING AN OUTSIDER INTO THE HOUSE WITHOUT PERMISSION?!!
ELDA...
I'M SORRY THIS IS SO SUDDEN.
I CAN'T BELIEVE YOU!! IT WAS SUPPOSED TO BE THE THREE OF US LIVING HERE TOGETHER FOREVER!
PLEASE, LISTEN–
HENRY IS NOT GETTING MARRIED!
ELDA!

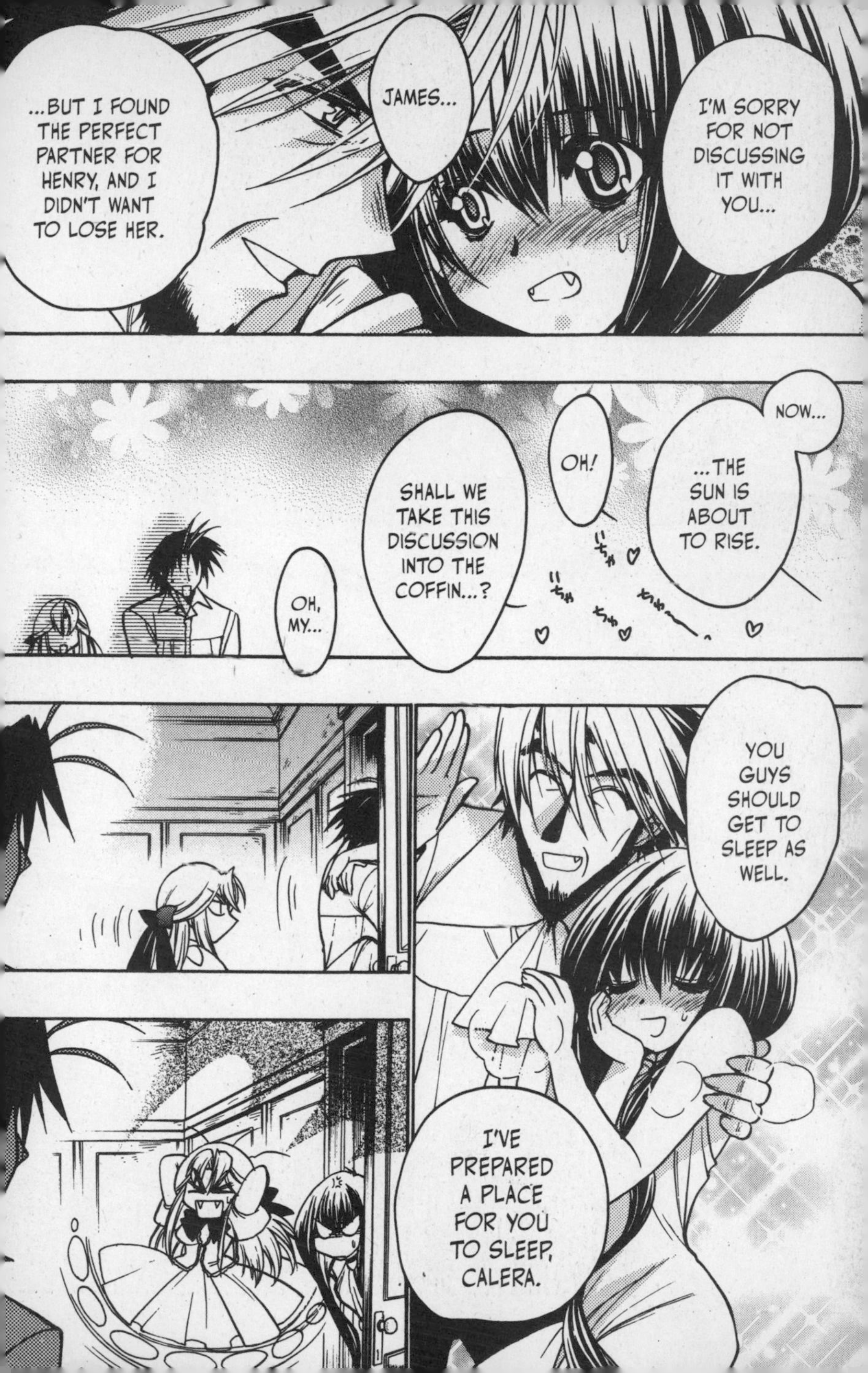
I'M SORRY FOR NOT DISCUSSING IT WITH YOU...
JAMES...
...BUT I FOUND THE PERFECT PARTNER FOR HENRY, AND I DIDN'T WANT TO LOSE HER.
NOW...
...THE SUN IS ABOUT TO RISE.
OH!
SHALL WE TAKE THIS DISCUSSION INTO THE COFFIN...?
OH, MY...
YOU GUYS SHOULD GET TO SLEEP AS WELL.
I'VE PREPARED A PLACE FOR YOU TO SLEEP, CALERA.

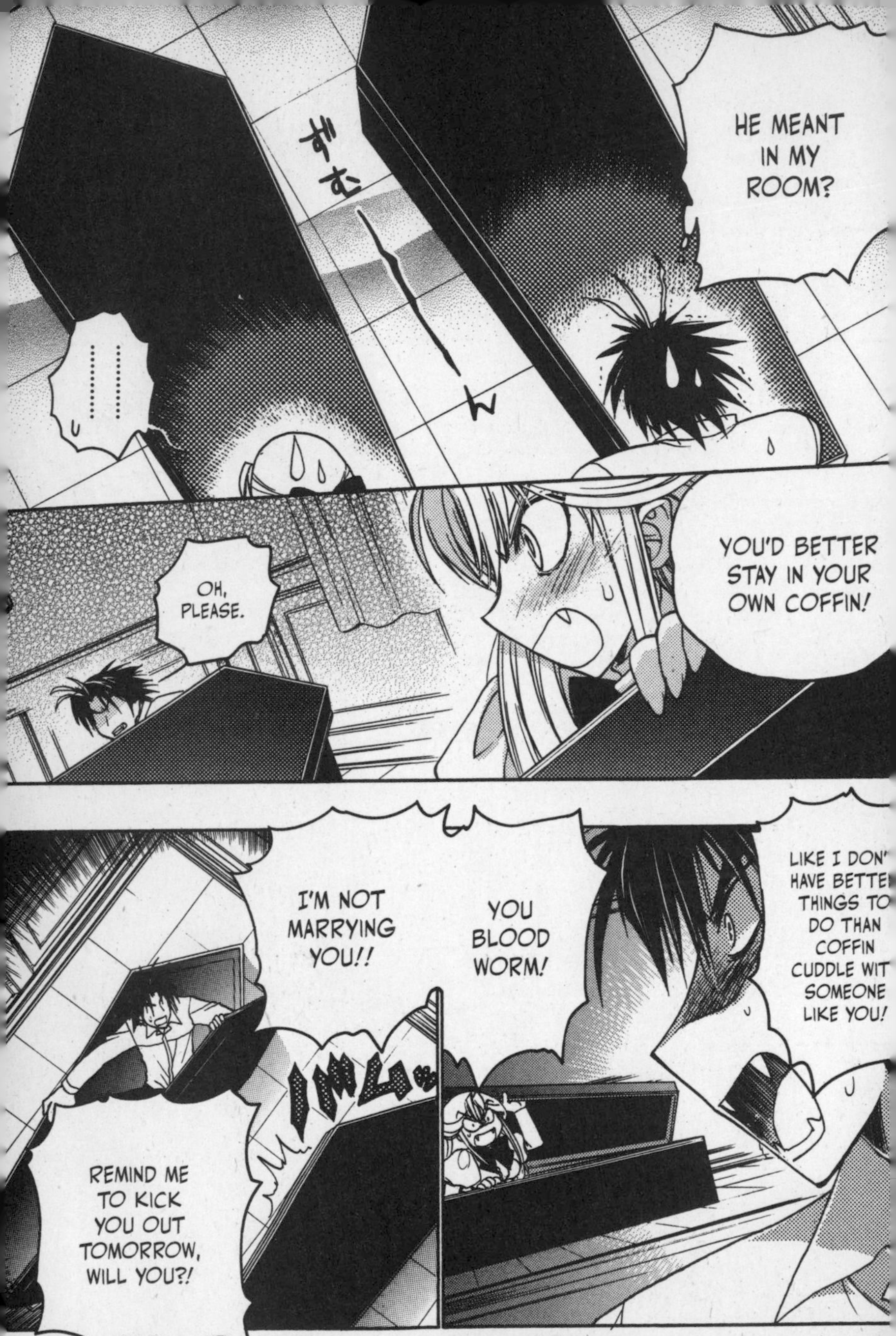
HE MEANT IN MY ROOM?
ずむーーん
……
YOU'D BETTER STAY IN YOUR OWN COFFIN!
OH, PLEASE.
LIKE I DON' HAVE BETTE THINGS TO DO THAN COFFIN CUDDLE WIT SOMEONE LIKE YOU!
YOU BLOOD WORM!
I'M NOT MARRYING YOU!!
REMIND ME TO KICK YOU OUT TOMORROW, WILL YOU?!

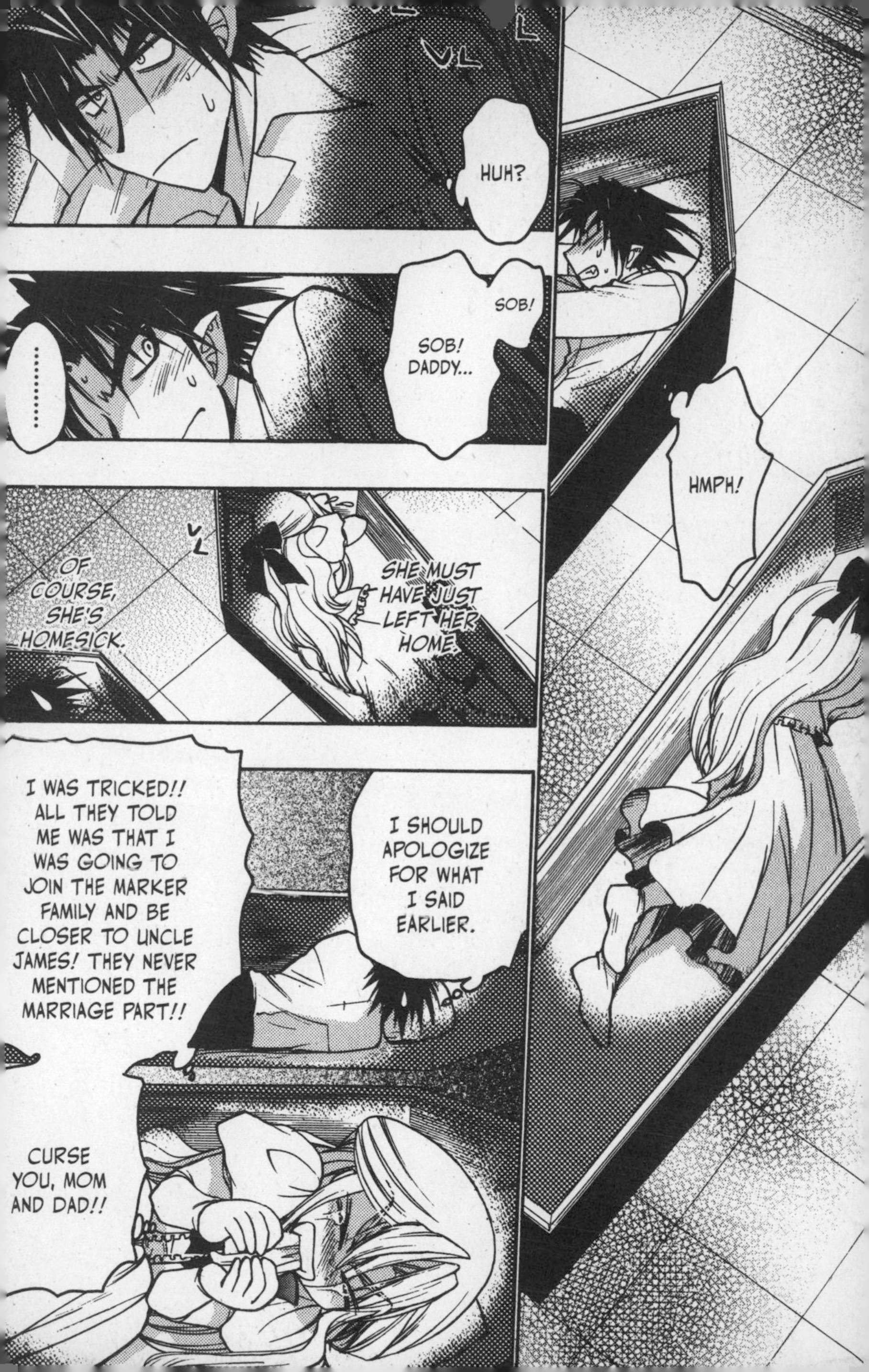
HMPH!
HUH?
SOB! SOB! DADDY...
......
SHE MUST HAVE JUST LEFT HER HOME.
OF COURSE, SHE'S HOMESICK.
I SHOULD APOLOGIZE FOR WHAT I SAID EARLIER.
I WAS TRICKED!! ALL THEY TOLD ME WAS THAT I WAS GOING TO JOIN THE MARKER FAMILY AND BE CLOSER TO UNCLE JAMES! THEY NEVER MENTIONED THE MARRIAGE PART!!
CURSE YOU, MOM AND DAD!!

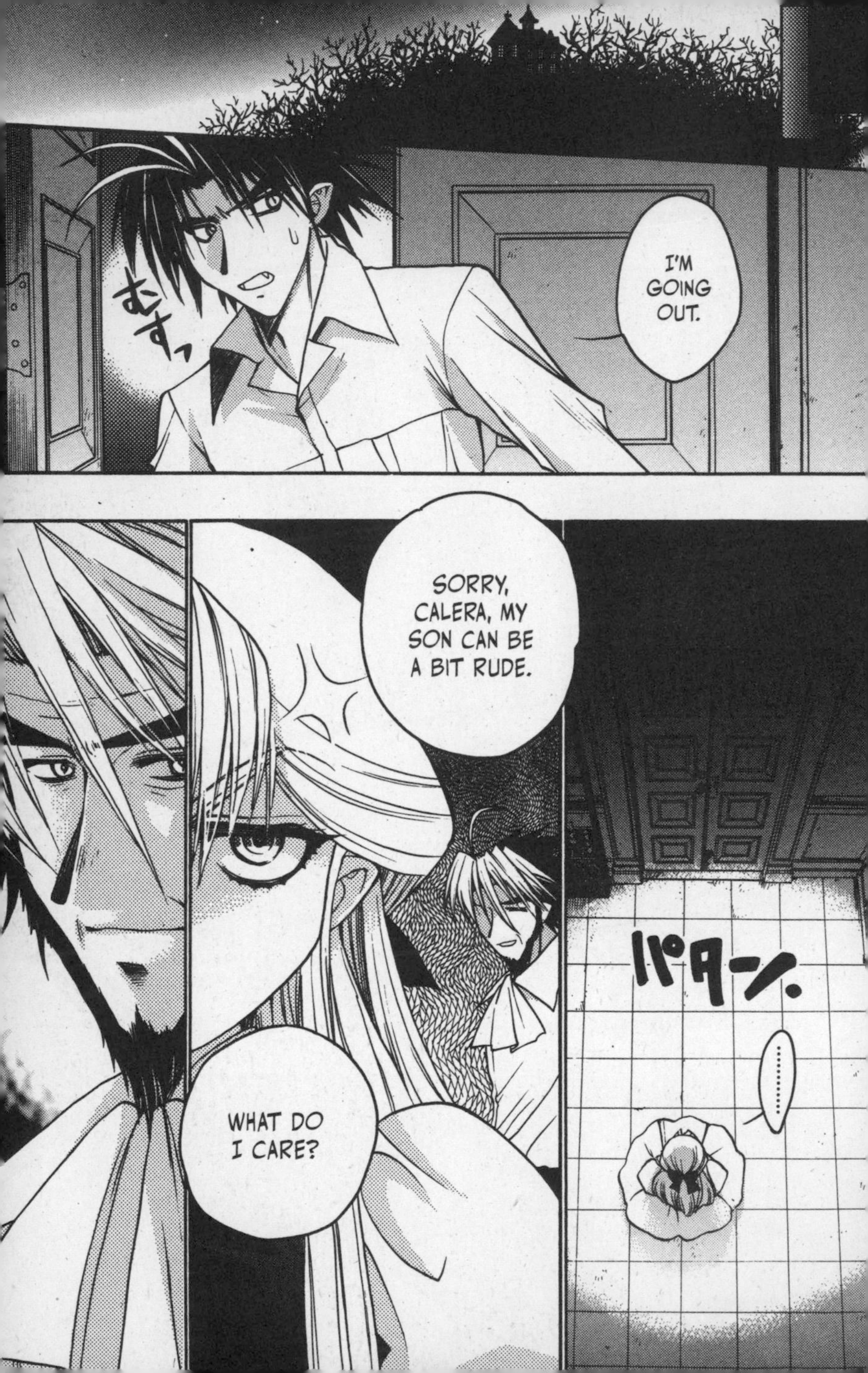
I'M GOING OUT.
むすっ
パターン
......
SORRY, CALERA, MY SON CAN BE A BIT RUDE.
WHAT DO I CARE?

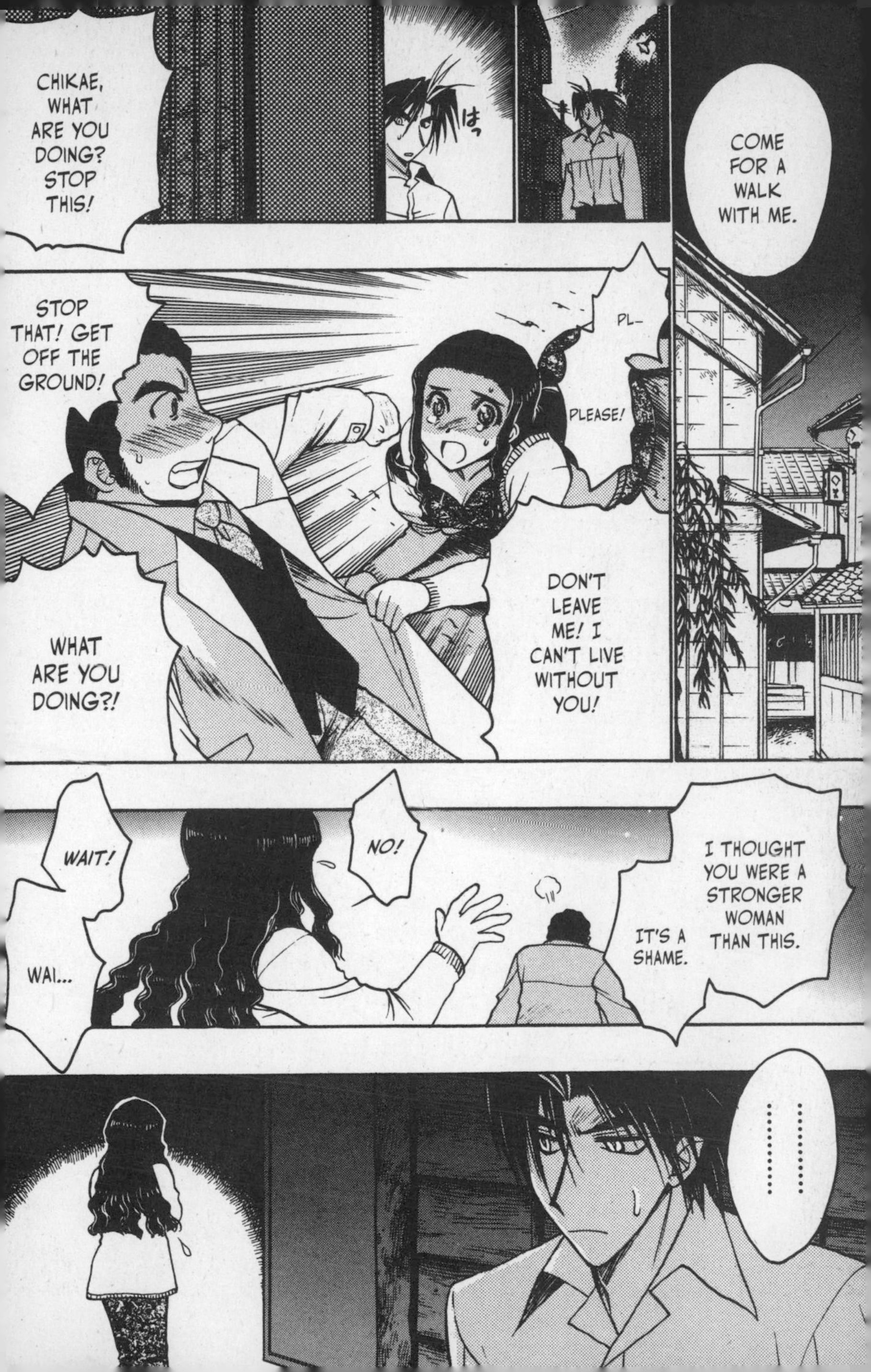
COME FOR A WALK WITH ME.
はっ
CHIKAE, WHAT ARE YOU DOING? STOP THIS!
PL—
PLEASE!
DON'T LEAVE ME! I CAN'T LIVE WITHOUT YOU!
STOP THAT! GET OFF THE GROUND!
WHAT ARE YOU DOING?!
I THOUGHT YOU WERE A STRONGER WOMAN THAN THIS.
IT'S A SHAME.
NO!
WAIT!
WAI...
......

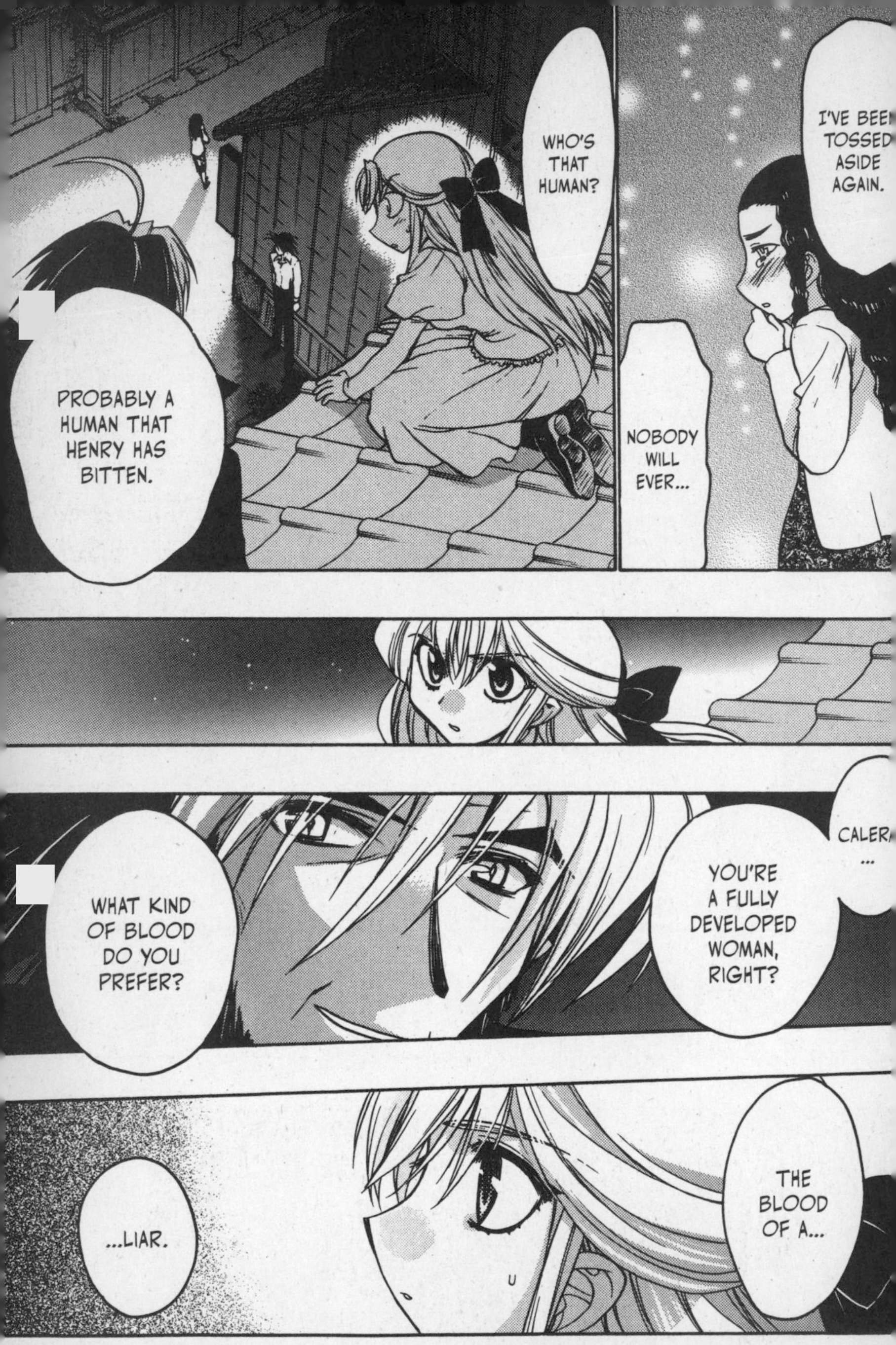
I'VE BEE TOSSED ASIDE AGAIN.
NOBODY WILL EVER...
WHO'S THAT HUMAN?
PROBABLY A HUMAN THAT HENRY HAS BITTEN.
CALER ...
YOU'RE A FULLY DEVELOPED WOMAN, RIGHT?
WHAT KIND OF BLOOD DO YOU PREFER?
THE BLOOD OF A...
...LIAR.

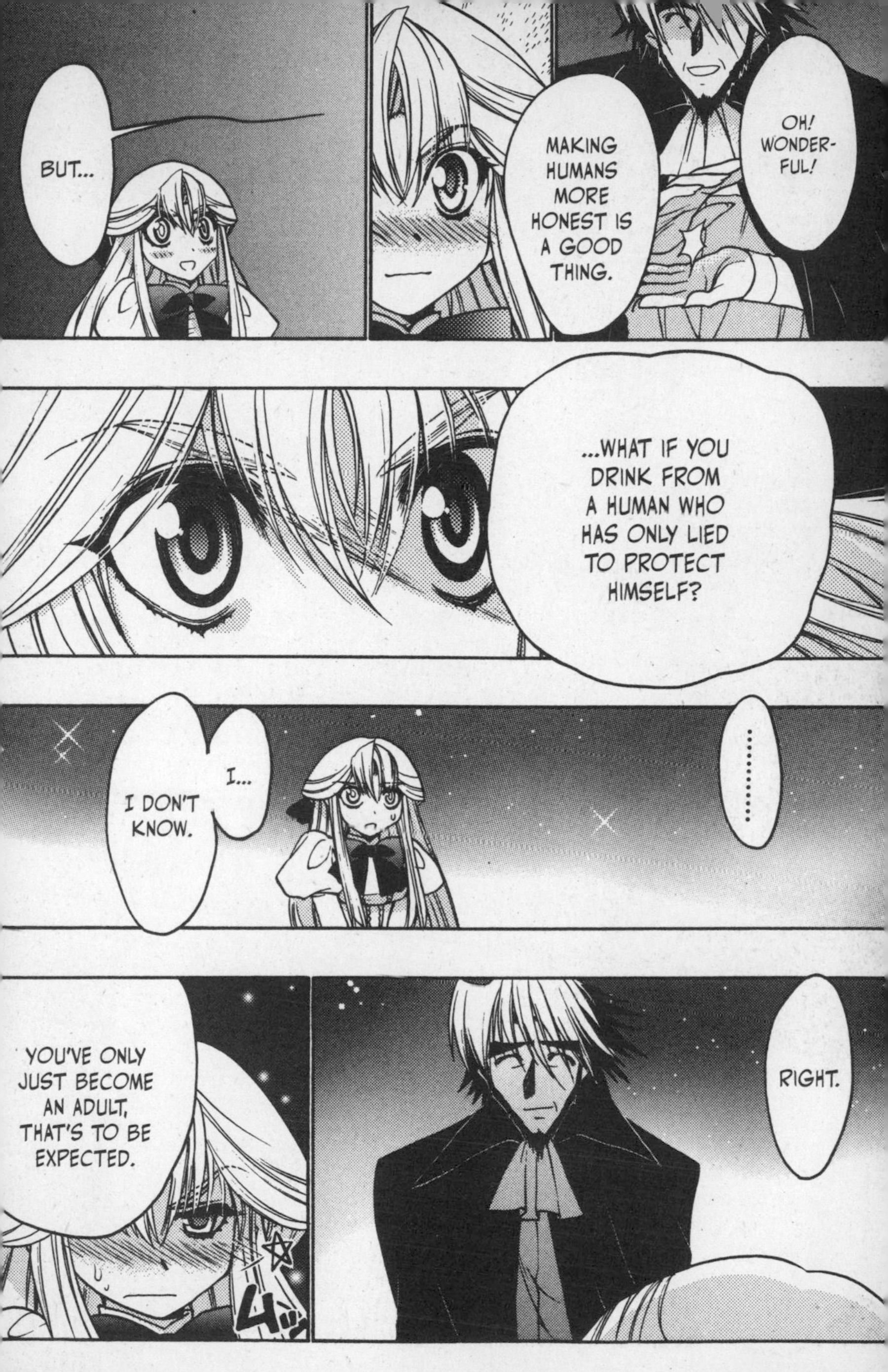
OH! WONDERFUL!
MAKING HUMANS MORE HONEST IS A GOOD THING.
BUT...
...WHAT IF YOU DRINK FROM A HUMAN WHO HAS ONLY LIED TO PROTECT HIMSELF?
......
I... I DON'T KNOW.
RIGHT.
YOU'VE ONLY JUST BECOME AN ADULT, THAT'S TO BE EXPECTED.

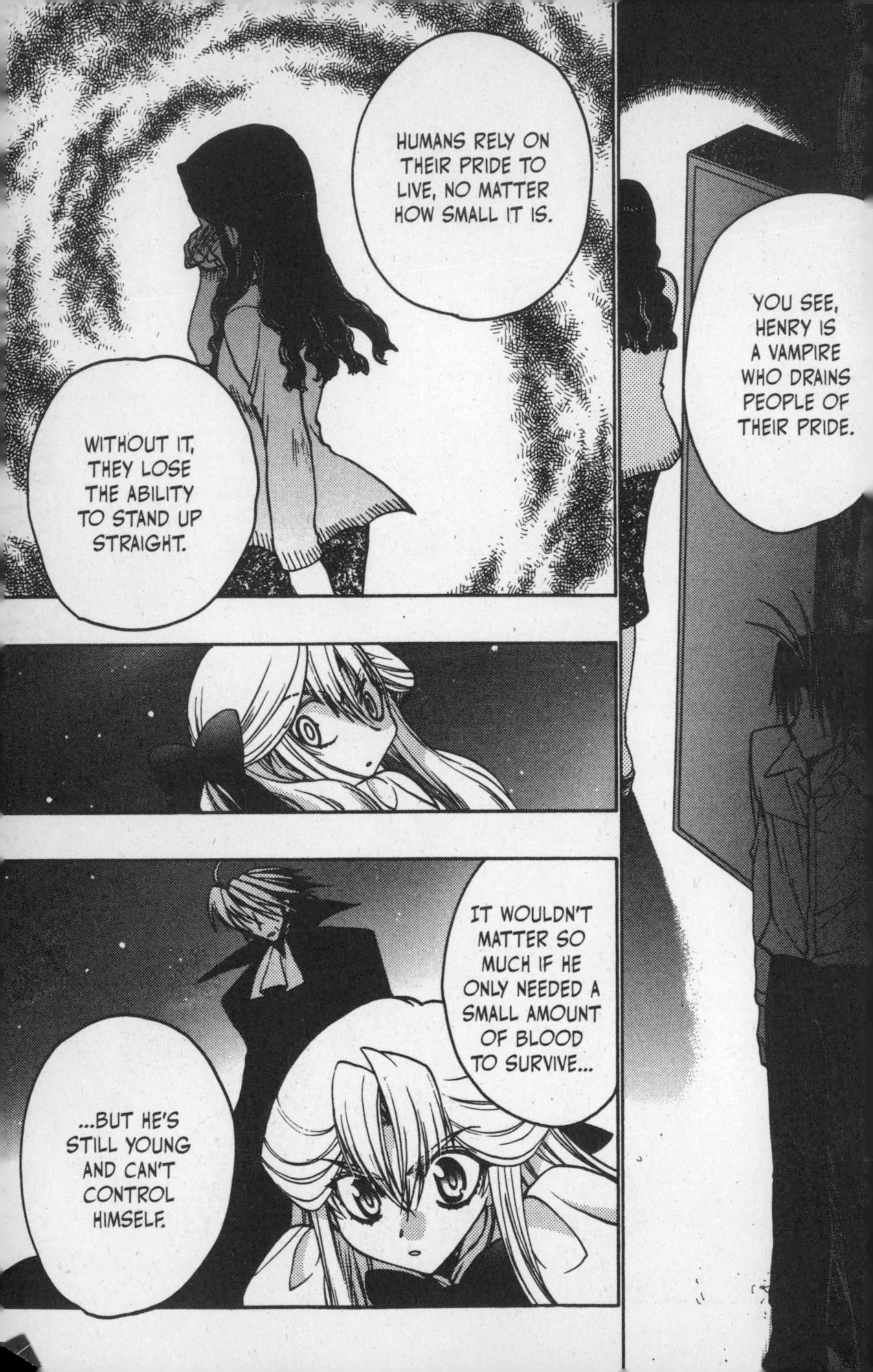
YOU SEE, HENRY IS A VAMPIRE WHO DRAINS PEOPLE OF THEIR PRIDE.
HUMANS RELY ON THEIR PRIDE TO LIVE, NO MATTER HOW SMALL IT IS.
WITHOUT IT, THEY LOSE THE ABILITY TO STAND UP STRAIGHT.
IT WOULDN'T MATTER SO MUCH IF HE ONLY NEEDED A SMALL AMOUNT OF BLOOD TO SURVIVE...
...BUT HE'S STILL YOUNG AND CAN'T CONTROL HIMSELF.

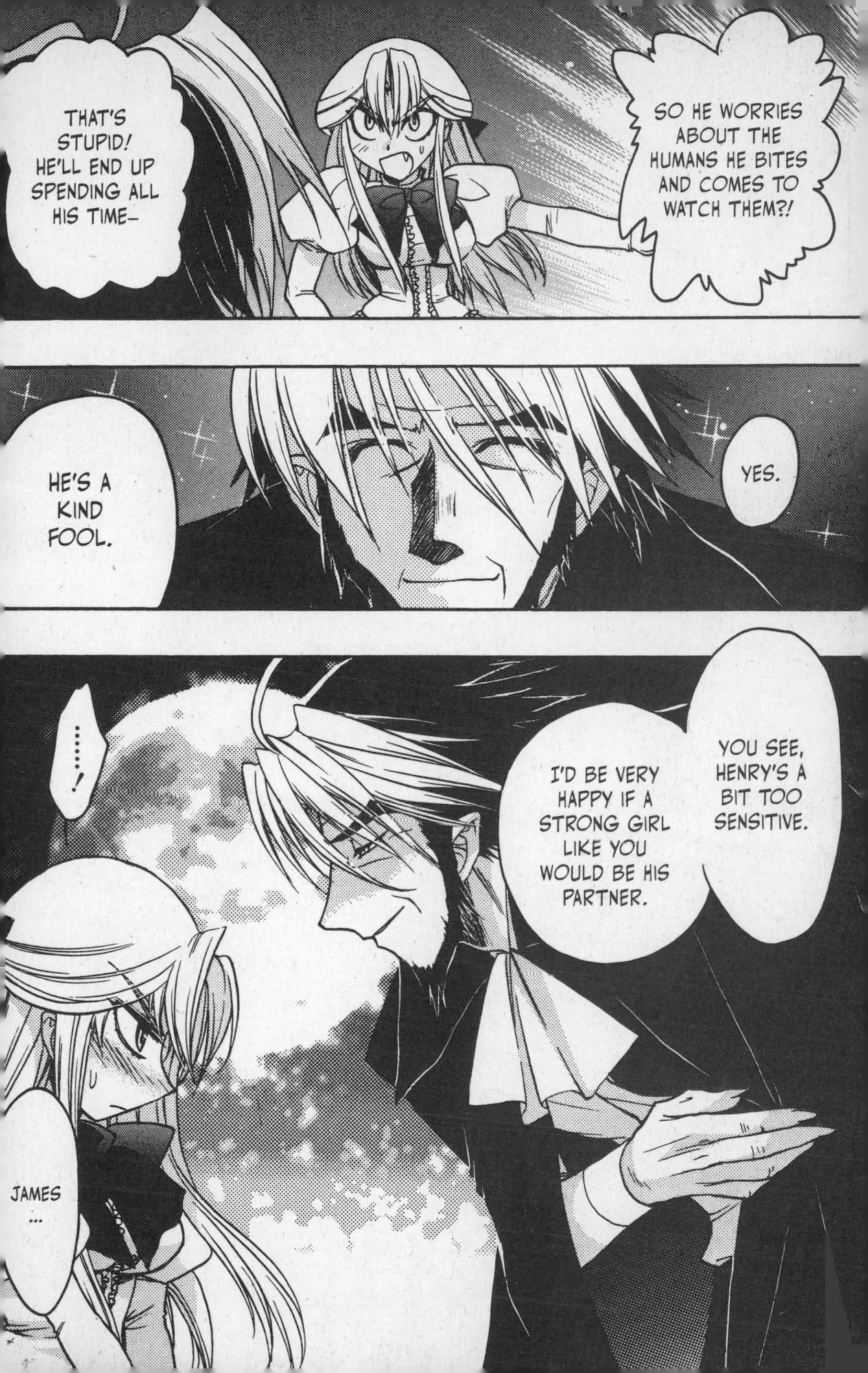
SO HE WORRIES ABOUT THE HUMANS HE BITES AND COMES TO WATCH THEM?!
THAT'S STUPID! HE'LL END UP SPENDING ALL HIS TIME–
YES.
HE'S A KIND FOOL.
YOU SEE, HENRY'S A BIT TOO SENSITIVE.
I'D BE VERY HAPPY IF A STRONG GIRL LIKE YOU WOULD BE HIS PARTNER.
......!
JAMES ...

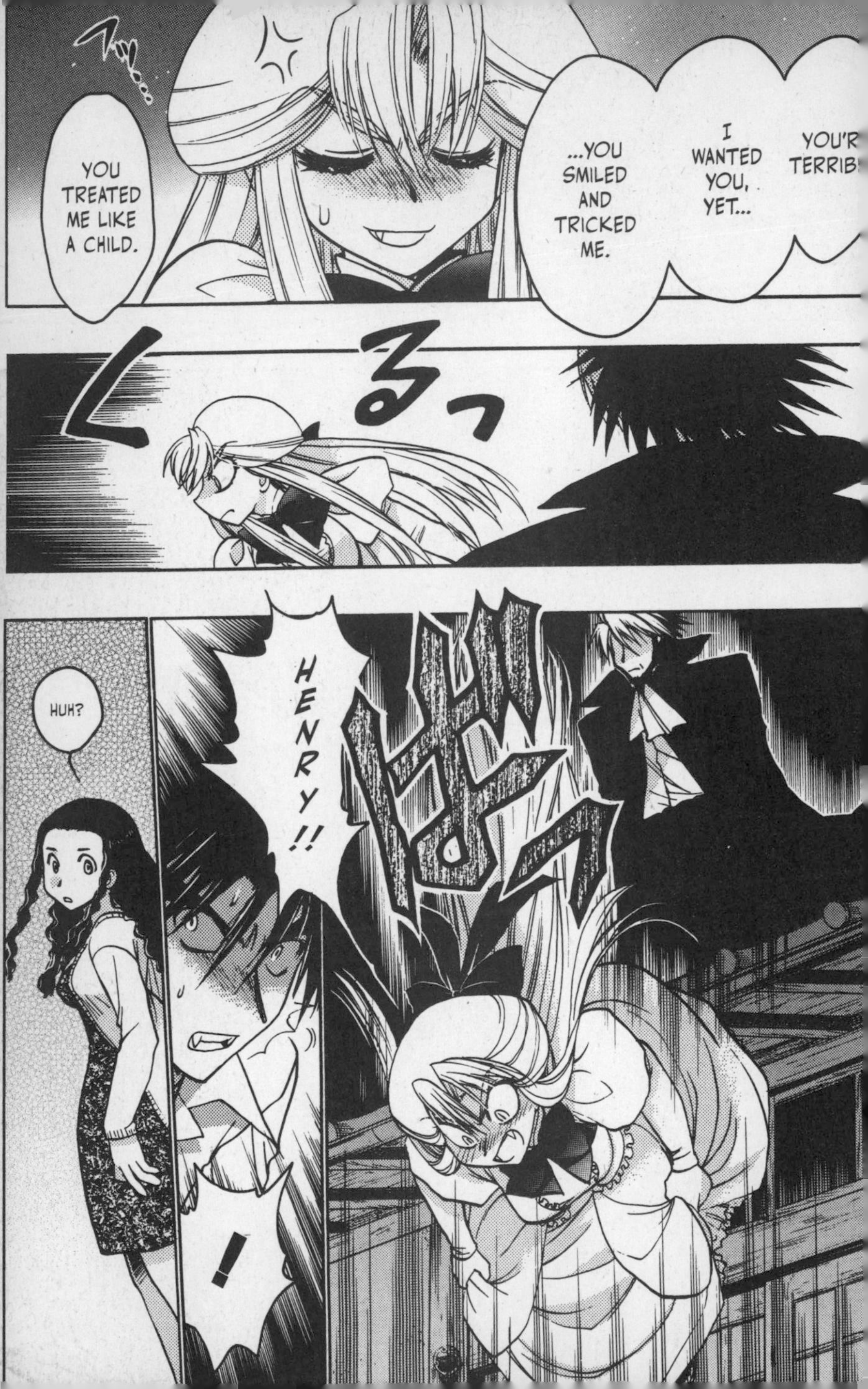
YOU'R TERRIB
I WANTED YOU, YET...
...YOU SMILED AND TRICKED ME.
YOU TREATED ME LIKE A CHILD.
くるっ
HENRY!!
!
HUH?

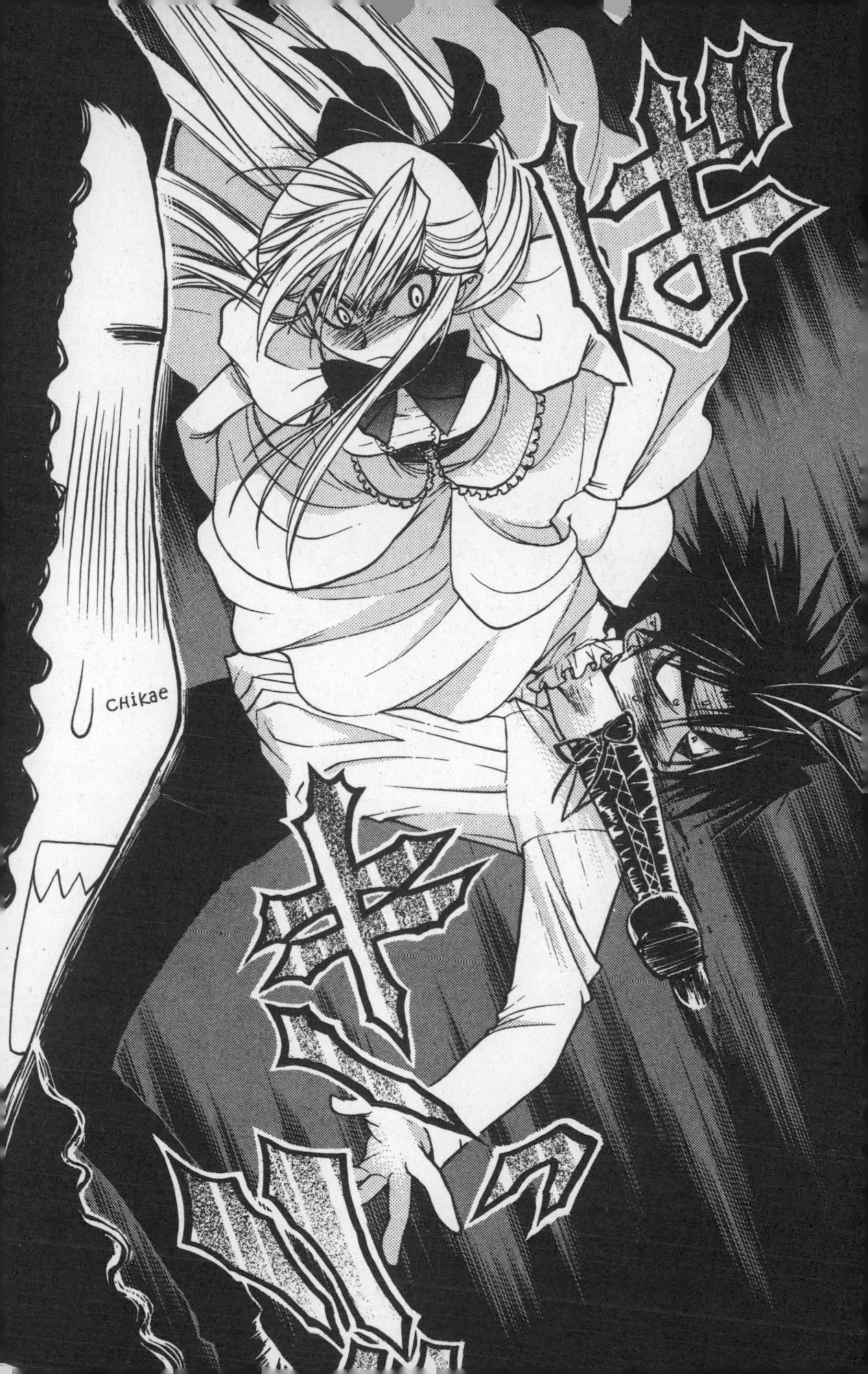
CHIKAE

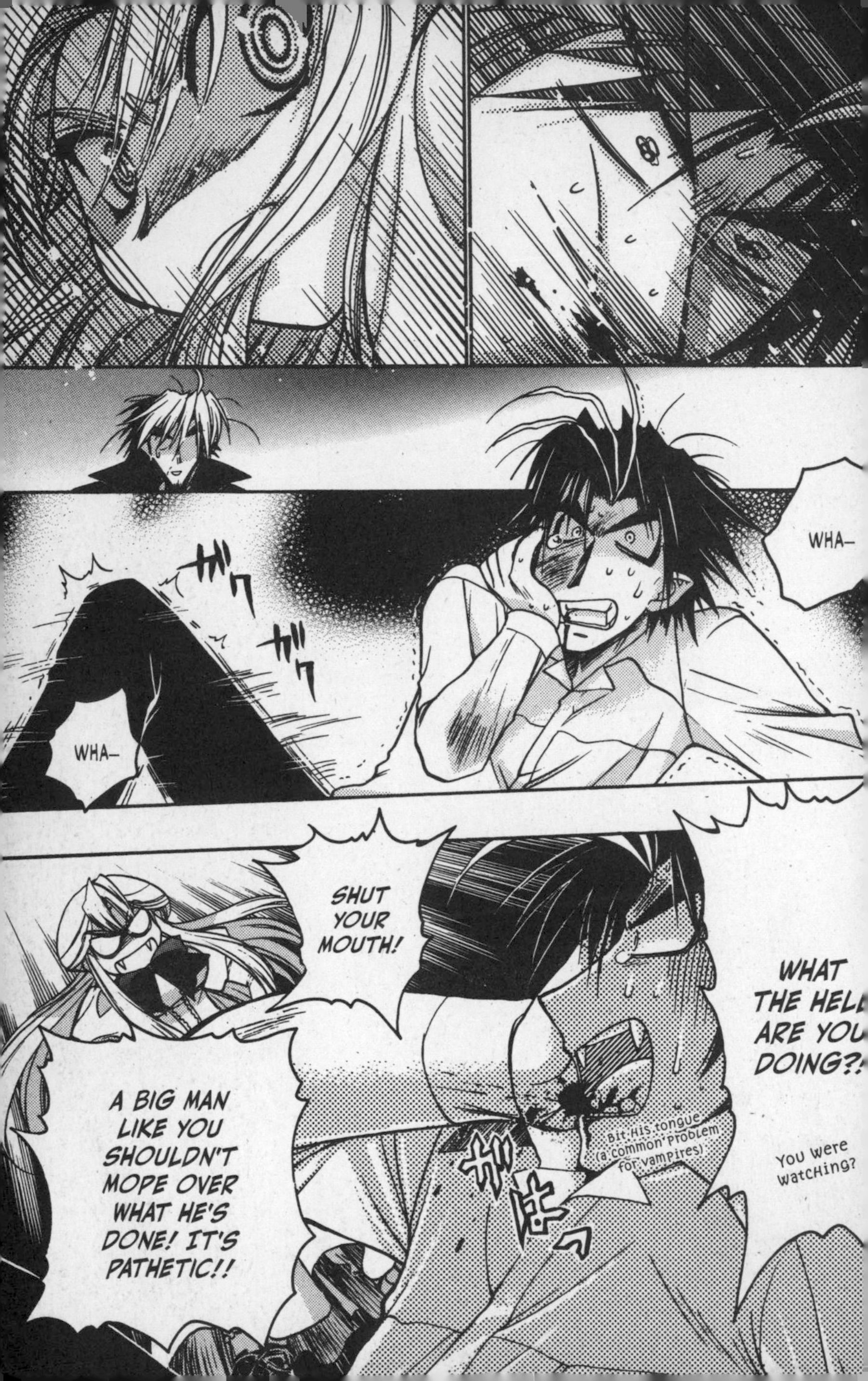
WHA—
WHA—
WHAT THE HELL ARE YOU DOING?!
You were watching?
SHUT YOUR MOUTH!
Bit his tongue (a common problem for vampires)
A BIG MAN LIKE YOU SHOULDN'T MOPE OVER WHAT HE'S DONE! IT'S PATHETIC!!

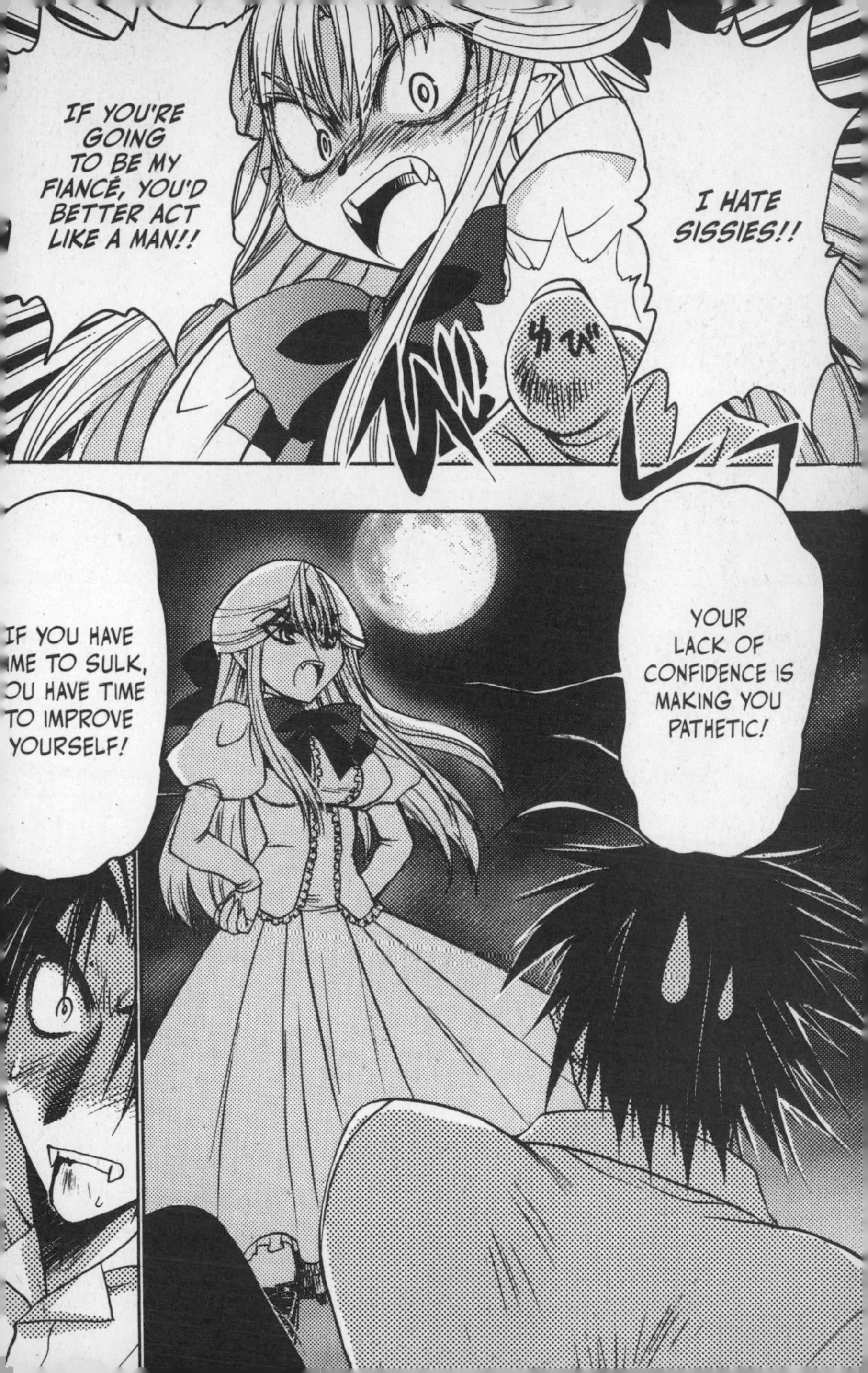
I HATE SISSIES!!
IF YOU'RE GOING TO BE MY FIANCÉ, YOU'D BETTER ACT LIKE A MAN!!
ゆび
YOUR LACK OF CONFIDENCE IS MAKING YOU PATHETIC!
IF YOU HAVE IME TO SULK, OU HAVE TIME TO IMPROVE YOURSELF!

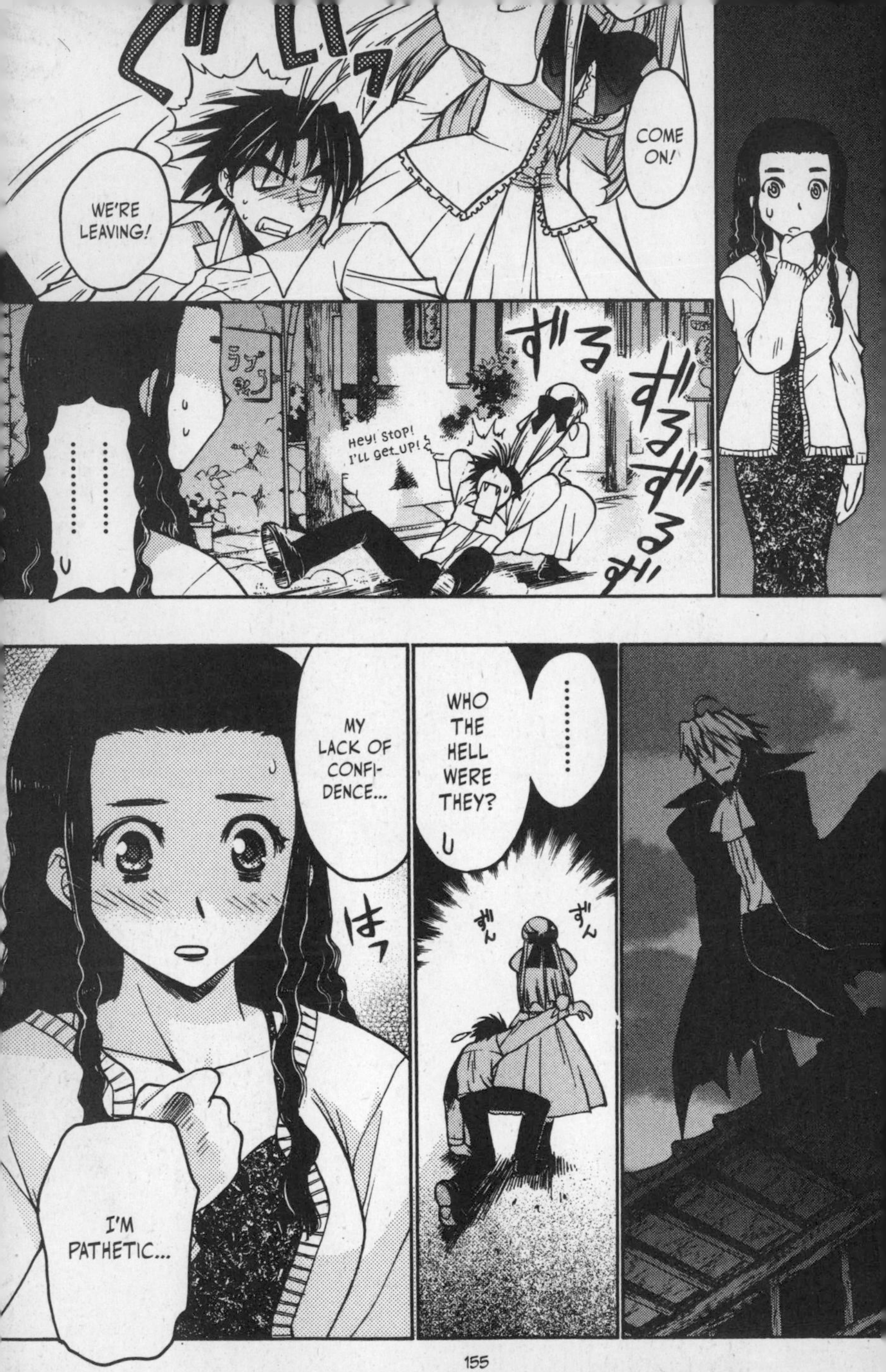
COME ON!
WE'RE LEAVING!
ずる ずるずる ずるずる ず
Hey! Stop! I'll get up!
......
......
WHO THE HELL WERE THEY?
ずん ずん
はっ
MY LACK OF CONFIDENCE...
I'M PATHETIC...

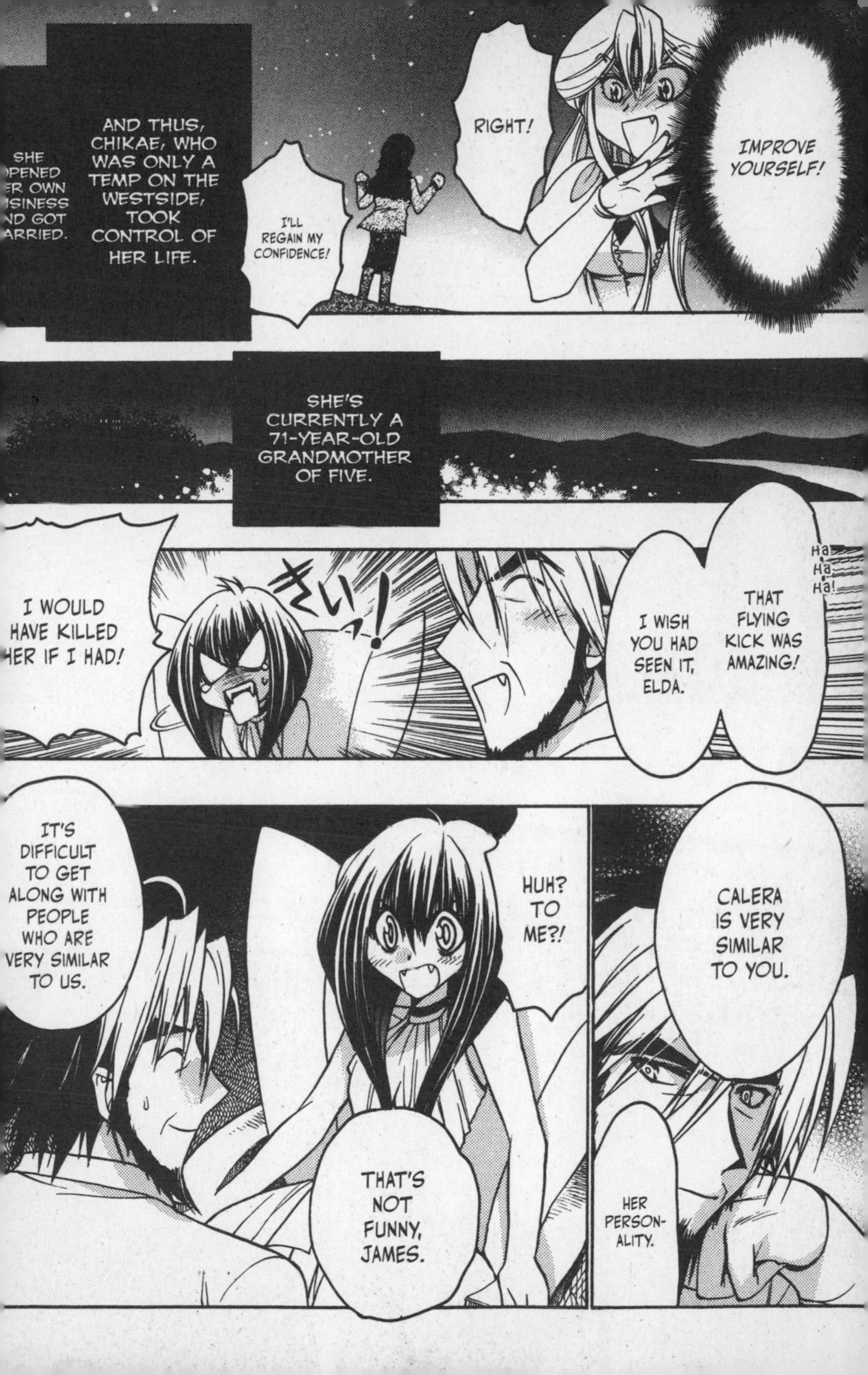
IMPROVE YOURSELF!
RIGHT!
I'LL REGAIN MY CONFIDENCE!
AND THUS, CHIKAE, WHO WAS ONLY A TEMP ON THE WESTSIDE, TOOK CONTROL OF HER LIFE.
SHE'S CURRENTLY A 71-YEAR-OLD GRANDMOTHER OF FIVE.
Ha Ha Ha!
THAT FLYING KICK WAS AMAZING!
I WISH YOU HAD SEEN IT, ELDA.
I WOULD HAVE KILLED HER IF I HAD!
CALERA IS VERY SIMILAR TO YOU.
HER PERSON-ALITY.
HUH? TO ME?!
IT'S DIFFICULT TO GET ALONG WITH PEOPLE WHO ARE VERY SIMILAR TO US.
THAT'S NOT FUNNY, JAMES.

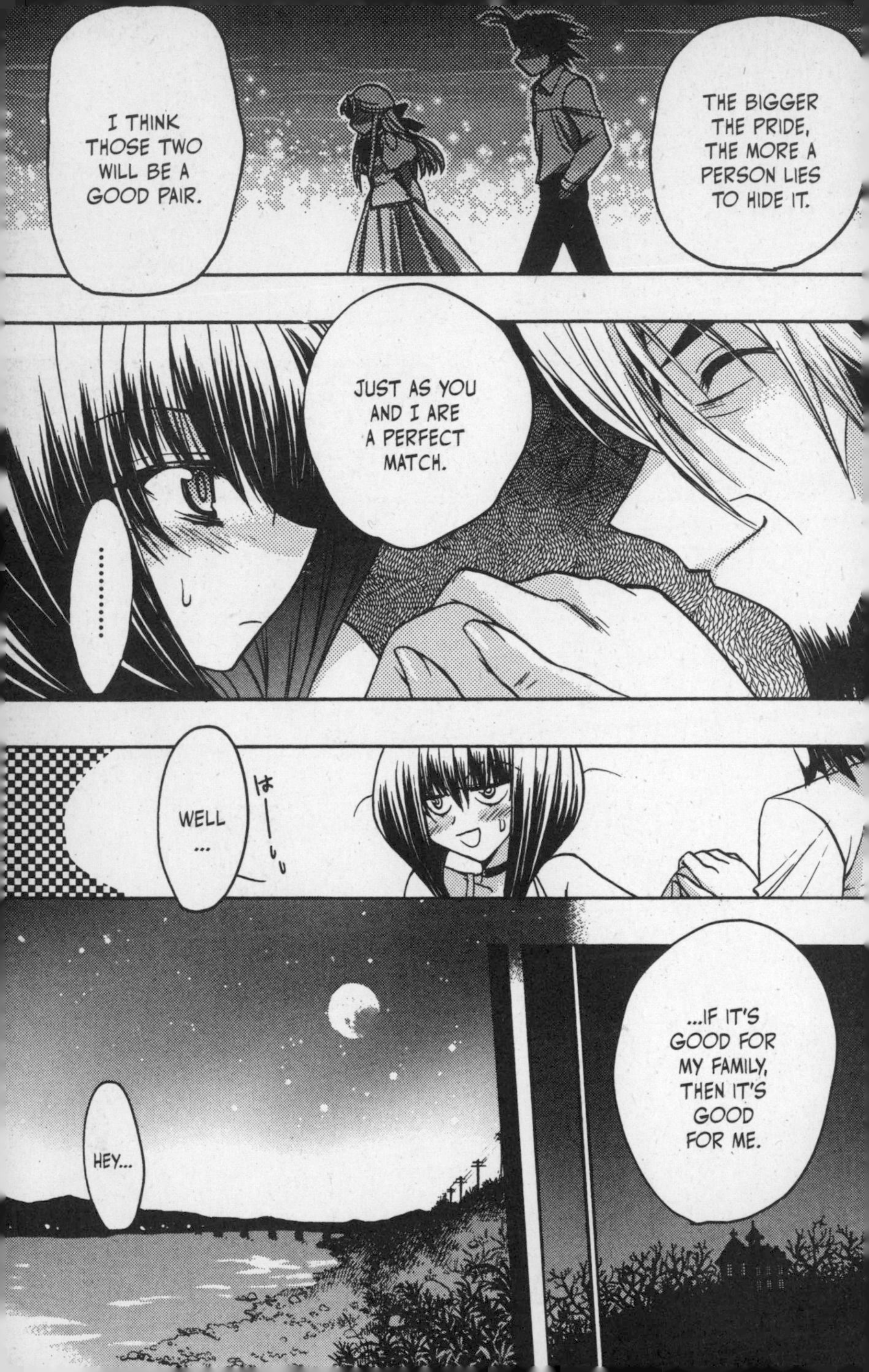
THE BIGGER THE PRIDE, THE MORE A PERSON LIES TO HIDE IT.
I THINK THOSE TWO WILL BE A GOOD PAIR.
JUST AS YOU AND I ARE A PERFECT MATCH.
....
はーぃ
WELL ...
...IF IT'S GOOD FOR MY FAMILY, THEN IT'S GOOD FOR ME.
HEY...

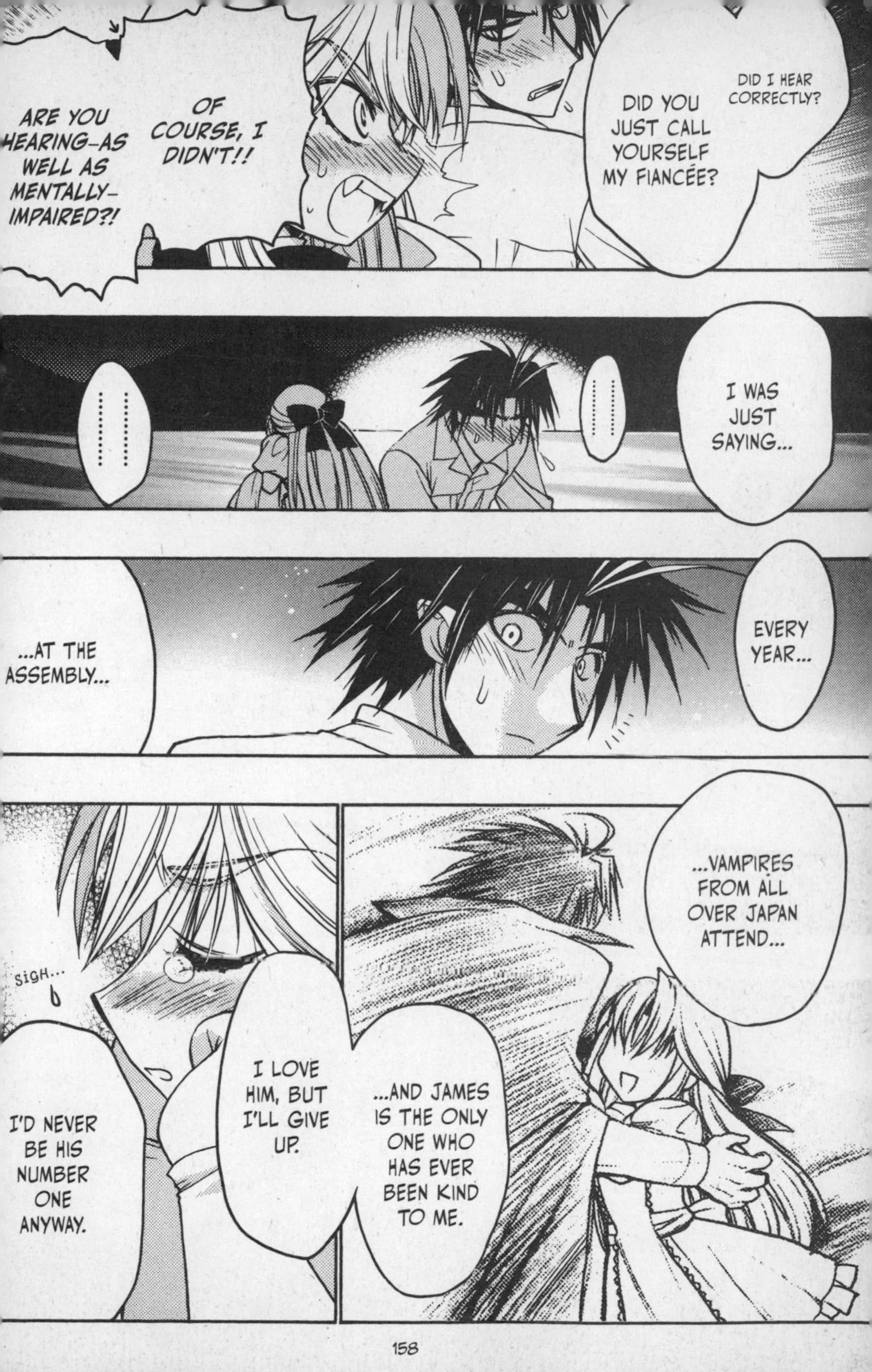
DID I HEAR CORRECTLY?
DID YOU JUST CALL YOURSELF MY FIANCÉE?
OF COURSE, I DIDN'T!!
ARE YOU HEARING—AS WELL AS MENTALLY—IMPAIRED?!
I WAS JUST SAYING...
......
......
EVERY YEAR...
...AT THE ASSEMBLY...
...VAMPIRES FROM ALL OVER JAPAN ATTEND...
...AND JAMES IS THE ONLY ONE WHO HAS EVER BEEN KIND TO ME.
I LOVE HIM, BUT I'LL GIVE UP.
SIGH...
I'D NEVER BE HIS NUMBER ONE ANYWAY.

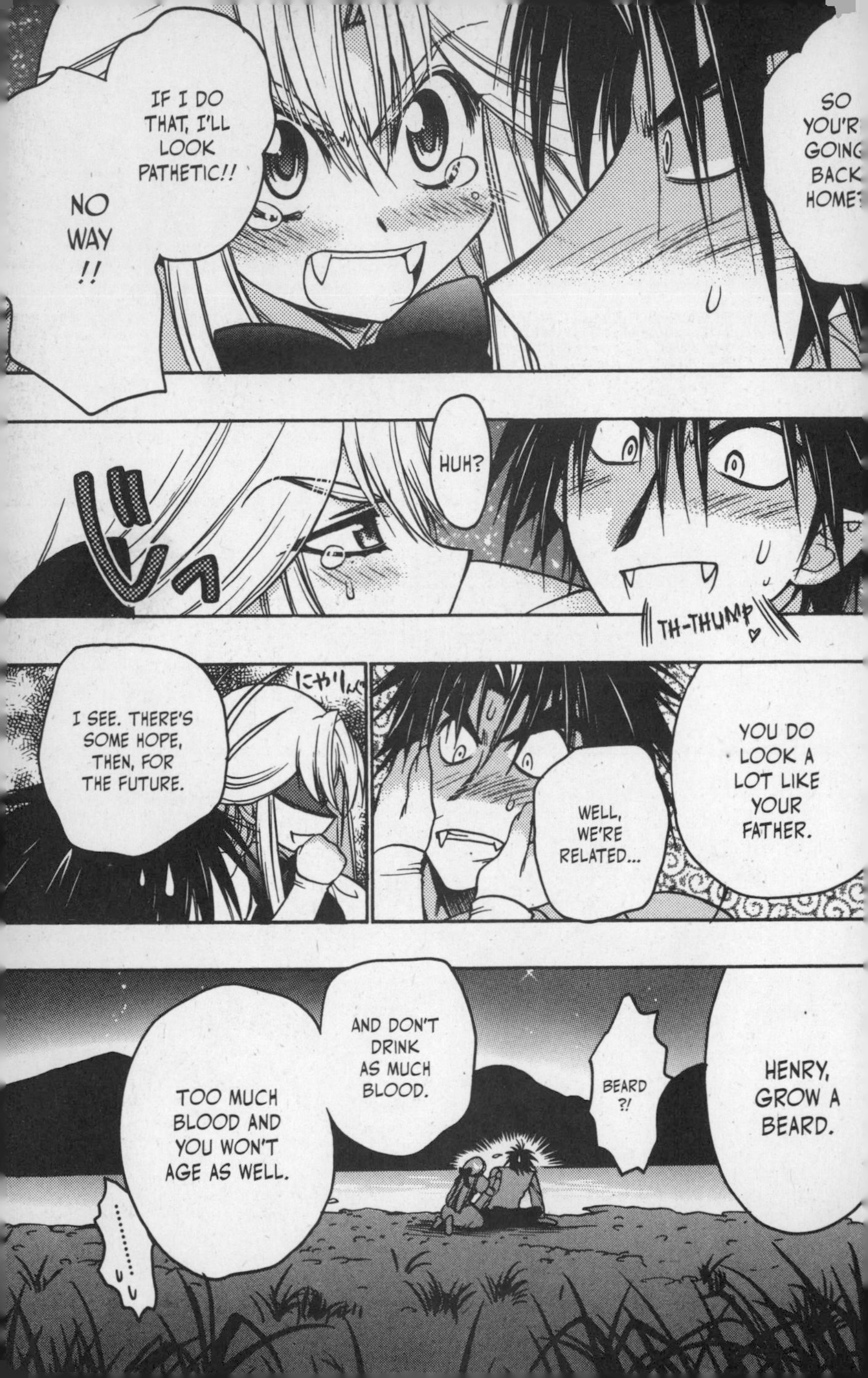
SO YOU'R GOING BACK HOME
IF I DO THAT, I'LL LOOK PATHETIC!!
NO WAY!!
HUH?
TH-THUMP
YOU DO LOOK A LOT LIKE YOUR FATHER.
WELL, WE'RE RELATED...
I SEE. THERE'S SOME HOPE, THEN, FOR THE FUTURE.
HENRY, GROW A BEARD.
BEARD?!
AND DON'T DRINK AS MUCH BLOOD.
TOO MUCH BLOOD AND YOU WON'T AGE AS WELL.
......

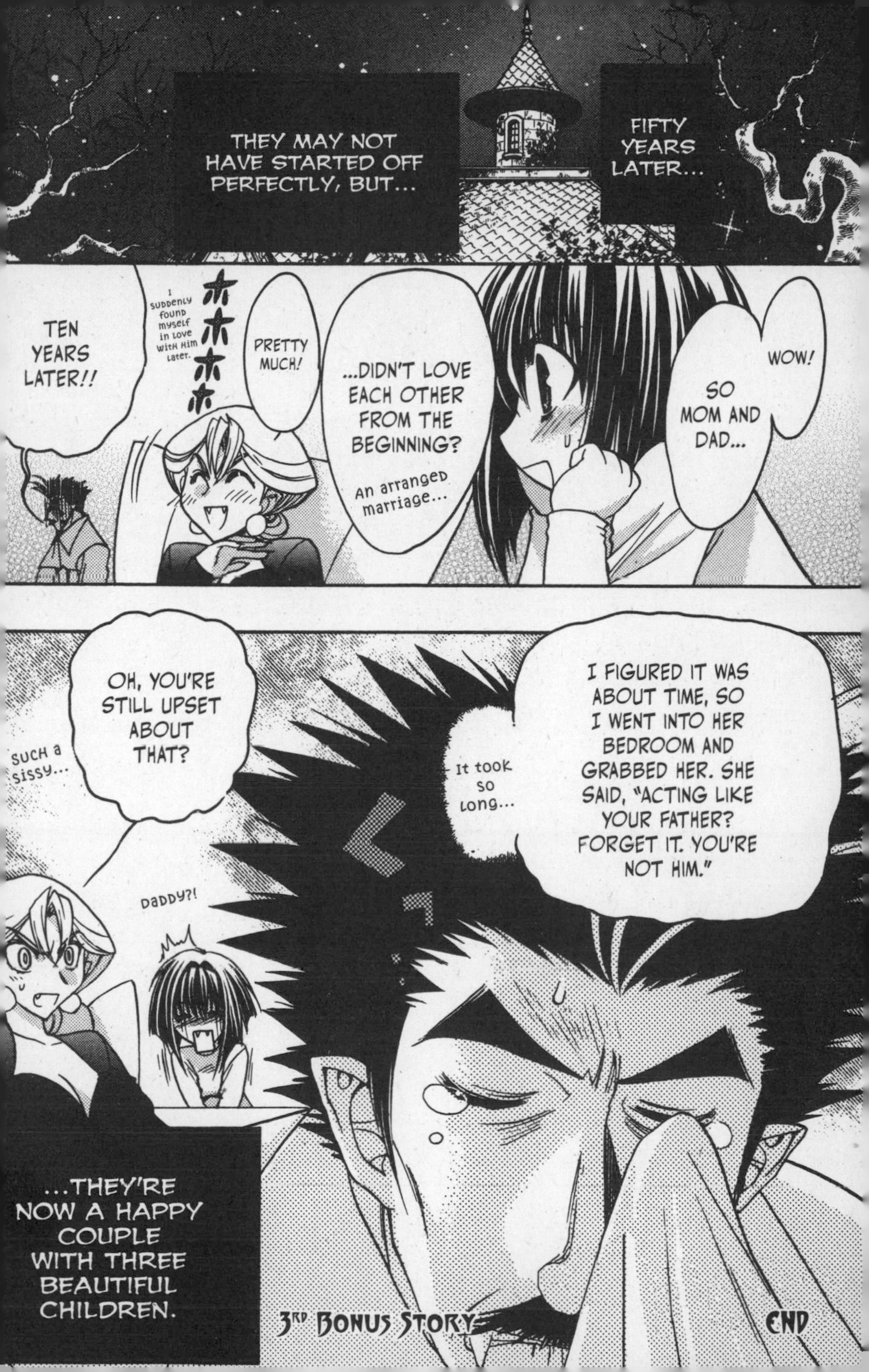
FIFTY YEARS LATER...
THEY MAY NOT HAVE STARTED OFF PERFECTLY, BUT...
WOW!
SO MOM AND DAD...
...DIDN'T LOVE EACH OTHER FROM THE BEGINNING?
An arranged marriage...
PRETTY MUCH!
ホホホホ
I suddenly found myself in love with him later.
TEN YEARS LATER!!
I FIGURED IT WAS ABOUT TIME, SO I WENT INTO HER BEDROOM AND GRABBED HER. SHE SAID, "ACTING LIKE YOUR FATHER? FORGET IT. YOU'RE NOT HIM."
It took so long...
OH, YOU'RE STILL UPSET ABOUT THAT?
Such a sissy...
Daddy?!
...THEY'RE NOW A HAPPY COUPLE WITH THREE BEAUTIFUL CHILDREN.
3RD BONUS STORY END

BONUS

KARIN'S GRANDMOTHER, ELDA

I BASICALLY DREW KARIN WITH LONGER HAIR AND DIFFERENT FACIAL EXPRESSIONS. IT WAS A LOT OF FUN.

I THOUGHT OF HER AS "DARK KARIN."

WHO KNEW A PERSONALITY FLIP WOULD BE SO FUN?

I want to awaken her again. Frankly, I'm bored of drawing you.

Meanie!

Memories of Yuna Kagesaki's Cultural Festival

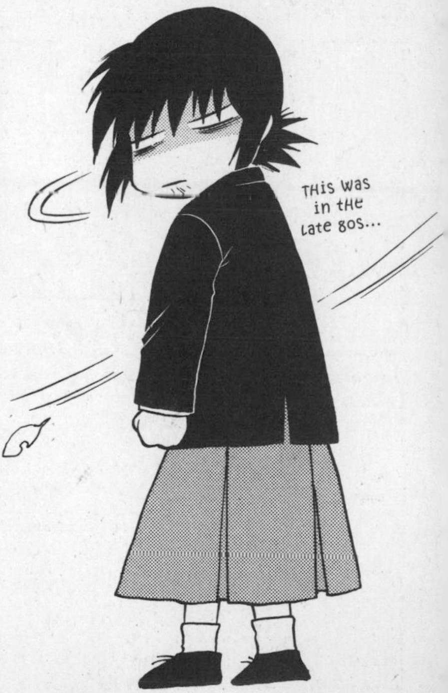
I ACTUALLY HAVE NO MEMORIES OF IT FROM HIGH SCHOOL.
This was in the late 80s...

School Wars

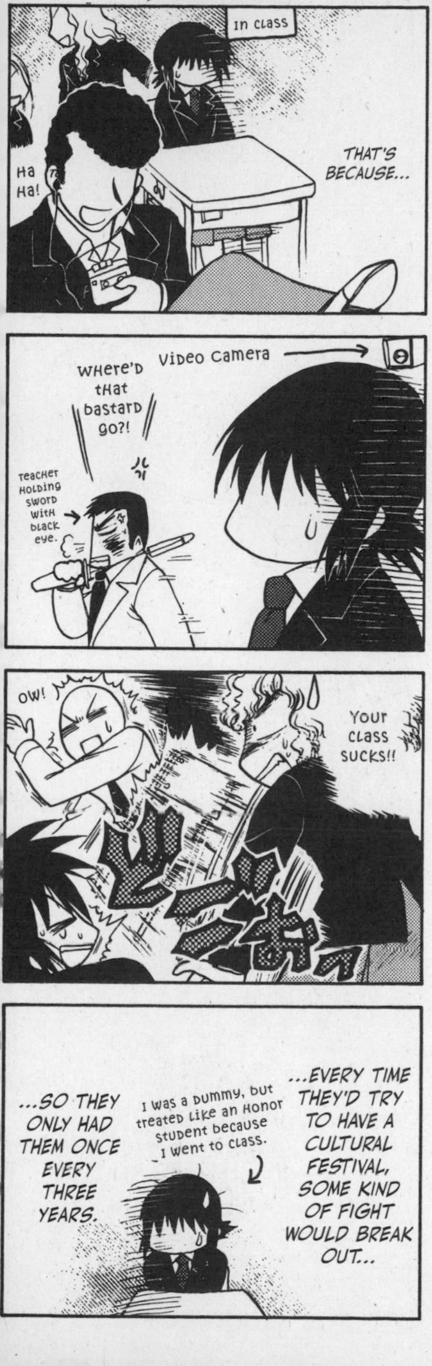
In class
THAT'S BECAUSE...
Ha Ha!
Video Camera
Where'd that bastard go?!
Teacher holding sword with black eye.
Your class sucks!!
OW!
...EVERY TIME THEY'D TRY TO HAVE A CULTURAL FESTIVAL, SOME KIND OF FIGHT WOULD BREAK OUT...
I was a dummy, but treated like an honor student because I went to class.
...SO THEY ONLY HAD THEM ONCE EVERY THREE YEARS.

My Parents Would Cry if They Read This

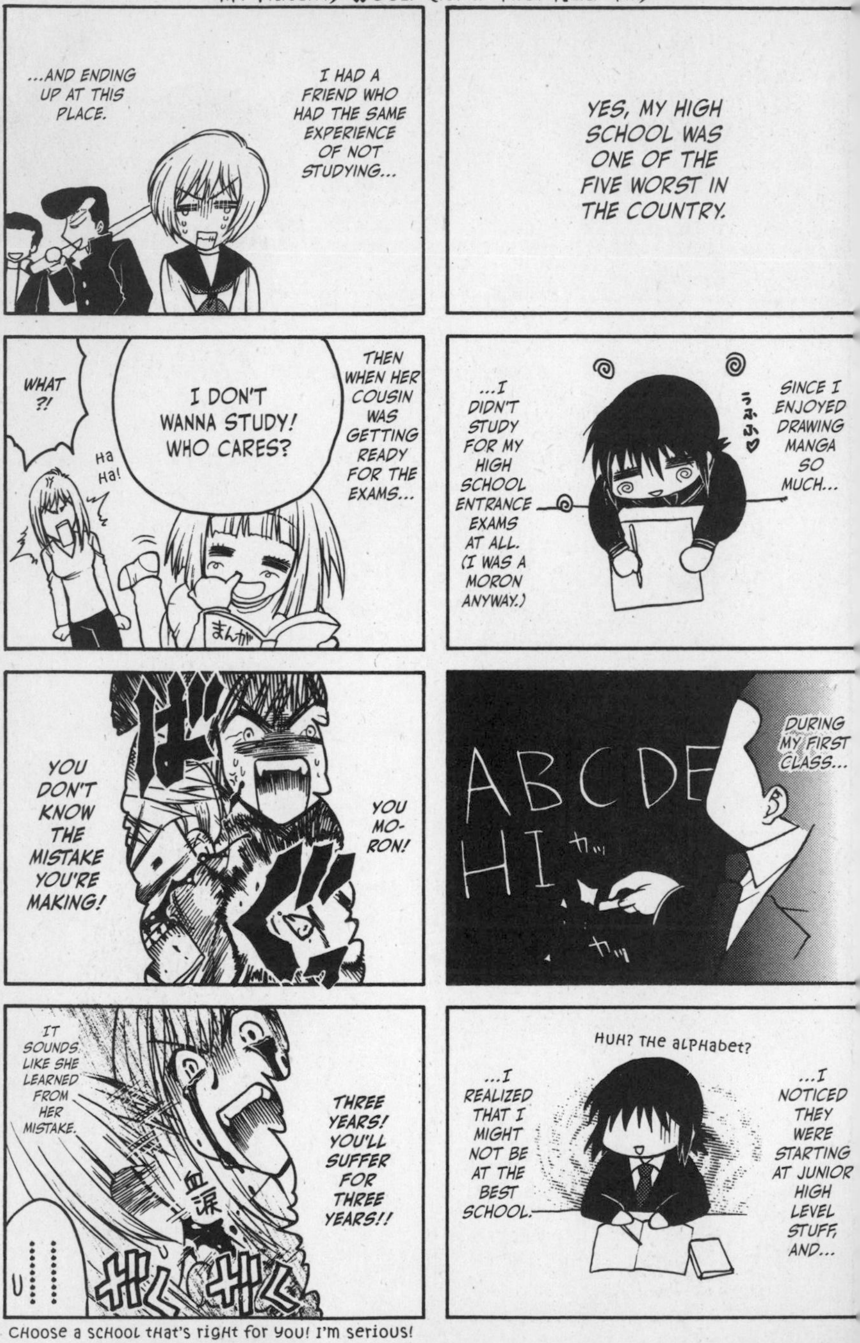
YES, MY HIGH SCHOOL WAS ONE OF THE FIVE WORST IN THE COUNTRY.
I HAD A FRIEND WHO HAD THE SAME EXPERIENCE OF NOT STUDYING...
...AND ENDING UP AT THIS PLACE.
SINCE I ENJOYED DRAWING MANGA SO MUCH...
うふふ♡
...I DIDN'T STUDY FOR MY HIGH SCHOOL ENTRANCE EXAMS AT ALL. (I WAS A MORON ANYWAY.)
THEN WHEN HER COUSIN WAS GETTING READY FOR THE EXAMS...
I DON'T WANNA STUDY! WHO CARES?
WHAT ?!
Ha Ha!
まんが
DURING MY FIRST CLASS...
ABCDE
HI
YOU MO-RON!
YOU DON'T KNOW THE MISTAKE YOU'RE MAKING!
HUH? The alphabet?
...I NOTICED THEY WERE STARTING AT JUNIOR HIGH LEVEL STUFF, AND...
...I REALIZED THAT I MIGHT NOT BE AT THE BEST SCHOOL.
THREE YEARS! YOU'LL SUFFER FOR THREE YEARS!!
血涙
IT SOUNDS LIKE SHE LEARNED FROM HER MISTAKE.
U.......

Choose a school that's right for you! I'm serious!

Lone Woman

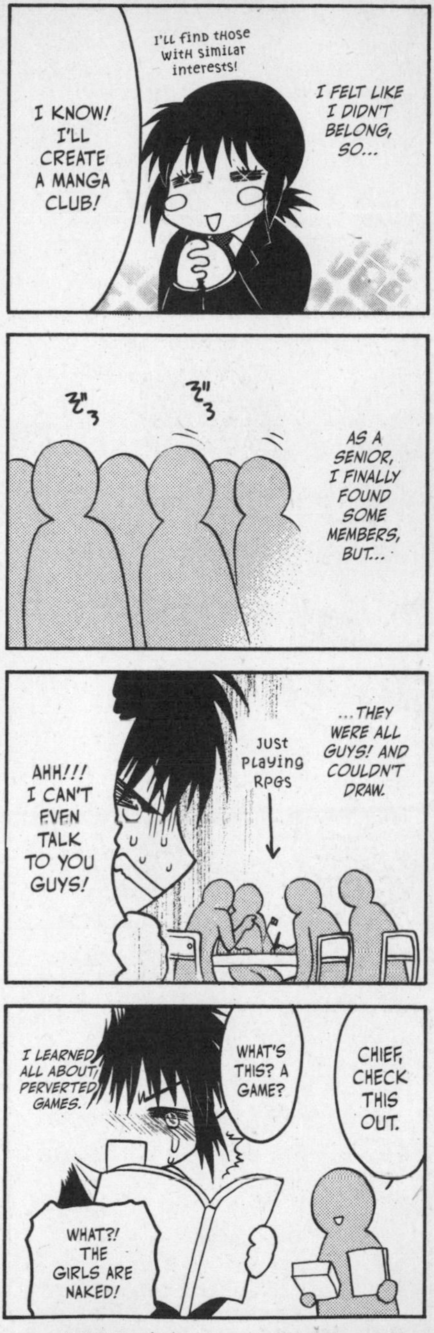
I FELT LIKE I DIDN'T BELONG, SO...
I'll find those with similar interests!
I KNOW! I'LL CREATE A MANGA CLUB!
AS A SENIOR, I FINALLY FOUND SOME MEMBERS, BUT...
...THEY WERE ALL GUYS! AND COULDN'T DRAW.
JUST PLAYING RPGS
AHH!!! I CAN'T EVEN TALK TO YOU GUYS!
CHIEF, CHECK THIS OUT.
WHAT'S THIS? A GAME?
I LEARNED ALL ABOUT PERVERTED GAMES.
WHAT?! THE GIRLS ARE NAKED!

I guess this is where it all started...

Only Once Every Three Years, Yet...

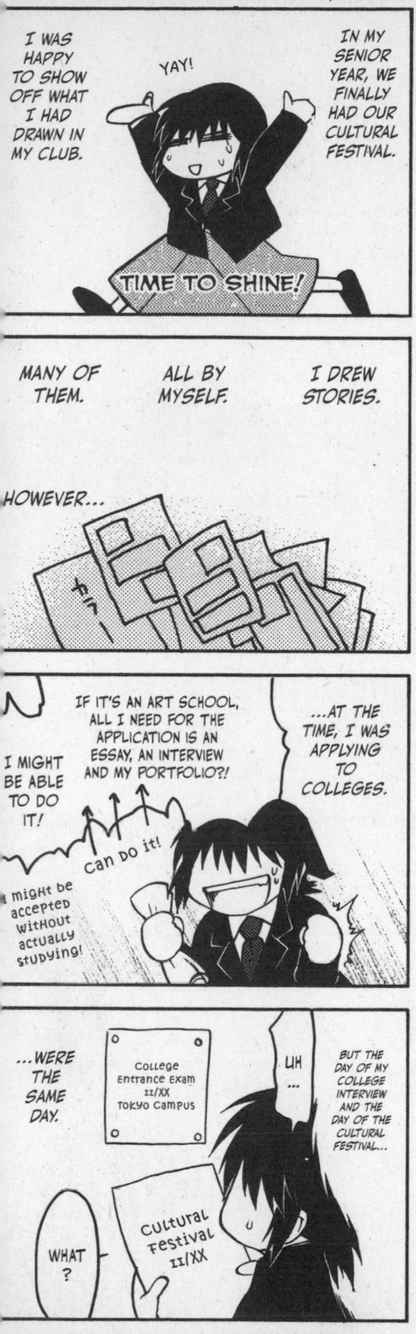
IN MY SENIOR YEAR, WE FINALLY HAD OUR CULTURAL FESTIVAL.
YAY!
I WAS HAPPY TO SHOW OFF WHAT I HAD DRAWN IN MY CLUB.
TIME TO SHINE!
I DREW STORIES.
ALL BY MYSELF.
MANY OF THEM.
HOWEVER...
...AT THE TIME, I WAS APPLYING TO COLLEGES.
IF IT'S AN ART SCHOOL, ALL I NEED FOR THE APPLICATION IS AN ESSAY, AN INTERVIEW AND MY PORTFOLIO?!
I MIGHT BE ABLE TO DO IT!
Can do it!
I might be accepted without actually studying!
BUT THE DAY OF MY COLLEGE INTERVIEW AND THE DAY OF THE CULTURAL FESTIVAL...
UH ...
College Entrance Exam 11/XX Tokyo Campus
...WERE THE SAME DAY.
Cultural Festival 11/XX
WHAT ?

That's why I have no memories of it.

A World Kagesaki Knows Little About

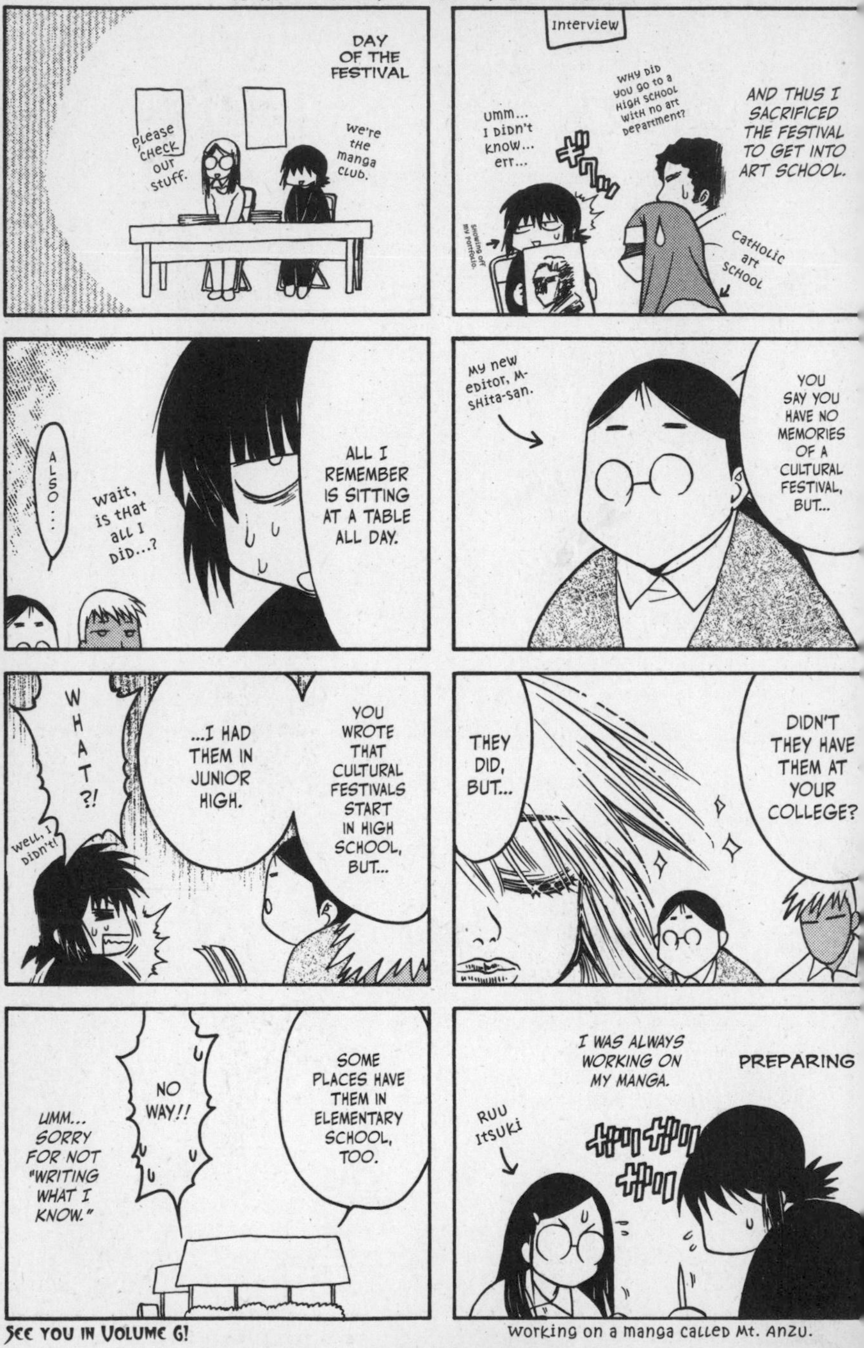
Interview
WHY DID YOU GO TO A HIGH SCHOOL WITH NO ART DEPARTMENT?
UMM... I DIDN'T KNOW... ERR...
SHOWING OFF MY PORTFOLIO.
CATHOLIC ART SCHOOL
AND THUS I SACRIFICED THE FESTIVAL TO GET INTO ART SCHOOL.
YOU SAY YOU HAVE NO MEMORIES OF A CULTURAL FESTIVAL, BUT...
MY NEW EDITOR, M-SHITA-SAN.
DIDN'T THEY HAVE THEM AT YOUR COLLEGE?
THEY DID, BUT...
I WAS ALWAYS WORKING ON MY MANGA.
PREPARING
RUU ITSUKI
DAY OF THE FESTIVAL
WE'RE THE MANGA CLUB.
PLEASE CHECK OUT STUFF.
ALL I REMEMBER IS SITTING AT A TABLE ALL DAY.
WAIT, IS THAT ALL I DID...?
ALSO...
YOU WROTE THAT CULTURAL FESTIVALS START IN HIGH SCHOOL, BUT...
...I HAD THEM IN JUNIOR HIGH.
WHAT?!
WELL, I DIDN'T!
SOME PLACES HAVE THEM IN ELEMENTARY SCHOOL, TOO.
NO WAY!!
UMM... SORRY FOR NOT "WRITING WHAT I KNOW."

Working on a manga called Mt. Anzu.

See you in Volume 6!

IN OUR NEXT VOLUME...

TOKYOPOP
chibi Vampire
6
Created By:
Yuna Kagesaki

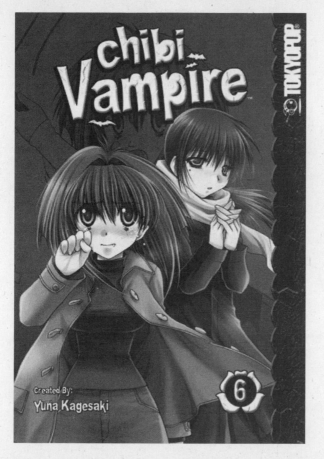

OUR NEXT VOLUME FEATURES PLENTY OF DRAMA, ANGST AND ONE ENORMOUS NOSEBLEED. KARIN FINALLY DECIDES TO TELL KENTA HOW SHE FEELS ABOUT HIM, ONLY TO HAVE THE EXPERIENCE RUINED BY A CASE OF MISTAKEN IDENTITY. WHO IS THIS MAN THAT LOOKS REMARKABLY LIKE KENTA? AND HOW WILL KARIN EVER BE ABLE TO RECOVER FROM HER EMBARRASSMENT (NOT TO MENTION HER UNBELIEVABLE LOSS OF BLOOD)? THE EMOTIONS RUN DEEP AND RICH AS BLOOD WHEN CHIBI VAMPIRE RETURNS!

DNA POSSIBILITIES

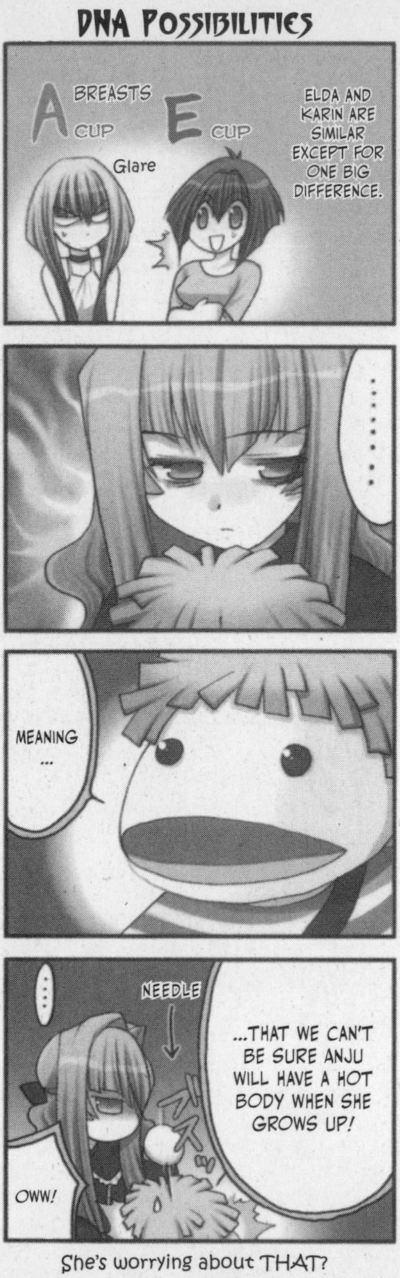
ELDA AND KARIN ARE SIMILAR EXCEPT FOR ONE BIG DIFFERENCE.
E CUP
BREASTS
A CUP
Glare
......
MEANING ...
...THAT WE CAN'T BE SURE ANJU WILL HAVE A HOT BODY WHEN SHE GROWS UP!
NEEDLE
....
OWW!

She's worrying about THAT?

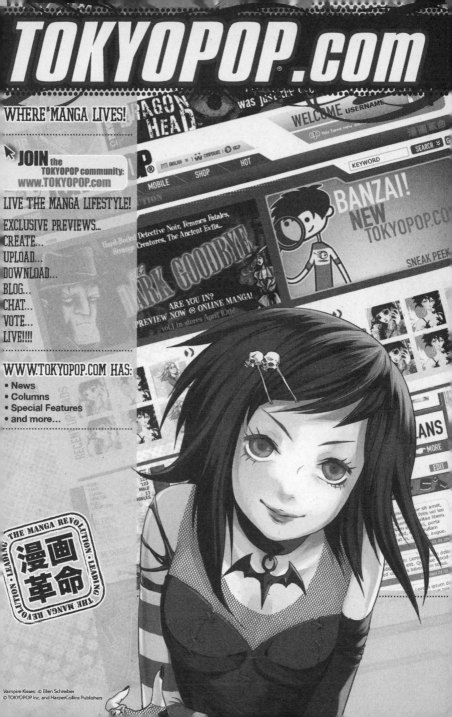

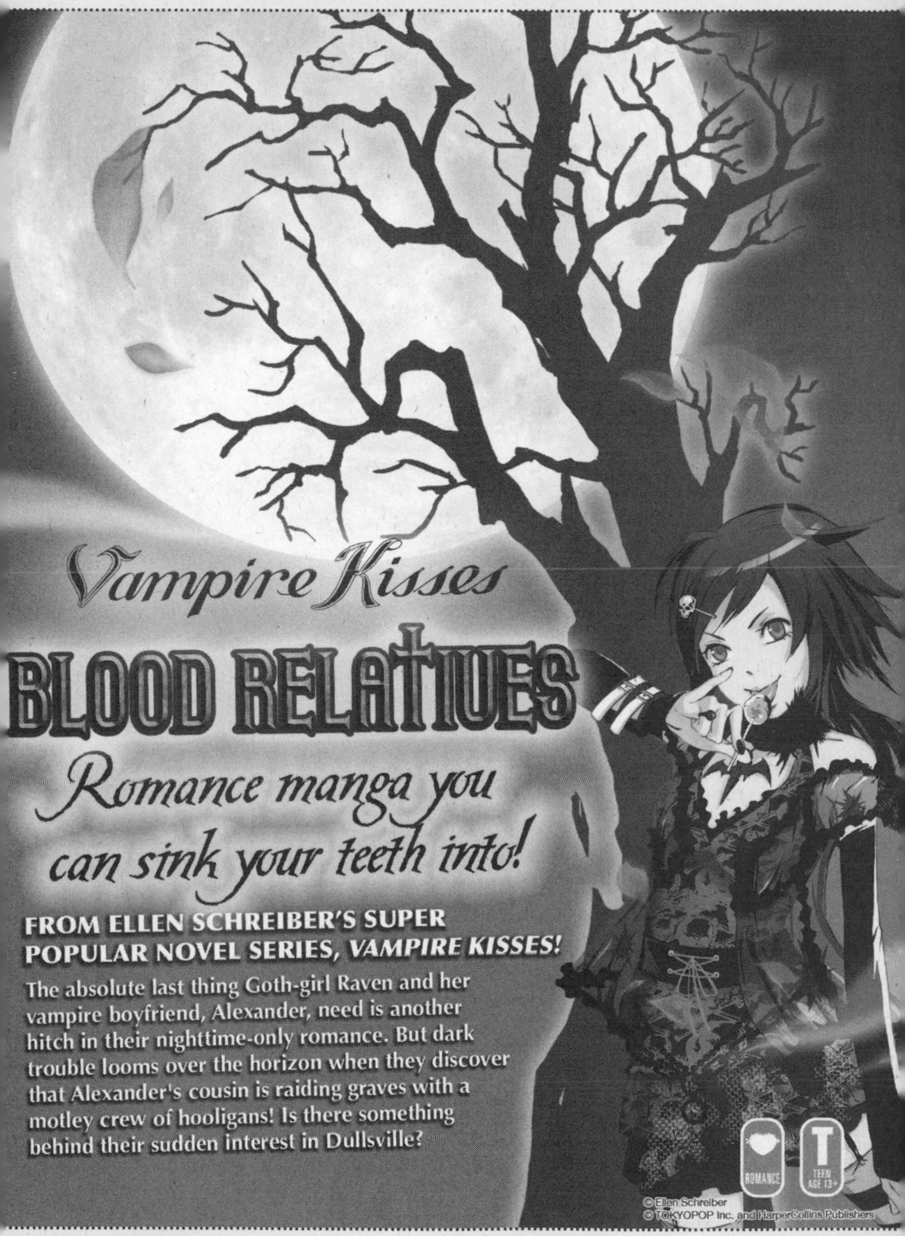
Vampire Kisses
BLOOD RELATIVES
Romance manga you can sink your teeth into!
FROM ELLEN SCHREIBER'S SUPER POPULAR NOVEL SERIES, VAMPIRE KISSES!
The absolute last thing Goth-girl Raven and her vampire boyfriend, Alexander, need is another hitch in their nighttime-only romance. But dark trouble looms over the horizon when they discover that Alexander's cousin is raiding graves with a motley crew of hooligans! Is there something behind their sudden interest in Dullsville?
ROMANCE
T
TEEN AGE 13+
© Ellen Schreiber
© TOKYOPOP Inc. and HarperCollins Publishers

DARK MOON DIARY ™

After losing her parents in a tragic accident, Priscilla goes to live in a new town with her aunt's family. As if adjusting to a new family wouldn't be tough enough, her relatives turn out to be vampires who live in the ghoul-filled town of Nachtwald! Priscilla tries hard to assimilate, but with a ghost for a teacher, a witch as a friend, and food that winks at you, can she ever adapt to life in her new town? Or will she pack her garlic and head back to normal-ville?

© Che Gilson and TOKYOPOP Inc.

FOR MORE INFORMATION VISIT: WWW.TOKYOPOP.COM

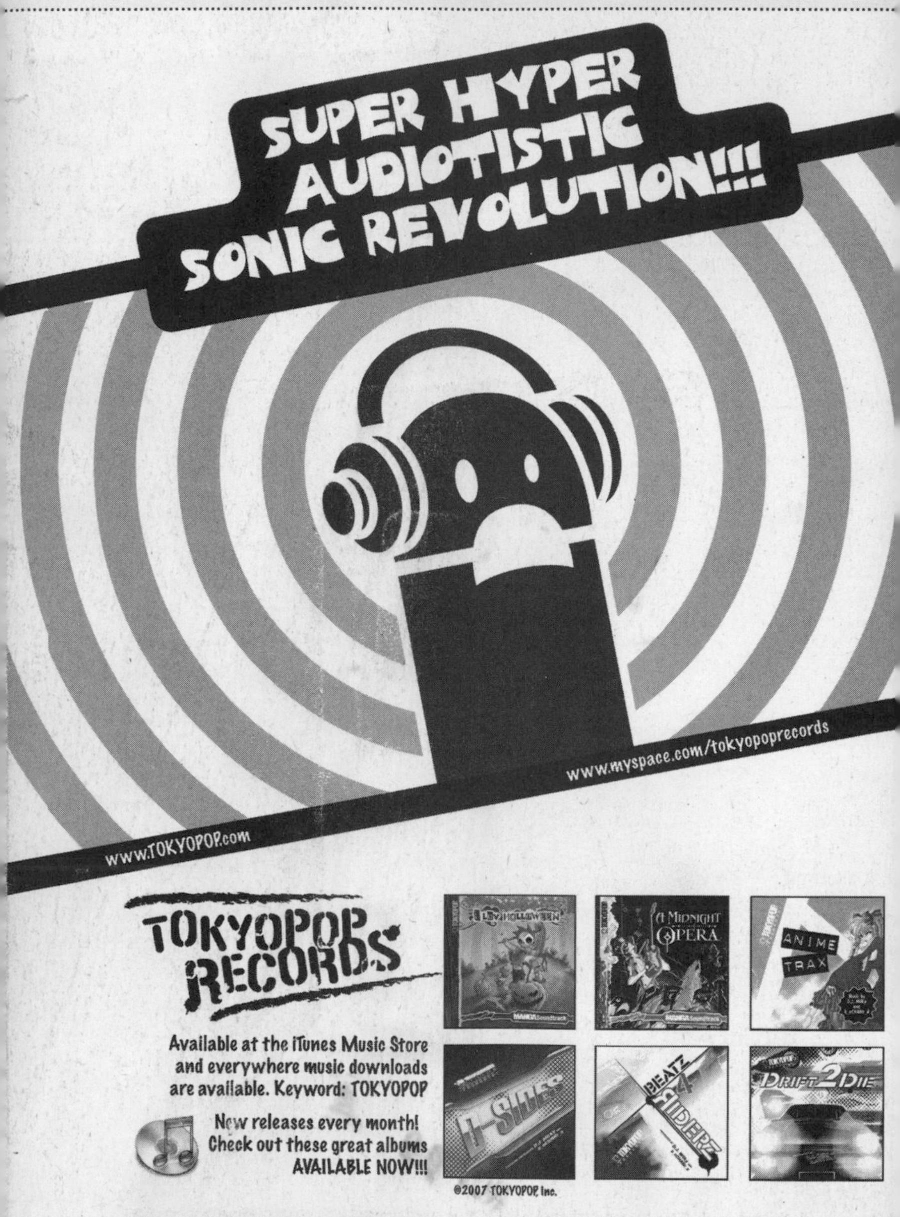
SUPER HYPER
AUDIOTISTIC
SONIC REVOLUTION!!!
www.myspace.com/tokyopoprecords
www.TOKYOPOP.com
TOKYOPOP RECORDS
Available at the iTunes Music Store
and everywhere music downloads
are available. Keyword: TOKYOPOP
New releases every month!
Check out these great albums
AVAILABLE NOW!!!
A MIDNIGHT OPERA
ANIME TRAX
B-SIDES
BEATZ 4 RIDERZ
DRIFT 2 DIE
©2007 TOKYOPOP Inc.

STOP!

This is the back of the book.
You wouldn't want to spoil a great ending!

This book is printed "manga-style," in the authentic Japanese right-to-left format. Since none of the artwork has been flipped or altered, readers get to experience the story just as the creator intended. You've been asking for it, so TOKYOPOP® delivered: authentic, hot-off-the-press, and far more fun!

DIRECTIONS

If this is your first time reading manga style, here's a quick guide to help you understand how it works.

It's easy... just start in the top right panel and follow the numbers. Have fun, and look for more 100% authentic manga from TOKYOPOP®!

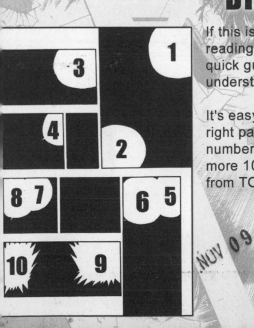

漫画革命

THE MANGA REVOLUTION · LEADING · LEADING · THE MANGA REVOLUTION